Secrets

of

Heaven

T0351835

SECRETS OF HEAVEN

The Portable New Century Edition

EMANUEL SWEDENBORG

Volume 5

Translated from the Latin by Lisa Hyatt Cooper

SWEDENBORG FOUNDATION

West Chester, Pennsylvania

Originally published in Latin as *Arcana Coelestia*, London, 1749–1756. The volume contents of this and the original Latin edition, along with ISBNs of the annotated version, are as follows:

Volume number in this edition	Text treated	Volume number in the Latin first edition	Section numbers	ISBN (hardcover)
1	Genesis 1–8	1	§§1–946	978-0-87785-486-9
2	Genesis 9–15	1	§§947–1885	978-0-87785-487-6
3	Genesis 16–21	2 (in 6 fascicles)	§§1886–2759	978-0-87785-488-3
4	Genesis 22–26	3	§§2760–3485	978-0-87785-489-0
5	Genesis 27–30	3	§§3486–4055	978-0-87785-490-6
6	Genesis 31–35	4	§§4056–4634	978-0-87785-491-3
7	Genesis 36–40	4	§§4635–5190	978-0-87785-492-0
8	Genesis 41–44	5	§§5191–5866	978-0-87785-493-7
9	Genesis 45–50	5	§§5867–6626	978-0-87785-494-4
10	Exodus 1–8	6	§§6627–7487	978-0-87785-495-1
11	Exodus 9–15	6	§§7488–8386	978-0-87785-496-8
12	Exodus 16–21	7	§§8387–9111	978-0-87785-497-5
13	Exodus 22–24	7	§§9112–9442	978-0-87785-498-2
14	Exodus 25–29	8	§§9443–10166	978-0-87785-499-9
15	Exodus 30–40	8	§§10167–10837	978-0-87785-500-2

ISBN (e-book of library edition)   Volume 5: 978-0-87785-727-3
ISBN (Portable)   **Volume 5: 978-0-87785-421-0**
ISBN (e-book of Portable Edition)   Volume 5: 978-0-87785-726-6

(The ISBN in the Library of Congress data shown below is that of volume 1.)

Library of Congress Cataloging-in-Publication Data

Swedenborg, Emanuel, 1688–1772.
     [Arcana coelestia. English]
     Secrets of heaven / Emanuel Swedenborg ; translated from the Latin by
Lisa Hyatt Cooper. — Portable New Century ed.
          p. cm.
     Includes bibliographical references and indexes.
     ISBN 978-0-87785-408-1 (alk. paper)
     1. New Jerusalem Church—Doctrines. 2. Bible. O.T. Genesis—Commentaries—Early works
to 1800. 3. Bible. O.T. Exodus—Commentaries—Early works to 1800. I. Title.
     BX8712.A8 2010
     230'.94—dc22
                                                                                                    2009054171

Senior copy editor, Alicia L. Dole
Text designed by Joanna V. Hill
Typesetting by Mary M. Wachsmann and Sarah Dole
Ornaments from the first Latin edition, 1749–1756
Cover design by Karen Connor
Cover photograph by Magda Indigo

For information about the New Century Edition of the Works of Emanuel Swedenborg, contact the Swedenborg Foundation, 320 North Church Street, West Chester, PA 19380 U.S.A.
Telephone: (610) 430-3222 • Web: www.swedenborg.com • E-mail: info@swedenborg.com

Contents

Volume 5

Genesis Chapter 30

Conventions Used in This Work

MOST of the following conventions apply generally to the translations in the New Century Edition Portable series. For introductory material on the content and history of *Secrets of Heaven,* and for annotations on the subject matter, including obscure or problematic content, and extensive indexes, the reader is referred to the Deluxe New Century Edition volumes.

Volume designation *Secrets of Heaven* was originally published in eight volumes; in this edition all but the second original volume have been divided into two. Thus Swedenborg's eight volumes now fill fifteen volumes, of which this is the fifth. It corresponds to approximately the second half of Swedenborg's volume 3.

Section numbers Following a practice common in his time, Swedenborg divided his published theological works into sections numbered in sequence from beginning to end. His original section numbers have been preserved in this edition; they appear in boxes in the outside margins. Traditionally, these sections have been referred to as "numbers" and designated by the abbreviation "n." In this edition, however, the more common section symbol (§) is used to designate the section numbers, and the sections are referred to as such.

Subsection numbers Because many sections throughout Swedenborg's works are too long for precise cross-referencing, Swedenborgian scholar John Faulkner Potts (1838–1923) further divided them into subsections; these have since become standard, though minor variations occur from one edition to another. These subsections are indicated by bracketed numbers that appear in the text itself: [2], [3], and so on. Because the beginning of the first *subsection* always coincides with the beginning of the *section* proper, it is not labeled in the text.

Citations of Swedenborg's text As is common in Swedenborgian studies, text citations of Swedenborg's works refer not to page numbers but to section numbers, which unlike page numbers are uniform in most editions. In citations the section symbol (§) is generally omitted after the title of a work by Swedenborg. Thus "*Secrets of Heaven* 29" refers to section 29 (§29) of Swedenborg's *Secrets of Heaven,* not to page 29 of any edition. Subsection numbers are given after a colon; a reference such as "29:2" indicates subsection 2 of section 29. The reference "29:1" would indicate the first subsection of section 29, though that subsection is not in fact labeled in the text. Where section numbers stand alone without titles, their function is indicated by the prefixed section symbol; for example, "§29:2".

Citations of the Bible Biblical citations in this edition follow the accepted standard: a semicolon is used between book references and between chapter references, and a comma between verse references. Therefore "Matthew 5:11, 12; 6:1; 10:41, 42; Luke 6:23, 35" would refer to Matthew chapter 5, verses 11 and 12; Matthew chapter 6, verse 1; Matthew chapter 10, verses 41 and 42; and Luke chapter 6, verses 23 and 35. Swedenborg often incorporated the numbers of verses not actually represented in his text when listing verse numbers for a passage he quoted; these apparently constitute a kind of "see also" reference to other material he felt was relevant. This edition includes these extra verses and also follows Swedenborg where he cites contiguous verses individually (for example, John 14:8, 9, 10, 11), rather than as a range (John 14:8–11). Occasionally this edition supplies a full, conventional Bible reference where Swedenborg omits one after a quotation.

Quotations in Swedenborg's works Some features of the original Latin text of *Secrets of Heaven* have been modernized in this edition. For example, Swedenborg's first edition generally relies on context or italics rather than on quotation marks to indicate passages taken from the Bible or from other works. The manner in which these conventions are used in the original suggests that Swedenborg did not belabor the distinction between direct quotation and paraphrase; but in this edition, directly quoted material is indicated by either block quotations or quotation marks, and paraphrased material is usually presented without such indicators. In passages of dialog as well, quotation marks have been introduced that were not present as such in the original. Furthermore, Swedenborg did not mark his omissions from or changes to material he quoted, a practice in which this edition generally follows him. One exception consists of those instances in which Swedenborg did not include a complete sentence at the beginning or end of a Bible quotation. The omission in such cases has been marked in this edition with added points of ellipsis.

Grammatical anomalies Swedenborg sometimes uses a singular verb with certain dual subjects such as love and wisdom, goodness and truth, and love and charity. The wider context of his works indicates that his reason for doing so is that he understands the two given subjects as forming a unity. This translation generally preserves such singular verbs.

Italicized terms Any words in indented scriptural extracts that are here set in italics reflect a similar emphasis in the first edition.

Special use of vertical rule The opening passages of the early chapters of *Secrets of Heaven,* as well as the ends of all chapters, contain material that derives in some way from Swedenborg's experiences in the spiritual world. Swedenborg specified that the text of these and similar passages be set in continuous italics to distinguish it from exegetical and other material. For this edition, the heavy use of italic text was felt to be antithetical to modern tastes, as well as difficult to read, and so such passages are instead marked by a vertical rule in the margin.

Changes to and insertions in the text This translation is based on the first Latin edition, published by Swedenborg himself (1749–1756); it also reflects emendations in the third Latin edition, edited by P. H. Johnson, John E. Elliott, and others, and published by the Swedenborg Society (1949–1973). It incorporates the silent correction of minor errors, not only in the text proper but in Bible verse references. The text has also been changed without notice where the verse numbering of the Latin Bible cited by Swedenborg differs from that of modern English Bibles. Throughout the translation, references or cross-references that were implied but not stated have been inserted in brackets; for example, [John 3:27]. In many cases, it is very difficult to determine what Swedenborg had in mind when he referred to other passages giving evidence for a statement or providing further discussion on a topic. Because of this difficulty, the missing references that are occasionally supplied in this edition should not be considered definitive or exhaustive. In contrast to such references in square brackets, references that occur in parentheses are those that appear in the first edition; for example, (1 Samuel 30:16), (see §42 above). Occasionally square brackets signal an insertion of other material that was not present in the first edition. These insertions fall into two classes: words likely to have been deleted through a copying or typesetting error, and words supplied by the translator as necessary for the understanding of the English text, though they have no direct parallel in the Latin. The latter device has been used sparingly, however, even at the risk of some inconsistency in its application. Unfortunately, no annotations concerning these insertions can be supplied in this Portable edition.

Biblical titles Swedenborg refers to the Hebrew Scriptures as the Old Testament and to the Greek Scriptures as the New Testament; his terminology has been adopted in this edition. As was the custom in his day, he refers to the Pentateuch (Genesis, Exodus, Leviticus, Numbers, and Deuteronomy) simply as "Moses"; for example, in §3862:7 he writes "as can be seen in Moses" and then quotes a passage from Numbers. Similarly, in sentences or phrases introducing quotations he sometimes refers to the Psalms as "David," to Lamentations as "Jeremiah," and to the Gospel of John, the Epistles of John, and the Book of Revelation as simply "John." Conventional references supplied in parentheses after such quotations specify their sources more precisely.

Problematic content Occasionally Swedenborg makes statements that, although mild by the standards of eighteenth-century theological discourse, now read as harsh, dismissive, or insensitive. The most problematic are assertions about or criticisms of various religious traditions and their adherents—including Judaism, ancient or contemporary; Roman Catholicism; Islam; and the Protestantism in which Swedenborg himself grew up. These statements are far outweighed in size and importance by other passages in Swedenborg's works earnestly maintaining the value of every individual and of all religions. This wider context is discussed in the introductions and annotations of the Deluxe edition mentioned above. In the present format, however, problematic statements must be retained without comment. The other option—to omit them—would obscure some aspects of Swedenborg's presentation and in any case compromise its historicity.

Secrets
of
Heaven

Genesis 27

[Matthew 24:8–14]

AN explanation of the Lord's words in Matthew 24:3–7 predicting the close of the age, or final days of the church, was prefixed to the previous chapter, Genesis 26, in §§3353–3356 there. Now, with the Lord's divine mercy, let me explain the words that follow next in verses 8–14 of the same chapter in that Gospel: 3486

> All these things will be the beginning of woes. Then they will hand you over to tribulation and kill you, and you will be hated by all the nations because of my name. And many will then stumble and betray each other and hate each other. And many false prophets will arise and lead many astray. And because of the multiplying of wickedness, many people's charity will go cold. But those persisting to the end will be saved. And this gospel of the kingdom will be preached in the whole inhabited [earth] for testimony to all the nations. And then will be the end. (Matthew 24:8, 9, 10, 11, 12, 13, 14)

The previous verses, explained in §§3353–3356, described the first stage in the corruption of the church, which was to occur when people began to forget what was good and true and quarreled about it. This would lead to falsities. 3487

The verses here, though, describe the second stage of the church's corruption, in which people will despise and oppose what is good and true, and faith in the Lord will gradually die out as neighborly love comes to an end.

The inner meaning makes it clear that these words of the Lord's in the Gospel describe the second stage in the corruption of the church. This is the inner meaning: 3488

All these things will be the beginning of woes symbolizes what has already been said about the first stage in the church's ruination: People started to forget what was good and true and quarreled about it, which led to falsities and heresies. This corrupted the religion many centuries ago, it is plain, since the church in the Christian world became divided, and opinions about

3

goodness and truth are what drove the divisions. So you can see that the church's decay began a long time ago.

[2] *Then they will hand you over to tribulation and kill you* means that goodness and truth will be destroyed—first by *tribulation,* or by being corrupted, and then by being *killed,* or denied. In relation to goodness and truth, killing is failing to accept and therefore denying; see §§3387, 3395. *You,* the apostles, symbolize all aspects of faith taken as a whole and accordingly both the goodness and the truth that faith teaches. For this symbolism of the twelve apostles, see §§577, 2089, 2129, 2130 at the end, 3272, 3354. The fact that they symbolize such things is obvious here, because the topic under discussion is not a prediction concerning the apostles but concerning the close of the age.

[3] *And you will be hated by all the nations because of my name* symbolizes contempt for and opposition to everything good and true. *Hating* means feeling contempt for and opposing, because these are facets of hatred. *By all the nations* means by people engaged in evil. For this meaning of nations, see §§1259, 1260, 1849, 1868, 2588 at the end. *Because of my name* means because of the Lord and therefore because of everything that comes from him. The Lord's name means everything by which he is worshiped—everything in his church—taken as a whole; see §§2724, 3006.

[4] *And many will then stumble and betray each other and hate each other* symbolizes different kinds of antagonism because of all this. *Many will stumble* means the antagonism itself, which is aimed at the Lord's humanity itself. The Word predicts in various places that his [divine] humanity will be a stumbling block and impediment. *They will betray each other* means mutual hostility sparked by falsity's opposition to truth; *and hate each other* means mutual hostility sparked by evil's opposition to goodness.

[5] *And many false prophets will arise and lead many astray* symbolizes the preaching of falsity. *False prophets* mean people who teach falsity, and their false teachings; see §2534. *And lead many astray* means that this preaching will produce further falsity.

[6] *And because of the multiplying of wickedness, many people's charity will go cold* means that charity passes away when faith does. *Because of the multiplying of wickedness* means in proportion to the falsity in one's faith. *Many people's charity will go cold* means the death of charity. The two go hand in hand, because where faith is absent, charity is absent, and where charity is absent, so is faith. Charity is what welcomes faith, and a lack of charity is what rejects faith. This is the source of all falsity and evil.

[7] *But those persisting to the end will be saved* symbolizes the salvation of people who love their neighbor. *Those persisting to the end* means those who do not let themselves be led astray, who do not give way in times of trial.

[8] *And this gospel of the kingdom will be preached in the whole inhabited [earth] for testimony to all the nations* means that the Christian world will learn it first. *It will be preached* means it will become known. *This gospel of the kingdom* means the truth of this, the gospel meaning a proclamation and a kingdom meaning truth. (On the point that a kingdom means truth, see §§1672, 2547.) *In the whole inhabited* earth means the Christian world. The earth means the area where the church exists, so it means the Christian world; see §§662, 1066, 1068, 1262, 1733, 1850, 2117, 2118, 2928, 3355. The church is described as inhabited here because of its religious life—in other words, because of the good that results from its truth. In an inner sense, inhabiting means living, and residents mean the good that comes of truth (1293, 2268, 2451, 2712, 3384). *For testimony* means in order to let people know, so that they cannot feign ignorance. *To all the nations* means to the evil (1259, 1260, 1849, 1868, 2588), because when people wallow in falsity and evil, they no longer know what is true and good. Under those circumstances, they believe falsity to be true and evil to be good, and the reverse. When the church reaches this stage, *then will come the end.*

The words that follow these—to be explained at the beginning of the next chapter of Genesis [§§3650–3655], by the Lord's divine mercy—deal with the church's third stage, called a ruinous abomination.

People in the church do not see that the church is like this—despising and opposing everything good and true, and harboring antagonism toward goodness and truth and especially toward the Lord. They go to church, listen to sermons, maintain an air of reverence while there, attend Holy Supper, occasionally talking with each other about these activities in a perfectly appropriate way, regardless of whether they are evil or good; and they live together in polite kindness or friendship. As a result, they never see any evidence of contempt, let alone opposition, least of all hostility, toward what faith values as good and true or toward the Lord. However, these are the outward forms of conduct by which one person misleads another. The inward forms among people in the church are completely different and are even diametrically opposed to the outward ones. The inward forms are the ones depicted here and are the ones that have this character.

3489

The nature of the inward forms is vividly apparent in the heavens, because angels pay attention only to people's inner depths, or their goals—that is, to their intent and will and their resulting thoughts. [2] The extent of the discrepancy between these and superficial appearances can be seen from people coming into the other life from the Christian world; to learn about them, see §§2121, 2122, 2123, 2124, 2125, 2126. In the next life, we think and speak only in accord with our inner values, because we left outward appearances behind with our bodies. No matter how peace loving such people seemed in this world, in the next it is clear that they hated each other and also hated everything involved in faith. Most of all they hated the Lord. When anyone simply mentions him to their face in the other world, a wave not only of contempt but even of opposition and antagonism toward him pours from them and spreads outward—even if they kept up appearances by speaking and also preaching reverently about him. The same thing happens when neighborly love and faith are mentioned.

[3] That is what they are like inside, and in the other world their inner form is as plain to see as it would have been while they were living in the world if they had been released and freed from outward constraints. In the world they feared for their life and feared the law. Most of all they feared for their reputation, which brought them the high rank they were aiming and competing for and the riches they envied and eagerly sought. Without these constraints, they would have attacked one another with mutual hatred, as they were actually attempting and planning to do. They would have robbed others without a single pang of conscience and butchered them—especially the innocent—again without a pang of conscience. That is what today's Christians are like inside, except for a few who are unknown. From this it is clear what the church is like.

Genesis 27

1. And it happened, because Isaac grew old and his eyes grew too dim for seeing, that he called Esau, his older son, and said to him, "My son!" and [Esau] said to him, "Here I am."

2. And he said, "Look, please; I am getting old; I don't know the day of my death.

3. And now please take up your weapons, your quiver and your bow, and go out to the field and hunt me game.

4. And make me delicacies such as I have loved and bring them to me and let me eat, in order that my soul can bless you before I die."

5. And Rebekah was listening as Isaac spoke to Esau his son. And Esau went to the field to hunt game to bring.

6. And Rebekah said to Jacob her son, saying, "Look, I heard your father speaking to Esau your brother, saying,

7. 'Bring me game and make me delicacies and let me eat and bless you in the presence of Jehovah before my death.'

8. And now, my son, listen closely to my voice, to what I command you:

9. Please go to the flock and fetch me from there two good goats' kids and let me make them into delicacies for your father, such as he loves.

10. And you are to bring them to your father and let him eat, in order that he can bless you before his death."

11. And Jacob said to Rebekah his mother, "Look, Esau my brother is a hairy man and I am a smooth man.

12. Perhaps my father might feel me, and I will be in his eyes as a deluder and bring on myself a curse and not a blessing."

13. And his mother said to him, "On me be your curse, my son; only listen closely to my voice and go, fetch them for me."

14. And he went and fetched them and brought them to his mother, and his mother made delicacies such as his father loved.

15. And Rebekah took the clothes of Esau her older son, the desirable ones that were with her in the house, and dressed Jacob her younger son.

16. And the hides of goats' kids she made him put on his hands and on the smoothness of his neck.

17. And she gave the delicacies and the bread that she had made into the hand of Jacob her son.

18. And he came to his father and said, "My father!" and [his father] said, "Here I am. Who are you, my son?"

19. And Jacob said to his father, "I am Esau, your firstborn; I did as you spoke to me. Rise, please; sit and eat of my game, in order that your soul can bless me."

20. And Isaac said to his son, "How did you hurry to find this, my son?" and he said, "Because Jehovah your God made it happen before my face."

21. And Isaac said to Jacob, "Come close, please, and I will feel you, my son, [to tell] whether you are he, my son Esau, or not."

22. And Jacob came close to Isaac his father, and [Isaac] felt him and said, "The voice is Jacob's voice, but the hands are Esau's hands."

23. And he did not recognize him, because his hands were like the hands of Esau his brother: hairy; and [Isaac] blessed him.

24. And he said, "Are you he, my son Esau?" And [Jacob] said, "I am."

25. And he said, "Carry it to me and let me eat of my son's game so that my soul can bless you." And [Jacob] carried it to him, and he ate; and he brought him wine, and he drank.

26. And Isaac his father said to him, "Come close, please, and kiss me, my son."

27. And he came close and kissed him, and [Isaac] smelled the smell of his clothes and blessed him and said, "See: the smell of my son, like the smell of a field that Jehovah has blessed.

28. And God will give you of the dew of the sky and of the fatness of the earth and an abundance of grain and new wine.

29. Peoples will serve you, and peoples will bow down to you; be master to your brothers, and your mother's sons will bow down to you. A curse on those cursing you, and a blessing on those blessing you!"

30. And it happened as Isaac finished blessing Jacob, and Jacob had just barely gone out from the presence of Isaac his father, that Esau his brother came from his hunting.

31. And he too made delicacies and brought them to his father and said to his father, "Let my father rise and eat of his son's game in order that your soul can bless me."

32. And Isaac his father said to him, "Who are you?" and he said, "I am your son, your firstborn, Esau."

33. And Isaac shuddered a very great shudder and said, "Then who was that who hunted game and brought it to me, and I ate of it all before you came, and blessed him? Blessed he also will be."

34. As Esau heard his father's words, he also shouted a very great and bitter shout and said to his father, "Bless me too, my father!"

35. And [Isaac] said, "Your brother came in deceit and took your blessing."

36. And [Esau] said, "Is it because they call his name Jacob? And he has supplanted me two times; my birthright he took, and look—now he has taken my blessing!" And he said, "Haven't you saved me a blessing?"

37. And Isaac answered and said to Esau, "Here, I have made him master to you, and all his brothers I have given him as slaves, and with

grain and new wine I have sustained him; and for you, then, what shall I do, my son?"

38. And Esau said to his father, "Is this the one blessing you have, my father? Bless me too, my father!" And Esau lifted his voice and wept.

39. And Isaac his father answered and said to him, "Watch: of the fatness of the earth your dwelling will consist, and of the dew of the sky from above.

40. And by your sword you will live, and your brother you will serve; and it will happen when you gain the dominance that you will tear his yoke off your neck."

41. And Esau hated Jacob because of the blessing with which his father had blessed him, and Esau said in his heart, "The days of mourning for my father will come near, and I will kill Jacob my brother."

42. And to Rebekah were told the words of Esau her older son, and she sent and called to Jacob her younger son and said to him, "Look, Esau your brother is consoling himself over you that he will kill you.

43. And now, my son, listen closely to my voice and get up, flee to Laban, my brother, to Haran.

44. And you must stay with him several days until your brother's wrath withdraws.

45. Your brother's anger may yet withdraw from you, and he may forget what you have done to him, and I will send and take you from there. Why should I be bereaved of you both in one day?"

46. And Rebekah said to Isaac, "I despise my life, thanks to the daughters of Heth. If Jacob takes a woman from the daughters of Heth like those from among the daughters of the land, why should I have lives?"

Summary

EARLIER, where the focus was on Isaac and Rebekah, the inner meaning had to do with the way the Lord made the rationality in himself divine. Now it has to do with the way he made the earthly level in himself divine. Esau means the goodness on that level, and Jacob, the truth. When the Lord was in the world, he made his entire humanity divine—the inner or rational part, the outer or earthly part, and even the bodily part. This he did according to the divine plan by which he also remakes us, or regenerates us. So in a representative sense, the chapter

3490

also talks about the rebirth of a person's earthly plane, and in that sense Esau again means goodness on the earthly level, and Jacob, truth on that level. This truth and goodness are still divine, because everything good and true belonging to a person reborn comes from the Lord.

✾✾✾✾✾✾✾✾✾✾✾✾✾✾✾✾✾✾✾✾✾✾✾✾✾✾✾✾✾✾

Inner Meaning

3491 GENESIS 27:1. *And it happened, because Isaac grew old and his eyes grew too dim for seeing, that he called Esau, his older son, and said to him, "My son!" and [Esau] said to him, "Here I am."*

It happened, because Isaac grew old means when the state arrived. *And his eyes grew too dim for seeing* means in which the rational part wanted to shed divine light on the earthly part. *That he called Esau, his older son,* symbolizes a desire for goodness on the earthly plane, or a well-lived life. *And said to him, "My son!" and [Esau] said to him, "Here I am,"* symbolizes presence as a result of foresight and providence.

3492 *It happened, because Isaac grew old* means when the state arrived. This can be seen from the symbolism of *growing old* as the arrival of a new state. In the Word, old age symbolizes both sloughing off previous conditions and taking on new ones. The reason for the symbolism is that old age is the end of an era, when we start to put off bodily concerns and with them the kinds of love belonging to the previous era, and when our inner depths begin to be enlightened. When bodily concerns have been removed, our inner levels are bathed in light. Another reason for the symbolism is that angels, who perceive the Word's contents in a spiritual way, no longer think about old age as such but replace it with the idea of new life. In the current verse, then, they think about the arrival of the stage at which the Lord's divine rationality (represented by Isaac) longed for an earthly part that corresponded to it—that is, an earthly part that was also divine.

3493 *And his eyes grew too dim for seeing* means in which the rational part wanted to shed divine light on the earthly part. This can be seen from the symbolism of *eyes* as inner or rational sight (dealt with in §2701) and from that of *seeing* as discerning and understanding (dealt with in §§2150, 2325, 2807). When the eyes are said to grow dim, it means that there is no longer any discernment. In the current case it symbolizes an inability to discern what lay on the earthly level, and since that is the symbolism of the words, it means that the rational part wanted to shed divine light on the earthly part.

The situation here can be clarified by earlier remarks and explanations concerning the rational and earthly dimensions in a person being reborn: Our rational side is reborn before our earthly side because the rational part is deeper and therefore closer to the Divine than the earthly part. It is also purer and therefore better suited to receiving the Divine. In addition, the earthly plane can be regenerated only through the rational plane. See §§3286, 3288, 3321.

[2] So when the rational dimension has been reborn and the earthly dimension has not, the rational mind seems to itself to grow dim, because there is no correspondence. Our rational part sees by heaven's light; our earthly part, by the world's light. If they do not correspond, the rational cannot see anything in the earthly; everything there is shadowy or even blacked out. When they do correspond, however, the rational sees the contents of the earthly in light, because the objects of earthly light are then lit by those of heavenly light and become virtually transparent.

These concepts, though, become clearer from previous discussions and demonstrations of correspondence; see §§2987, 2989, 2990, 2991, 3002, 3138, 3167, 3222, 3223, 3225, 3337, 3485.

From these ideas you can now grasp to some extent how "Isaac's eyes grew too dim for seeing" means that the rational level wanted to shed divine light on the earthly level. To be specific, the rational level wanted to make the earthly level divine too, since in the highest sense the subject is the Lord. This process can be illustrated by the one that takes place in a person being reborn—the process discussed here. After all, human rebirth is an image of the Lord's glorification (§§3043, 3138, 3212, 3296, 3490).

That he called Esau, his older son, symbolizes a desire for goodness on the earthly plane, or a well-lived life. This is established by the representation of *Esau* as divine goodness on the earthly plane (discussed in §§3300, 3302, 3322). Since goodness on the earthly plane is goodness that is visible in what we want and how we live, a desire for goodness on that plane, or living a good life, is what Esau represents here.

3494

A desire for goodness on the earthly plane and accordingly goodness in one's life is what is called the *older son,* but a desire for truth and consequently truth in one's theology is what is called the *younger son.* The fact that wanting what is good and living a good life is the older or firstborn son is obvious from what happens with children. They start off having goodness, because they are in a state of innocence, of love for their parents and other caregivers, and of mutual kindness toward their little companions. As a result, goodness is the firstborn in every human being. This goodness that we are initiated into when young lasts forever, because anything we absorb in early childhood permeates our life; and because it lasts, it becomes the goodness in our [adult] life. If we lacked the kind of goodness we acquired in infancy, we would not be human but more wild than any beast in the forest. We do not see that it is present, since everything we absorb in our earliest years looks as if we came by it naturally. Look at our ability to walk or move in other ways, the customs and manners we use in our social life, the way we talk, and so on. You can see, then, that goodness is the older or firstborn son and consequently that truth is the younger or later-born son. We do not learn truth until youth, early adulthood, and full maturity.

[2] Both goodness and truth in the earthly or outer self are "sons," the offspring of the rational or inner self. Anything that emerges in the earthly or outer self comes from the rational or inner self; it is born and exists from that self. What is not born into existence from the inner self is not living or human. That would be like saying that an entity with physical senses and a body could exist without a soul.

That is why both goodness and truth are called sons, the offspring of the rational mind. Still, it is not rationality that produces and gives birth to the earthly part but an inflow coming by way of the rational mind into the earthly part, and that inflow originates in the Lord. So every baby born is the Lord's child. Later, when we develop wisdom, the Lord adopts us as his children to the extent that we continue to be childlike, that is, with childhood's innocence, its love for our parent (who is now the Lord), and its mutual kindness toward our infant companions (who are now our neighbors).

3495   *And said to him, "My son!" and [Esau] said to him, "Here I am,"* symbolizes presence as a result of foresight and providence, as can be seen from the following: *He called him and said to him, "My son!"* means as a result of foresight and providence, because the words are attributed to the Lord's divine side. And the answer, *he said to him, "Here I am,"* symbolizes presence.

3496   Genesis 27:2, 3, 4. *And he said, "Look, please; I am getting old; I don't know the day of my death. And now please take up your weapons, your quiver and your bow, and go out to the field and hunt me game. And make me delicacies such as I have loved and bring them to me and let me eat, in order that my soul can bless you before I die."*

He said, "Look, please; I am getting old," means that the state had arrived. *I don't know the day of my death* symbolizes life on the earthly plane. *And now please take up your weapons, your quiver and your bow,* symbolizes the doctrines concerning goodness known to it. *And go out to the field* means where there is good ground. *And hunt me game* symbolizes the truth that comes of something good. *And make me delicacies such as I have loved* symbolizes results that are appealing because they come from something good. *And bring them to me and let me eat* means adopting them. *In order that my soul can bless you* means connecting them to one's life. *Before I die* symbolizes the first stage of revival on the earthly plane.

He said, "Look, please; I am getting old," means that the state had arrived, as can be seen from the remarks about the symbolism of *getting old* above in §3492.

3497

I don't know the day of my death symbolizes life on the earthly plane. This can be seen from the symbolism of a *day* as a state (discussed in §§23, 487, 488, 493, 893, 2788) and from that of *death* as rising again, or being restored to life (discussed in §3326). So the day of someone's death symbolizes a state in which one is restored to life—in other words, life itself. That it is on the earthly plane is clear, because life on that plane is the theme here.

3498

No one can see how matters stand in regard to this without knowing how they stand in regard to the life of our rational level and the life of our earthly level, or the life of our inner and outer selves. The life of our rational or inner self is distinct from that of our earthly or outer self— so distinct that the life of our rational or inner self exists independently from the life of our earthly or outer self, though the latter cannot exist without the former. The outer self lives off the inner, and in fact if life were to cease in the inner self, it would instantly disappear in the outer self. The outer surface depends on the inner depths the way later things depend on prior ones, or the way an effect depends on its efficient cause; if the efficient cause were to cease, the effect would immediately disappear. The case is the same with life in the outer self as it relates to that of the inner self.

[2] Human beings offer clear illustration of this principle. While we are living in the world, in our bodies, our rational dimension is so distinctly different from our earthly dimension that we can leave behind our outer, physical senses (and even the inner senses of our earthly self, to an extent) and immerse ourselves in our rational dimension, or spiritual thought. An even clearer illustration is the fact that we totally lose any outward, physical sensation when we die but hold on to the life of our inner self. We do

keep the facts stored in our outward, earthly memory but do not use them (see §§2475, 2476, 2477, 2479, 2480, 2481, 2482, 2483, 2485, 2486).

Plainly, then, the rational, inner self is distinct from the outer self.

While living in our bodies, though, our rational plane does not look different from our earthly plane because we are inhabiting the world, the realm of nature. Accordingly, the life present in our rational level appears on the earthly level; there does not seem to be a hint of life on the rational level that is not also present on the earthly level. The rational level is seen as possessing life to the extent that the earthly level corresponds to it (see above at §3493).

This shows that Isaac's words to Esau, "I don't know the day of my death," symbolize a corresponding life or vitality on the earthly plane. After all, Isaac represents what is rational, and Esau represents what is earthly—specifically, the goodness involved in what is rational and what is earthly.

3499   *And now please take up your weapons, your quiver and your bow,* symbolizes the doctrines concerning goodness known to it. This can be seen from the symbolism of *weapons, quiver and bow,* as doctrines (discussed in §§2686, 2709)—here, as doctrines concerning goodness known to the earthly-level goodness represented by Esau.

3500   *And go out to the field* means where there is "good ground." This is established by the symbolism of a *field* as what is good in the church and as what is good in its theology (discussed in §§2971, 3196, 3310, 3317), and therefore as good ground.

3501   *And hunt me game* symbolizes the truth that comes of something good. This can be seen from the symbolism of *hunting* and *game* as truth on the earthly level that leads to goodness in one's life (discussed in §3309). Here it symbolizes the truth that *comes of* something good because the words are addressed to Esau, who represents goodness on the earthly level, as mentioned before.

3502   *And make me delicacies such as I have loved* symbolizes results that are appealing because they come from something good. This can be seen from the symbolism of *delicacies* as things that are appealing. Since they were to come from Esau, who represents goodness on the earthly plane, it means that they come from something good. In the original language, *delicacies* are pleasant, agreeable flavors. In an inner sense, they mean the pleasures of goodness and the attractiveness of truth, because like the other physical senses, taste corresponds to heavenly and spiritual attributes. The correspondence is to be dealt with later, by the

Lord's divine mercy [§§4318–4331, 4403–4421, 4523–4534, 4622–4634, 4652–4660, 4791–4806].

To understand this, it is necessary to know how the earthly part is made new or receives life from the rational part, or rather from the Lord through the rational part. [2] The earthly part becomes new or receives life corresponding to the rational part—is reborn, that is—only through doctrines, or knowledge of what is good and true. In the heavenly person, it is the knowledge of goodness that first accomplishes this; in the spiritual person, it is the knowledge of truth. Doctrines, or knowledge of goodness and truth, cannot be communicated to the earthly person, and therefore cannot be internalized and adopted, except through pleasures and delights suited to the earthly self. The reason they cannot is that they are instilled by the external route of the senses. If an idea does not enter through some kind of pleasure or delight, it does not stick, so it does not last. That is what is meant by the truth that comes of something good and by results that are appealing, which are the focus in what follows.

Bring them to me so that I can eat means adopting them. This can be seen from the symbolism of *eating* as adopting (dealt with in §§2187, 2343, 3168).

3503

In order that my soul can bless you means connecting them to one's life, so it symbolizes life that corresponds to the rational level. This can be seen from the symbolism of being *blessed* as being gifted with heavenly and spiritual goodness (discussed in §§981, 1731, 2846, 3017, 3406).

3504

The goodness that we have in childhood and therefore live by is the same as the goodness of the earthly dimension represented by Esau. It is not spiritual goodness, because the goodness of childhood lacks knowledge and understanding, and so it lacks wisdom. Childhood goodness becomes spiritual by having truth grafted onto it and consequently by regeneration (see §§1616, 1802, 2280, 2290, 2291, 2299, 2304, 2305, 2307, 3494 at the end). This creates a correspondence between rational and earthly qualities and so a connecting of the earthly self with life in the rational self. This connection to one's life is what is symbolized by *for my soul to bless you.*

Before I die symbolizes the first stage of revival on the earthly plane. This can be seen from the symbolism of *dying* as rising again or being brought back to life (discussed in §§3326, 3498). Clearly this is the first stage, because goodness in childhood, and therefore a well-lived life, is the first step in rebirth, and so far Esau has represented that phase. The stages that follow it are what the current chapter deals with in order.

3505

3506   Genesis 27:5, 6, 7. *And Rebekah was listening as Isaac spoke to Esau his son. And Esau went to the field to hunt game to bring. And Rebekah said to Jacob her son, saying, "Look, I heard your father speaking to Esau your brother, saying, 'Bring me game and make me delicacies and let me eat and bless you in the presence of Jehovah before my death.'"*

Rebekah was listening as Isaac spoke to Esau his son symbolizes a desire for truth and the life that results from it. *And Esau went to the field to hunt game to bring* symbolizes the effort that the desire for goodness made to acquire truth, which was to form a connection with divine rationality. *And Rebekah said to Jacob her son, saying,* symbolizes a perception the Lord received from divine truth concerning earthly truth. *Look, I heard your father speaking to Esau your brother, saying,* means that divine goodness in the Lord's divine rationality wanted there to be a desire for goodness [on the earthly level]. *Bring me game* symbolizes the truth that comes of goodness. *And make me delicacies* symbolizes a longing for and delight in the appealing qualities of that truth. *And let me eat* means adoption of it. *And bless you in the presence of Jehovah* means union with it. *Before my death* means life on the earthly plane as a result.

3507   *Rebekah was listening as Isaac spoke to his son* symbolizes a desire for truth and the life that results from it. This can be seen from the representation of *Rebekah* as divine truth united with divine goodness in the Lord's divine rational mind and therefore as the desire itself for truth, and from the symbolism of *listening as Isaac spoke* as the life that results from it. In an inner sense, listening as someone speaks means [accepting] an influence, because in a representative sense, *listening* means submitting (§2542) and *speaking* means willing and influencing (§§2626, 2951, 3037). So in the highest sense, listening as someone speaks means the life that results—the life present in divine truth that results from divine goodness. *To his son* in an inner sense means having to do with goodness on the earthly level and consequently with truth there.

[2] This meaning of the words departs rather widely from their literal meaning, or the story line, so it is not very apparent. Nevertheless it *is* the meaning. Angelic ideas are completely different from human ideas. Angelic ideas are spiritual, and if they go deep enough, they are heavenly, but human ideas are earthly, and if they come from the narrative, they are sense based. However, the Lord through the Word has created a correspondence between the spiritual things of heaven and the earthly things of the world, and the correspondence is such that earthly thoughts very quickly turn into spiritual ones. That is how heaven unites

with the world through humankind, through the Word, and so through the church, which has the Word.

In absolutely everything we can possibly grasp and perceive with our minds, there is a correspondence of earthly and spiritual elements. With the Lord's divine mercy, this will become clear from the remarks based on experience concerning the universal human at the ends of the following chapters.

And Esau went to the field to hunt game to bring symbolizes the effort **3508** that the desire for goodness made to acquire truth, which was to form a bond with divine rationality, as can be seen from the following: *Esau* represents goodness on the earthly plane, as noted above, so he represents a desire on the earthly plane for goodness on the rational plane. The goodness that exists on the earthly plane does not belong to that plane but to the rational plane within it (see §3498). *Going out to the field to hunt game to bring* symbolizes an effort to acquire truth, since a *field* means a place where the ground is good (3500). *Hunting* and *game* mean truth that comes of goodness (3501). *To bring* means to acquire, and therefore to connect it to divine rationality.

The focus of the highest meaning here, as noted before, is the glorification of the Lord's earthly dimension, and the focus of the representative meaning is the rebirth of the earthly dimension in us (3490). The plan is for this to be accomplished by means of truth, or by concepts of what is good and true, because without them, the earthly level cannot be enlightened by the rational level (or rather *through* the rational level). So without them, the earthly level cannot be reborn. These concepts are vessels designed to receive goodness and truth flowing in from the rational mind. The quality and quantity of what the vessels receive determines the quality and quantity of the light shed on them.

The vessels that receive goodness and truth from the rational mind are the truths of the earthly level, which are nothing but facts, religious concepts, and doctrines. The arranging of what flows into them and the hierarchy they maintain among themselves is what converts these types of truth into goodness. That is the source of goodness on the earthly level.

And Rebekah said to Jacob her son symbolizes a perception the Lord **3509** received from divine truth concerning earthly truth. This can be seen from the representation of *Rebekah* as divine truth in the Lord's divine rational mind (discussed in §§3012, 3013, 3077), from the symbolism of *saying* as perceiving (discussed in §§1791, 1815, 1819, 1822, 1898, 1919, 2080, 2506, 2515, 2552, 2619), and from the representation of *Jacob* as truth in the Lord's earthly mind (discussed in §3305). This shows that *Rebekah said to Jacob her son* symbolizes a perception the Lord received from divine truth concerning earthly truth.

Inspired by the divine goodness in his divine rationality (represented by Isaac), the Lord wanted to use goodness on the earthly level (represented by Esau) to acquire truth by which in turn he could glorify his earthly plane (or make it divine). But inspired by the divine *truth* in his divine rationality (represented by Rebekah), he wanted to use *truth* on the earthly level (represented by Jacob) to acquire truth by which in turn his *rational* plane could be glorified (or become divine). This can be comprehended only when it is illustrated by processes that occur in a person whom the Lord is regenerating or remaking. Even then it cannot be understood unless one knows about goodness and truth in the rational mind, so this needs to be stated briefly.

[2] The rational mind is divided into two capacities, one called the will, and the other, the intellect. What issues from the will of a person being reborn is called goodness, and what issues from the intellect is called truth. Until we have been reborn, our will does not act in unison with our intellect. Rather, our will wants goodness but our intellect wants truth—so much so that we sense the efforts of our will as being quite separate from those of our intellect. However, we sense this only if we reflect on it and only if we know what the will and its desires are, and what the intellect and its thoughts are. If we do not know any of this and so do not reflect on it, we cannot sense the separation. Another reason we do not is that the earthly mind is regenerated by the rational mind (see §3493) according to the following pattern: Rational goodness does not act directly on the goodness of the earthly plane to regenerate it but works through truth in the intellect; so to all appearances it operates from rational truth.

Such is the theme of the current chapter in its inner sense. Isaac means the rational mind in respect to goodness belonging to the will; Rebekah, the rational mind in respect to truth belonging to the intellect. Esau means goodness on the earthly plane emerging from goodness on the rational plane; Jacob means truth on the earthly plane emerging from goodness on the rational plane by means of the truth there.

[3] This discussion shows what kind of secrets the Word holds in its inner meaning, but there are very few that can be described intelligibly to people on earth. The number of transcendent, indescribable secrets is boundless. The further the Word penetrates, or the deeper into heaven it goes, the more inexhaustible and ineffable they are—not only to us but

even to angels of the lower heaven. When the Word reaches the deepest heaven, the angels there perceive that the secrets are infinite in number and completely incomprehensible to them because of being divine.

That is what the Word is like.

Look, I heard your father speaking to Esau your brother, saying, means that divine goodness in the Lord's divine rationality wanted there to be a desire for goodness [on the earthly level]. This is established by the representation of Isaac, the *father* here, as divine goodness in the Lord's divine rationality (dealt with before), by the symbolism of *speaking* as willing (discussed in §§2626, 2951, 3037), and by the representation of *Esau* as a desire for goodness on the earthly level (discussed above at §3508). **3510**

Bring me game symbolizes the truth that comes of goodness, which can be seen from the symbolism of *game* presented above at §3501 as the truth that comes of goodness. **3511**

And make me delicacies symbolizes a longing for and delight in the appealing qualities of that truth. This can be seen from the symbolism of *delicacies* as things that are appealing (discussed above at §3502) and so as a longing for and delight in its appealing qualities (the appeal of that truth). As noted in the section cited, truth is introduced into our earthly mind through enticements suited to it, and whatever is not introduced in an appealing way does not stick. As a consequence it is not internalized by our rational mind through correspondence. **3512**

Truth, like any other kind of fact, is assigned a place in our earthly self's memory on the basis of the attractions and pleasure that introduced it. Consider that when that appeal and those pleasures return, the ideas introduced by them come back, and the reverse: when the ideas are recalled, the pleasures or appeal attached to them are also stirred up.

And let me eat means adoption of it. This can be seen from the symbolism of *eating* as being adopted (dealt with at §§2187, 2343, 3168, 3503). Adoption occurs when truth (knowledge of what is good and true) is instilled into a person's earthly mind by means of appealing qualities and delights, and when it is connected to the goodness there. This establishes communication with the truth and goodness of the rational mind and therefore with the rational mind itself. Such communication is what is called adoption, because the truth belongs to the rational plane but exists on the earthly plane. **3513**

You see, the contents of the rational plane relate to those of the earthly plane as particulars relate to what is general. People recognize that a general whole grows out of its particular components, and that without particulars, nothing general exists. A general whole embracing the particulars of the rational level is what presents itself on the earthly level. Since it is generalized, it looks different, and what it looks like depends on the way the particular components are arranged. As a result it depends on the form they take. If particulars and their component details consisting of heavenly goodness and spiritual truth are what make up the general whole on the earthly level, it results in a heavenly, spiritual form. Some measure of heaven is represented as a kind of image in the individual elements of the whole. On the other hand, if particulars and details consisting not of goodness and truth but of evil and falsity are what make up the general whole on the earthly level, some measure of hell is represented as an image in the individual elements of the whole.

[2] This is what eating and drinking symbolize in the Holy Supper, where they again symbolize adoption. The eating symbolizes adoption of goodness, and the drinking symbolizes adoption of truth. If goodness— love for the Lord and charity for our neighbor—form our inner, rational self and through it form a corresponding outer, earthly self, then as a whole and in all our parts we become an image of heaven and therefore of the Lord. Conversely, if our inner and outer self are formed by contempt for the Lord, contempt for what faith teaches as good and true, and hatred for our neighbor, then as a whole and in all our parts we become an image of hell. It is even worse if this is our state while we are engaging in sacred ceremonies, because profanation is the result. That is what it means to say that people who eat and drink [the Holy Supper] worthily receive eternal life as their own, while those who eat and drink unworthily make death their own.

3514   *And bless you in the presence of Jehovah* means union with it. This can be seen from the symbolism of *let me bless you* as connecting [truth] to one's life (mentioned above at §3504). Since it says *let me bless you in the presence of Jehovah* this time, it now symbolizes full union. The communication of truth on the earthly plane with goodness on the rational plane is characterized as a connection, but that of goodness on the earthly plane with goodness on the rational plane is characterized as union. There is a parallelism between the Lord and us when it comes to the heavenly attributes of goodness but not in regard to the spiritual qualities of truth; see §1832.

3515   *Before my death* means life on the earthly plane as a result. This can be seen from the symbolism of *death* as being brought back to life (discussed above at §§3498, 3505).

Genesis 27:8, 9, 10. *"And now, my son, listen closely to my voice, to what* **3516** *I command you: Please go to the flock and fetch me from there two good goats' kids and let me make them into delicacies for your father, such as he loves. And you are to bring them to your father and let him eat, in order that he can bless you before his death."*

Now, my son, listen closely to my voice, to what I command you symbolizes a longing for and delight in earthly truth, perceived by the divine truth present in the divine rational mind. *Please go to the flock* means to a familial type of earthly goodness that is unconnected with divine rationality. *And fetch me from there two good goats' kids* symbolizes the truth belonging to that goodness. *And let me make them into delicacies for your father, such as he loves* means that it will make something nice out of it. *And you are to bring them to your father and let him eat* means for the divine goodness belonging to divine rationality, and adoption. *In order that he can bless you* means a resulting union. *Before his death* symbolizes revival on the earthly plane.

Now, my son, listen closely to my voice, to what I command you symbol- **3517** izes a longing for and delight in earthly truth, perceived by the divine truth present in the divine rational mind. This can be seen from the representation of Rebekah, the speaker, as divine truth in the divine rational mind (mentioned before) and from that of Jacob, to whom she is speaking, as earthly truth (also mentioned before). It is clear without explanation that longing and delight are involved.

Please go to the flock symbolizes a familial type of earthly goodness **3518** that is unconnected with divine rationality. This can be seen from the symbolism of a *flock* as goodness (discussed in §§343, 415, 1565)—here, because the words are addressed to Jacob, as earthly goodness, and in fact familial goodness, since he stayed at home. The field, which supplied Esau with his game and symbolizes goodness on the earthly plane (§§3500, 3508), was a goodness unconnected with family.

In other Scripture passages, a flock is used to portray goodness on the rational plane, but those passages use a herd to portray goodness on the earthly plane (see §2566).

Earthly goodness of a familial type is the goodness we inherit from our parents, the goodness we are born with. It differs radically from the goodness on the earthly plane that flows in from the Lord. (For a definition and description of earthly goodness, see §§3470, 3471.) In order to distinguish them, then, one kind is being called *goodness on the earthly plane,* the other, *earthly goodness.*

We each receive familial goodness from our father and from our mother, and these two kinds also differ. The goodness we receive from our father is deeper; that from our mother is shallower. In the Lord these two kinds of goodness were very clearly distinguished. The goodness he took from his Father was divine, but what he took from his mother was tainted with inherited evil. The goodness that the Lord had from his Father on the earthly plane was his own proper goodness, because it was his actual life, and this goodness is what Esau represents. The earthly goodness the Lord acquired from his mother, being stained with inherited evil, was in reality evil, and that is what is meant by familial goodness. Although it was evil, it was still of service when his earthly dimension was reforming; but after it completed its service, it was rejected.

[2] The case is the same with every person being reborn. The goodness we receive from the Lord as our new Father is deeper, and the goodness we inherit from our parents is shallower. The goodness we receive from the Lord is called spiritual goodness, but the goodness we inherit from our parents is called earthly goodness. The latter, the goodness we inherit from our parents, is of service at first when we are reforming, because with all its sweetness and pleasure it provides a mode for introducing factual knowledge and, later, the knowledge of truth. When it has finished serving as a means to this end, it is removed. Then spiritual goodness emerges and reveals itself.

Experience provides ample proof. For instance, simply consider that when the young are starting their education, they are eager to learn, and not, at first, for any purpose they can see but out of an almost physical pleasure, an inborn delight, and other promptings. When they grow up, their eagerness to learn takes on a goal, which is to outdo their peers and rivals. Later they develop goals involving worldly success. During the process of rebirth, they are motivated by the pleasure and appeal of truth, and when that process is complete (in adulthood), by the love of truth and subsequently by the love of goodness. Their preceding goals and the pleasure that went with them are then taken away bit by bit, to be replaced by inner goodness from the Lord, which displays itself in their desires.

Clearly, then, the prior pleasures, which looked good on the outside, served as means. New means are constantly replacing one another in this way.

[3] The situation resembles that of a tree, which in the early stages of spring adorns its branches with leaves, and then, as spring advances, with flowers. When summer arrives, it produces the rudiments of fruit, which

mature, and finally it places seeds in them. In these it secures itself new trees of the same kind, and a whole potential garden—or an actual garden, if the seeds are scattered.

Metaphors like this, which are also representations, exist in nature, because the whole material world is a theater representing the Lord's kingdom in the heavens and therefore his kingdom on the earth (that is, in the church) and his kingdom in everyone reborn.

This clarifies how earthly goodness of a familial type serves as a means for producing goodness on the earthly level, which unites with goodness on the rational level to become regenerate or spiritual goodness—goodness from the Lord—even though familial goodness consists merely of shallow and even worldly pleasure.

That is what Esau and Jacob represent and symbolize in the current chapter.

And fetch me from there two good goats' kids symbolizes the truth belonging to that goodness. This can be seen from the symbolism of *goats' kids* as truth associated with goodness, discussed below. There were *two* because like the rational plane, the earthly plane has attributes of both will and intellect. Those relating to the will on the earthly plane are pleasures, and those relating to the intellect there are facts. These two have to join together to have any reality.

3519

[2] The meaning of goats' kids as the truth belonging to goodness can be shown in Scripture passages mentioning kids and goats.

You need to know that in a positive sense all tame, useful animals mentioned in the Word symbolize heavenly qualities of goodness and spiritual qualities of truth (see §§45, 46, 142, 143, 246, 714, 715, 2180, 2781, 3218). There are different kinds of heavenly qualities, or goodness, and consequently of spiritual qualities, or truth, so one animal has a different symbolism than another. One thing is meant by a lamb, another by a kid, another by a ewe, she-goat, ram, he-goat, young ox, or adult ox, another by a horse or camel, another by birds, and another by sea creatures like whales and fish. The kinds of heavenly and spiritual phenomena and therefore of goodness and truth are beyond counting, but when heavenliness or goodness is spoken of, or when spirituality or truth is, it does not seem to be complex but plain and simple. In reality they are both quite complex and come in countless varieties, as can be seen from the remarks on heaven in §3241: Heaven is divided into countless communities. The divisions are determined by the different types of heavenly and spiritual traits, or the types of good done out of love and the types of truth that lead to faith.

Each category of goodness and each category of truth has unlimited subcategories, into which communities of every kind are divided; and the same goes for each subcategory.

[3] The most comprehensive categories of goodness and truth are what the animals offered as burnt offerings and sacrifices represented. Because the categories are inherently and distinctly different, it was explicitly commanded that one type and not another was to be used. Male and female lambs and male and female goats' kids were to be used in some; rams and ewes or he-goats in others; calves, young cattle, and adult cattle in yet others; and pigeons and turtledoves too (see §§922, 1823, 2180, 2805, 2807, 2830).

The symbolism of kids and goats can be seen both from the sacrifices in which they were offered and from other places in the Word. These passages make it plain that male and female lambs symbolized innocence in the inner, rational self, while kids and goats symbolized innocence in the outer, earthly self, and accordingly the truth and goodness associated with that innocence.

[4] The following passages in the Word show that a kid and a goat symbolize the truth and goodness that go with innocence in the outer, earthly self. In Isaiah:

> The wolf will stay with the *lamb,* and the leopard will lie down with the *kid,* the calf also and the young lion and the sheep [will live] together, and a little child will lead them. (Isaiah 11:6)

The subject here is the Lord's kingdom and conditions in which people no longer fear evil, or dread hell, because they are with the Lord. The lamb and the kid stand for people with innocence, and because they are kept the safest of all, these animals come up first.

[5] When every firstborn in Egypt was struck, the people were commanded to slaughter a sound member of the flock, a male one, from the *lambs* or *kids,* and put some of the blood on the doorposts and lintel of their houses so that they would not be given the plague by the striker (Exodus 12:5, 7, 13). The firstborn of Egypt mean the goodness of love and charity, snuffed out (§3325). Lambs and kids mean states of innocence, and people in those states are safe from evil. After all, states of innocence are what the Lord uses to protect everyone in heaven. That protection was represented by the slaughtering of the lamb or kid and of the blood on the doorposts and lintel of the houses.

[6] Whenever Jehovah appeared to people in the form of an angel, they would sacrifice a *kid of the goats* to keep from dying. Examples are his

appearance to Gideon (Judges 6:19) and Manoah (Judges 13:15, 16, 19). The reason was that Jehovah, or the Lord, cannot appear to anyone—not even an angel—who is not in a state of innocence. As soon as the Lord presents himself, the individual is brought into a state of innocence, because it is through innocence that the Lord enters, even with angels in heaven. So no one can go to heaven without some trace of innocence, as the Lord said in Matthew 18:3; Mark 10:15; Luke 18:17. For people's belief that they would die if they failed to offer this burnt offering when Jehovah appeared to them, see Judges 13:22, 23.

[7] Since true marriage love is innocence (§2736), it was customary in the representative church to go in to one's wife with the gift of a *goats' kid,* as we read of Samson in Judges 15:1 and of Judah when he went in to Tamar in Genesis 38:17, 20, 23.

The symbolism of a kid and goat as innocence is also evident from the fact that people would offer them as guilt sacrifices when they sinned by mistake (Leviticus 1:10; 4:28; 5:6). A sin committed by mistake is an unknowing sin, which has innocence in it. The same symbolism is evident from this divine command in Moses:

> The very first of the first fruits of your land you shall bring to the house of Jehovah your God. You shall not boil a *kid* in its mother's milk. (Exodus 23:19; 34:26)

The first fruits of the land that they were to bring to Jehovah's house symbolize the state of innocence that exists in childhood. Not boiling a kid in its mother's milk means not destroying that innocence. This symbolism is the reason the one command follows directly after the other in both of the cited passages. In the literal sense, they seem to have nothing in common, but in the inner sense they go together.

[8] Since kids and goats symbolized innocence, as noted, it was also ordered that the curtains on the dwelling place of the tabernacle be made with *goats' wool* (Exodus 25:4; 26:7; 35:5, 6, 23, 26; 36:14) as a sign that every sacred quality represented in the tabernacle took its essential nature from innocence. Goats' wool symbolizes the very outermost surface of innocence, which is lacking in knowledge. That is what innocence is like among people outside the church, who in an inner sense are the tabernacle's curtains.

This now clarifies the identity and nature of the truth belonging to goodness that is symbolized by the two good goats' kids of which Rebekah, the mother, spoke to her son Jacob. It is the truth of innocence, or early childhood, which Esau was to bring to his father Isaac; see §§3501, 3508.

Actually, it was not that truth, but at first it seemed to be, which is why Jacob used it to impersonate Esau.

3520   *And let me make them into delicacies for your father, such as he loves* means that it will make something nice out of it. This can be seen from the symbolism of *delicacies* as the appealing quality that comes from goodness (discussed above in §3502). Here it is called something nice because the truth came not from real but from familial goodness (§3518).

3521   *And you are to bring them to your father and let him eat* means for the divine goodness belonging to divine rationality, and adoption. This is established by the representation of Isaac, the *father* here, as divine goodness in the divine rationality (discussed before) and by the symbolism of *eating* as adopting (discussed above at §3513). The truth that grew out of familial goodness was *not* adopted, though, as will become clear below [§§3536, 3556, 3570].

3522   *In order that he can bless you* means a resulting union, which is established by the symbolism of *blessing* as union (discussed above at §§3504, 3514).

3523   *Before his death* symbolizes revival on the earthly plane, which can be seen from the symbolism of *death* as revival (also dealt with above, at §§3498, 3505). The fact that it was on the earthly plane is clear.

3524   Genesis 27:11, 12, 13. *And Jacob said to Rebekah his mother, "Look, Esau my brother is a hairy man and I am a smooth man. Perhaps my father might feel me, and I will be in his eyes as a deluder and bring on myself a curse and not a blessing." And his mother said to him, "On me be your curse, my son; only listen closely to my voice and go, fetch them for me."*

Jacob said to Rebekah his mother symbolizes a perception the Lord received from divine truth about earthly truth. *Look, Esau my brother is a hairy man* symbolizes the relative quality of earthly goodness. *And I am a smooth man* symbolizes the relative quality of earthly truth. *Perhaps my father might feel me* symbolizes the deepest level of perception. *And I will be in his eyes as a deluder* symbolizes a rejection [of earthly truth] because it seems to break the rules. *And bring on myself a curse and not a blessing* symbolizes a rift. *And his mother said to him* symbolizes a perception received from divine truth. *On me be your curse, my son* means no rift. *Only listen closely to my voice and go, fetch them for me* means in effect.

3525   *Jacob said to Rebekah his mother* symbolizes a perception the Lord received from divine truth about earthly truth. This can be seen from the symbolism of *saying* in scriptural narrative as perceiving (discussed in §3509), from the representation of *Jacob* as earthly truth (discussed in

§3305), and from that of *Rebekah* as divine truth in the Lord's divine rationality (discussed in §§3012, 3013, 3077).

A perception from divine truth concerning earthly truth is symbolized, rather than one coming from earthly truth and having to do with divine truth, as the literal meaning seems to suggest. All discernment on the earthly level comes from the rational level. Here, where it applies to the Lord, the meaning is that it came from divine truth known to his divine rational mind.

Look, Esau my brother is a hairy man symbolizes the relative quality of goodness on the earthly level. This becomes clear from the symbolism of *Esau* as goodness on the earthly level (dealt with above in §§3494, 3504) and from that of a *hairy man* as its quality—the quality of goodness. For the symbolism of *hairy* as the earthly level and especially the truth there, see §3301 and the section that now follows. **3526**

And I am a smooth man symbolizes the relative quality of truth on the earthly level. This becomes clear from the representation of Jacob—*I*—as truth on the earthly level (discussed in §3305) and from the symbolism of a *smooth man* as its quality, a symbolism discussed below. **3527**

To learn the meaning of these words, one first has to learn what *hairy* and *smooth* mean. Our inward depths present a kind of portrait of themselves on our surface, especially in our face and facial expression. Our *inmost* depths no longer appear there, but to some extent our inward depths do, unless we have learned since infancy to dissemble. Under the latter circumstances we more or less assume another frame of mind and consequently put on another face, because one's frame of mind is what appears in one's face. Through practice and so through custom, hypocrites develop more ability at this than others; and the more deceitful they are, the more ability they develop. In people who are not deceptive, rational goodness appears in the face as a kind of animating fire, and rational truth, as the light cast by its flame. This is something we realize from an almost innate knowledge, acquired without effort. It is the living energy of the goodness and truth in a person's spirit that displays itself this way, and since we are spirits clothed with a body, we recognize such things by perceiving them with our spirit, which is to say, spontaneously. That is why we are sometimes affected by another's countenance—though it is not the countenance that affects us but the mind shining through it. Our earthly level, on the other hand, appears in our face as a dimmer animating fire and the dimmer light of that animation. Our bodily level can barely be seen except as a warmth and brightness and as changes in their intensity, depending on the changes in our emotions.

[2] The very earliest people were heavenly people, totally ignorant of pretense and even more so of hypocrisy and deceit. So because one's inner reaches reveal themselves in a kind of portrait this way, especially in one's face, those people were able to see the different levels of another's mind in visible form in his or her face. Accordingly, the face also symbolized matters of will and matters of intellect, or the deeper rational levels and the goodness and truth there (§§358, 1999, 2434). The goodness on those deeper levels was symbolized by the blood in the face and its ruddiness; the truth there, by the shape of the face and its glow. The inner earthly levels, on the other hand, were symbolized by things that grow on the surface, like hair and the outer layer of skin. Hair symbolizes what grows out of earthly goodness, and the outer layer of skin symbolizes what grows out of earthly truth. So people who had devoted themselves to earthly goodness were called hairy men, while those who had devoted themselves to earthly truth were called smooth men. This shows what *Esau my brother is a hairy man and I am a smooth man* symbolizes on an inner level: the relative quality of goodness on the earthly level and of truth there.

The same thing clarifies Esau's representation as goodness on the earthly level, because he was called Esau for his hairiness (Genesis 25:25) and Edom for his ruddy color (Genesis 25:30). Mount Seir, where he lived, symbolizes something similar—bushiness. Because of this, there was a mountain leading up to Mount Seir called Bald or Smooth Mountain, as mentioned in Joshua 11:17, 12:7, and it represented truth leading up to goodness.

[3] It was shown in §3301 that *hairy* is used to describe goodness and the resulting truth, and in a negative sense, evil and the resulting falsity. The following passages in the Word make it clear that *smooth* is used to describe truth, and in a negative sense, falsity. In Isaiah:

> You were growing hot for your gods under every green tree; in the *smooth places of the valley* was your allotment. (Isaiah 57:5, 6)

Being hot has to do with evil; the smooth places of the valley, with falsity. In the same author:

> The crafter strengthens the metalsmith, who is *polishing a mallet* by pounding on an anvil, saying to the joint, "It is good." (Isaiah 41:7)

"The crafter strengthens the metalsmith" has to do with evil; one polishing or smoothing a mallet, with falsity. In David:

> Butter makes *his mouth smooth;* when his heart approaches, his words are softer than oil. (Psalms 55:21)

The smooth mouth (flattery) has to do with falsity; the heart and its soft words, with evil. In the same author:

> Their throat is an open grave; with their tongue they speak *smoothly*. (Psalms 5:9)

The open grave of their throat has to do with evil; the tongue speaking smoothly, with falsity. In Luke:

> Every valley will be filled in, and every mountain and hill will be lowered. And the circuitous will become direct, and the rough will turn *into flat paths*. (Luke 3:5)

The valley stands for what is lowly (§§1723, 3417). The mountain and hill, for what is lofty or proud (1691). The circuitous made direct stands for the conversion of unknowing evil into goodness, because length and everything connected with it has to do with goodness (1613). The rough turned into flat paths stands for the conversion of unknowing falsity into truth, since a path relates to truth (627, 2333).

Perhaps my father might feel me symbolizes the deepest level of perception. This can be seen from the symbolism of *feeling* as the deepest core and all-in-all of perception, and from that of a *father* as goodness—here, divine goodness, since the Lord is the subject. **3528**

Feeling means the deepest core and all-in-all of perception because all physical sensitivity relates to the sense of touch, which stems and springs from perceptiveness. Sensation is just outward perceptiveness, and perceptiveness is just inward sensation. For a definition of perceptiveness, or perception, see §§104, 371, 495, 503, 521, 536, 1383–1398, 1616, 1919, 2145, 2171, 2831 at the beginning.

Although sensation and perception seems to take many forms, it all relates to the one pervasive, universal sense, which is touch. The different varieties—taste, smell, hearing, and sight—which are outward sensory abilities, are simply the general categories of touch, rising from inner sensation, or perception. Much experience is available to confirm this, but it will be discussed in its own place, by the Lord's divine mercy.

This shows that in an inner sense, *feeling* means the deepest core and the whole of perception.

What is more, all perceptiveness, or inward sensation, comes from goodness rather than truth (unless it comes from goodness *through* truth), because the Lord's divine life flows into what is good and through goodness into truth and in the process establishes perception. This indicates what *if my father feels me* symbolizes: the deepest core and the whole of perception springing from goodness and so from the Lord's divinity.

3529   *And I will be in his eyes as a deluder* symbolizes a rejection [of earthly truth] because it seems to break the rules, as can be seen from the following. *Being in his eyes* means having its character perceived, because an *eye* symbolizes the perception of inward vision (§§212, 2701, 2789, 2829, 3198, 3202). And a *deluder* means that it breaks the rules (or in this case, seems to). That is exactly what it is to delude someone. This would lead to rejection.

What an apparent breaking of the rules means will become clear in what follows [§§3539, 3563].

3530   *And bring on myself a curse and not a blessing* symbolizes a rift. This can be seen from the symbolism of a *curse* as a rift with or turning from what is good (discussed in §§245, 379, 1423) and from that of a *blessing* as union with goodness (discussed in §§3504, 3514).

3531   *And his mother said to him* symbolizes a perception received from divine truth. This can be seen from the symbolism of *saying* as perceiving, mentioned many times before, and from the representation of Rebekah, the *mother* here, as divine truth known to the Lord's divine rationality (discussed at §§3012, 3013).

3532   *On me be your curse, my son* means no rift. This can be seen from the symbolism of a *curse* as a rift (mentioned just above in §3530). Since the perception came from something divine (§3531), it means that there would be no rift.

3533   *Only listen closely to my voice and go, fetch them for me* means in effect. This can be seen from the symbolism of *listening closely to a voice* as obeying and from that of *going and fetching them for me* as doing. The words are addressed to truth on the earthly level, represented by Jacob, and are spoken by truth on the rational level (divinely rational, in this case), represented by Rebekah, so they can only mean "in effect." The earthly mind looks at things from the effect, but the rational mind, from causes.

3534   Genesis 27:14, 15, 16, 17. *And he went and fetched them and brought them to his mother, and his mother made delicacies such as his father loved. And Rebekah took the clothes of Esau her older son, the desirable ones that were with her in the house, and dressed Jacob her younger son. And the hides of goats' kids she caused to be put on his hands and on the smoothness of his neck. And she gave the delicacies and the bread that she had made into the hand of Jacob her son.*

He went and fetched them and brought them to his mother symbolizes a state in which truth on the earthly plane obeys. *And his mother made delicacies such as his father loved* symbolizes what is enjoyable but not the object of genuine desire. *And Rebekah took the clothes of Esau her older son, the desirable ones,* symbolizes genuine truth-from-goodness. *That were with her in the house* means which came from divine goodness by way of the divine truth known to the divine rationality. *And dressed Jacob her younger son* symbolizes a desire for truth, or the vital force of goodness that comes from truth. *And the hides of goats' kids she caused to be put* symbolizes the shallower truth belonging to familial goodness. *On his hands* means according to one's ability to receive it. *And on the smoothness of his neck* means so that the truth would not appear divisive. *And she gave the delicacies* symbolizes enjoyable results. *And the bread* symbolizes a good result. *That she had made* means that came from divine truth. *Into the hand of Jacob her son* means this is what the desire for earthly truth was like.

He went and fetched them and brought them to his mother symbolizes a state in which truth on the earthly plane obeys, as is established by the remarks just above at §3533 without further explanation.

3535

And his mother made delicacies such as his father loved symbolizes what is enjoyable but not the object of genuine desire. This is established by the representation of Rebekah, the *mother* here, as truth in the divine rational mind, and from the symbolism of *delicacies* as the appealing qualities of truth (discussed above at §3502). Here they mean something enjoyable that is not the object of genuine desire because they come not from Esau's hunting, or from the truth associated with real goodness (§3501), but from goats' kids taken out of the flock, or from the truth associated with familial goodness (§§3518, 3519).

3536

How these matters stand can be seen from discussions above at §§3502, 3512, 3518, 3519.

And Rebekah took the clothes of Esau her older son, the desirable ones, symbolizes genuine truth-from-goodness. This can be seen from the symbolism of *desirable clothes* as genuine truth. *Clothes* mean relatively superficial truth (see §2576). *The desirable ones* are genuine, because this truth belonged to genuine goodness on the earthly level, which *Esau her older son* represents (§§3300, 3302, 3322, 3494, 3504, 3527).

3537

That were with her in the house means which came from divine goodness by way of the divine truth known to the divine rationality. This can be seen from the representation of Rebekah ("her") as divine truth in the divine rational mind (discussed previously) and from the symbolism of the *house* as divine goodness, since it is being ascribed to the Lord. A *house* means what is good (see §§710, 2233, 2559, 3128).

3538

The reason the phrase *that were with her in the house* has this symbolism is that a house symbolizes the rational level in respect to both goodness
and truth. To put the same thing another way, it symbolizes both the volitional part of the rational mind (because the will has to do with goodness)
and the intellectual part (because the intellect has to do with truth). When
the rational mind acts from the will, or goodness, by means of the intellect, or truth, that mind is called a single house. [2] For the same reason,
heaven itself is called the house of God, since only what is good and
true exists there, and goodness acts through the truth that unites or
becomes one with it. It is also represented in marriages of husband and
wife, who make up a single household, because marriage love springs
from the divine marriage between goodness and truth (§§2728, 2729, 3132).
Each partner has a will motivated by goodness, but with a difference reflecting the relationship goodness has to its truth. So a husband symbolizes
what is good, and a wife symbolizes what is true. When the house is
united, goodness is the all-in-all there, and even the truth is good, because
it is composed of goodness.

The text says *with her in the house* rather than *with him* or *with them*
because the message has to do with a state in which truth and goodness
are joining—in other words, a state preceding their full oneness or union.
A discussion of that state now follows.

3539   *And dressed Jacob her younger son* symbolizes a desire for truth, or
the vital force of goodness that comes from truth, as can be seen from
the following: Rebekah represents divine truth in the Lord's divine rationality. *Jacob* represents divine truth in his earthly divinity. And *dressing*
here means communicating and imparting—imparting the truth-from-
goodness symbolized by Esau's clothes (§3537) and therefore a desire for
earthly truth, which is the same here as the vital force of goodness that
comes from truth.

What was said above in §3518 shows how to understand these ideas,
but since there is deep ignorance today about such things, let me explain
them a little more intelligibly. The current chapter tells how the Lord
made his earthly dimension divine, and in a representative sense it speaks
of the rebirth of a person's earthly level (see §3490). The situation with a
person is this:

[2] The goal of rebirth is for us to develop a new inner self and therefore a new soul, or spirit, but our inner self cannot be remade or reborn
unless our outer self is too. Although we are spirits after death, we take

with us into the other life aspects of our outer self: earthly emotions, doctrines, facts—in short, all the contents of our outer, earthly memory (see §§2475–2483). These form the foundation on which our inner depths rest. Whatever priorities determine their arrangement, then, those are the priorities that inner things take on when they flow in, because inner things are modified on the outer plane. This shows that not only our inner, rational self needs to be reborn or remade but our outer, earthly self as well. Otherwise there would be no correspondence. For the correspondence between our inner self with its spiritual qualities and our outer self with its earthly qualities, see §§2987, 2989, 2990, 2991, 3002, 3493.

[3] Esau and Jacob in this chapter depict the conditions of human regeneration, in a representative sense. Here they depict the nature of the first stage, when we are being reborn, or before we have finished the process. This stage is all upside-down compared to the stage we reach when we have been reborn. At the stage in which we are being reborn, before we have reached the end, intellectual forces related to truth seem to take the leading role. Once we have been reborn, forces of the will related to goodness do. Jacob's takeover of Esau's birthright represented the apparent dominance of intellectual forces related to truth at the first stage (see §§3325, 3336). So did his theft of the blessing, which is the current theme. Jacob's impersonation of Esau by wearing Esau's clothes and the hides of the goats' kids represents the complete topsy-turviness of that stage. In it, rational truth is not yet closely united with rational goodness; that is, the intellect is not yet closely united with the will. So when rational truth flows into and acts on the earthly dimension, it turns the contents of that dimension the other way up.

[4] Abundant experience can provide evidence too. Consider in particular that with our intellect we can discern much that is good and true, and our earthly side can therefore know about it, even when our will is not yet able to live by it. For instance, love and charity are imperative. Our intellectual capacity can see and confirm this, but until we have been reborn, our voluntary capacity cannot acknowledge it. There are people completely lacking in love for the Lord and charity for their neighbor who grasp it firmly.

Again, love is our very life, and the quality of our love determines the quality of our life. All pleasure and pleasantness and therefore all joy and happiness come from love, so the quality of our love also determines the quality of our joy and happiness. This too we can grasp with our intellect, even when our will disputes or outright opposes [the logical consequence:] that the happiest life results from love for the Lord and for our neighbor (because divinity itself flows into that life), and conversely that the unhappiest life results from love for ourselves and for worldly advantages (because hell flows into that life).

Another concept perceptible to the intellect but not to the will is that love for the Lord is therefore the life of heaven, while mutual love is heaven's soul, animated by that life. The less the vital energy of our will guides our thoughts, and the less we reflect on the life our will has led us to live, the better we perceive this with our intellect. The more the energy of our will guides our thoughts, the less we perceive it; in fact, we deny it.

[5] Furthermore, humility is the attribute in us that the Divine can flow into, because self-love and materialism—hellish qualities that block that inflow—are removed in a humble state. This is clearly visible to the intellect, but until we develop a new will and our intellect unites with it, we cannot achieve heartfelt humility. The worse our life is, or the more our will turns toward evil, the less capable we are of true humility. To that extent the whole idea becomes obscure to us and we deny it.

From this we can also perceive with our intellect that we are asked to be humble not because the Lord loves glory but because of his divine love. Humility in us enables him to flow in with goodness and truth, bless us, and make us happy. The more we consult our will, though, the harder it is to see this. The same is true with very many other concepts.

[6] This ability to understand what is good and true even when we do not will it is given to us so that we can reform and regenerate. As a result, it exists in both the evil and the good. In fact, the ability is sometimes more keenly honed in the evil. The difference is that evil people do not desire truth for the sake of living by it, that is, for the sake of the good deeds to which truth can lead. Consequently they cannot reform. Good people, however, do desire truth for the sake of living by it, or for the sake of doing good, so they *can* reform.

When good people are going through the first stage of reformation, they see theological truth as coming first and living a good life as second, because truth inspires them to do good. During their second stage, though, a good life comes first and theological truth second, because goodness (or rather a desire for goodness) inspires them to do good. At that point, since their will unites with their intellect in a kind of marriage, they have been reborn.

These two stages are discussed in the inner meaning of Esau and Jacob's story.

And the hides of goats' kids she caused to be put symbolizes the shallower truth belonging to familial goodness. This can be seen from the symbolism of *hides* as what lies on the surface (discussed below) and from that of *goats' kids* as the truth belonging to familial goodness, since they came from a family flock. The latter symbolism was discussed at §§3518, 3519, which also show what familial goodness and the truth that grows out of it are. Every kind of goodness has its truth and every truth its goodness, and they need to unite if they are to amount to anything.

`3540`

Hides symbolize what lies on the surface because they form the outermost covering of an animal, the outer boundary of its inward parts, just as the layers of skin do in a human being. They take their symbolism from a representation in the other world: There are individuals there belonging to the region of the skin, who will be discussed where the universal human is described at the ends of the following chapters, by the Lord's divine mercy. They are those who focus exclusively on superficial goodness and the truth that goes with it. So the skin, and also a hide, symbolizes what lies on the surface. This stands out clearly in the Word, as in Jeremiah:

> Because of the abundance of your wickedness, the fringes of your skirt have been lifted to expose you, your heels have been violated. Will Ethiopians change *their skin,* and leopards, their spots? Even you can do good, schooled as you are in doing evil. (Jeremiah 13:22, 23)

The fringes are superficial truth; the heels are the shallowest forms of goodness. For the meaning of the heel and shoes as the lowest earthly factors, see §§259, 1748. Since this truth and goodness come from evil, as the text says, they are compared to black Ethiopians and their skin, and to leopards and their spots. [2] In Moses:

> If you go so far as to take your companion's garment as collateral, before the sun sets you shall restore it to him, because it alone is his covering; it is *his garment used as a hide, in which he must lie down.* (Exodus 22:26, 27)

All laws in the Word, both civil and criminal, correspond to the laws of goodness and truth in heaven and were laid down from heaven, so the same is true of this one. Otherwise it would be impossible to figure out why before the sun set they had to restore a garment taken as collateral and why it says that it is his garment used as a hide, in which he must lie down. The correspondence becomes clear from the inner meaning, which is that we are not to defraud our companions of the shallower truth that makes up the doctrines they live by and their rituals. For the meaning of a garment as this kind of truth, see §§297, 1073, 2576. The sun means the resulting goodness that they love or live by (§§1529, 1530, 2441, 2495). Not letting it die out is symbolized by restoring the garment before the sun sets. Since that truth is the outer covering or border of something deeper, the text says that the garment is "used as a hide, in which he must lie down."

[3] Since hides symbolized something superficial, it was commanded that the tabernacle covering be made of red *rams' hides*, and on top of them, *badgers' hides* (Exodus 26:14). The tabernacle represented the three heavens and therefore the heavenly and spiritual qualities found in the Lord's kingdom. The curtains surrounding it represented earthly qualities, which are outward traits (§3478), which in turn are the rams' and badgers' hides. Superficial traits are what sheathe inward ones—earthly traits are what sheathe spiritual and heavenly ones—just as a body cloaks its soul; and that was the reason for the command. Again, whenever the [Israelites'] camp set out on a journey, Aaron and his sons would cover the ark of the testimony with the curtaining veil and put on it a blanket of *badger hide*. On the table [for the bread] and everything atop it, they would spread a cloth of double-dyed scarlet and cover it with a blanket of *badger hide*. They would put the lampstand and all its utensils under a blanket of *badger hide*. And all the utensils for ministry they would put under a cloth of blue-violet and cover them with a blanket of *badger hide* (Numbers 4:5, 6, 8, 10, 11, 12). Anyone who thinks reverently about the Word can see that all these articles represented divine attributes. The ark, the table, the lampstand, and the utensils for ministry did, and so did the coverings of double-dyed scarlet and blue-violet and the blankets of badgers' hide, which represented the outer parts of the divine dimension.

[4] The prophets represented people who teach and consequently scriptural teachings about goodness and truth (§2534). Elijah represented the Word itself (§2762), as did John [the Baptist], who is therefore called the Elijah who was to come (Matthew 17:10, 11, 12, 13). So in order to represent the Word as it is outwardly, or in its literal text, Elijah was girded at his hips with a *belt of hide* (2 Kings 1:8), and John had clothing of camel's hair and a *belt of hide* around his hips (Matthew 3:4).

Hide and skin, then, symbolized superficial things—which earthly things are by comparison with what is spiritual and heavenly. So since it was customary in the ancient church to speak and write symbolically, hide and skin have the same symbolism in Job, a book of the ancient church. This can be seen from several places in Job, including this:

> I know my Redeemer; he is alive and in the end will rise over the dust, and afterward all this will be wrapped in *my skin,* and from *my flesh* I will see God. (Job 19:25, 26)

Being wrapped in skin stands for being wrapped in the earthly element we take with us after death, as described in §3539. Seeing God from one's flesh means seeing him from a sense of one's autonomy brought to life. For this symbolism of flesh, see §§148, 149, 780. As just mentioned, Job's representational, symbolic manner of writing shows it to be a book of the ancient church, but it is not among the books called the Law and the Prophets, because it does not have an inner meaning dealing exclusively with the Lord and his kingdom. This is the only criterion for a true book of the Word.

On his hands means according to one's ability to receive [that truth]. This can be seen from the symbolism of a *hand* as power (discussed in §§878, 3091) and so the ability to receive.

3541

And on the smoothness of his neck means so that the truth would not appear divisive. This can be seen from the use of "smooth" or *smoothness,* which has to do with truth (discussed in §3527), and from the symbolism of a *neck* as a connector (discussed below). In this case, since the smoothness of his neck only *appeared* [to be hairy], it means so that truth would not *appear* divisive.

3542

Statements and illustrations above at §3539 show how matters stand in all this: Goodness and truth that flow out from the intellect and not at the same time from the will are not good or true, however much they may appear so on the outside. When there is a will for evil, goodness and truth divide rather than unite. When there is any will for goodness, though, they do not divide but unite, even if they are arranged upside down, because they are the means of our rebirth. So arranged, they serve to regenerate us in the beginning, which is why I said just above that the truth would not appear divisive under those circumstances. There will be more on this below.

[2] The reason a *neck* symbolizes a connector is that everything up in our head communicates back and forth with everything down in our body through the neck in between. So this middle part symbolizes inflow, communication, and union, all three. This will become even clearer from the correspondence of the universal human with various aspects of the

human body, as discussed at the ends of the chapters. The neck symbolizes the same thing in the Word, as in Isaiah:

> His spirit is like a flooding river; *right at the neck he will cut [them] in half.* (Isaiah 30:28)

The flooding river stands for falsity overflowing. Cutting in half at the neck stands for blocking and cutting off contact and therefore connection between what is higher and what is lower. Contact and connection is blocked and broken when spiritual goodness and truth are not accepted. [3] In Habakkuk:

> You struck the head off the house of ungodliness, laying the foundation bare *right to the neck.* (Habakkuk 3:13)

Striking the head off the house of ungodliness stands for destroying the roots of falsity. Laying the foundation bare right to the neck stands for breaking all connection. In Jeremiah:

> Transgressions, intertwined, *rose onto my neck;* he made my strength stumble. God gave me into their hands; I cannot rise again. (Lamentations 1:14)

"Transgressions, intertwined, rose onto my neck" stands for the idea of falsities opposing deeper, rational concepts.

[4] Since the neck symbolized this communication and interconnection, chains on the neck symbolized a break in it and therefore the abandonment of truth. We abandon truth when we no longer admit spiritual influences—constantly flowing in from the Lord—into our rational mind or consequently into our earthly mind. A break in contact, or the desertion of truth, is what the following command in Jeremiah represents:

> He was to make himself bonds and yokes and *put them on his neck* and send them to different peoples and say that those people were to serve Nebuchadnezzar, king of Babylon, and any who did not *lay their neck* under his yoke would be punished with sword, famine, and contagion. But any who *submitted their neck* would be left on the land. (Jeremiah 27:2, 3, 8, 11)

Putting one's neck under the yoke of Babylon's king and serving him stands for being purged of truth and stripped of goodness. Babylon means that which strips goodness away (see §1327 at the end), and it is stripped from people to prevent them from profaning what is holy (§§301, 302,

303, 1327, 1328, 2426, 3398, 3399, 3402). Since evil and falsity are served when the inflow of goodness and truth is broken off, putting one's neck under the yoke also means serving them. [5] In the same author:

> Jehovah has said, "I will break the yoke of Nebuchadnezzar, king of Babylon, within two years of days, *off the neck* of all the nations." (Jeremiah 28:11)

This stands for the necessity of delivering people from that devastation. In Isaiah:

> Shake yourself from the dirt; rise, sit, Jerusalem! *Open the bonds on your neck,* captive daughter of Zion! (Isaiah 52:2)

Opening the bonds on one's neck stands for letting in and welcoming what is good and true. In Micah:

> Here, now, I am planning on this family an evil *from which you will not remove your necks,* and you will not go upright; because it will be a time of evil. (Micah 2:3)

Not removing their necks from the evil stands for not letting truth in. Not going upright stands for a resulting failure to turn our gaze up toward the things of heaven (§248).

And she gave the delicacies symbolizes enjoyable results. This is established by the symbolism of *delicacies* as something appealing and enjoyable (dealt with above at §§3502, 3536).   **3543**

And the bread symbolizes a good result. This is established by the symbolism of *bread* as what is good (dealt with in §§276, 680, 1798, 2165, 2177, 3464, 3478).   **3544**

That she had made means that came from what was divine. This can be seen from the representation of Rebekah as divine truth in the Lord's divine rational mind. Since it says that Rebekah *made* it, the meaning is that it came from what was divine.   **3545**

Into the hand of Jacob her son means this is what the desire for earthly truth was like, as can be seen from the fact that these words are the conclusion to the preceding verses. This is what Jacob, representing earthly truth (§§3305, 3509, 3525), was then like: on his hands and neck he wore the hides of goats' kids, and he held in his hand some delicacies that he would carry to his father Isaac.   **3546**

Genesis 27:18, 19, 20. *And he came to his father and said, "My father!" and [his father] said, "Here I am. Who are you, my son?" And Jacob said to*   **3547**

his father, "I am Esau, your firstborn; I did as you spoke to me. Rise, please;
sit and eat of my game, in order that your soul can bless me." And Isaac said
to his son, "How did you hurry to find this, my son?" and he said, "Because
Jehovah your God made it happen before my face."
          He came to his father and said, "My father!" and he said, "Here I am.
Who are you, my son?" symbolizes a state of perception at the presence of
that truth. *And Jacob said to his father* means what earthly truth sensed. *I*
am Esau, your firstborn means that it believed it was genuine earthly goodness. *I did as you spoke to me* symbolizes obedience. *Rise, please; sit and eat*
of my game symbolizes truth belonging to the desire for such goodness.
In order that your soul can bless me symbolizes union. *And Isaac said to his*
son symbolizes a perception. *How did you hurry to find this, my son?* means
that it was produced so fast. *And he said, "Because Jehovah your God made*
it happen before my face," symbolizes providence.

3548   *He came to his father and said, "My father!" and he said, "Here I am.*
Who are you, my son?" symbolizes a state of perception at the presence of
that truth. This can be seen from the representation of Isaac, the *father*
here, and of Jacob, the *son* here (both dealt with several times earlier), and
from the symbolism of *saying* as perceiving (also dealt with before). This
and the rest of the evidence shows that it means a state of perception at
the presence of the truth represented by Jacob. The nature of the truth
currently represented by Jacob is clear from the inner meaning of the preceding and following parts of the story: In outward form it looks like the
goodness and truth-from-goodness represented by Esau and symbolized
by his hunting; but it was not like that on the inside.

          Truth on the earthly level appears to be good and true in people being
reborn, before they reach the end of the process, not that it looks that
way to the people themselves. They know nothing of goodness and truth
in themselves when they are being reborn, but it does seem so in the eyes
of angels, who view such things by heaven's light. We on earth do not even
know what earthly goodness and truth are. Not knowing, we cannot perceive them; and not perceiving them generally, we cannot perceive their fine
points, so we cannot see differences between them, let alone their changing
states. As a consequence, we have a hard time grasping how matters stand
with this goodness and its truth, no matter how they are described. However, the chapter does focus on this, so I will explain it as intelligibly as
possible in what follows.

3549   *And Jacob said to his father* means what earthly truth sensed, as can be
seen from the following: *Saying* means perceiving, as mentioned before.

Here it means sensing, since it is being done by the earthly level. And *Jacob* represents earthly truth, as also mentioned before [§3305].

I am Esau, your firstborn means that it believed it was genuine earthly goodness. This can be seen from the representation of *Esau* and the symbolism of a *firstborn* as goodness, and in fact the earthly goodness represented by Esau.

3550

The truth we possess before we have been reborn, you see, is something we believe to be genuine goodness. People with perception know it is not genuine goodness but truth in the guise of goodness. People without perception, though, are fully convinced that it is.

This too will become clearer in what follows.

I did as you spoke to me symbolizes obedience, as can be seen without explanation.

3551

Rise, please; sit and eat of my game symbolizes truth belonging to the desire for such goodness, as can be seen from the following symbolism: *Rising* involves some kind of elevation, as discussed in §§2401, 2785, 2912, 2927, 3171. *Sitting* involves a measure of calm. *Eating* symbolizes adoption, as discussed in §§2187, 3168. And *game* symbolizes the truth that rises out of goodness, as mentioned in §3501. Here, then, is symbolized a desire for the type of goodness out of which truth rises. Everything that rising, sitting, and eating mean in an inner sense has to do with desire, so "desire" by itself stands for all three.

3552

In order that your soul can bless me symbolizes union. This can be seen from the symbolism of being *blessed* as union (discussed before at §§3504, 3514, 3530).

3553

And Isaac said to his son symbolizes a perception, or what the rationality represented by *Isaac* perceived about the earthly plane represented by Jacob. The symbolism of *saying* as perceiving has been shown many times before.

3554

How did you hurry to find this, my son? means that it was produced so fast, as stands to reason without explanation.

3555

And he said, "Because Jehovah your God made it happen before my face," symbolizes providence, as can also be seen without explanation.

3556

The providential measure depicted here is that of arranging goodness and the truth that grows out of it in such a pattern in people being reborn that it looks on the outside as if it were genuine goodness and the genuine truth that grows out of it. That is to say, it presents itself superficially with such a face even though it is not so but is familial goodness (as noted above) and the truth growing out of it. These are of use only to people undergoing regeneration; they serve only to introduce goodness and truth of a rather coarse nature, because they are helpful then.

3557   Genesis 27:21, 22, 23. *And Isaac said to Jacob, "Come close, please, and I will feel you, my son, [to tell] whether you are he, my son Esau, or not." And Jacob came close to Isaac his father, and [Isaac] felt him and said, "The voice is Jacob's voice, but the hands are Esau's hands." And he did not recognize him, because his hands were like the hands of Esau his brother: hairy; and [Isaac] blessed him.*

Isaac said to Jacob symbolizes a perception about this earthly dimension. *Come close, please, and I will feel you, my son* symbolizes a very deep perception resulting from presence. *Whether you are he, my son Esau, or not,* means that it was not earthly goodness. *And Jacob came close to Isaac his father* symbolizes a state of presence. *And he felt him* symbolizes comprehensive perception as a result. *And said, "The voice is Jacob's voice, but the hands are Esau's hands,"* means that the intellectual part there deals with inward truth, but the volitional part there deals with outward goodness, which is upside-down. *And he did not recognize him, because his hands were like the hands of Esau his brother: hairy,* means that from the volitional part on the outside [the Lord] perceived it as earthly goodness. *And he blessed him* symbolizes consequent union.

3558   *Isaac said to Jacob* symbolizes a perception about this earthly dimension. This can be seen from the symbolism of *saying* as perceiving (dealt with before) and from the representation of *Jacob* as truth in the earthly dimension. Here it means simply the earthly dimension, because he also seemed to represent—pretended outwardly to be—Esau. So he also appeared to represent the goodness in the earthly dimension that is Esau and also Esau's game, which is the truth that comes of that goodness (§3501).

The reason "she said" or "he said" recurs so many times is also because with this phrase there begins a new stage or new perception; see §§2061, 2238, 2260.

3559   *Come close, please, and I will feel you, my son* symbolizes a very deep perception resulting from presence. This is established by the symbolism of *coming close* as presence and by that of *feeling* as very deep and comprehensive perception (discussed in §3528).

3560   *Whether you are he, my son Esau, or not,* means that it was not earthly goodness. This can be seen from the doubt expressed in these words and those that directly follow. Since the rational mind is what perceives the identity and nature of the earthly level, the phrase means a perception that it was not so—not earthly goodness, or Esau.

And Jacob came close to Isaac his father symbolizes a state of presence, as can be seen from the above without further explanation.

3561

And he felt him symbolizes comprehensive perception. This can be seen from the symbolism of *feeling* as deep and comprehensive perception (mentioned above in §§3528, 3559). Here it symbolizes a comprehensive perception, because such perception develops out of the deepest kind. In other words, people who perceive inwardly perceive everything below, because what lies below is nothing but an offshoot and composite of what lies inside. The inmost core is the all-in-all in everything below itself, because nothing lower exists that does not spring from what is inside or (to put it another way) what is higher, as an effect from its efficient cause.

3562

This shows why our purpose determines our happiness or unhappiness in the next life. The purpose is the core of every cause. In fact, if the purpose is not present in the cause—is not the all-in-all of the cause—it is not a cause. The purpose is likewise the core of every effect, because the effect stems from a purpose-dependent cause. As a result, everything we have in us draws its existence from our purpose. So in the other world we live in a state that mirrors the state of our purpose (see §§1317, 1568, 1571, 1645, 1909, 3425).

From this it stands to reason that since feeling symbolizes the deepest perception, it symbolizes comprehensive perception.

And said, "The voice is Jacob's voice, but the hands are Esau's hands," means that the intellectual part there deals with inward truth, but the volitional part there deals with outward goodness, which is upside-down. This can be seen from the association of the word *voice* with truth and of the word *hand* with goodness. The use of *voice* for truth is clear from quotations in §§219, 220 of the first volume and from the fact that the voice is said to be that of *Jacob,* who represents earthly truth, as shown in various places above. The use of *hand* for goodness is due to its symbolism as power and ability (§§878, 3541), which come exclusively from goodness. Truth acquires all its power and ability from goodness, even though it seems to come from truth. The association is also due to the fact that the hands are said to be those of *Esau,* who represents goodness, as also shown above.

3563

This arrangement is plainly upside-down, because the proper pattern is for goodness in the will to lie on the inside, and truth in the intellect to lie on the outside. As noted above, though [§3548], few know anything about such topics, so they cannot be explained very intelligibly. Even if they are explained with perfect clarity, they cannot be understood when knowledge is lacking. Still, something needs to be said about it, since it is the subject here.

[2] Goodness on our earthly level comes only from deeper goodness, or goodness on our rational level. Our earthly level cannot acquire anything good from anywhere else. However, the inflow gives that goodness its character. And since goodness on the earthly level comes from nowhere else, truth on the earthly level has the same source. After all, wherever there is goodness there is truth. Both have to exist in order for them to be anything. But the inflow into the truth there gives it the character *it* has.

Here is how spiritual inflow works: Goodness on the rational plane flows into the earthly plane by two routes. The short path leads directly into the goodness there and through this into the truth there. This goodness and truth are what Esau and his hunting represent. Goodness on the rational plane also flows into the earthly plane by a longer route leading through truth on the rational plane. By this inflow, it forms something that resembles goodness but is actually truth.

[3] It is orderly, then, for goodness on the rational plane to flow directly into goodness on the earthly level and at the same time directly into truth; also to flow indirectly into the goodness there through truth on the rational plane; and likewise to flow both directly and indirectly into truth on the earthly plane. When this happens, the inflow is going by the ordained pattern, and that is how it operates in people who have been reborn. It operates differently, however, in people who have not yet been reborn, as noted earlier [§3539]. With them, goodness in the rational dimension does not flow directly into the goodness of the earthly dimension, only indirectly through truth in the rational dimension. In this way it establishes something similar to goodness on the earthly plane but not genuine goodness and therefore not genuine truth. The thing it establishes does have goodness at its core, because this goodness flows in by way of truth on the rational plane, but nothing more. So goodness exists there in a different form. On the outside it resembles the goodness represented by Esau, but on the inside it resembles the truth represented by Jacob. Since this is not the proper pattern, it is said to be upside-down. Yet considering that we cannot regenerate otherwise, it *is* the proper pattern.

[4] I realize that, although these ideas have been expressed clearly and can therefore be perceived clearly by people who know about them, they are dark and dim to people who do not know what spiritual inflow is. They are even dimmer to people who do not know that the rational plane

is different from the earthly plane, and dimmest of all to those who cannot distinguish goodness from truth.

The nature of earthly goodness and truth before rebirth can be revealed simply by the desires that affect us at that stage. When we seek truth not for the sake of living by it but for other purposes—to become well educated out of a kind of competitive urge or childish jealousy or desire for glory—then goodness and truth on our earthly level take on the pattern represented here by Jacob. So the two are more or less upside-down. Our intentions, which relate to goodness, are on the outside, while our intellect, which relates to truth, is on the inside. [5] The stage we reach after rebirth is different. At that point we do not merely want truth for the sake of living by it; even more ardently we long for real goodness in our lives. Our earlier feelings of rivalry, childish envy, and pride detach themselves and even seem to disappear. Then the good we intend is on the inside and the truth we understand is on the outside. Still, the truth acts in unison with the goodness, because it acts *from* goodness. This pattern is truly orderly. The previous pattern works toward the formation of this later pattern, because our intentions, which then lie on the outside, let in much that is useful for our regeneration. It is like a sponge that in soaking up both clear and muddy water absorbs material that would be rejected otherwise. Nevertheless, these things serve as means and help us form ideas about what is good and true, not to mention other functions they perform.

He did not recognize him, because his hands were like the hands of Esau **3564**
his brother: hairy, means that from the volitional part on the outside [the Lord] perceived it as earthly goodness. This is clear from the fact that he did not recognize Jacob as Jacob (that is, the truth that Jacob represents) but perceived him to be Esau (earthly goodness on the outside) because of the inflow discussed just above at §3563.

Communication exists between inner goodness and outer goodness, because they have symmetry (§§1831, 1832, 3514), but not between goodness and truth, unless the inflow of goodness into truth is as described just above.

And he blessed him symbolizes consequent union. This can be seen **3565**
from the symbolism of being *blessed* as union (dealt with in §§3504, 3514, 3530); but at this stage there was no union other than the kind described in §3563. There was inmost union with the truth Jacob represented but not intermediate union. Inmost union was achieved through the purpose (the deepest good), which was something that could be accomplished in this way and no other. When there is a purpose, at first there is a union of

the deepest with the shallowest levels. The intervening connection then comes more slowly, accomplished by the purpose, because all progress lies hidden in the goal. The Lord acts through purposes, gradually arranging intervening layers in order by means of them. This leads to the union symbolized by Isaac's blessing of Jacob.

3566   Genesis 27:24, 25. *And he said, "Are you he, my son Esau?" And [Jacob] said, "I am." And he said, "Carry it to me and let me eat of my son's game so that my soul can bless you." And [Jacob] carried it to him, and he ate; and he brought him wine, and he drank.*

He said, "Are you he, my son Esau?" And he said, "I am," means that the desire for earthly truth was then at a stage in which it believed itself to be earthly goodness, because of its outward appearance. *And he said, "Carry it to me and let me eat of my son's game,"* symbolizes a longing to bind earthly truth to itself through goodness. *So that my soul can bless you* symbolizes union. *And he carried it to him, and he ate* means being united with goodness first. *And he brought him wine, and he drank* means being united with truth next.

3567   *He said, "Are you he, my son Esau?" And he said, "I am,"* means that earthly truth was then at a stage in which it believed itself to be earthly goodness, because of its outward appearance, as can be seen from the following: Isaac asks, *"Are you he, my son Esau?"* which on an inner level can symbolize only the inflow of goodness in the rational mind into the earthly truth represented by Jacob. The answer—*he said, "I am"*—[means] that it then believed itself to be a form of goodness; see what is said above at §3550.

3568   *And he said, "Carry it to me and let me eat of my son's game,"* symbolizes a longing to bind earthly truth to itself through goodness. This can be seen from the symbolism of *eating* as uniting and adopting (discussed in §§2187, 2343, 3168, 3513 at the end) and from that of *my son's game* as the truth that comes of goodness (discussed at §§3309, 3501, 3508). The element of longing is obvious.

3569   *So that my soul can bless you* symbolizes union. This can be seen from the symbolism of being *blessed* as union (discussed at §§3504, 3514, 3530, 3565).

3570   *And he carried it to him, and he ate* means being united with goodness first. *And he brought him wine, and he drank* means being united with truth next. This is established by the following: *Eating* symbolizes union with and adoption of what is good (as noted just above at §3568). *Wine* symbolizes truth that develops out of goodness (as mentioned at §§1071, 1798). And *drinking* symbolizes union with and adoption of truth (§3168).

Here is how matters stand with the fact that goodness on the rational level (represented by Isaac) first binds goodness to itself and then truth, by means of the earthly plane (Jacob): When our earthly part is at a stage where goodness is on the outside and truth on the inside (a situation described above at §§3539, 3548, 3556, 3563), it lets in much that is not good but is still useful as means to a good end, arranged in its own hierarchy. However, goodness on the rational plane binds to itself and adopts only such material from there as conforms with its own goodness. It does not accept any other goodness. Anything that clashes, it rejects. The rest it leaves on the earthly level to serve as means for admitting and introducing further compatible material.

[2] Rationality is located in our inner self. Our earthly part has no idea what goes on there, because the inner self lies above the realm the earthly part is aware of. So people who lead only an earthly life cannot know anything about activity in their inner self, or rational mind. The Lord manages such activity without the person's least knowledge. That is why we have no idea how we are reborn and scarcely even *that* we are.

If you do want to know, just look at what your goals and intentions are, which you likely do not reveal to anyone. If you aim at something good, if you care more about your neighbor and the Lord than yourself, you are at some stage of rebirth. If you aim at something bad, if you care more about yourself than your neighbor or the Lord, be aware that you are not at any stage of rebirth. [3] Our life goals determine our place in the other world. Good goals put us in heaven with the angels; evil goals put us in hell with the devils. The purposes we have are actually the different kinds of love we feel, because what we love, we hold as our purpose. And since the things we love constitute the core of our life, so do our goals; see §§1317, 1568, 1571, 1645, 1909, 3425, 3562, 3565.

People's good aims are part of their rational dimension and are what I am calling goodness on the rational plane, or goodness in the rational mind. The Lord uses our good aims (or the goodness on that plane) to organize everything in the earthly dimension. A purpose is like a soul, and the earthly element is like that soul's body. The nature of the soul determines the nature of the body that surrounds it. So the character of the goodness on the rational plane determines the character of the earthly plane that clothes it.

[4] People know that the human soul takes its start in the mother's egg, then develops in her uterus, where a tender little body envelops it, a body that provides a suitable vehicle through which the soul can act in the

world into which it is born. The same thing happens when we are being born again, or regenerating. The new soul we then receive is an intention to do good, which takes its start in our rational mind, where it first exists in a kind of egg, then develops in a kind of uterus. The soft little body that surrounds this soul is the earthly dimension and the goodness in it, which eventually comes to act in conformity with the soul's purposes. The truth present in that dimension resembles fibers in the body, because truth is formed out of goodness (§3470).

This shows that the formation of a human being in the womb presents an image of human reformation. Believe it or not, heavenly goodness together with spiritual truth from the Lord is what forms us and then plants in us the ability to receive both [goodness and truth] gradually, so far and so well as we focus on heavenly goals like human beings and not on worldly goals like brute animals.

[5] The way goodness on the rational level uses the earthly level to first bind goodness to itself and then truth—the process symbolized by "Jacob carried delicacies and bread to Isaac, and he ate; and he brought him wine, and he drank"—can also be illustrated by functions the body performs for its soul. The soul is what gives the body the urge to seek food and also the ability to taste it. The pleasures of appetite and flavor— shallow types of goodness—put the food inside us, but not all the food we swallow becomes part of our life. Some of it serves as a solvent for digesting the food, some for modifying it, some for breaking it down, and some for introducing it into the blood vessels. The food selected as beneficial is introduced into and becomes part of the blood, from which the soul binds to itself the useful components. [6] The same thing occurs with the rational and earthly levels. A longing and desire to know truth correspond to appetite and flavor, and secular and religious knowledge correspond to food (§1480). Because they correspond, they also function the same way. The soul, or the goodness in our rational dimension, makes us long for and desire that knowledge. So it introduces the concepts of the academic disciplines and of theology through the pleasure we long for and the good we desire. Not all the information it brings in, though, is suited to becoming part of a good life; some of it serves as a means for digesting and modifying the rest, so to speak, some for breaking it down and introducing it. But the soul takes the beneficial parts, which have to do with life, applies them to itself, binds them to itself, and forms them into truth for itself.

This clarifies how the rational mind as the soul—in other words, as the aim (which is the soul)—organizes the earthly mind to serve in perfecting it for usefulness in the Lord's kingdom.

Genesis 27:26, 27, 28, 29. *And Isaac his father said to him, "Come close, please, and kiss me, my son." And he came close and kissed him, and [Isaac] smelled the smell of his clothes and blessed him and said, "See: the smell of my son, like the smell of a field that Jehovah has blessed. And God will give you of the dew of the sky and of the fatness of the earth and an abundance of grain and new wine. Peoples will serve you, and peoples will bow down to you; be master to your brothers, and your mother's sons will bow down to you. A curse on those cursing you, and a blessing on those blessing you!"*

3571

Isaac his father said to him, "Come close, please," symbolizes a still deeper level of perception. *And kiss me, my son* means as to whether they could become one. *And he came close and kissed him* symbolizes presence and oneness. *And he smelled the smell of his clothes* symbolizes a sense of pleasure from the truth that comes of goodness, as [the Lord] perceived it. *And blessed him* symbolizes union then. *And said, "See: the smell of my son,"* symbolizes a sense of pleasure from the truth that comes of goodness. *Like the smell of a field* means as from the good ground in which truth sprouts. *That Jehovah has blessed* means which the Divine causes to multiply and be fruitful. *And God will give you of the dew of the sky* means with divine truth. *And of the fatness of the earth* means with divine goodness. *And an abundance of grain* symbolizes earthly goodness as a result. *And new wine* symbolizes earthly truth as a result. *Peoples will serve you* symbolizes religious truth, or spiritual religions. *And peoples will bow down to you* symbolizes the truth that comes of goodness. *Be master to your brothers* symbolizes the dominance that a desire for truth on the earthly level apparently has at first over any desire for goodness on the earthly level. *And your mother's sons will bow down to you* means over all other desire for truth. *A curse on those cursing you* means that those who disconnect themselves will be disconnected. *And a blessing on those blessing you* means that those who connect themselves will be connected.

Isaac his father said to him, "Come close, please," symbolizes a still deeper level of perception. This can be seen from the symbolism of *saying that he should come close* as a deeper level of perception due to presence. *Coming close* means nothing else.

3572

And kiss me, my son means as to whether they could become one. This can be seen from the symbolism of *kissing* as uniting and becoming one

3573

out of desire. A kiss, which is an outward act, simply means a desire for closeness, which is an inward feeling. The two also correspond.

The subject here in the highest sense is the glorification of the Lord's earthly part, as stands out clearly from remarks above [§§3490, 3508, 3509]; in other words, the text tells how the Lord made the earthly level in himself divine. In a representative sense, though, it deals with the rebirth of a person's earthly part and therefore talks about the union of the earthly part with the rational. The earthly plane, you see, is not reborn until it unites with the rational plane. They are united through a direct and indirect inflow from the rational plane into the goodness and truth of the earthly plane. Goodness on the rational plane flows directly into goodness on the earthly plane and through this into truth there. It flows indirectly through truth on the rational plane into truth on the earthly plane and from there into goodness on the earthly plane. These are the types of union being discussed. [2] They can occur only through means provided by the Divine—means of which we are totally unaware. We cannot really form any notion of them through objects of worldly light, or objects of the earthly glimmer we enjoy, but through objects of heavenly light, or of rational light. All these means are revealed in the Word's inner sense, however. They lie open to the view of those who focus on that sense—in other words, angels, who see and perceive countless facets of the topic, hardly any of which can be unfolded and explained in a way that we on earth can understand.

[3] On the other hand, we can to some extent see how matters stand with that union from its effects and their outward signs. The rational mind—the deeper will and intellect in us—ought to manifest itself in our earthly mind just as our earthly mind manifests itself in our face and its expression. In fact, just as the face is the countenance of the earthly mind, so the earthly mind ought to be the countenance of the rational mind. When they unite, as they do when we have been reborn, then whatever we intend and think deep in our rational mind displays itself openly in our earthly mind, which displays itself openly in our face. That is what the faces of angels are like, and that is what the faces of the earliest people (who were heavenly individuals) were like. They were not at all afraid to let others know their aims and purposes, because they wished nothing but good. None who allow the Lord to lead them ever intend or think anything else.

When this is the situation, goodness in the rational dimension unites directly with goodness in the earthly dimension and through this with truth there; and through truth joined to itself in the rational dimension it also unites indirectly with truth in the earthly dimension and through this with goodness there. This makes the union unbreakable.

[4] The width of the gap between this state—the heavenly state—and that of humankind today stands out clearly from this: People consider it a matter of social prudence to talk one way and act another, and to show something different on their face from what they think and intend. They even go so far as to control their earthly mind in such a way that it acts in unison with their face to contradict what they think and aim at deep inside from evil purposes. The earliest people considered this a heinous crime, and people who committed it were thrown out of their communities as devils.

These practices are results (and outward signs of the results) of the union between our rational, inner self and our earthly, outer self in regard to goodness and truth. As such, they reveal what that union is like and consequently what the person who is an angel and the person who is a devil are like.

And he came close and kissed him symbolizes presence and oneness. This can be seen from the symbolism of *coming close* as presence and from that of *kissing* as oneness, or uniting out of desire (§3573). This symbolism of *kissing* can also be seen from other passages in the Word. In David, for instance:

3574

> Serve Jehovah with fear, and *kiss his Son* or he might grow angry and you might be destroyed along the way, because his anger will blaze instantly. Fortunate are all who trust in him. (Psalms 2:[11,] 12)

This is about the Lord, whose divine humanity is the Son. Kissing him means being united to him through the faith that comes of love. In the same author:

> Let mercy and truth meet; let justice and peace *kiss.* (Psalms 85:10)

Letting justice and peace kiss stands for having them unite. In Hosea:

> Ephraim spoke a horror and acquired guilt through Baal. And now they commit further sin. They make for themselves a cast image from their silver; with their intelligence [they make] idols, the work of artisans, all of it, saying to them, "Those who sacrifice a human *kiss calves.*" (Hosea 13:1, 2)

Ephraim stands for intelligence—here, arrogant intelligence, or people who do not want their wisdom to come from the Lord and do not believe that it does. A cast image from their silver stands for falsified goodness.

The work of artisans, all of it, stands for arrogant intelligence. People with such intelligence are said to kiss calves, or to embrace witchcraft and become attached to it. In 1 Kings:

> Jehovah said to Elijah, "I have left seven thousand in Israel—all the knees that have not bowed *down* to Baal, and every mouth that has not *kissed him.*" (1 Kings 19:18)

Kissing something stands for uniting with it out of desire and so for worshiping it.

3575　　*And he smelled the smell of his clothes* symbolizes a sense of pleasure from the truth that comes of goodness, as [the Lord] perceived it. This can be seen from the symbolism of a *smell* as something pleasing (discussed in §925) and of *smelling* as perceiving something pleasant, and from that of *clothes* as truth (discussed in §§297, 1073, 2576). Because the clothes were Esau's—*his*—and Esau represents goodness on the earthly level, the truth that grows out of goodness is what is meant.

The truth that grows out of goodness is truth produced on the earthly level by a direct and indirect inflow from the rational level, as described above in §3573. This truth was what [the Lord] longed for, but it could not be produced simply by a direct inflow from goodness on the rational plane; it had to arise also from an indirect inflow from that goodness through truth on the rational plane. This inflow required many different means, which are what Esau and Jacob depict in the inner meaning here. So *smelling the smell of his clothes* symbolizes truth from goodness as it was perceived.

3576　　*And blessed him* symbolizes union then, as can be seen from the symbolism of being *blessed* as uniting (discussed in §§3504, 3514, 3530, 3565).

Everything said about Esau and Jacob here shows that goodness on the rational plane united at the deepest level with goodness on the earthly plane and through that goodness with truth. Isaac represents goodness on the rational plane; Rebekah represents truth on the rational plane; Esau represents the earthly plane's goodness; and Jacob represents its truth. The goodness on the rational level meant by Isaac united at the deepest level with the earthly level's goodness meant by Esau but not with the earthly level's truth meant by Jacob, except in an indirect way. Take as evidence the fact that Isaac had Esau in mind when he pronounced a blessing on Jacob; he was not thinking of Jacob but of Esau.

If you deliver a blessing, you bless the person you are thinking about, not one you are not thinking about. All blessing issues from within. The words of blessing on your lips receive life from your intention and thought, so the blessing really belongs to the person for whom you intend it, the person you are thinking of. If someone intercepts and appropriates the blessing, it is like stolen goods that ought to be restored.

Everything up to this point indicates that when Isaac said his blessing, he was thinking of Esau rather than Jacob. In verses 18, 19, for instance, Isaac says to Jacob, "'Who are you, my son?' And Jacob said to his father, 'I am Esau, your firstborn.'" In verses 21, 22, 23: "Isaac said to Jacob, 'Come close, please, and I will feel you, my son, [to tell] whether you are he, my son Esau, or not.'" And after he had felt him he said, "'The voice is Jacob's voice, but the hands are Esau's hands.' And he did not recognize him." In verse 24: "And he said, 'Are you he, my son Esau?' And he said, 'I am.'" And finally [in verse 27] when he kissed him, "he smelled the smell of his (Esau's) clothes," and when he then blessed him, he said, "*See: the smell of my son.*" This shows that by the son he blessed, none other was meant than Esau. Then too, when he heard from Esau that it had been Jacob, "Isaac shuddered a very great shudder" (verse 33). "And he said, 'Your brother came in deceit'" (verse 35).

Jacob kept the blessing, though, as can be seen in verses 33 and 37, and that is because the truth represented by Jacob was destined to seem dominant for a while, as shown several times before. [2] There is a period of reformation and rebirth, during which genuine goodness lies hidden and from deep within imposes order on everything in general and particular that appears true or that truth claims as its own. When this period ends, genuine goodness comes out in the light and openly takes charge. That is the meaning of Isaac's message to Esau in verse 40: "By your sword you will live, and your brother you will serve; and it will happen when you gain the dominance that you will tear his yoke off your neck." The inner meaning of these words is that as long as truth unites with goodness, goodness will seem to occupy a lower position, but it needs to take first place. When it does, the rational plane will connect with goodness on the earthly plane and through this with truth. As a result, truth will become an outgrowth of goodness. Then Esau will represent real goodness on the earthly level, and Jacob, real truth there, both of them connected with the rational level. In the highest sense they will represent the Lord's earthly divinity—Esau, the divine goodness in it, and Jacob, the divine truth there.

Like the smell of a field means as from the good ground in which truth sprouts. This can be seen from the symbolism of the *smell of a field* as a perception of the truth that springs from what is good, resembling the perception of the fragrance given off when a field is harvested. For the symbolism of a *field* as good ground, see §3500.

A smell means perception because in the other life the pleasure we sense in goodness and the delight we sense in truth express themselves as corresponding scents; see §§1514, 1517, 1518, 1519. This phenomenon and the correspondences involved show that a smell actually means perceptiveness—but an earthly perceptiveness corresponding to spiritual perceptiveness.

3578   *That Jehovah has blessed* means which the Divine causes to multiply and be fruitful. This can be seen from the symbolism of *Jehovah's blessing something* as the multiplication of its truth and fruitfulness of its goodness (discussed in §§2846, 3406).

3579   *And God will give you of the dew of the sky* means with divine truth. *And of the fatness of the earth* means with divine goodness. This can be seen from the symbolism of the *dew of the sky* as truth (discussed below) and from that of *fat* as what is good (discussed in §353)—both of them divine, in the highest sense, since in that sense they apply to the Lord.

To take up the multiplication of truth and fruitfulness of goodness: When the rational dimension flows into the earthly, it makes its goodness manifest there in a general form. Through this goodness it produces truth there, almost the same way the life force constructs fibers in the human body and organizes them into forms according to their functions. Through this truth, arranged into a heavenly pattern, that goodness produces new goodness, and through this goodness it produces new truth, which consists of inferences. In this way we are able to construct an earthly picture of the way truth is formed out of goodness, new goodness out of the truth, and yet more truth out of the goodness. Only people in the other world can construct a spiritual picture, though, since their ideas are shaped by heavenly light, which contains understanding.

[2] The symbolism of *dew* as truth can also be seen from elsewhere in the Word, as in Zechariah:

> The seed of peace; the grapevine will yield its fruit, and the earth will yield its produce, and the *heavens will yield their dew*. (Zechariah 8:12)

This is about a new religion. "The grapevine will yield its fruit" means that the spiritual side of the religion—the truth taught by faith—will yield goodness. "The earth will yield its produce" means that its heavenly side—good done out of neighborly love—will yield truth. These things are the dew that the heavens will yield. In Haggai:

> Because of my House, which has been devastated, *the heavens* above you *have been shut off from their dew* and the earth has been shut off from its produce. (Haggai 1:9, 10)

The heavens' dew and the earth's produce that have been held back stand for the same things. [3] In David:

> Out of the womb of the dawn you receive the *dew of your birth.* (Psalms 110:3, 4)

This is about the Lord. The dew of his birth stands for love's heavenly quality. In Moses:

> A blessing from Jehovah on his land in the precious worth of the sky, *in the dew,* and in the underlying abyss. (Deuteronomy 33:13)

The subject here is Joseph. The precious worth of the sky means the spiritual dimension (§3166), which is the dew. The underlying abyss means the earthly dimension. In the same author:

> Israel has lived safely, alone, at Jacob's spring, in a land of grain and new wine; the *skies were* also *drizzling dew.* (Deuteronomy 33:28)

Here too the dew that the heavens were drizzling stands for the spiritual dimension, which has to do with truth.

[4] In its core sense, dew means the truth that grows out of goodness in a state of innocence and peace, because those states are symbolized by the morning or dawn, when the dew falls (§§2333, 2405, 2540, 2780). The manna from heaven also came with the dew that fell at morning time, as indicated in Moses:

> In the *morning there was a layer of dew* around the camp, and when the *layer of dew* vanished, look! On the face of the wilderness, something crumbly, round; something crumbly like frost on the earth. (Exodus 16:13, 14)

> When *dew fell on the camp* at night, manna fell on it. (Numbers 11:9)

Since manna was heavenly bread, in the highest sense it symbolized the Lord's divine goodness, so it also symbolized heavenly love in people, since this comes from the Lord's divine quality (§§276, 680, 1798, 2165, 2177, 3464, 3478). The dew on which and with which the manna fell stands in the highest sense for divine truth, and in a secondary sense for spiritual truth known to humankind. Morning time means a state of peace containing those benefits (§§92, 93, 1726, 2780, 3170).

[5] Since dew symbolizes the truth that develops out of goodness, or spirituality that develops out of heavenliness, the Word also *compares* spiritual truth to dew. Symbols serve also as similes for the thing they symbolize. In Isaiah, for example:

> This is what Jehovah has said to me: "I will rest and watch in my dwelling place, like a sheen of heat on the light, *like a cloud of dew* when the harvest heats up." (Isaiah 18:4)

In Hosea:

> What shall I do with you, Ephraim? What shall I do with you, Judah? For your holiness is like a *cloud at dawn,* and *like dew settling in the morning.* (Hosea 6:4; 13:3)

In the same author:

> *I will be like dew to Israel;* it will bud like a lily and fix roots like Lebanon. (Hosea 14:5)

In Micah:

> The survivors of Jacob in the midst of many peoples will be *like dew* from Jehovah, like raindrops on the grass. (Micah 5:7)

In David:

> . . . like good oil on the head that ran down onto the mouth of Aaron's garments, *like Hermon's dew* that ran down on Mount Zion, because there Jehovah commanded the blessing of life eternal. (Psalms 133:2, 3)

In Moses:

> My teaching will flow down like rain; *my word will shower like dew,* like dewdrops on the grain and like raindrops on the grass. (Deuteronomy 32:2)

The dew stands for multiplication of the truth that comes from goodness and for the fruitfulness of the goodness that comes through truth. And

since dew is what makes field and vineyard fertile every morning, goodness itself and truth itself are symbolized by the grain and new wine dealt
with next.

And an abundance of grain symbolizes earthly goodness as a result;   **3580**
and new wine symbolizes earthly truth as a result. This can be seen from
the symbolism of *grain* as something good and of *new wine* as something
true. When mentioned in connection with the earthly plane, they symbolize earthly goodness and truth, and in that case, bread and mature
wine are used to depict the rational plane. Bread means heavenly goodness (see §§276, 680, 1798, 2165, 2177, 3464, 3478), and wine means what
is spiritual and therefore truth that grows out of goodness (§§1071, 1798).

[2] This symbolism of grain and new wine can also be seen from the
following passages in the Word. In Haggai:

> The heavens have been shut off from their dew and the earth has been
> shut off from its produce, and I have summoned a drought on the earth
> and on the mountains and *on the grain* and *on the new wine* and on
> what the earth brings forth. (Haggai 1:10, 11)

The drought stands for a lack of dew and rain and so for a lack of any
truth that stems from something good. A drought on the grain means a
lack of goodness, and one on the new wine, a lack of truth. In Moses:

> Israel will live safely, alone, at Jacob's spring, *in a land of grain and new
> wine,* and its skies will drizzle dew. (Deuteronomy 33:28)

"Alone" stands for people who are not plagued by evil and falsity (§§139,
471). A land of grain and new wine stands for the goodness and truth in
a religion. [3] In Hosea:

> I will be like dew to Israel; it will bud like a lily and fix its roots like
> Lebanon. Its branches will spread, and its honor will resemble an olive
> tree, and it will have a *scent* like Lebanon's. Those living in its shade will
> return. They will *bring the grain to life* and blossom like a *grapevine;* its
> memory will be like the *wine* of Lebanon. (Hosea 14:5, 6, 7)

The grain stands for spiritual goodness; the wine, for spiritual truth. In
Isaiah:

> A curse will devour the land, *the new wine will mourn,* the *grapevine* will
> droop, everyone glad at heart will groan. (Isaiah 24:6, 7)

This is about the ruination of a spiritual religion. "The new wine will mourn" means that truth will die out. [4] In Jeremiah:

> Jehovah has ransomed Jacob; they will come and sing on Zion's height and stream together toward Jehovah's goodness—*toward grain* and *toward new wine* and toward oil and toward the offspring of flock and herd. (Jeremiah 31:11, 12)

The grain and new wine stand for goodness and the truth that comes from it. The oil stands for the goodness from which they come and to which they lead. The offspring of flock and herd stand for the resulting truth. Because they symbolize these things, they are called Jehovah's goodness. [5] In Hosea:

> She does not know that I am the one who gave her *grain* and *new wine* and oil. And her silver I multiplied, and the gold that they made for Baal; therefore I will return and take back *my grain* and *my new wine* in its season and snatch away my wool and my flax. (Hosea 2:8, 9)

The subject here is a corrupt religion. The grain obviously does not mean grain, nor the new wine, new wine; nor do the oil, silver, gold, wool, or flax mean those things. Instead, they symbolize what is spiritual, or what relates to goodness and truth. [6] Likewise where the same author speaks of a new religion:

> I will betroth you to me in faith, and you will know Jehovah; and it will happen on that day that I will hear the heavens, and they will hear the earth, and the earth will hear the *grain* and *new wine* and oil, and these will hear Jezreel. (Hosea 2:20, 21, 22)

Jezreel stands for the new religion. In Joel:

> Wake up, drunkards, and cry and howl, all you wine bibbers, *because of the new wine* that has been cut off from your mouth. The field has been devastated, the earth mourns, because *the grain has been devastated, the new wine has dried up,* the oil droops. (Joel 1:5, 10)

[7] In the same author:

> Children of Zion, rejoice and be glad in Jehovah your God, because he has given you the morning rain as a matter of justice, and he will make the morning rain and late rain fall for you in the first [month], and the threshing floors will be filled with *pure grain,* and the presses will overflow with *new wine* and oil. (Joel 2:23, 24)

In the same author:

> It will happen on that day that *the mountains will shower down new wine,* and the hills will stream with milk, and all the brooks of Judah will stream with water, and a spring will issue from Jehovah's house. (Joel 3:18)

This is about the Lord's kingdom. The new wine, milk, and water symbolize spiritual qualities, whose abundance is being depicted. [8] In Zechariah:

> Jehovah their God will save them on that day; like a flock [will he save] his people, because how great is their goodness, and how great their beauty! *Grain* will cause young men—and *new wine,* young women—to sprout. (Zechariah 9:16, 17)

In David:

> You visit the earth and take pleasure in it; you greatly enrich it. God's brook is full of water. You prepare *their grain.* Meadows clothe the flock, and the valleys are covered with *grain.* Let them clap, let them also sing. (Psalms 65:9, 13)

All this now shows what grain and new wine mean.

Peoples will serve you symbolizes religious truth. *And peoples will bow down to you* symbolizes the truth that comes of goodness. This can be seen from the use of *serve,* which has to do with truth (as discussed in §§2567, 3409), and from the symbolism of *peoples* as truth (discussed in §§1259, 1260, 2928, 3295). The peoples mentioned first symbolize religious truth, which is called spiritual truth, and the peoples mentioned second symbolize the truth that comes of goodness. This truth is spiritual goodness and is called truth, by comparison [with heavenly goodness]. Good done out of love for others is this kind of truth. Since there is a difference, the Hebrew does not use the same word to express the idea of *peoples* the first time as it does the second time but another, related word. **3581**

Be master to your brothers symbolizes the dominance that a desire for truth on the earthly level apparently has at first over any desire for goodness on the earthly level. This can be established from the symbolism of *being master* as dominance and from that of *brothers* as the desire for goodness—here, for goodness on the earthly level—see §§367, 2360, 3303. Concerning the apparent dominance of truth over goodness in the beginning, see §§3324, 3325, 3330, 3332, 3336, 3470, 3539, 3548, 3556, 3563, 3570. **3582**

3583   *And your mother's sons will bow down to you* means over all other desire for truth, as can be seen from the following: *Sons* also symbolize truth, as noted in §§489, 491, 533, 1147, 2623, 3373. And a *mother* symbolizes a desire for spiritual truth, so she also symbolizes a religion, since it is on account of truth and a desire for it that a religion *is* a religion and is called one, as noted at §§289, 2691, 2717.

3584   *A curse on those cursing you* means that those who disconnect themselves will be disconnected; *and a blessing on those blessing you* means that those who connect themselves will be connected. This can be seen from the symbolism of being *cursed* as being disconnected and from that of being *blessed* as being connected (dealt with in §§3504, 3514, 3530, 3565). These words relate to the subject of truth. *Those cursing* symbolize falsity, which isolates itself from truth, while *those blessing* symbolize truth, which attaches itself to all other truth.

True ideas and good desires form a community among themselves and eventually make a kind of unified city. That is how they associate with each other. This effect traces its cause to the form of heaven, which arranges angels according to the relationships and connections of their goodness and truth and consequently makes them into a single kingdom or city. From that kingdom or city, truth and goodness flow into us, and when they reach us, they are arranged in a similar pattern by the Lord alone. The way this works will become clearer from the correspondence of the universal human (heaven) with everything large and small in the human being. A treatment of this correspondence will appear at the ends of the chapters, with the Lord's divine mercy.

These remarks now show what is involved in the blessing Isaac pronounced on Jacob, intending it for Esau: the fruitfulness of goodness through the multiplication of truth, followed by further fruitfulness.

3585   Genesis 27:30, 31, 32, 33. *And it happened as Isaac finished blessing Jacob, and Jacob had just barely gone out from the presence of Isaac his father, that Esau his brother came from his hunting. And he too made delicacies and brought them to his father and said to his father, "Let my father rise and eat of his son's game in order that your soul can bless me." And Isaac his father said to him, "Who are you?" and he said, "I am your son, your firstborn, Esau." And Isaac shuddered a very great shudder and said, "Then who was that who hunted game and brought it to me, and I ate of it all before you came, and blessed him? Blessed he also will be."*

It happened as Isaac finished blessing Jacob means when the first bond had been formed in this way. *And Jacob had just barely gone out from the presence of Isaac his father* symbolizes forward movement and change in the state. *That Esau his brother came from his hunting* symbolizes the truth that grows out of goodness, and its arrival. *And he too made delicacies and brought them to his father* symbolizes what was desirable and enjoyable to divine rationality. *And said to his father, "Let my father rise and eat of his son's game,"* means to make the truth that comes of earthly goodness its own. *In order that your soul can bless me* means in order to unite with it. *And Isaac his father said to him, "Who are you?" and he said, "I am your son, your firstborn, Esau,"* symbolizes a state of perception concerning earthly goodness and the truth that comes out of it. *And Isaac shuddered a very great shudder* symbolizes the immense change entailed in turning that state around. *And said, "Then who was that who hunted game and brought it to me?"* symbolizes inquiry concerning that truth. *And I ate of it all before you came* means that it had been adopted. *And blessed him; blessed he also will be* means that it had been united.

And it happened as Isaac finished blessing Jacob means when the first **3586** bond had been formed in this way. This is established by the symbolism of *blessing* as union (discussed above at §§3504, 3514, 3530, 3565, 3584). So *as he finished blessing* means when the union had been formed. The first union was with the truth represented by Jacob, as the discussion above makes plain.

And Jacob had just barely gone out from the presence of Isaac his father **3587** symbolizes forward movement and change in the state. This can be seen from the symbolism of *barely having gone out from someone's presence* as the point at which the things that Jacob represented came to an end and therefore when the state changed. After all, the text now turns to Esau and, in an inner sense, to the way goodness on the earthly level comes out from deep within (as noted before [§3576]), reveals itself, and takes charge once reformation has been brought to completion through the ministry of truth.

That Esau his brother came from his hunting symbolizes the truth that **3588** grows out of goodness, and its arrival, as is established by the following: *Esau* represents goodness on the earthly plane, as noted above. *Coming* means its arrival. And *hunting* symbolizes the truth that grows out of goodness, as noted in §3501.

And he too made delicacies and brought them to his father symbolizes **3589** what was desirable and enjoyable to divine rationality. This can be seen from the symbolism of *delicacies* as the pleasures of goodness and the appealing qualities of truth (discussed in §§3502, 3536). The pleasures of goodness are desirable, and the appealing qualities of truth are enjoyable, because a predilection for goodness is what has longings or desires, and a predilection for truth is what takes delight or enjoyment.

3590 *And said to his father, "Let my father rise and eat of his son's game,"* means to make the truth that comes of earthly goodness its own, as can be seen from the following: Isaac, the *father* here, represents goodness on the rational plane, as noted many times. *Eating* means adopting, as noted in §§2187, 2343, 3168, 3513 at the end. And *game* symbolizes the truth that develops out of goodness on the earthly level, as noted just above at §3588.

3591 *In order that your soul can bless me* means in order to unite with it. This can be seen from the symbolism of being *blessed* as being united (also dealt with above, at §§3504, 3514, 3530, 3565, 3584).

3592 *And Isaac his father said to him, "Who are you?" and he said, "I am your son, your firstborn, Esau,"* symbolizes a state of perception concerning earthly goodness and the truth that comes out of it. This is established by remarks above at §§3548, 3549, 3550 concerning verses 18 and 19, where similar words occur.

3593 *And Isaac shuddered a very great shudder* symbolizes immense change entailed in turning that state around. This can be seen from the symbolism of a *shudder* as a change. The fact that it is entailed in turning that state around is evident from earlier statements about the two states we go through when being reborn, one before we have finished the process, and the other, after. Before rebirth, truth seems to dominate, but afterward, truth yields control and goodness takes over. See the many previous explanations of this at §§1904, 2063, 2189, 2697, 2979, 3286, 3288, 3310 at the end, 3325, 3330, 3332, 3336, 3470, 3509, 3539, 3548, 3556, 3563, 3570, 3576, 3579.

3594 *And said, "Then who was that who hunted game and brought it to me?"* symbolizes inquiry concerning that truth. This can be seen from the representation of Jacob, to whom the question *who was that?* refers, as truth on the earthly level (mentioned above [§3305]), and from the symbolism of *hunting* and *game* as the truth that comes of goodness (discussed at §3501). Here there was an inquiry concerning that truth to find out whether it came from goodness.

3595 *And I ate of it all before you came* means that it had been adopted, which can be seen from the symbolism of *eating* as being adopted (discussed in §§2187, 2343, 3168, 3513 at the end).

And blessed him; blessed he also will be means that it had been united, **3596** which can be seen from the symbolism of being *blessed* as being united (discussed in §§3504, 3514, 3530, 3565, 3584).

How matters stand with the adoption and uniting of the truth that Jacob represents can be seen from what has already been said. Those remarks are such that they lie beyond the grasp of the earthly self and can be seen only in the light by which the rational, inner self sees. Few today have the use of that light because few have been reborn, so it will be best not to elucidate the subject any further. To explain the unknown and unintelligible is to cast not light but greater shadow. Besides, these ideas need to build on concepts of earthly truth that enable the mind to comprehend them, and such concepts are also lacking in modern times.

That is why the explanations just above have not been very extensive and have dealt only with the inner meaning of the words.

[2] Isaac asked his son for game to eat before blessing him; he did not bless his son until after he had eaten, so the meal was followed by a blessing on the one who had made it and carried it to him. This is clear from what Isaac says here about Jacob: "He brought it to me, and I ate of it all before you came, and blessed him; and blessed he also will be." Preceding discussions show what is involved in this situation, and the reason for it becomes clear from a deep understanding of the ancient church's customs. Among the people of that church, eating symbolized adoption and union—union with the person with whom they had eaten, or whose bread they had eaten. Food in general symbolized aspects of love and charity—that is, the same thing that heavenly and spiritual food symbolizes. The bread they ate symbolized aspects of love for the Lord, and the wine symbolized aspects of charity toward one's neighbor. When they adopted these qualities, they were united. Accordingly they talked affectionately to each other and formed ties with each other. Banquets held by the ancients meant nothing else; the eating of consecrated food in the Jewish religion represented nothing else; and the luncheons and dinners of the early Christian church involved nothing else.

Genesis 27:34, 35, 36, 37, 38, 39, 40. *As Esau heard his father's words,* **3597** *he also shouted a very great and bitter shout. And he said to his father, "Bless me too, my father!" And [Isaac] said, "Your brother came in deceit and took your blessing." And [Esau] said, "Is it because they call his name Jacob? And he has supplanted me two times. My birthright he took, and look—now he has taken my blessing!" And he said, "Haven't you saved me a blessing?" And*

Isaac answered and said to Esau, "Here, I have made him master to you, and all his brothers I have given him as slaves, and with grain and new wine I have sustained him; and for you, then, what shall I do, my son?" And Esau said to his father, "Is this the one blessing you have, my father? Bless me too, my father!" And Esau lifted his voice and wept. And Isaac his father answered and said to him, "Watch: of the fatness of the earth your dwelling will consist, and of the dew of the sky from above. And by your sword you will live, and your brother you will serve; and it will happen when you gain the dominance that you will tear his yoke off your neck."

[2] *Esau heard his father's words* symbolizes what earthly goodness sensed from divine goodness. *He also shouted a very great and bitter shout* symbolizes the immense change required in it when the state was turned around. *And he said to his father, "Bless me too, my father!"* means that earthly goodness longed for union, even though truth was what was united in the process. *And he said, "Your brother came in deceit,"* symbolizes an upside-down arrangement. *And took your blessing* symbolizes union under this arrangement. [3] *And he said, "Is it because they call his name Jacob?"* symbolizes its quality. *And he has supplanted me two times* means that it turns things upside down. *My birthright he took* symbolizes priority. *And look— now he has taken my blessing* symbolizes union. *And he said, "Haven't you saved me a blessing?"* means, was it not possible to unite in any way in this first state? [4] *And Isaac answered and said to Esau* symbolizes instruction. *Here, I have made him master to you* means that in this state [truth] would dominate. *And all his brothers I have given him for slaves* means that any desire for goodness would apparently be subordinate to a desire for truth at this time. *And with grain and new wine I have sustained him* as before symbolizes its goodness and truth [§3580]. *And for you, then, what shall I do, my son?* means that there is nothing left for goodness in that state. [5] *And Esau said to his father* symbolizes what earthly goodness sensed. *Is this the one blessing you have, my father?* means whether some other facet of earthly goodness could be attached at that point. *Bless me too, my father!* means that it longed for union, even though truth was what was united in the process. *And Esau lifted his voice and wept* symbolizes a state of further change. [6] *And Isaac his father answered and said to him* symbolizes a perception that earthly goodness would become divine. *Watch: of the fatness of the earth your dwelling will consist* means that life rises out of divine goodness. *And of the dew of the sky from above* means out of divine truth. [7] *And by your sword you will live, and your brother you will serve* means that as long as truth unites with goodness, goodness will seem to occupy a lower position. *And it will happen when you gain the dominance*

means that it needs to take first place. *That you will tear his yoke off your neck* means that there will then be union through goodness, and truth will be an outgrowth of it.

Since the contents of verses 34, 35, 36, 37, 38 resemble things previously explained, and since prior discussions show what is involved, it would be superfluous to explain their inner meaning any further. Only the contents of verses 39 and 40, concerning the blessing of Esau by his father Isaac, are to be explained.

3598

And Isaac his father answered and said to him symbolizes a perception that earthly goodness would become divine, as can be seen from the following: *Isaac* symbolizes divine goodness in the Lord's divine rationality, as discussed at §§3012, 3194, 3210. *Saying,* in scriptural narrative, means perceiving, as noted many times before. And Esau, *to whom* Isaac spoke, represents earthly goodness, as also discussed quite a few times above. The blessing, dealt with next, shows that this goodness became divine.

3599

It was said above that Esau represents divine goodness in the Lord's earthly divinity, while Jacob represents divine truth in his earthly divinity. Here, though, it is said that Esau represents earthly goodness that would become divine, and in preceding sections, that Jacob represented earthly truth that also would become divine. How this matter stands can be seen from the remarks above in §§3494 and 3576. To make it even clearer, I must say a few words.

[2] The earthly goodness that Esau first represents is that of the Lord's childhood. It was divine from his Father but human from his mother, and so far as it came from his mother, it was steeped in inherited evil. As such, it could not instantly conform to a pattern enabling it to accept the divine nature lying at its core; the Lord first had to reduce it into that pattern. It is the same with the truth that Jacob represents, because where goodness exists, truth has to exist, if it is to be anything. Even in children, all thought involves truth and is linked to a desire of the will, which involves something good.

Consequently, the Lord reduced the goodness and truth on his earthly plane into a pattern in which that plane could accept divinity, so that the Lord could flow into it from his divine side. He gradually banished everything human he received from his mother, too. After that, Esau represents goodness in the Lord's earthly divinity, and Jacob represents truth there.

[3] However, Esau and Jacob represent divine goodness and truth belonging to the Lord's earthly divinity joined together as brothers. Viewed

in themselves they are nothing but a single, united capacity to fashion and receive applied goodness and truth. This applied goodness and truth will be discussed later.

These remarks show how many secrets the Word's inner meaning holds—secrets inaccessible to our intellect in even their broadest outlines (as may be the case with those just discussed). How are countless other details concerning them to be explained, then? They are suited instead to the understanding and grasp of angels, who on these and similar subjects receive heavenly ideas from the Lord, illuminated with indescribably appealing, blissful representations. From this you can contemplate the nature of angelic wisdom, though only in a distant way, since the human intellect sees such things in shadow.

3600 *Watch: of the fatness of the earth your dwelling will consist* means that life rises out of divine goodness, and *of the dew of the sky from above* means out of divine truth, as can be seen from the following: *Fatness* symbolizes something good, as noted in §353. Here it symbolizes divine goodness, since it is mentioned in connection with the Lord. The act of *dwelling* [or settling] symbolizes life, as discussed in §§1293, 3384, and dwelling [or residing] is mentioned in connection with goodness (§§2268, 2451, 2712). And the *dew of the sky* symbolizes truth that comes from goodness in a state of peace and innocence, as discussed above in §3579. Here it symbolizes divine truth, because it is mentioned in connection with the Lord.

Similar words were addressed to Jacob above at verse 28: *God will give you of the dew of the sky and of the fatness of the earth.* There, the dew and accordingly truth came first, and the fatness of the earth or goodness came second. It also says that God would give of them to him. In the current verse, on the other hand, Esau is told first about the fatness of the earth, or goodness, and second about the dew of the sky, or truth, and not that God would give of them but that his dwelling would be from them. This too shows that Jacob represents truth and Esau goodness. It also shows that truth is apparently in first place at the beginning, and that this is upside-down, as demonstrated many times before.

3601 *And by your sword you will live, and your brother you will serve* means that as long as truth unites with goodness, goodness will seem to occupy a lower position, as is established by the following: A *sword* symbolizes truth engaged in battle (treated of in §2799). So *living by a sword* happens when truth unites with goodness. The union is achieved through battle, or inward trials, because without them truth cannot possibly be united.

And *serving one's brother* means occupying a lower position. Goodness is not really but only apparently in a lower position, as is established by remarks made many times before; see §3582.

And it will happen when you gain the dominance means that it needs to take first place, which can be seen from the symbolism of *dominating* as being in first place. See directly below for a discussion.

3602

That you will tear his yoke off your neck means that there will then be union through goodness, and truth will be an outgrowth of it. This can be seen from the symbolism of *tearing a yoke off one's neck* as being freed. The *neck* symbolizes inflow, communication, and therefore union, while a *yoke on the neck* symbolizes blocking and interrupting them; see §3542. So tearing the yoke off one's neck means being freed of that blockage and interruption and consequently being united through goodness. It also means that truth becomes an outgrowth of goodness, because when there is no longer any blockage or interruption, goodness flows in and unites with truth.

3603

[2] Remarks and explanations up to this point show what the situation is in all this, but few understand what the apparent primacy of truth or temporary inferiority of goodness is. The main reason is that few think deeply on such subjects. No, they do not even reflect on the fact that goodness is distinct from truth. People who live lives of love for themselves and for worldly advantages never know what goodness is, because they do not believe anything good exists that does not stem from that love. Since they do not know what goodness is, they also do not know what truth is, because truth grows out of goodness. They do know from revelation that loving the Lord and their neighbor is goodness, and that doctrines from the Word are truth, but because they do not live according to them they have no perception of that goodness or truth, only knowledge detached from perception. In fact, even people being reborn do not know what goodness is until they have completed the process. Beforehand they imagine that truth is goodness and that obeying truth is goodness, when in reality it is not good they are then doing but truth. When we are at that stage, we are at the stage depicted by Jacob and described in the blessing he received. But when we arrive at the stage where we do good because we want what is good—when we have been reborn—we arrive at the stage described in the blessing Esau received.

[3] This can be illustrated by evidence that appears in us in the first and second stages of our life and then in the third and fourth stages. In the first stage, we know what is in the Word or what our faith teaches

only by memory. We consider ourselves good when we know a lot and can apply some of it not to our own life but to the lives of others. In the second stage, when we mature somewhat, we are not content with a ready memory of the Word's contents and the teachings of doctrine but start to think more deeply and personally about them. The more original thought we can add on to them, the better it pleases us. So we have a desire for truth sparked by a more or less worldly love, which also acts as a means for inspiring us to learn much that we would otherwise ignore. In the third stage, however, if we are among those who can be reborn, we start to consider usefulness; we start to reflect on what we read in the Word and absorb from doctrine, and our purpose then is to put it to use. At this stage, everything turns the other way up. That is, we no longer put truth so much in first place. The fourth stage is that of rebirth, because then our state is complete, as described in §2636. In that stage we love the Word and doctrines drawn from the Word—that is, truth—for the sake of the good it can do in our life and consequently because of the goodness in our life. So the goodness that up to that point seemed to come second takes first place.

[4] The reason goodness seemed to come second is that it lay at the heart of every emotion we had. It could not reveal itself because it was surrounded on the outside by traits with which it could not harmonize— empty, worthless traits like those that characterize worldly glory and self-importance. After we have been reborn, these things fade and the goodness that lay at their heart emerges from a kind of prison. It flows into everything outside it, makes truth its own, and in this way reveals itself.

[5] In the meantime, the goodness in us is like the involuntary drive residing in our voluntary desires, in everything we think, and so in everything we do. We do not know we have this drive, because we do not perceive anything in us that is not our own—in other words, that is not voluntary. This involuntary drive has two sides. One is what we inherit from our father and mother; the other flows in through heaven from the Lord. When we grow up, if we are such that we refuse to be reborn, the involuntary element we inherited from our parents comes out more and more. From it we extract evil, which we make our own. The involuntary side that comes through heaven from the Lord, on the other hand, comes out in adulthood among people who are being reborn. In the meantime, it organizes and rules absolutely everything they think and will, even though it is not evident.

Genesis 27:41, 42, 43, 44, 45. *And Esau hated Jacob because of the bless-* **3604**
ing with which his father had blessed him. And Esau said in his heart, "The
days of mourning for my father will come near, and I will kill Jacob my
brother." And to Rebekah were told the words of Esau her older son, and she
sent and called to Jacob her younger son and said to him, "Look, Esau your
brother is consoling himself over you that he will kill you. And now, my son,
listen closely to my voice and get up, flee to Laban, my brother, to Haran.
And you must stay with him several days until your brother's wrath with-
draws. Your brother's anger may yet withdraw from you, and he may forget
what you have done to him, and I will send and take you from there. Why
should I be bereaved of you both in one day?"

Esau hated Jacob because of the blessing with which his father had blessed
him means that earthly goodness opposed truth's reversed connection.
And Esau said in his heart symbolizes thought. *The days of mourning for*
my father will come near, and I will kill Jacob my brother means a reversal,
and depriving truth of the life it possesses from itself. *And to Rebekah*
were told the words of Esau her older son symbolizes a perception the Lord
received from divine truth concerning the mindset of earthly goodness at
that time. *And she sent and called to Jacob her younger son and said to him*
symbolizes a state in which he sensed a desire for truth as a result of an
inflow coming through divine truth. *Look, Esau your brother is consoling*
himself over you that he will kill you symbolizes an intent to reverse the
state and deprive truth of the life it possesses from itself. *And now, my son,*
listen closely to my voice and get up symbolizes waiting a bit. *Flee to Laban,*
my brother, to Haran means to a desire for superficial, tactile goodness.
And you must stay with him several days symbolizes what came next. *Until*
your brother's wrath withdraws means until the state turns. *Your brother's*
anger may yet withdraw from you symbolizes the next state for earthly
goodness. *And he may forget what you have done to him* means becoming
accustomed as a result of the wait. *And I will send and take you from there*
means coming to an end then. *Why should I be bereaved of you both in one*
day? means that otherwise there would be no union.

Esau hated Jacob because of the blessing with which his father had blessed **3605**
him means that earthly goodness opposed truth's reversed connection, as
can be seen from the following: In the inner sense here, *hating* means
opposing, as explained below. *Esau* represents earthly goodness, and *Jacob*
represents earthly truth, as noted above [§§3232, 3300, 3305]. And a *bless-*
ing symbolizes union, as discussed above in §§3504, 3514, 3530, 3565, 3584.

Here it means the upside-down union of truth represented by Jacob, as can be seen from statements and explanations above in §§3539, 3548, 3556, 3563, 3570, 3576, 3603.

[2] The reason *hating* means opposing, in an inner sense, is that it is being attributed to the goodness represented by Esau, and goodness does not even know what hatred is. Hatred is the direct opposite of goodness, and direct opposites can never exist in the same entity. Instead of feeling hatred, goodness (or people with goodness) puts up a type of opposition, and that is why hatred in an inner sense here means opposition. The inner meaning is mainly for the inhabitants of heaven, so when it filters down from there and is channeled into a literal meaning, a feeling of resistance is expressed as hatred, if that is what the story calls for. Yet this is done in such a way that for those in heaven it contains no suggestion of hatred.

The situation resembles the account in the second volume, §1875, of an experience involving the sentence in the Lord's Prayer, *Do not lead us into crisis but free us from evil* [Matthew 6:13; Luke 11:4]. The idea of crisis and evil was so thoroughly rejected that what remained was purely angelic; specifically, what was left was goodness, without a hint of crisis or evil. Attached to their idea was a kind of indignation and sense of repugnance that anyone should mentally link evil with the Lord.

[3] It is the same where we read in the Word that Jehovah (the Lord) feels hatred, as in Zechariah:

"Do not think evil in your heart, a man of his companion, and do not love a lying oath, *because all this I hate,*" says Jehovah. (Zechariah 8:17)

In Moses:

You shall not set up for yourself a pillar, *which Jehovah your God hates.* (Deuteronomy 16:22)

In Jeremiah:

My inheritance has become to me like a lion in the forest. It uttered its voice against me; *therefore I hate it.* (Jeremiah 12:8)

In Hosea:

In Gilgal *I hated them.* Because of the wickedness of their deeds I will drive them from my house; I will not love them anymore. (Hosea 9:15)

In an inner sense, the hatred ascribed here to Jehovah (the Lord) is not hatred but mercy, because the Divine is mercy. When mercy flows into people under the sway of evil and they incur the penalty for their evil, the mercy looks like hatred, and because that is the appearance, the literal meaning speaks in accord with it. [4] The case resembles that in the Word, which ascribes anger, wrath, and fury to Jehovah (the Lord)—attributes discussed in §§245, 592, 696, 1093, 1683, 1874, 2335, 2395, 2447. More than any others, the people of Judah and Israel were such that as soon as they detected any hostility, even among their companions, they believed they had the right to torture and not only kill them but also expose their bodies to the wild animals and birds. Since in them the Lord's inflowing mercy would be turned into this kind of hatred not only against their enemies but even against their friends, as I said, they could not help believing that Jehovah also felt hatred, anger, wrath, and fury. Accordingly, the Word speaks this way in keeping with the appearance. Whatever we are like, that is what the Lord seems like to us (§§1838, 1861, 2706).

The character of hatred in people devoted to love and charity, or people with goodness, can be seen from the Lord's words in Matthew:

> You have heard that it was said, "You shall love your neighbor and *hate your enemy.*" But I tell you, love your enemies, bless those who curse you, do good to those who hate you, and pray for those who wound and persecute you, so that you may be the children of your Father who is in the heavens. (Matthew 5:43, 44, 45)

And Esau said in his heart symbolizes thought, which can be seen from the symbolism of *saying in one's heart* as thinking. **3606**

The days of mourning for my father will come near, and I will kill Jacob my brother means a reversal, and depriving truth of the life it possesses from itself. This can be seen from the symbolism of the *days of mourning* as a reversal of the state and from that of *killing Jacob my brother* as depriving truth of the life it possesses from itself. **3607**

It was said just above [§3605] that in its inner sense hatred does not mean hatred, and the case is similar here. This can also be seen from a common incident in the other world. Anything good that flows down from heaven to people caught up in evil there turns into something evil and, among those in hell, into something opposed to goodness. Truth likewise turns into falsity. (See §2123.) Conversely, then, anything evil or false among such people becomes good and true in heaven. To convert it into something good, spirits stationed along the way discard any thought of evil or falsity, so that the idea of what is good and true can assert itself. (Concerning this riddance, see §§1393, 1875.) In addition, when evil and falsity washes up against those devoted to goodness and truth, it does not look evil or false but appears under a different guise, in keeping with the character and state of their goodness.

[2] This also indicates that on an inner level, *killing Jacob my brother* means not killing but taking away a type of life that is incompatible with truth. Truth possesses life not from itself but from goodness, because truth is only a vessel for receiving what is good (see §§1496, 1832, 1900, 2063, 2261, 2269, 2697, 3049, 3068, 3128, 3146, 3318, 3387). Life resides in goodness, not in truth, except for the life that truth receives from goodness (§1589 and many other places). So depriving truth of the life it possesses from itself is not snuffing truth out but bringing it to life. When truth appears to itself to possess inherent life, it does not have any life except the kind that is not inherently alive. When it is deprived of that life, it receives the gift of genuine life, life that comes by way of goodness from the Lord, who is life itself.

[3] This is very plain to see in people in the other life who focus solely on truth. Their thoughts seem to be shut so tight that nothing from heaven can touch them except in such a general way that the people hardly know the inflow comes from there. By contrast, the thoughts of those who also focus on goodness appear so wide open that what comes from heaven flows into a kind of miniature heaven, or essentially into an image of itself, because in them it flows through what is good into what is true; see §§1869, 2429.

The fact that truth is deprived of the life it possesses from itself when goodness starts to take first place or dominate can be seen from earlier discussions and explanations about the seeming initial priority of truth and the eventual priority of goodness. That is what is meant here by the removal from truth of the life it possesses from itself.

This is called a *mourning for my father* because the *days of mourning* symbolize a reversal of state, the same reversal symbolized above by the very great shudder Isaac shuddered (verse 33; §3593) and the very great and bitter shout Esau shouted (verse 34; §3597).

3608 *And to Rebekah were told the words of Esau her older son* symbolizes a perception the Lord received from divine truth concerning the mindset of earthly goodness at that time, as can be seen from the following: *Being told* means thinking and reflecting, as noted in §2862, and therefore perceiving. *Rebekah* represents divine truth in the Lord's divine rational mind, and *Esau* represents earthly goodness, as noted above. This shows that *Rebekah was told about the words of Esau her older son* means a perception the Lord received from divine truth concerning the mindset of earthly goodness.

And she called to Jacob her younger son and said to him symbolizes a
state in which he sensed a desire for truth as a result of an inflow coming
through divine truth, as can be seen from the following: Rebekah, who
called and *said,* represents divine truth in the Lord's divine rationality,
united with divine goodness there. *Jacob* represents earthly truth, or a
desire for truth on that plane. These have both been explained before.
And *calling to him and saying to him* symbolizes a state of perception, also
discussed before. In this instance, it means a state in which one senses
something, since the text is dealing with the earthly plane.

3609

Look, Esau your brother is consoling himself over you that he will kill you
symbolizes an intent to reverse the state and deprive truth of the life it
possesses from itself, as can be seen from the following: *Consoling oneself
over someone* or something means calming one's agitated mind with the
hope of someone or something. *Over you* involves a state of reversal for
truth. And *killing you* (Jacob) means depriving truth of the life it possesses
from itself, as explained just above at §3607, where it was shown that
depriving truth of such life is not snuffing it out but bringing it to life.

3610

This is how matters stand with the life that truth possesses: When
people with truth, or with a desire for truth, fail to live according to the
truth they know—the truth to which they are drawn—they gain a certain
gratification and pleasure from self-love or materialism that fastens itself
to their desire for truth. This feeling looks good, although it is not. The
only good thing about it is the role it plays in enabling us to be introduced
to truth and to learn about truth, which can later serve real goodness and
a good life. When truth (or the people who are drawn to it) is in this condition, it is said to have life from itself. Such life is not life. This can be
seen from the fact that love for ourselves and for worldly advantages (or
the gratification and pleasure of that love) does not contain life; heavenly
and spiritual love and its gratification and pleasure do. So when the life
that truth possesses from itself is taken away from it, or rather from people
with this desire for truth, at that point they receive life for the first time,
or first come to life.

[2] People who are fond of themselves and of material advantages cannot possibly comprehend these ideas, because they do not think any other
kind of life exists. If it were taken from them, they believe, they would not
have any life at all. People with this kind of life have no way of knowing
what spiritual and heavenly life is. The reality, though, is that when they
are deprived of a life of attachment to themselves and the world, a life
resembling angelic, heavenly life flows in from the Lord along with inexpressible wisdom and happiness. When they view their former life from

this life, it looks lifeless, or else seems to resemble the squalid life of brute animals. It contains nothing divine except for the power they receive to think and speak and in this way appear outwardly like others.

[3] To continue with the idea that goodness was intending to reverse the state and deprive truth of its inherent life, as symbolized by *Esau is consoling himself over you that he will kill you:* In a person being reborn, goodness always has an urge to overturn the existing state of affairs and reorganize it to remove truth from first place and put it second, as fits with the state of affairs in heaven. The urge lies deeply hidden, however, and does not rise to the person's awareness until the reversal is accomplished.

It is like the love that leads to marriage, which does not appear in childhood and youth but lies in wait, not emerging until everything has been arranged so that it can reveal itself. In the meanwhile it produces all necessary means—or rather, they are produced.

It is the same in the plant kingdom. Hidden deep in every tree and plant lies an impetus for producing fruit or seed, but this impetus cannot manifest itself until it has first produced all the means—stems, leaves, flowers. When these have been brought forth, the effort emerges into actuality.

[4] It is the same with people who are being born anew. The "marriage" of goodness and truth lies in hiding for a long time but is present as a force in the efficient cause and so in the effect, although it does not become visible until everything has been arranged. When arrangements are complete, it emerges for the first time and reveals itself. This impetus is what is meant by the intent to reverse the state and deprive truth of its inherent life.

This makes it plain that the inner meaning here is completely different from what the literal meaning suggests: it speaks of reducing truth into order and bringing it to life, not destroying it and taking away its life.

3611 *And now, my son, listen closely to my voice and get up* symbolizes waiting a bit. This can be seen from the symbolism of *listening closely to someone's voice* as obeying, by waiting a while longer in that reversed state. This is discussed in what follows.

3612 *Flee to Laban, my brother, to Haran* means to a desire for superficial, tactile goodness. This is established by the representation of *Laban* as a desire for goodness in the earthly self (discussed at §§3129, 3130, 3160) and by the symbolism of *Haran* as something superficial and therefore relatively dim (discussed in §1430).

Later passages mentioning Laban and Haran show what they properly symbolize: goodness branching off from the same stock [§§3665, 3777, 3778].

Goodness and truth are interconnected the way parents, siblings, blood relations, and other kin are in their families (§§685, 917, 2508, 2524, 2556, 2739). However, these relationships are completely hidden from people who are not living good lives. They do not even know what goodness is, so they also do not know what truth is. If they first knew these things—and knew them from a theology bound up with life, or from a life bound up with theology—they would know and intuit countless things about goodness and truth. This knowledge would gradually come into sharper and sharper focus, as would the interconnections and interrelationships, and finally the closest ties, in their series. Each of these ties would again offer countless things to learn, so that in the end it would hold heaven in its [entire] form, which is to say, in its beauty and bliss.

And you must stay with him several days symbolizes what came next, as can be seen from the following: *Staying* means the same thing as residing [or settling], so it means living (discussed in §§1293, 2268, 2451, 2712, 3384), although "staying" describes a life of truth accompanied by goodness, while "residing" describes a life of goodness accompanied by truth. And *days* symbolize periods and states (discussed in §§23, 487, 488, 493, 2788, 3462). So it is life in its subsequent periods and states—that is, what came next—that *staying with him several days* means. **3613**

The following chapters speak of this aftermath, or Jacob's stay with Laban.

Until your brother's wrath withdraws means until the state turns; and *your brother's anger may yet withdraw from you* symbolizes the next state for earthly goodness. This can be seen from the symbolism of *wrath* and *anger* as states that repel (discussed below). When these states no longer repel but start to unite, wrath and anger are said to withdraw. That is why *until your brother's wrath withdraws* means until the state turns, and *your brother's anger may yet withdraw* symbolizes the next state for earthly goodness. **3614**

Wrath plainly involves something different from *anger,* since otherwise the words are synonyms, and "until your brother's *wrath* withdraws" would be redundant with "your brother's *anger* may yet withdraw." What they involve becomes clear from the general explanation and also from the contexts in which each is used. *Wrath* is used of truth—here, truth that develops out of the goodness represented by Esau. *Anger* is used of that goodness itself.

[2] The Word mentions *wrath* and *anger* many times. In an inner sense they do not mean wrath and anger but that which repels, because anything repellent to one of our emotions arouses wrath or anger. So in an inner

sense they simply mean opposition. Anything repellent to truth is called wrath, and anything repellent to goodness is called anger. In an opposite sense, wrath means what is repellent to falsity or to a desire for falsity (that is, to distorted premises) while anger means what is repellent to evil or to a craving for evil (that is, to self-love and materialism). In this sense, wrath really does mean wrath, and anger does mean anger. When they apply to what is good and true, wrath and anger mean zeal, which looks the same on the outside, so wrath and anger is what the literal meaning calls it.

[3] The following places in the Word show that in an inner sense wrath and anger simply mean opposition. In Isaiah:

> *Jehovah's rage* is against all the nations, and his *wrath,* against each of their armies. (Isaiah 34:2)

Jehovah's rage against the nations stands for opposition to evil. For nations meaning evil, see §§1259, 1260, 1849, 1868, 2588 at the end. His wrath against each of their armies stands for opposition to the falsity that results. "The army of the heavens" there [Isaiah 34:4] refers to stars; for stars meaning knowledge and therefore truth, or in a negative sense falsity, see §§1128, 1808, 2120, 2495, 2849. In the same author:

> Who has made Jacob into plunder, and given Israel to looters? Is it not Jehovah, against whom we sinned? And he has *poured out onto them the wrath of his anger.* (Isaiah 42:[24,] 25)

The wrath of his anger stands for opposition to the falsity that comes of evil. Jacob stands for people immersed in evil, and Israel, for those immersed in falsity. [4] In the same author:

> The winepress I have trodden alone, and from among the peoples no man was with me, and I trod them in *my anger* and destroyed them in *my wrath.* And I trampled the peoples in *my anger* and made them drunk in *my wrath.* (Isaiah 63:3, 6)

This is about the Lord and the victories he won in his times of trial. Treading and trampling in his anger stand for his victories over evil; destroying and causing drunkenness in his wrath, for his victories over falsity. In the Word, trampling has to do with evil, and causing drunkenness, with falsity. In Jeremiah:

> This is what the Lord Jehovih has said: "Here, now, *my anger* and *my wrath* have been poured out on this place—on human and on animal

and on the tree of the field and on the fruit of the ground—and it will burn and not be put out." (Jeremiah 7:20)

This passage mentions both anger and wrath because it is dealing with both evil and falsity. [5] Where the Prophets speak of evil they also speak of falsity, just as where they speak of goodness they also speak of truth. This is because of the heavenly marriage of goodness and truth in every detail of the Word (§§683, 793, 801, 2173, 2516, 2712). That is why both anger and wrath are spoken of; otherwise just one would have been enough. In the same author:

> I myself will fight with you with an outstretched hand and a strong arm and *in anger* and *in wrath* and in *great rage,* and I will strike the residents of this city, both human and animal. (Jeremiah 21:5, 6)

Here too anger refers to the punishment of evil; wrath, to the punishment of falsity; and rage, to that of both. Since anger and wrath means opposition, it also means punishment, because things that are opposed to each other clash, and evil and falsity are then punished. Evil contains an opposition to goodness, and falsity, to truth, and since they oppose each other, they also clash. Punishment is the natural consequence; see §§696, 967. [6] In Ezekiel:

> And *my anger* will be fulfilled, and I will make *my wrath* rest on them and *comfort myself,* and they will know what I Jehovah have said in *my zeal,* in my fulfilling *my wrath* on them, in carrying out judgments on you, in *anger* and in *wrath* and in fits of *temper.* (Ezekiel 5:13, 15)

Again in this passage anger stands for the punishment of evil, and wrath, for that of falsity, because of their opposition and the antipathy that results from it. In Moses:

> It will not please Jehovah to pardon that one, because then *Jehovah's anger* and *his zeal will smoke* against that man, and Jehovah will separate him from all the tribes of Israel for evil. Sulfur and salt; the whole of its land a conflagration. It will not be sown and will not sprout, and no grass will come up in it, as in the overthrow of Sodom and Gomorrah, Admah and Zeboiim, which *Jehovah overthrew in his anger* and *his wrath.* And all the nations will say, "Why did Jehovah do so to this land? What is the *heat of this great anger?*" (Deuteronomy 29:20, 21, 23, 24)

Sodom means evil, and Gomorrah means the falsity that grows from it (§§2220, 2246, 2322), and the nation Moses is talking about here is being compared with them in regard to evil and falsity. So the text speaks of anger in relation to evil, of wrath in relation to falsity, and of anger's heat in relation to both. It ascribes these emotions to Jehovah, or the Lord, because that fits with the appearance; we see him as angry and wrathful when we ourselves plunge into evil and the evil punishes us (see §§245, 592, 696, 1093, 1683, 1874, 2335, 2395, 2447, 3605).

3615   *And he may forget what you have done to him* means becoming accustomed as a result of the wait. This can be seen from the symbolism of *forgetting* here as the gradual ebbing of opposition. Opposition fades because the wait accustoms one to the situation, so that is what *he may forget what you have done to him* means.

3616   *And I will send and take you from there* means coming to an end then, as can be seen from the context above and below. The end symbolized here by *sending and taking you from there* comes when truth conforms with goodness and serves goodness as an underling. It is represented by Esau *when* (after Jacob had finished his stay with Laban) *he ran to meet Jacob and hugged him and fell on his neck and kissed him, and they cried* (Genesis 33:4). When the finale of union arrives, goodness on the rational plane flows directly into goodness on the earthly plane and through this into truth there. It also flows indirectly through truth on the rational plane into truth on the earthly plane and through this into the goodness there. (See §3573.)

This clarifies why Rebekah, representing truth on the rational plane, said to Jacob, representing truth on the earthly plane, "I will send and take you from there."

3617   *Why should I be bereaved of you both in one day?* means that otherwise there would be no union. Consider this: In the inner sense of what follows, Jacob's stay with Laban represents certain processes, and if those processes did not take place, truth could not unite with goodness. Goodness, then, would be unable to unite with the earthly level's truth, and the rational level would be bereaved of both. Unless truth unites with goodness, and goodness with the earthly level's truth, rebirth does not occur. That is what the secondary meaning of the current chapter deals with.

This is also the conclusion to the preceding verses.

3618   Genesis 27:46. *And Rebekah said to Isaac, "I despise my life, thanks to the daughters of Heth. If Jacob takes a woman from the daughters of Heth like those from among the daughters of the land, why should I have lives?"*

Rebekah said to Isaac symbolizes a perception the Lord received from divine truth. *I despise my life, thanks to the daughters of Heth* symbolizes the attachment earthly truth forms in some other places. *If Jacob takes a woman from the daughters of Heth* means that earthly nontruth would be associated with them. *Like those from among the daughters of the land* means because they were not from the same ground. *Why should I have lives?* means then there would be no union.

Rebekah said to Isaac symbolizes a perception the Lord received from divine truth. This is established by the symbolism of *saying* as perceiving; the representation of *Rebekah* as divine truth in the Lord's divine rational mind; and the representation of *Isaac* as divine goodness there. These have been discussed before. Divine goodness is reality itself, and divine truth is the life force that flows from it, so the Lord is the Lord mainly because of his divine goodness. That is why it says that the Lord received the perception from divine truth.

Perception from divine truth on the rational plane is perception with the intellect, but perception from divine goodness is perception with the will. Still, perception with the intellect is not a function of the intellect but of the will that influences it. The intellect is just the will in a form— at least when bonded to the will. Before then it looks as though it exists by itself, and the will, by itself, even though the fact of the matter is simply that the outer shell isolates itself from the inner core. When the intellect contemplates and considers anything deep inside, a goal supplied by the will is what constitutes its life and regulates its thinking. The reason the intellect takes its life from the goal is that our goal is our life (see §§1909, 3570). This gives some idea what it is for a person to perceive from truth (the secondary meaning here) and for the Lord to perceive from divine truth (the highest meaning).

I despise my life, thanks to the daughters of Heth symbolizes the attachment earthly truth forms in some other places, as can be seen from the following: *Despising life* symbolizes the lack of an attachment—an attachment between earthly truth and truth on the rational plane. When this attachment is missing, the rational mind sees its life as worthless, as the discussion above at §3493 indicates. And the *daughters of Heth* symbolize desires for truth from a source that is not genuine—here, desires for earthly truth, since the statement has to do with Jacob, who represents earthly truth, as shown before [§3305]. *Daughters* mean desires (see §2362), and *Heth* or a Hittite means truth from a nongenuine source (§3470). You can see, then, that *I despise my life, thanks to the daughters of*

3619

3620

Heth means that the earthly level does not form any connection through truth from a nongenuine source. So it means that earthly truth's connection has to lie in some other quarter.

The attachment earthly truth does form comes up later, in the story of Jacob's stay with Laban; to be specific, truth from the same stock attaches to it. The truth represented by the daughters of Heth was not of the same stock, so no attachment could be formed through it, because it was unequal and incompatible. After all, the children of Heth represent a spiritual religion among people outside the church (§§2913, 2986). Since such a religion does not have the Word, the truth it possesses does not originate there.

3621   *If Jacob takes a woman from the daughters of Heth* means that earthly nontruth would be associated with them. This can be seen from the symbolism of *taking a woman* as being associated, and from that of the *daughters of Heth* as desires for truth from a nongenuine source (discussed just above in §3620)—in other words, as truth, since truth cannot be internalized without a desire for it (§§3066, 3336). What the case is here can be seen from the remarks just above on the daughters of Heth.

3622   *Like those from among the daughters of the land* means because they were not from the same ground—that is, from the truth known to a genuine religion. This is established by the symbolism of the *daughters of a land* as religions. *Daughters* symbolize a desire for what is good and true (§2362), and a *land* symbolizes the area where a religion exists, so it symbolizes a religion (as discussed in §§662, 1066, 1068, 1262, 1733, 1850, 2117, 2118 at the end, 2928, 3355). The daughters of the land, then, are the goodness and truth promoted by a religion.

3623   *Why should I have lives?* means then there would be no union. This can be seen from the symbolism of *lives* as union through truth and goodness. If truth from the same stock—from a genuine origin—could not be attached to earthly truth, the earthly level would also lack connection with truth on the rational level, and the rational dimension would see its life as worthless (§§3493, 3620). So *Why should I have lives?* means that then there would be no union.

This verse and others use *lives* in the plural because we have two capacities for life in us: one (relating to truth) called the intellect; the other (relating to goodness) called the will. These two "lives," or capacities for life, make one life when the intellect is subordinate to the will or, to put it another way, when truth is subordinate to goodness.

That is why Hebrew idiom sometimes speaks of life and sometimes of lives. The following places show that it speaks of lives:

Jehovah God formed a human, dirt from the ground, and he breathed into the human's nostrils the *breath of lives,* and the human was made into a living soul. (Genesis 2:7)

Jehovah God caused to sprout from the ground every tree desirable in appearance and good for food, and the *tree of lives* in the middle of the garden. (Genesis 2:9)

Here, I am bringing a flood of water on the earth, to destroy all flesh that has the *breath of lives* in it. (Genesis 6:17)

They entered to Noah in the ark, two each, two each of all flesh that had the *breath of lives* in it. (Genesis 7:15; §780)

Everything that had the breath of the *spirit of lives* in its nostrils breathed its last. (Genesis 7:22)

In David:

I believe I will see Jehovah's goodness in the *land of lives.* (Psalms 27:13)

In the same author:

Who is the man *desiring lives,* loving [to have many] days, in order to see good? (Psalms 34:12)

In the same author:

Yours, Jehovah, is the *fountain of lives;* in your light we see light. (Psalms 36:9)

In Malachi:

"My *compact* with Levi was one *of lives* and peace." (Malachi 2:5)

In Jeremiah:

This is what Jehovah has said: "Here, I am putting before you the *way of lives* and the way of death." (Jeremiah 21:8)

In Moses:

. . . to love Jehovah your God, to obey his voice, and to cling to him because he is *your lives* and the length of your days, to live on the land. (Deuteronomy 30:20)

In the same author:

> This word is not too empty for you [to listen to], because it is *your lives*. And through this word you will lengthen your days on the land. (Deuteronomy 32:47)

And other places. These speak of lives in the plural because life is two (as just mentioned) and yet also one—just as "heavens" in Hebrew is plural and yet also singular. So are the "waters that were above and below" (Genesis 1:7, 8, 9), meaning spiritual attributes of the rational and earthly dimensions, which also need to unite as one.

"Lives" in the plural symbolizes both what belongs to the will and what belongs to the intellect, so it symbolizes matters of goodness and matters of truth. Our life is nothing but goodness and truth, which hold life from the Lord. Without goodness and truth and the life they contain, we are non-human, because without them we could not will or think. All our power to will comes from what is good or what is not good, and our power to think comes from what is true or what is not true. These provide us with our two lives, which constitute one life when our thinking grows out of our willing, or when the truth we believe grows out of the goodness we love.

The Correspondence of All Our Organs and Parts, both Internal and External, with the Universal Human, Which Is Heaven

3624 LET me now relate and describe some amazing things that so far as I am aware have never been known to anyone or even entered anyone's head: The whole of heaven has been formed to correspond with the Lord and his divine humanity. Human beings have been formed to correspond in absolutely every particular with heaven, and through heaven with the Lord.

This is a huge mystery that needs to be revealed at this time and will be treated of here and at the ends of the following chapters.

3625 That explains why it was said several times in preceding sections describing heaven and communities of angels that they belonged to some region of the body, like that of the head, chest, abdomen, or some part or organ there [§§956, 1385, 1525, 1977, 3351]; the reason is the above-mentioned correspondence.

The existence of this correspondence is very well known in the other world not only to angels but also to spirits, even evil ones. From it angels learn the deepest secrets about the body and the deepest secrets about the world and everything in nature, as I have often been able to observe. For example, when I talked about some part of the body, they knew not only its whole structure, operation, and purpose but also immeasurably more about it than a person would ever be capable of researching or understanding. The information was properly arranged and organized, and they acquired it by observing the design of heaven (to which they conformed), since the design of the body part corresponded with it.

As their attention is on first origins, those origins teach them about everything that results.

3626

It is an overarching rule that nothing can emerge or last from itself but only from something else (that is, *through* something else) and that it can be held together only from something else (that is, *through* something else). This can be deduced from all the evidence of the material world.

On the outside, the human body is held together by atmospheres, as people recognize. If some active, living force did not also hold it together from within, it would collapse in a moment.

Anything lacking connection with what is prior to itself, and through everything prior, to what is first, perishes instantly. That something prior is the universal human, or inflow from it, and through that everything in us, in whole and in part, connects with what is first, or the Lord. This will become clear in what follows.

3627

All this I learned through much experience, as I also learned that it is not only the contents of our mind—not only our thoughts and feelings—that correspond to the spiritual and heavenly attributes heaven receives from the Lord. It is our entire self in general and everything in us in particular. In fact, not the least part exists, not even the least part of a part, that does not correspond. It is because of correspondence that we come into existence and continue to survive.

3628

Experience has also taught me that if we did not correspond this way with heaven and through heaven with the Lord—or with what is prior to us and through this with what is first—we would not survive for even a moment but would disintegrate into nothing.

[2] As noted above, there are always two forces that keep everything connected and hold it together, one acting on the outside, and one on

the inside. Between them is the object being maintained. This includes human beings, with all their individual parts, even the very smallest.

The atmospheres are what keep the whole body together from the outside by their constant pressure or weight and so by their active force. The atmosphere called air does this for the lungs by flowing into them, and also for its own unique organ, which is the ear, and all the structures it contains for detecting modifications in the air. By the same token, the atmosphere called ether maintains the deeper connections. It flows in freely through all the pores and keeps the inner organs of the whole body intact in their structures by almost the same kind of pressure, and so by its active force. It does the same for its own unique organ, which is the eye, and all the structures it contains for detecting modifications in the ether. All this is known.

Unless there were inner forces that corresponded to the atmospheres and counteracted the outer forces the atmospheres exert, containing and balancing the objects lying between, the objects would not last a moment. [3] Clearly, then, there absolutely have to be two forces for anything to emerge and survive. The forces whose influence and action are internal come from heaven and through heaven from the Lord. They possess intrinsic life.

The lesson becomes even more obvious from the organ of hearing. If it were not affected from inside by life, as it is correspondingly affected from outside by air, we would not hear anything. It also becomes clear from the organ of sight, since if this did not enjoy the inner light of life, to which the outer light of the sun corresponds, we would not see anything.

The same holds true for all the other organs and parts of the human body; there are earthly forces working on the outside that are not intrinsically alive and forces working on the inside, intrinsically alive, that hold everything together and enable it to live, in accordance with the form given it for its function.

3629   Few can believe this, because people do not know what the spiritual and earthly planes are, let alone how they differ, what correspondence is, or what inflow is. They do not know that when the spiritual level acts on the organic forms of the body, it enables them to function in a living way, to all appearances; or that without this inflow and correspondence, not even the smallest particle of the body could live or move.

Personal experience has taught me the situation in all this—not only that heaven exerts a general influence, but also that the individual communities

exert a specific one. I have also learned which communities act on this physical organ or that, on this part or that, and what those communities are like.
Each organ or part has not one community but many acting on it, and each
community has many members. The more there are, the stronger and more
perfect the correspondence, because strength and perfection result from a
large, like-minded multitude of people joining forces in a heavenly form.
So the impetus flowing into each part becomes stronger and more perfect
the more people there are.

This showed me that our individual viscera and parts—the motor and **3630**
sensory organs—correspond to communities in heaven, each virtually a
separate heaven. From these communities (or rather through them) come
heavenly and spiritual influences on us, which act on the forms adapted
and fitted to them, bringing about effects that we are able to see. The effects
seem completely earthly to us, though; they appear under a shape and guise
so entirely different that we do not realize they come from heaven.

Once I was shown with utter clarity the identity and character of the **3631**
communities that make up the region of the face and affect the muscles
of the forehead, cheeks, chin, and neck. I saw how they flow in and act
and how they communicate with each other. Wanting to present this
vividly to me, they were allowed to reproduce a face in various ways by
flowing in.

Likewise they showed me the identity and character of the communities acting on the lips, tongue, eyes, and ears. I was allowed to talk with
them and in this way be fully instructed.

The experience also showed me the following: All those going to
heaven are organs or body parts of the universal human. Heaven never
closes; instead, the more inhabitants it has, the more powerful its impetus, force, and action. And the Lord's heaven is immense—so immense
as to surpass all belief. The inhabitants of our planet are very few, by
comparison—almost like a pond in relation to the ocean.

The divine and therefore the heavenly pattern actually comes to rest **3632**
in us in bodily phenomena—our deeds, acts, facial expressions, words,
physical sensations, and resulting pleasures. These form the outermost
border of that pattern and of spiritual inflow, which come to a halt in
them. The deeper entities flowing in are not the same as they look on the
outside, though. They have a completely different face, different countenance, different sensations, and different gratifications. Correspondences
and representations teach what their nature is, as already described.

The difference can be shown in actions that flow from the will, and in speech that flows from thought. Physical action is not physical in the will, and verbal speech is not verbal in one's thoughts.

This also makes it evident that earthly deeds flow from spiritual ones, because desires of the will and ideas of thought are spiritual. The latter are mirrored in the former by correspondence, but in a different form.

3633   All spirits and angels see themselves as human, with a human face and a human body containing its organs and limbs, because their inmost core aims at such a form. In the same way, the rudiments of a human being, which come from the parent's soul, strive to form the whole person in the egg and uterus, even though they themselves are not in the form of the body but in a different, exquisitely perfect form known to the Lord alone. Since the inmost core in everyone aims and strives toward the human form, all see themselves as human in the other world.

In addition, the whole of heaven is such that each member is like a focal point for all the others, since each is a focal point for influences coming from all the others by way of heaven's form. This brings the image of heaven out in everyone, causing each individual to resemble heaven—in other words, to be human. Whatever the whole is like, that is what each part is like, because the parts have to resemble the whole in order to belong to it.

3634   People who are in correspondence—that is, people who love the Lord, have charity for their neighbor, and therefore believe—are in heaven as to their spirit and in the world as to their body. Accordingly, they make common cause with angels, so they are also images of heaven. As noted, all in general influence the individual, or the whole influences the parts, so these same people are miniature heavens in human form. (It is goodness and truth that make us human and distinguish us from brute animals.)

3635   All movement of the human body, all its actions and outward or purely physical sensations spring from two physical sources: the heart and the lungs. These two correspond to the universal human (the Lord's heaven) in such a way that the heavenly angels there constitute one kingdom, and the spiritual angels, another—the Lord's kingdom being both heavenly and spiritual. The heavenly kingdom consists of angels who love the Lord; the spiritual kingdom, of those who feel charity for their neighbor (§§2088, 2669, 2715, 2718, 3235, 3246). In the body, the heart and its kingdom correspond to heavenly qualities; the lungs and their kingdom, to spiritual qualities. Those are also the qualities that act on the domains of the heart and the lungs—so much so that these domains come into existence and remain in existence as a result of that action. The correspondence of the heart and lungs with the universal human will be dealt with in detail elsewhere, the Lord in his divine mercy willing [§§3883–3896].

It is an absolutely universal rule that the Lord is the sun of heaven; **3636** that all light in the next life comes from this sun; that angels and spirits or those in the next life see nothing whatever of worldly light; and that light from the world's sun is nothing but darkness to angels.

The sun of heaven, or the Lord, radiates heat as well as light, but it is a spiritual light and a spiritual heat. The light looks to angels' eyes like light but contains understanding and wisdom, because it comes from that sun. The warmth feels to their senses like warmth but contains love, because it comes from that sun. So love is called spiritual warmth and provides us with vital heat, while understanding is called spiritual light and provides us with the light of life.

From this universal correspondence extend all others, because everything relates to goodness, which is a matter of love, and to truth, which is a matter of understanding.

The universal human is the whole of the Lord's heaven as it relates **3637** to a human being, but in the highest sense it is the Lord alone, because heaven comes from him, and everything in it corresponds to him.

The Lord had to come into the world because the human race had wholly corrupted itself by its evil life and resulting distorted convictions. People's lower levels started to rule their upper levels; their earthly dimension started to rule their spiritual dimension. In fact, Jehovah (the Lord) could no longer flow into them through the universal human, or heaven, and restore those elements to order. So the Lord had to come so as to take on a human dimension and make it divine. By this means he would restore order, so that all of heaven would relate to him as the only human and correspond to him alone. People taken up with evil and therefore with falsity would be thrown down underfoot, outside the universal human.

As a result, those in the heavens are said to be in the Lord and even in his body, because the Lord is the whole of heaven, and in him they are all allotted regions and functions.

That is why all communities in the other world without exception **3638** maintain their own constant position in relation to the Lord, who appears to the whole of heaven as the sun. What is surprising—and hardly any will believe it, since they cannot understand it—is that the communities there maintain this same position in relation to *everyone* there. No matter where you are, which way you turn, or how you move around, communities that appear on your right are always on your right, and those on your left are always on your left, even when you turn your face or move your body from quarter to quarter.

This too I was allowed to observe many times by turning my [spiritual] body.

Plainly, then, the form of heaven is such that it constantly portrays a universal human in relation to the Lord. Equally clearly, all angels are not only *with* the Lord but *in* the Lord. To put it another way, the Lord is with them and in them. Otherwise things would not work this way.

3639 All locations in heaven therefore relate to the human body as determined by two things. One is direction: on the right or left, in front, behind, in any position. The other is levels. For instance, a place could be on a level with the head and its parts, such as forehead, temples, eyes, or ears; or on a level with the body, such as shoulder blades, chest, abdomen, hips, upper legs, lower legs, or feet. It could also be above the head or underfoot, at any angle. Or it could be at the back, from the occiput on down.

From location alone it can be known which communities are which and what body part's region they belong to, without error; but this can be seen even better from their emotional makeup and character.

3640 The hells, which are very numerous, also have their constant position, so that from it alone their identity and nature can be known. Location works the same way for them. Everything beneath a person lies on different levels in all directions under the sole of the foot.

Some from hell also appear overhead and in other scattered locations, but not because they have their place there. Persuasive fantasy is what creates the illusion and lie that this is their place.

3641 Everyone in both heaven and hell appears upright, head above and feet below, but in reality and in the eyes of angels, the orientations are different. Those in heaven have their heads toward the Lord, who is the sun there and consequently the common center that determines all position and location. The hellish, on the other hand, appear in angels' eyes with their head down and their feet up. So they appear to be oriented the opposite way, or at least at a steep angle. What is "up" to the heavenly, you see, is "down" to the hellish; and what is "down" to the heavenly is "up" to the hellish.

This shows a little more clearly how heaven can make a kind of unit with hell, or how together they can represent a single whole in location and orientation.

3642 One morning I joined a group of angelic spirits who were thinking and speaking in unison, as is their custom. Their activity also reached hell and permeated it so fully that they seemed to join forces with the inhabitants there. The fact of the matter, though, was that what was good and true among the angels turned into evil and falsity among the hellish by gradually flipping in the most amazing way as it sank down. There hell joined forces with it through distorted convictions and evil cravings.

Although the hells are outside the universal human, they are forced into a semblance of unity this way, which keeps them in order, which in turn decides what alliances they form. So the Lord from his divinity also rules the hells.

I have observed that the inhabitants of the heavens enjoy an aura of **3643** clear light resembling the light of morning and midday continuing almost till dusk, and likewise a warmth resembling that of spring, summer, and fall. Hell's inhabitants, though, live in a dense, foggy, dark atmosphere and in the cold.

I have noticed that these balance each other overall. The more love, charity, and resulting faith angels have, the more they live in an aura of springtime light and warmth. The more the hellish live in hatred and therefore in falsity, the more they live in the dark and cold.

In the other world, light contains understanding (as noted above [§3636]), warmth contains love, the dark contains craziness, and the cold contains hatred.

In regard to their soul—the spirit that will live on after physical death— **3644** all humans in the entire world have a place either in the universal human (heaven) or outside it in hell. We are not aware of this as long as we are living in the world, but we *are* there and are governed from there. The goodness we love and the truth we therefore believe determines our place in heaven. The evil we hatefully seek and the falsity we therefore adopt determines our place in hell.

The Lord's whole kingdom is a kingdom of purposes and usefulness. **3645** I was given the opportunity to sense clearly this divine environment of purpose and usefulness, along with certain other features that I cannot put into words.

Everything large and small flows from that environment and is regulated by it. To the extent that the feelings, thoughts, and deeds of a person, spirit, or angel embody a heartfelt intent to do good, that individual is in the universal human, or heaven. To the extent that a person or spirit intends from the heart to do evil, however, that individual is outside the universal human, or in hell.

Influence and correspondence are the same for animals as for humans: **3646** the spiritual world flows into them, the physical world brushes up against them, and these two forces hold them together, enabling them to live. However, the actual operation of the forces expresses itself variously, depending on the form of a being's soul and therefore of its body. The situation resembles that of sunlight, which shines on the earth's various objects with the same strength and in the same manner but acts on different forms in different ways, producing beautiful colors in some and ugly colors in others. When spiritual light shines on the souls of brute animals, they receive it in an entirely different way than when it shines on the soul of a human and are therefore activated in a different manner. [2] Human souls are at a higher level and in a more perfect state and are capable of looking up to heaven and the Lord, so the Lord can attach them to himself and give them eternal life. The souls of unreasoning animals can look only downward to earthly things and connect only with them. Accordingly they perish when their bodies die.

Goals are what demonstrate the nature of human and animal life. We humans can form spiritual and heavenly goals and see, acknowledge, believe, and be affected by them, but the only goals animals can form are earthly ones. So we can enjoy the divine environment of purpose and usefulness that exists in heaven and makes heaven, but the only environment animals can enjoy is that of earth's purposes and functions. Goals are the same thing as what one loves, because anything that is loved is held as a goal.

[3] Most people do not know the difference between human and animal life because like animals they focus on the surface of things. They put all their care and concern into earthly, bodily, and worldly interests, and people who do that also believe they have the same kind of life animals do. They expect to disappear like animals after death, because they do not know or care about spiritual and heavenly dimensions. From this comes the insanity of our era, that people compare themselves with animals and see no inner distinction. But people who believe in what is heavenly and spiritual, letting spiritual light flow in and act on them, see exactly the opposite; they recognize how far above heedless animals they are.

The life of brute animals is to be treated of separately, though, with the Lord's divine mercy.

3647   The way these matters stand was also demonstrated to me. I was allowed to see and perceive certain individuals who were then entering the other life. During bodily life they had focused exclusively on earthly concerns, which formed their only goal; and no one had ever taught them what was good and true. They were of sailor and peasant stock. As they appeared, and as I perceived them, they had so little vitality I supposed they could not be dealt eternal life, the way other spirits are. They resembled machines, barely animated. However, angels were taking excellent care of them and making use of the capacity these spirits had as human beings, in order to introduce them to a life of goodness and truth. So they were being led further and further from animal-like life into human life.

The Lord, working through heaven, also flows into members of the **3648** plant kingdom—all kinds of trees as they reproduce themselves, and different types of smaller plants as they multiply. If a spiritual force from the Lord were not constantly acting within the rudimentary forms of those plants in their seeds, they would never sprout and grow in such an amazing series of steps. Vegetative forms are such that they do not actually receive any life, though.

As a result of this inflow from the Lord, they contain within themselves an image of eternity and infinity. This can be seen from the fact that they are constantly trying to reproduce their kind and species in order to live forever (so to speak) and fill the universe. Every seed harbors this urge.

[2] Yet people attribute all these wonderful marvels to nature itself. They do not believe in any influence from the spiritual world, because they privately deny its existence, even though they ought to know that nothing can survive except by emerging into existence. In other words, survival is perpetual emergence; or again, productivity is constant creation. Consequently, the whole material world is a theater representing the Lord's kingdom (see §3483).

These phenomena and the way they correspond with the universal human will also be discussed elsewhere, by the Lord's divine mercy.

There is more on the universal human and the way things correspond **3649** with it at the ends of the following chapters.

Genesis 28

[Matthew 24:15–18]

3650 THE preliminaries to the previous chapter, Genesis 27, explained what the Lord taught in Matthew 24:8–14 when he predicted the Last Judgment, or the church's last days (§§3486–3489). Here before the upcoming chapter I need to continue the pattern by explaining what comes next, in Matthew 24:15, 16, 17, 18:

> So when you see the ruinous abomination (told of by Daniel the prophet) standing in the Holy Place—reader, take note!—then those in Judea should flee into the mountains. Those on the roof of the house should not go down to take anything from their house. And those in the field should not turn back behind to take their garment. (Matthew 24:15, 16, 17, 18)

3651 Anyone can see that these words hold secrets. Unless the secrets are revealed, no one can possibly know what is meant by the command for those in Judea to flee into the mountains, those on the roof of the house not to go down to take anything from the house, and those in the field not to turn back behind to take their garment.

Without the inner meaning to teach them what these images symbolize and involve, scholars and translators of the Word could be misled and fall into outlandish opinions about it. In fact, those too who at heart deny the Word's holiness could conclude that such words describe only flight and escape in the face of an enemy, so that the text contains nothing holier than that. The reality is that with these words the Lord gives a comprehensive picture of a state in which the church is purged of any love for goodness or belief in truth. The following explanation will demonstrate this meaning.

3652 According to the inner meaning:

So when you see the ruinous abomination symbolizes the purging of the church. This purging [or devastation] takes place when people no longer acknowledge the Lord (and so do not love or believe in him), no longer show any charity toward their neighbor, and consequently have no goodness or truth in their faith. In the church, or more precisely in regions where the Word exists, these traits take hold in people's private thoughts (though not in their public theology), and then comes ruin. The traits mentioned are the abomination that accompanies that ruin. "When you see the ruinous abomination," therefore, means when anyone observes these signs. The steps such a person then needs to take follow in verses 16, 17, 18.

[2] *Told of by Daniel the prophet* in an inner sense means by the Prophets. When the Word refers to a prophet by name, it does not mean that prophet but the Word's prophetic parts themselves. Names never penetrate to heaven (§§1876, 1888). Still, one prophet does not symbolize the same thing as another. For the symbolism of Moses, Elijah, and Elisha, see the preface to Genesis 18 and §2762. Daniel symbolizes all prophecy about the Lord's Coming and about the church's state—here, its final state. The prophets have a lot to say about devastation. In the literal sense of those passages, the devastation means the destruction of the religion of Judah and Israel, but on an inner level it symbolizes the destruction of religion in general, and this is true of the devastation that is looming now.

[3] *Standing in the Holy Place* means being purged of everything connected with goodness and truth. The Holy Place is a state of love and faith. In an inner sense, a place means a state (see §§2625, 2837, 3356, 3387). The holiness of that state is the goodness that we love and the truth we therefore believe. Holy things in the Word have no other meaning, because goodness and truth come from the Lord, who is holiness itself, or the sanctuary itself.

Reader, take note means that people in the church—especially those with love and faith (the people discussed here)—need to observe these things carefully.

[4] *Then those in Judea should flee into the mountains* means that people in the church will rely on the Lord alone and accordingly on love for him and charity for their neighbor. Judea symbolizes the church, as will be shown below. A mountain symbolizes the Lord himself, but mountains in the plural symbolize love for him and charity for one's neighbor; see §§795, 796, 1430, 2722. Taken literally, this prophecy would mean that if Jerusalem were besieged—as it actually was by the Romans—people would run not to the city but onto the mountains, in accord with these words in Luke:

> When you see Jerusalem surrounded by armies, then know that devastation is near. Then let those in Judea flee onto the mountains, and those in its midst leave; but those in the territories should not enter it. (Luke 21:20, 21)

[5] It is the same with Jerusalem here; literally, it means Jerusalem, but in an inner sense it means the Lord's church (see §§402, 2117).

Each and every mention of the people of Judah and Israel in the Word represents the Lord's kingdom in the heavens and the Lord's kingdom on earth, or the church, as shown many times. That is why Jerusalem never means Jerusalem, and Judea never means Judea, in an inner sense. Instead they were something that could (and did) represent the heavenly and spiritual qualities of the Lord's kingdom. This made it possible for the Word to be written in such a way that people reading it on earth could grasp it and the angels present with them could truly understand it. The Lord spoke in the same way for the same reason. Had it been otherwise, the message would not have been suited to the grasp of readers—especially at that time—or to the comprehension of angels; people would not have accepted it, and angels would not have understood it.

[6] *Those on the roof of the house should not go down to take anything from their house* means that people motivated by good that is done out of neighborly love were not to turn from that to matters of religious doctrine. In the Word, the roof of a house symbolizes a higher state in us, or a state of goodness. What is below symbolizes a lower state in us, or a state of truth. For the meaning of a house, see §§710, 1708, 2233, 3142, 3538.

Here is the case with the state of people in the church: When they are being reborn, they learn truth for the sake of goodness, because they desire truth as a means to goodness. When the process of rebirth is complete, though, they act on both truth and goodness. Having reached this stage, they ought not to return to the previous one. If they did, they would use truth to debate the goodness in which they live, corrupting their state. All debate ends, as it should, when we reach a stage in which we will what is true and good. At that point we base our thoughts and deeds on our will and so on conscience, not on our intellect, as we did before. If we resort to our intellect again, we fall prey to trials in which we fail. That is the meaning of "Those on the roof of the house should not go down to take anything from their house."

[7] *And those in the field should not turn back behind to take their garment* (their coat) means that likewise people motivated by the good that truth advocates were not to turn from that aspect of truth to doctrinal truth. In the Word, a field symbolizes this state of goodness in a person. (For the meaning of a field, see §§368, 2971, 3196, 3310, 3317, 3500, 3508.) A garment or coat symbolizes that which clothes goodness—in other words, doctrinal truth, because this is like a garment for goodness. (For this meaning of a garment, see §§297, 1073, 2576, 3301.)

Anyone can see that a deeper message than appears in the literal text lies hidden in these words, since the Lord himself spoke them.

These considerations now show that the verses offer a comprehensive **3653** picture of a state in which the church is purged of any love for goodness or belief in truth, and that the passage calls on people with that love and belief to take the next, necessary steps.

There are three kinds of people in the church: those with love for the Lord, those with charity for their neighbor, and those with a desire for truth. *Those in Judea should flee into the mountains* specifically symbolizes people in the first category—those with love for the Lord. *Those on the roof of the house should not go down to take anything from their house* symbolizes those in the second category, with charity for their neighbor. *Those in the field should not turn back behind to take their garment* symbolizes those in the third category, with a desire for truth.

See previous remarks and explanations of this in §2454 of the third volume, where the meaning of turning back behind and looking back behind oneself is also given.

In the Word's inner meaning, Judea does not mean Judea, and Jeru- **3654** salem does not mean Jerusalem, and many scriptural passages can illustrate this fact.

The Word speaks more often in terms of the land of Judah than of Judea. Like the land of Canaan it symbolizes the Lord's kingdom and consequently the church (since the church is the Lord's kingdom on earth). Judah, or the Jewish nation, represented the Lord's heavenly kingdom, while Israel, or the Israelite people, symbolized his spiritual kingdom, and since this is what they represented, they mean that and nothing else in the inner sense of the Word wherever they are mentioned. [2] What later sections say about Judah and the land of Judah will establish this symbolism, by the Lord's divine mercy. Meanwhile, these few passages from the Prophets will do. In Isaiah:

> My beloved had a vineyard on a horn of the offspring of oil. He surrounded it and de-stoned it and planted it with a choice grapevine and built a tower in the middle of it and also hollowed out a winepress in it and waited for it to produce grapes; but it produced wild grapes. And now, *resident of Jerusalem* and *man of Judah,* judge, please, between me and my vineyard. I will make it a *ruin;* for Jehovah Sabaoth's vineyard is the *house of Israel,* and the *man of Judah* is his delightful plant. And he waited for judgment, but look: an abscess! For justice, but look: an outcry! (Isaiah 5:1, 2, 3, 6, 7)

The literal meaning of this passage concerns the corrupt state of the Israelites and Jews, but the inner meaning concerns the corrupt state of the church that Israel and Judah represented. The resident of Jerusalem means goodness in the church—a resident meaning goodness or, to put it another way, people with goodness (see §§2268, 2451, 2712, 3613), and Jerusalem meaning the church (402, 2117). The house of Israel has the same meaning, a house standing for goodness (710, 1708, 2233, 3142, 3538) and Israel, for the church (3305). The same is true of the man of Judah, since a man symbolizes truth (265, 749, 1007, 3134, 3310, 3459) and Judah symbolizes goodness. The difference is that the man of Judah means truth deriving from the good we do out of love for the Lord (called heavenly truth), or people with that truth. [3] In the same author:

> He will lift up a banner for the nations and assemble the *exiles of Israel,* and the *scattered elements of Judah* he will gather from the four wings of the earth. Then Ephraim's envy will withdraw, and *Judah's foes* will be cut off. Ephraim will not show envy toward *Judah,* and *Judah* will not assail Ephraim. Jehovah will exterminate the tongue of Egypt's sea. And he will wave his hand over the river in the fierceness of his breath. Then there will be a path for the survivors of his people who will remain from Assyria. (Isaiah 11:12, 13, 15, 16)

In its literal meaning, this passage tells about the return of the Israelites and Jews from their captivity. In its inner meaning it has to do in general with a new religion and in particular with everyone who is regenerating, or becoming a church. The exiles of Israel stand for the truth such people know; the scattered elements of Judah, for the good they do. Ephraim stands for their intellect, which will no longer rebel. Egypt stands for secular knowledge, and Assyria, for reasoning based on that knowledge, which they corrupted. The exiles, scattered elements, survivors, and remainder stand for the truth and goodness left standing. The meaning of Ephraim as the intellect will become clear elsewhere [§5354]. For the meaning of Egypt as secular knowledge, see §§1164, 1165, 1186, 1462, 2588, 3325. For that of Assyria as reasoning, 119, 1186. And for that of survivors [or a remnant] as the traces of goodness and truth the Lord stores away in our inner self, 468, 530, 560, 561, 660, 661, 798, 1050, 1738, 1906, 2284. [4] In the same author:

> Listen to this, house of Jacob, you who are called by the name of *Israel* (and *they issued from the waters of Judah*), because after the holy city they are called, and on the God of Israel they lean. (Isaiah 48:1, 2)

The waters of Judah stand for truth that develops from the good we do out of love for the Lord. That truth is itself the goodness of neighborly love, which is called spiritual goodness. Spiritual goodness makes a spiritual religion, whose inner depths are Israel and whose outer surface is the house of Jacob. This clarifies what is symbolized by "the house of Jacob who are called by the name of Israel" and "from the waters of Judah they issued." [5] In the same author:

> From Jacob I will produce seed, and *from Judah, the heir to my mountains;* and the ones I have chosen will own it, and my servants will live there. (Isaiah 65:9)

In its highest sense, the heir of [Jehovah's] mountains, from Judah, stands for the Lord. In a representative sense it stands for people who love him and are therefore devoted to good done out of both kinds of love. Mountains mean that goodness, as shown above at §3652. [6] In Moses:

> A lion's cub is *Judah;* fueled by prey, you have risen, my son. He crouched; he lay like a lion and like an aging lion. Who will rouse him? (Genesis 49:9)

Obviously in the highest sense Judah means the Lord here, and in a representative sense it means people motivated by the goodness that comes from love for him. In David:

> When Israel came out from Egypt—the house of Jacob, from a barbarous people—*Judah became [God's] sanctuary; Israel,* his ruling power. (Psalms 114:1, 2)

Again Judah stands for heavenly goodness, which is the goodness of loving the Lord, and Israel, for heavenly truth, or spiritual goodness. [7] In Jeremiah:

> "Look! The days are coming," says Jehovah, "when I will raise up for *David* a righteous offshoot who will reign as monarch and prosper and exercise judgment and justice in the land; in his days *Judah will be saved* and *Israel will live in safety.* And this is his name that they will call him: Jehovah our Righteousness." (Jeremiah 23:5, 6; 33:15, 16)

This is about the Lord's Coming. Judah stands for people committed to the goodness required by love for the Lord; Israel, for those awake to the truth that stems from that goodness. Judah clearly does not mean Judah, nor does Israel mean Israel, since Judah was *not* saved, and Israel fared no better. Likewise in the same author:

> I will bring *Judah* back from *captivity* and *Israel* back from *captivity* and rebuild them as before. (Jeremiah 33:7)

Again, in the same author:

> "In those days and in that time," says Jehovah, "*Israel's children will come,* they and *Judah's children* together; crying along the way they will go, and Jehovah their God they will seek, and Zion they will seek by this way, where their faces [turn]." (Jeremiah 50:4, 5)

In the same author:

> In that time they will call *Jerusalem* Jehovah's throne, and all the nations will be gathered to it because of Jehovah's name, to *Jerusalem;* they will no longer go after the hardness of their evil heart. In those days the *house of Judah will go toward the house of Israel,* and they will come as one from the land of the north onto [this] land. (Jeremiah 3:17, 18)

[8] In the same author:

> "Look! The days are coming," says Jehovah, "on which I will sow the *house of Israel* and the *house of Judah* with the seed of human and the seed of animal. And I will strike a new pact with the *house of Israel* and with the *house of Judah.* This is the pact that I will strike with the *house of Israel* after those days: I will put my law in the midst of them, and upon their heart I will write it." (Jeremiah 31:27, 31, 33)

Obviously it is not Israel (or the house of Israel) that is meant here, because its people were scattered among the surrounding nations, never to return from captivity. Neither is Judah (or the house of Judah) meant, then. Instead, on an inner level these symbolize people from the Lord's spiritual and heavenly kingdoms. They are the ones with whom he makes a new pact, the ones on whose hearts he writes his law. A new pact stands for union with the Lord through goodness (§§665, 666, 1023, 1038, 1864, 1996, 2003, 2021, 2037). The law written on a person's heart stands for a resulting perception of goodness and truth and also for conscience. [9] In Joel:

> It will happen on that day that the mountains will shower down new wine, and the hills will stream with milk, and *all the brooks of Judah will stream with water,* and a spring will issue from Jehovah's house and water the river of the sheetim. Egypt will become a wasteland, and Edom will become a wilderness of a wasteland, because of violence to the *children of Judah,* whose innocent blood they shed on their land. And *Judah will abide forever* and *Jerusalem* for generation after generation. (Joel 3:18, 19, 20)

Each detail again shows that Judah does not mean Judah, and Jerusalem does not mean Jerusalem. They mean people with reverent love and charity, since these are the people who will abide forever, for generation after generation. [10] In Malachi:

> Watch: I am sending my angel, who will prepare the way before me; and suddenly to his temple will come the Lord, whom you are seeking, and the Angel of the Covenant, whom you desire. *Then the minha of Judah and Jerusalem will be sweet to Jehovah,* as in the days of old and as in former years. (Malachi 3:1, 4)

This passage describes the Lord's Coming. Clearly Judah's and Jerusalem's minha was not sweet to Jehovah at that time, so Judah and Jerusalem plainly symbolize characteristics of the Lord's church.

The same holds true in all other Scripture passages mentioning Judah, Israel, or Jerusalem.

This now shows what Judea means in Matthew: the Lord's church. In the current passage it means the church when it has been devastated.

The verses preceding this passage in the Gospel dealt with the first **3655** and second stages in the corruption of the church. In the first stage, people started to forget what was good and true and quarreled about it, which gave rise to falsity; see §3354. In the second, people despised and opposed what is good and true, and faith in the Lord gradually died out as neighborly love came to an end; see §§3487, 3488.

The current passage accordingly deals with the third stage, which is one in which the church is stripped of its goodness and truth.

Genesis 28

1. And Isaac called to Jacob and blessed him and commanded him and said to him, "You shall not take a woman from the daughters of Canaan.

2. Get up; go to Paddan-aram, to the house of Bethuel, your mother's father, and take yourself from there a woman from the daughters of Laban your mother's brother.

3. And God Shaddai will bless you and make you fruitful and multiply you, and you will become a throng of peoples.

4. And he will give you the blessing of Abraham—you and your seed with you—so that you inherit the land of your immigrant journeys, which God gave Abraham."

5. And Isaac sent Jacob, and he went to Paddan-aram, to Laban, son of Bethuel the Aramean, brother of Rebekah, Jacob and Esau's mother.

6. And Esau saw that Isaac had blessed Jacob and sent him to Paddan-aram to take himself a woman from there (when [Isaac] blessed him) and had commanded him, saying, "You shall not take a woman from the daughters of Canaan,"

7. and [that] Jacob listened to his father and to his mother and went to Paddan-aram.

8. And Esau saw that the daughters of Canaan were bad in the eyes of Isaac his father.

9. And Esau went to Ishmael and took Mahalath, daughter of Ishmael (son of Abraham), sister of Nebaioth—in addition to his women—to himself as his woman.

* * * *

10. And Jacob went out from Beer-sheba and went to Haran.

11. And he happened on a place and spent the night there because the sun went down, and he took one of the stones of the place and put it as his headrest and lay down in that place.

12. And he dreamed. And look: a ladder resting on the earth, and its head reaching the sky, and look: God's angels going up and going down on it!

13. And look: Jehovah standing above it; and he said, "I am Jehovah, God of Abraham your father and God of Isaac; the land that you are lying on, to you I will give it and to your seed.

14. And your seed will be like the dust of the earth, and you will burst out toward the sea and toward the east and toward the north and toward the south. And in you all the clans of the ground will be blessed, and in your seed.

15. And look: I am with you and will guard you in every [place] where you go and will bring you back to this ground, because I will not abandon you until I have done what I spoke to you."

16. And Jacob woke from his sleep and said, "Surely Jehovah is in this place and I didn't know."

17. And he was afraid and said, "How frightening this place is! This is nothing but the house of God, and this is the gate of heaven."

18. And Jacob got up early in the morning and took the stone that he had put as his headrest and put it as a pillar and poured oil on its head.

19. And he called the name of that place Bethel. And certainly Luz had been the name of the city earlier.

20. And Jacob vowed a vow, saying, "If God is with me and guards me on this way that I am walking and gives me bread to eat and clothing to wear,

21. and I return in peace to the house of my father, Jehovah will become my God.

22. And this stone that I have put as a pillar will be the house of God, and everything that you give me, I will make sure to tithe it to you."

Summary

I N the highest sense the theme here is the way the Lord started to make the truth and the goodness in his earthly level divine. The means are depicted in a general way. In a representative sense, though, the theme is the way the Lord regenerates or remakes the truth and the goodness of a person's earthly level. Again the process is dealt with in a general way (verses 1–10). **3656**

The highest inner sense describes how the Lord started with the outermost plane of the divine design in making the truth in his earthly level divine. Then he could organize the intermediate planes and unite everything with that which is first: his divinity itself. The representative inner sense tells how the Lord also regenerates a person's earthly level by starting with the outermost plane of the design. Then he can organize the intermediate planes so as to unite them with himself by means of the rational level (dealt with in verses 11–22). **3657**

Inner Meaning

G ENESIS 28:1, 2. *And Isaac called to Jacob and blessed him and commanded him and said to him, "You shall not take a woman from the* **3658**

daughters of Canaan. Get up; go to Paddan-aram, to the house of Bethuel,
your mother's father, and take yourself from there a woman from the daugh-
ters of Laban your mother's brother."

Isaac called to Jacob means perceiving what goodness-from-truth
received from the Lord was like. *And blessed him* means that it would
accordingly be united. *And commanded him and said to him* symbolizes
reflection and a resulting perception. *You shall not take a woman from the*
daughters of Canaan means as long as it did not unite with the desire for
falsity and evil. *Get up* means as long as he lifts that goodness higher. *Go*
to Paddan-aram symbolizes knowledge of that kind of truth. *To the house*
of Bethuel, your mother's father, and take yourself from there a woman from
the daughters of Laban your mother's brother symbolizes a side branch of
outward goodness, and from it, truth that was to be united.

3659   *Isaac called to Jacob* means perceiving what goodness-from-truth
received from the Lord was like, as can be seen from the following. *Call-*
ing to someone means perceiving the person's character (discussed in
§3609). *Isaac* represents divine goodness in the Lord's divine rationality
(discussed in §§1893, 2066, 2072, 2083, 2630, 3012, 3194, 3210). And *Jacob*
represents earthly truth in the Lord (discussed in §§1893, 3305, 3509, 3525,
3546, 3576, 3599), but here and in the rest of the chapter he represents
goodness based on that truth. This explanation shows, then, that the
words *Isaac called to Jacob* mean perceiving what goodness-from-truth
from the Lord was like.

[2] Jacob now represents goodness based on that truth because by
this point he had taken Esau's rights as firstborn and his blessing. In the
process he put on Esau's identity, although not yet in regard to anything
more than the goodness that came from the truth he had previously
represented. All truth, no matter what its identity and nature, contains
goodness. Goodness is the only thing that makes truth true. Truth is
called truth because of its goodness.

By taking the position of firstborn and the blessing, Jacob rather
than Esau became the one whose descendants would inherit the promise made to Abraham and Isaac concerning the land of Canaan. So he
became the one who would represent the Lord's earthly divinity, just as
Isaac represented the Lord's divine rationality, and Abraham his divinity itself. The aim in allowing Jacob to take the right of firstborn and
then the blessing from Esau was for the representation to fall onto one
person's shoulders.

That is why Jacob now represents goodness on the earthly level. At first, though, he represents goodness based on the truth he just finished representing.

Esau remains involved in the story (as below in verses 6, 7, 8, [9] of the current chapter) in order to represent the goodness that comes of truth and the truth that comes of deeper goodness on the Lord's earthly level. Jacob was not yet able to represent this.

What follows will clarify the identity and nature of the goodness-from-truth currently meant by Jacob.

And blessed him means that it would accordingly be united. This can be seen from the symbolism of being *blessed* as being united (discussed in §§3504, 3514, 3530, 3565, 3584).

	3660

Isaac the father now blesses Jacob his son, even though Jacob had come in deceit and stolen Esau's blessing, a deed at which Isaac shuddered, as verses 33 and 35 of the previous chapter (Genesis 27) make plain. Isaac blessed Jacob because he now perceived that Jacob's offspring rather than Esau's would be the ones to possess the land of Canaan. That is why he affirmed the blessing. However, the deceit at which Isaac shuddered symbolized and foreshadowed that nation's deceitful attitude toward its representation. In other words, Jacob's descendants represented the divine or heavenly qualities of the Lord's kingdom in a way that was anything but sincere or heartfelt. Just the opposite of the ancient church, they focused solely on outward compliance detached from any inward devotion—and not even that, since they so often sank into open idolatry.

[2] I have already said what is meant by the uniting or union symbolized on an inner level by being blessed: the Lord's earthly level had to form a connection with his rational level—his outer self with his inner self—in regard to goodness and truth. In order to make his earthly level divine, he had to supply it with the kind of goodness and truth that would correspond to the goodness and truth on his divine rational plane. Without corresponding goodness and truth, no union takes place.

The good urges and true ideas that exist in our earthly mind, or that characterize our earthly self, are countless. There are so many that we can barely learn their most general categories, even though when earthly goodness and truth are mentioned, people see them as simple and undivided. This is true of the whole earthly dimension and everything it contains. Because it is so diverse, naturally there is earthly goodness and truth that *can* hold rational goodness and truth, and there is earthly goodness and truth that *cannot* hold rational goodness and truth. Consequently, there is earthly goodness and truth that can be connected to rational goodness and truth by correspondence. They are discussed in this and following chapters.

[3] We cannot learn much about these kinds of goodness and truth, distinguish them from each other, examine their nature, and see how they adjust to their future union until we start to think deeply, or until heaven's light illuminates our thoughts. Before that, such ideas seem both impenetrable and boring. Nevertheless they are suited to being grasped and truly understood by angels, and also to being grasped by spirits. Angels and spirits do not have their thoughts interrupted by worldly, bodily, and earthly concerns, as they did before when living as people on earth. They revel in the delights of understanding and the blessings of wisdom when they glean ideas about goodness and truth from the Word's inner meaning. The Divine then showers them with light, because in its highest sense the Word tells about the Lord, and in a representative sense, about religion and rebirth. So they are then in the divine aura of the Lord and of his aims and objectives.

3661   *And commanded him and said to him* symbolizes reflection and a resulting perception. This can be seen in the stories of the Word, where *commanding* symbolizes reflecting and *saying* symbolizes perceiving (discussed in §§1791, 1815, 1819, 1822, 1898, 1919, 2080, 2619, 2862). To reflect is to consider how some matter stands and examine its nature—a process that results in perception.

3662   *You shall not take a woman from the daughters of Canaan* means as long as it did not unite with the desire for falsity and evil. This can be seen from the symbolism of *taking a woman* as being joined or united, from that of *daughters* as desires (discussed in §§568, 2362, 3024), and from that of *Canaan* as falsity and evil (discussed in §§1093, 1140, 1141, 1167, 1205, 1444, 1573, 1574, 1868).

3663   *Get up* means as long as he lifts that goodness higher. This can be seen from the symbolism of *getting up.* Wherever the term is used, it involves some type of elevation (as discussed in §§2401, 2785, 2912, 2927, 3171). Here it symbolizes rising up from the attributes symbolized by the daughters of Canaan to those symbolized by the daughters of Laban, treated of below.

3664   *Go to Paddan-aram* symbolizes knowledge of that kind of truth. This is established by the symbolism of *Aram* or Syria as knowledge (dealt with in §§1232, 1234, 3249). Paddan-aram symbolizes knowledge of truth because it was located in Syria of the Rivers, home of Nahor, Bethuel, and Laban, which symbolizes such knowledge (see §3051). Paddan-aram is also mentioned above in Genesis 25:20 and below in Genesis 31:18, and in those verses it again symbolizes knowledge of truth.

To the house of Bethuel, your mother's father, and take yourself from there a woman from the daughters of Laban your mother's brother symbolizes a side branch of outward goodness, and from it, truth that was to be united, as can be seen from the following: *Bethuel* represents goodness among people outside the church who belong to a first category (as mentioned in §2865). *Laban* represents a desire for goodness in the earthly self, or a desire for outward goodness. Strictly speaking, he represents goodness branching off from a shared stock. (These are discussed in §§3129, 3130, 3160, 3612.) And *taking a woman from his daughters* means joining or uniting with a desire for truth stemming from that goodness. *Taking a woman* means uniting, of course, and *daughters* symbolize desires (see §§568, 2362, 3024). Clearly, then, these words mean that the earthly goodness now represented by Jacob would unite with the truth that stems from a side branch of outward goodness.

[2] When we are being reborn, the Lord leads us first as children, then as youths, then as young adults, and finally as full adults. The truth a child learns when young is completely superficial and tactile, because he or she cannot yet grasp anything deeper. This truth is simply the knowledge of matters that have divine elements at their core.

There is knowledge that does not have anything divine at its core and knowledge that does. Knowledge that has something divine at its core is capable of letting in progressively deeper levels of truth, one after another in order. But knowledge that contains nothing divine spits truth out rather than letting it in. The knowledge of superficial, tactile goodness and truth resembles soil that accepts one kind of seed but not another, that nurtures one kind and chokes off the other. Knowledge that has something divine deep inside welcomes spiritual and heavenly truth and goodness, because the divinity within disposes it to do so. In contrast, knowledge that holds nothing divine welcomes only falsity and evil, because that is its nature.

The daughters of Laban, from the house of Bethuel, symbolize the knowledge of superficial, tactile truth that opens itself to spiritual and heavenly truth and goodness. The daughters of Canaan symbolize the knowledge that does not.

[3] The concepts we learn in childhood and youth are like very broad containers that need to be filled with goodness; as they fill, we become enlightened. If the vessels are such that they can contain genuine goodness, the divine quality within them gradually enlightens us more and more. If they are such that they cannot contain genuine goodness, we do not receive a glimmer of light. We appear to be enlightened, but the light is swamp light cast by falsity and evil, which in reality lead us into ever deeper darkness regarding what is good and true.

[4] Such concepts are numerous—so numerous that one can hardly list the broad categories, let alone distinguish the specific types. They stream in great profusion from the divine plane through the rational into the earthly. Some flow directly through rational goodness into earthly goodness, into the truth derived from this goodness, and from there into the outermost, tactile part of the earthly level, where they again drain into various rivulets. Others flow indirectly through rational truth into earthly truth, into the goodness derived from this truth, and from there into the outermost, tactile part of the earthly level. (See §§3573, 3616.)

Such concepts resemble nations, clans, and households with their blood ties and connections. Some descend in a direct line from the first ancestor, while some descend in an indirect line, or branch further and further off. In the heavens the interrelationships are very clear, because the communities there are all divided up according to the major and minor types—and therefore the relative closeness—of their goodness and truth (§§685, 2508, 2524, 2556, 2739, 3612). The earliest people, who were heavenly, represented these relationships by living divided into nations, clans, and households (§§470, 471, 483, 1159, 1246). This representation was also the reason for the command that the people of the representative religion contract marriage within the clans of their own nation; in doing so they could represent heaven and the bonds of goodness and truth among its communities. One example is the requirement here that Jacob go to the house of Bethuel, his mother's father, and take himself from there a woman from the daughters of Laban, his mother's brother.

[5] This knowledge of superficial, tactile truth coming from a side branch of goodness, which as noted holds something divine and can therefore open itself to genuine goodness, is like the knowledge that young children have who are later reborn. In general it is the kind of knowledge contained in Bible stories—what the Word says about paradise, the first

human in paradise, the tree of life in the middle of it, and the tree of knowledge with its deceitful snake [Genesis 2, 3]. These are the concepts that hold something divine and welcome spiritual and heavenly goodness and truth, since this goodness and truth are what they represent and symbolize.

Such concepts also include all other details of scriptural narrative: those concerning the tabernacle, the Temple, and their construction; those concerning the garments worn by Aaron and his sons; those concerning the feasts of booths, of the harvest's first fruits, and of unleavened bread; and so on. When young children know and think about this information and other information like it, the angels with them think about the divine attributes represented and symbolized. Because the angels are moved by these thoughts, their emotion is communicated to the children, creating the pleasure and delight the children feel in such knowledge, and preparing their minds to receive genuine truth and goodness.

These and many other concepts make up the knowledge of superficial, tactile truth stemming from a side branch of goodness.

Genesis 28:3, 4, 5. *"And God Shaddai will bless you and make you fruitful and multiply you, and you will become a throng of peoples. And he will give you the blessing of Abraham—you and your seed with you—so that you inherit the land of your immigrant journeys, which God gave Abraham." And Isaac sent Jacob, and he went to Paddan-aram, to Laban, son of Bethuel the Aramean, brother of Rebekah, Jacob and Esau's mother.* **3666**

God Shaddai will bless you symbolizes times when that truth and goodness are tested, which lead to union. *And make you fruitful and multiply you* symbolizes resulting goodness and truth. *And you will become a throng of peoples* symbolizes an abundance. *And he will give you the blessing of Abraham* symbolizes the union of divinity itself with earthly goodness and truth. *You and your seed with you* symbolizes [union] with the goodness and truth that develops next. *So that you inherit the land of your immigrant journeys* symbolizes a well-taught life. *Which God gave Abraham* means which comes from the Divine. *And Isaac sent Jacob* symbolizes the beginning of its existence. *And he went to Paddan-aram* here as before symbolizes a knowledge of that truth. *To Laban, son of Bethuel the Aramean,* symbolizes a side branch of goodness. *Brother of Rebekah, Jacob and Esau's mother,* symbolizes a connection through their mother with the goodness-from-truth that is Jacob and the truth-from-goodness that is Esau.

3667   *God Shaddai will bless you* symbolizes times when that truth and goodness are tested, which lead to union. This can be seen from the symbolism
of *God Shaddai* as times of testing (discussed below) and from that of
being *blessed* as union (discussed in §§3504, 3514, 3530, 3565, 3584). Since
Jacob now represents the goodness that comes of truth (as shown above in
§3659), *you* means that goodness and truth.

God Shaddai symbolizes times of testing, because in ancient times people referred to God the Highest (or the Lord) by various names according
to his attributes, or according to the goodness they received from him, or
according to various true ideas. These come in great variety, as everyone
knows.

People in the ancient church took all these names to mean only one
God—the Lord, whom they called Jehovah.

After that church fell away from what was good and true and from
this wisdom, they started to worship as many gods as there were names of
the one God. In fact, each nation and eventually each clan acknowledged
one of them as its own god. That is why so many gods sprang into existence, and their names come up throughout the Word.

[2] This happened in the clan of Terah, Abraham's father, and also
in Abraham's own household, whose members worshiped other gods (see
§§1356, 2559), especially God Shaddai (§1992). The following words in
Moses show that worship of him survived in that household:

> I appeared to Abraham, Isaac, and Jacob as God Shaddai, and by my
> name "Jehovah" I was not known to them. (Exodus 6:3)

That is why Abraham was told, "*I am God Shaddai;* walk before me and be
upright" (Genesis 17:1). It is also why Isaac now tells Jacob, "*God Shaddai
will bless you.*"

A very clear piece of evidence that this is so appears in the current chapter. Even after the Lord said in a dream, "I am Jehovah, God of Abraham
your father and God of Isaac" (verse 13), Jacob still said, "If God is with
me and guards me on this way that I am walking and gives me bread to
eat and clothing to wear, and I return in peace to the house of my father,
Jehovah will become my God" (verses 20, 21). This statement shows that
Jacob's household, too, did not acknowledge Jehovah but that Jacob was
ready to acknowledge Jehovah as his God if Jehovah treated him well.

It is exactly the same today in the world of Christian paganism.

To turn specifically to God Shaddai, that is what the ancient church
had called the Lord in regard to his role in trials and in the blessings and

benefits that follow trial, as shown in §1992 of the third volume. That is why God Shaddai on an inner level symbolizes times of trial.

For the idea that goodness and truth are united through times of trial, see the previous remarks and explanations concerning trial cited in §2819.

And make you fruitful and multiply you symbolizes resulting goodness and truth. This can be seen from the association of *being fruitful* with goodness and of *multiplying* with truth, as discussed in §§43, 55, 913, 983, 2846, 2847. **3668**

And you will become a throng of peoples symbolizes an abundance, as is evident without explanation. A *throng of peoples* has specifically to do with truth, because *peoples* in the Word symbolize those focused on truth (see §§1259, 1260, 2928, 3581), whereas nations symbolize those devoted to goodness (§§1259, 1260, 1416, 1849). **3669**

The reason this verse mentions a throng of peoples is that the subject is goodness based on truth, as represented by Jacob. Goodness that grows out of truth is one thing; goodness that gives rise to truth is another. The first is the goodness meant here by Jacob; the second is the goodness meant by Esau. The goodness that grows out of truth is the reverse of the goodness that gives rise to truth. People who are being reborn live in the former until they have achieved rebirth. The same people live in the latter when they have been reborn. To read about the reversal of their state, see §§3539, 3548, 3556, 3563, 3570, 3576, 3603.

And he will give you the blessing of Abraham symbolizes the union of divinity itself with earthly goodness and truth. This can be seen from the symbolism of a *blessing* as union (dealt with above at §§3660, 3667) and from the representation of *Abraham* as the Lord's divinity itself, which is called the Father (discussed in §§[2010,] 2011, 3251, 3439). These words are addressed to Jacob, who will later represent divine goodness and truth in the Lord's earthly divinity, so the union of divinity itself with earthly goodness and truth is what *he will give you the blessing of Abraham* symbolizes on an inner level. **3670**

In a literal sense, Abraham's blessing refers to the ownership of Canaan, as do the words below "so that you inherit the land of your immigrant journeys, which God gave Abraham." Everyone who denies that scriptural narrative involves anything more heavenly or secret than this takes the words literally. This is especially the case with the Jewish nation, which even claims superiority over all nations and peoples on this account. Their ancestors, particularly Jacob, understood the words the same way—and you can see from the remarks just above in §3667 what Jacob was like. He did not know Jehovah or want to acknowledge him unless Jehovah gave him bodily and worldly benefits. But it was not Abraham, Isaac, or Jacob who was meant. Instead, Jacob represents the Lord's earthly level, which the Lord made divine, as these explanations have made abundantly clear.

What kind of people are filling representative roles makes no difference, whether they are evil or good. Evil people can represent the Lord's divinity just as well and have done so. See §§665, 1097, 1361.

[2] The same conclusion can also be drawn from modern representations. All monarchs represent the Lord simply by virtue of the royalty invested in them, no matter who they are or what they are like. The same holds true for all priests simply by virtue of their priesthood, no matter who they are or what they are like. Royalty and priesthood themselves are holy, regardless of the character of the person serving in those positions. As a result, the Word is just as holy when an evil person is preaching it; the sacraments of baptism and Holy Supper are just as holy; and so on.

Another valid conclusion is that monarchs can never take credit for the holiness that attaches to their royalty, and priests can never take credit for the holiness that attaches to their priesthood. The more they claim that holiness for themselves, or attribute it to themselves, the more deeply they imprint on themselves the signs of a spiritual thief, or the mark of spiritual thievery. In addition, the more wrong they do—the more they violate justice and fairness, goodness and truth—the more they shed their representative role; a monarch sheds the representation of royal holiness, a priest sheds that of priestly holiness, and they come to represent the opposite.

That is why the representative Jewish religion had so many laws about reverent conduct, principally affecting priests as they carried out their ministry. More will be said on this subject later, by the Lord's divine mercy.

3671   *You and your seed with you* symbolizes [union] with the goodness and truth that develops next. This is established by the representation of Jacob—*you*—as goodness-from-truth, or the goodness that comes of truth (discussed above [§3659]) and from the symbolism of *seed* as the goodness and truth that belong to faith (discussed in §§1025, 1447, 1610, 2848, 3373). *With you* means that these were attached to the goodness-from-truth that is Jacob.

Goodness and truth interrelate the way seed and soil do. Inner goodness is like seed that produces fruit but only in good soil. Outward goodness and truth are like soil in which the seed of inward goodness and truth reproduces and without which it cannot put down roots.

That is why our rational level is reborn first of all, because that is where the seed is. The earthly level is regenerated later, to serve as soil (§§3286, 3288, 3321, 3368, 3493, 3576, 3620, 3623). Since the earthly level is like the ground, goodness and truth can become fruitful and multiply on the rational level, which they could not do if they did not have ground somewhere for the seed to sink its roots into.

In this comparison as in a mirror you can see the workings of regeneration and its many mysteries.

[2] Understanding and willing what is good and true is a function of the rational plane, and the resulting perceptions of goodness and truth are like seeds. Learning and doing what is good and true is a function of the earthly plane. The concepts we learn and deeds we do act as soil when we have a liking for facts that validate goodness and truth, and especially when we feel pleasure in carrying them out. Then the seeds live and grow in their soil, so to speak. Goodness consequently becomes fruitful, and truth multiplies, constantly reaching up from that soil to the rational level, which is perfected by them.

The case is very different when we understand what is good and true and even sense a certain inner will to act on them but do not like learning about them, let alone actually putting them into practice. Then goodness cannot become fruitful and truth cannot multiply on the rational plane.

So that you inherit the land of your immigrant journeys symbolizes a **3672** well-taught life, as can be seen from the following: *Inheriting* means receiving another's life, as discussed in §§2658, 2851—in this case, life from the Divine symbolized by the very next words. And *immigrant journeys* symbolize instruction, as discussed in §§1463, 2025. The *land* means where there is life.

The well-taught life mentioned here is a life of the goodness-from-truth represented by Jacob. When we live by the truth we have learned, we are living a well-taught life.

Which God gave Abraham means which comes from the Divine. This **3673** can be seen from the representation of *Abraham* as the Lord in regard to the Divine that the Word calls the Father (discussed in §§[2010,] 2011, 3251, 3439). *God gave* means it became the Lord's own, of course, because what is given belongs to the recipient. Clearly, then, *which God gave Abraham* symbolizes life that comes from the Divine.

3674   *And Isaac sent Jacob* symbolizes the beginning of its existence. This can be seen from the fact that Jacob now starts to represent the goodness that comes of truth and therefore the beginning of existence for the Lord's earthly divinity. Things said later about Jacob when he was staying with Laban contain this representation. That is why *Isaac sent Jacob* symbolizes the beginning of its existence.

3675   *And he went to Paddan-aram* symbolizes a knowledge of that truth. This is established by the symbolism of *Paddan-aram* as knowledge of truth (mentioned just above in §3664).

3676   *To Laban, son of Bethuel the Aramean,* symbolizes a side branch of goodness, as can be seen from the following: *Laban* represents goodness branching off from the same stock (as also mentioned above, in §3665). And *Bethuel* represents goodness among people outside the church who belong to a first category (as noted in §§2865, 3665). This is the shared stock from which the goodness represented by Laban branches off. Bethuel is surnamed *the Aramean* here because Aram, or Syria, symbolizes the knowledge of goodness and truth (§§1232, 1234, 3249) that is the focus of discussion here.

The outer truth from which comes the goodness that Jacob represents here is simply religious knowledge. This is the truth that people starting to be reborn absorb first and accept as true. Still, knowledge is not true on its own; its truth is due to its divine content. When the divine qualities within the concepts gleam through, they first become truth. Until then they are merely like broad vessels through which and in which truth can be received. Those mentioned above toward the end of §3665 are examples, and so are all the secular facts we first learn.

3677   *Brother of Rebekah, Jacob and Esau's mother,* symbolizes a connection through their mother with the goodness-from-truth that is Jacob and the truth-from-goodness that is Esau, as can be seen from the following: *Rebekah* represents divine truth in the Lord's divine rational mind (as dealt with many times before). *Jacob* represents goodness-from-truth, which is goodness that comes of truth, on the earthly level. And *Esau* represents truth-from-goodness, which is goodness that gives rise to truth, on the earthly level. (Both of these meanings are dealt with above in §3669.) Everything good and true in the outer, earthly self is conceived and born from the inner, rational self—from goodness on the rational plane as father and from truth on the rational plane as mother (§§3314, 3573, 3616). So these words symbolize a connection through the mother with the goodness-from-truth that is Jacob and the truth-from-goodness that is Esau. [2] What is more, the relationships are exactly the same. However, explaining them in an intelligible way is extremely difficult because not even the broadest outlines of the subject are presently known. For instance, people do not know what spiritual goodness is or what the truth that develops out of it is. They do not know that there are countless major categories of goodness and its truth, and even more subcategories. Nor do they know that these different types of goodness and truth are tied to each other by different degrees of kinship and family connection, so to speak. If this very general information is unknown, a description of the degrees and connections would fall into deep shadow. The darkness is all the deeper because scholars today do not even want to know such things. They love to rove about on the surface of a topic and argue, asking not what such and such is like but whether it even exists. As long as they remain in such a state of mind, they have no desire whatever to learn this boundless quantity of information.

Genesis 28:6, 7, 8, 9. *And Esau saw that Isaac had blessed Jacob and* **3678** *sent him to Paddan-aram to take himself a woman from there (when [Isaac] blessed him) and had commanded him, saying, "You shall not take a woman from the daughters of Canaan," and [that] Jacob listened to his father and to his mother and went to Paddan-aram. And Esau saw that the daughters of Canaan were bad in the eyes of Isaac his father. And Esau went to Ishmael and took Mahalath, daughter of Ishmael (son of Abraham), sister of Nebaioth— in addition to his women—to himself as his woman.*

Esau saw that Isaac had blessed Jacob symbolizes thoughts that earthly goodness had about union through the truth-based goodness that is Jacob. *And had sent him to Paddan-aram* symbolizes the beginning of its existence through a knowledge of that goodness. *To take himself a woman from there* symbolizes a resulting union through the desire for truth. *When he blessed him, and had commanded him, saying,* symbolizes reflection and then perception with a view to union. *You shall not take a woman from the daughters of Canaan* means that it was not to unite with the desire for falsity and evil. *And [that] Jacob listened to his father and to his mother* symbolizes obedience and desire. *And went to Paddan-aram* here as before [§3664] means in regard to acquiring that knowledge of goodness and truth. *And Esau saw that the daughters of Canaan were bad in the eyes of Isaac his father* means the Lord foresaw that the desire for truth to which earthly goodness had so far been united would not help bring about union, and he provided for this situation. *And Esau went to Ishmael and took Mahalath, daughter of Ishmael (son of Abraham),* symbolizes the union of earthly goodness with truth from a divine origin. *Sister of Nebaioth—in addition to his women—to himself as his woman* symbolizes a desire on a deeper level for heavenly truth.

3679   *Esau saw that Isaac had blessed Jacob* symbolizes thoughts that earthly goodness had about union through the truth-based goodness that is Jacob, as can be seen from the following: *Seeing* symbolizes thinking, since thinking is just inward seeing, or inner sight. *Esau* represents goodness on the earthly level, as discussed at §§3300, 3302, 3322, 3494, 3504, 3576, 3599. Being *blessed* symbolizes union, as noted at §§3504, 3514, 3530, 3565, 3584. *Isaac* represents divine goodness in the Lord's divine rationality, as noted before. And *Jacob* represents goodness based on truth, as discussed in §§3669, 3677. This shows that *Esau saw that Isaac had blessed Jacob* symbolizes thoughts that earthly goodness had about union through truth-based goodness.

[2] It is also impossible to explain in a fully intelligible way what the thoughts earthly goodness had about union through a goodness based on truth are, but a brief explanation is needed. The thinking of earthly goodness is the thinking of the inner, rational self within the outer, earthly self, and it is based on goodness in the latter. The inner, rational self is what thinks, not the outer, earthly self. The inner self enjoys heaven's light, which contains understanding and wisdom coming from the Lord (§§3195, 3339, 3636, 3643). The outer self uses the world's light, which does not contain any understanding or even life. So unless our inner self did the thinking in our outer self, we could not think at all. Our thoughts appear to take place in our outer self, though, because they are based on impressions that have entered through our senses and belong to the world.

[3] The case resembles that of physical sight. Sense-oriented people imagine that our eyes see on their own, but in reality the eye is merely a physical organ by which our inner self sees objects outside our bodies, in the world. The case also resembles that of language. Sense-oriented people imagine that our mouth and tongue produce speech on their own. If we raise our thoughts a little higher we suppose that our voice box and other inner organs produce speech using air from our lungs. In reality, our thoughts speak through those organs, because speech is nothing but our thoughts talking. Illusions of the senses like these are quite common.

The situation is the same with all life appearing in our outer self; the life of our inner self inhabits our outer self as its physical, bodily vehicle.

[4] As for our thoughts, as long as we are alive in our bodies, we think from our rational part in our earthly part—in one way when our earthly part corresponds to our rational part and in another when it does not. When our earthly part corresponds, we are rational and think spiritually, but when it does not correspond, we are not rational and cannot think spiritually. In people whose earthly side corresponds to their rational side, a channel of communication is open, allowing heaven's light to flow in from the Lord through their rational plane into their earthly plane, shedding the light of understanding and wisdom. The result is that they are rational and can think spiritually. In people whose earthly side does not correspond to their rational side, communication is shut off, allowing only a little unfocused light to flow through their rational plane around the edges and through small cracks into their earthly plane. The result is that they are not rational and do not think spiritually. The inflow of heaven's light into us determines the nature of our thoughts. Plainly, then, the thoughts of all depend on the state of correspondence between their earthly and rational dimensions in regard to goodness and truth.

[5] Spirits and angels do not think the way people on earth do. True, their thinking, too, rests on the earthly plane, because they keep their whole earthly memory and the emotions associated with it, but they are not allowed to use that memory (§§2475–2479). Still, although they are not allowed to use it, it serves as a basis or foundation for their thoughts to rest on. Accordingly, their thoughts are deeper, and their units of speech are not words (as ours are) but the ideas behind the words. This demonstrates clearly that the nature of their thoughts likewise depends on the correspondence of their earthly and rational planes. It also shows that there are rational spirits who think spiritually and irrational spirits who do not think spiritually. The sole determining factor is what they had desired and therefore thought about during bodily life—that is, what kind of life they had acquired for themselves in the world.

[6] To some extent you can now see what the thoughts earthly goodness has are; they are thoughts involving earthly goodness. (What are called "the thoughts earthly goodness has" according to a spirit's viewpoint are called "thoughts involving earthly goodness" according to the

viewpoint of a person in this world.) The rational mind involves earthly goodness in its thinking when it looks to goodness as its goal. The thoughts earthly goodness has about union through truth-based goodness, then, are thoughts on the earthly level about the goal. The question those thoughts focus on is how truth can be united to goodness according to the divine plan in the usual way, which starts (as noted many times before) with superficialities—in other words, with what comes last in line, furthest on the periphery. That is where all rebirth of the earthly level begins. This last in line or furthest periphery is the religious knowledge we first learn as children and youths (as discussed toward the end of §3665).

[7] At first, to all outward appearance, the truth based on goodness that Esau stands for lacks connection with the goodness based on truth that Jacob stands for, because the latter is the reverse of the former (§3669). But most inwardly, in their aims, they are united. The goal of the truth that comes from goodness is to attach truth to itself in an orderly way, as noted. The goal of the goodness that comes from truth is the same. Since goals have a unifying effect, these two also unite (§§3562, 3565). The reversed arrangement marking the early stages is only an intermediate step looking toward the final objective.

3680   *And had sent him to Paddan-aram* symbolizes the beginning of its existence through a knowledge of that goodness. This can be seen from the meaning of *sent him* as the beginning of its existence (discussed above at §3674) and from the symbolism of *Paddan-aram* as knowledge of truth (discussed in §3664). I am calling it a knowledge of goodness because all truth is knowledge about what is good; truth that does not rise out of something good, that does not look to something good as its goal, is not true. So far as it looks to doctrine, though, it is called knowledge of truth.

3681   *To take himself a woman from there* symbolizes a resulting union through the desire for truth. This can be seen from the symbolism of a *woman* as a desire for truth (dealt with in §§1468, 2517, 3236). *Taking* one means becoming attached to it.

3682   *When he blessed him, and had commanded him, saying,* symbolizes reflection and then perception with a view to union. This can be seen from the symbolism of being *blessed* as union (discussed in §§3504, 3514, 3530, 3565, 3584) and from that of *commanding* and *saying* as reflection and consequent perception (dealt with in §3661).

You shall not take a woman from the daughters of Canaan means that **3683**
[goodness based on truth] was not to unite with the desire for falsity and
evil. This can be seen from the symbolism of *taking a woman* as being
joined and united, and from that of the *daughters of Canaan* as desires for
what is false and evil (also discussed above, at §3662).

And [that] Jacob listened to his father and to his mother symbolizes **3684**
obedience and desire. This can be seen from the meaning of *listening to*
or paying attention to someone as obeying (discussed in §2542). Listening to his *father and mother* symbolizes obedience from desire.

And went to Paddan-aram means in regard to acquiring knowledge **3685**
of goodness and its truth. This can be seen from the symbolism of *going*
and traveling as the pattern and customs of a life (mentioned in §§1293,
3335). In this case it refers to acquiring knowledge—the knowledge of
goodness and its truth symbolized by *Paddan-aram* (§§3664, 3680)—in
accord with that pattern.

And Esau saw that the daughters of Canaan were bad in the eyes of Isaac **3686**
his father means the Lord foresaw that the desire for truth to which earthly
goodness had so far been united would not help bring about union, and
he provided for this situation, as can be seen from the following: In the
current verse, *seeing* symbolizes foresight and providence, as discussed
in §§2837, 2839. *Esau* represents divine goodness on the Lord's earthly
plane, as noted before. The *daughters of Canaan*—daughters of Heth, in
this case—symbolize a desire for truth from a source that is not genuine,
as discussed in §§3470, 3620, 3621, 3622. And *bad in the eyes of Isaac his*
father means that they would not help bring about union—union through
the earthly goodness that is Esau with the rational goodness that is Isaac.
These words clearly mean, then, that the Lord foresaw how the desire for
that truth, since it did not have a genuine source, would not help bring
about union, and that he provided for the situation.

How these matters stand can be seen from the explanation at Genesis
26:34, 35, which speaks of the daughters of Heth whom Esau took as his
women, and at Genesis 27:46, which says that Jacob was not to take himself a woman from the daughters of Canaan.

In this instance the daughters of Canaan symbolize a desire for truth
from a source that is not genuine, but above at §§3662, 3683 they symbolized a desire for falsity and evil. The reason for the discrepancy is that
Hittites—who were part of the church among non-Jews in the land of
Canaan—were not as weighed down with falsity and evil as other nations

there, such as the Canaanites, Amorites, and Perizzites. So Hittites also represented the Lord's spiritual church among Gentiles (§§2913, 2986).

[2] The earliest church, which was heavenly and preceded the Flood, inhabited the land of Canaan (see §567). The ancient church, which followed the Flood, also occupied that area as well as many other countries (1238, 2385). That is how it came about that all the nations, lands, and rivers there took on representative meanings. You see, the earliest people, who were heavenly, perceived properties of the Lord's kingdom in everything they looked at (920, 1409, 2896, 2897, 2995), including the lands and rivers of Canaan. [3] The representative meanings survived from their era into the time of the ancient church, including the meanings of the places. The Word of the ancient church (discussed in §§2897, 2898, 2899) kept the representative names of places, as did the next era's Scripture, called Moses and the Prophets. As a result, Abraham was ordered to go to that region and received a promise that his descendants would own the land. It was not that they were better than all other nations, because in reality they were among the worst of all (1167, 3373). Rather, the intent was to establish through them a representative religion in which nothing was implied about the person or places doing the representing, only about the entities being represented (3670). This would also preserve the names used by the earliest and ancient churches.

3687   *And Esau went to Ishmael and took Mahalath, daughter of Ishmael (son of Abraham),* symbolizes the union of earthly goodness with truth from a divine origin, as can be seen from the following: *Esau* represents goodness on the earthly level, as noted above. *Ishmael son of Abraham* represents truth from a divine origin. Ishmael represents the Lord's spiritual church and therefore truth (see §§1949, 1950, 1951, 2078, 2691, 2699, 3268), while Abraham represents the divine nature in the Lord that is called the Father (§§[2010,] 2011, 3251, 3439). So *Mahalath daughter of Ishmael (son of Abraham)* symbolizes truth from a divine origin. *Taking* a wife obviously means being joined and united.

This shows that *Esau went to Ishmael and took Mahalath, daughter of Ishmael (son of Abraham)* symbolizes the union of earthly goodness with truth from a divine origin.

3688   *Sister of Nebaioth—in addition to his women—as his woman* symbolizes a desire on a deeper level for heavenly truth, as can be seen from the following: A *sister* symbolizes intuitive or rational truth, as discussed in §§1495, 2508, 2524, 2556, 3386. *Nebaioth* represents goodness in a spiritual religion, as discussed in §3268. So *sister of Nebaioth* symbolizes a desire for heavenly truth—in other words, for spiritual goodness. The *women* or daughters of Heth symbolize a desire for truth from a source that is not genuine, as discussed in §§3470, 3620, 3621, 3622, 3686. And taking one's *woman* means being joined and united. Clearly, then, these words and those just above symbolize union of the goodness represented by Esau with truth from a divine source and consequently, on a deeper level, with a desire for heavenly truth.

[2] This subject has been discussed before, but it is a hard one to understand as long as one does not know even its broadest outlines. Besides, today's world does not care about such topics because its concern is for earthly rather than heavenly values; as people themselves even say, they see and know what is on earth but not what is in heaven. However, the contents of the Word's inner meaning need to be not only revealed but also explained, so let me use an example to illustrate how matters stand with the subjects discussed to this point—truth based on goodness, as represented by Esau; goodness based on truth, as represented by Jacob; and the fact that the latter is the reverse of the former until we have been reborn, although they afterward unite.

[3] The example: People who are capable of being reborn (the Lord foresees this, and because he foresees he provides for it) do not know at first, as young children, what deeds of charity toward their neighbor are, because they do not yet know what charity is or what their neighbor is. They know from the Word that one should give to the poor and that people who give to the poor receive a reward in heaven, so they do good mostly to beggars. Believing that beggars are the poverty-stricken meant in the Word, they fail to consider that most of the people who beg in the street live unholy, criminal lives, despise everything connected with worship of God, and have surrendered completely to idleness and ease. Even so, people in the first stages of rebirth do good to beggars from the heart. The good they do is inspired by the shallow truth with which they start. Truth originating in goodness, which is deeper, exerts an influence on this good, bringing it to fruition in a way that harmonizes with the knowledge they possess as children.

[4] Later, when they are more enlightened, they want to benefit everyone they consider needy and afflicted, still failing to differentiate much between the needy and afflicted who are godly and those who are ungodly. They believe everyone is their neighbor in the same respect and to the same degree.

When they become still more enlightened in these matters, though, they make distinctions, helping only those who are honest and good. They know that to help the evil is to wrong many, since aiding and benefiting the evil gives the evil the means of hurting others.

Eventually, when they are being reborn, they do good only to good, devout people, because by then they feel drawn not to the person they are helping but to the goodness in the person. Because the Lord is present in what is virtuous and godly, their attachment to goodness also bears witness to their love for the Lord. When they exercise this kind of neighborly love from their heart, they have been reborn.

[5] This shows that their earlier attitude was backward, compared to their current frame of mind. They considered what was not good to be good, but this was the "good" they had to do at the beginning of their regeneration because their knowledge of the subject went no further. A deeper feeling of neighborly kindness could not flow into any truth other than the truth they knew. The deeper goodness was there all along, doing the work, but it could not reveal itself until they had gradually gained the light of further knowledge about the nature of goodness and truth.

To some extent this explains goodness based on truth as represented here by Jacob, truth based on goodness as represented by Esau, the fact that each was the reverse of the other at first, and their eventual union.

*   *   *   *

3689   Genesis 28:10, 11. *And Jacob went out from Beer-sheba and went to Haran. And he happened on a place and spent the night there because the sun went down, and he took one of the stones of the place and put it as his headrest and lay down in that place.*

Jacob went out from Beer-sheba symbolizes a life more distant from divine teachings. *And went to Haran* symbolizes goodness and truth on that level. *And he happened on a place* symbolizes a state. *And spent the night there because the sun went down* symbolizes life in a dim situation. *And he took one of the stones of the place* symbolizes truth in that state. *And put it as his headrest* symbolizes the most general possible communication with the Divine. *And lay down in that place* symbolizes the calmness of the state.

3690   *Jacob went out from Beer-sheba* symbolizes a life more distant from divine teachings, as is established by the following: *Going* means living, as discussed in §§3335, 3685, so *going out* means living more distantly. And *Beer-sheba* symbolizes divine teachings, as noted in §§2723, 2858, 2859, 3466. This shows that *Jacob went out from Beer-sheba* symbolizes a life more distant from divine teachings.

Life is said to be more distant when shallow truth is its focus and the rule by which one lives. Such is the life of childhood and youth with people who are being reborn, as discussed just above at §3688.

[2] To describe that life and its quality somewhat more clearly, I need to add a little more.

All Bible stories are the kind of truth that is relatively distant from real, divine teachings. Still, they serve as a means for gradually introducing children and youths into deeper teachings about truth and goodness and eventually to truly divine teachings (since divinity is at the core of the teachings). When the stories are read by children and touch their innocent hearts, the angels with them experience heavenly delight, being drawn by the Lord to the inner meaning and therefore to the things that the narrative details represent and symbolize. The heavenly delight of the angels is what flows into the children and gives them pleasure.

The whole point of putting stories in the Word was to bring about this first stage, the childish and youthful stage of people who are to be reborn. That is why the stories were written in such a way that absolutely everything in them would contain something divine.

[3] The size of the gap between these stories and divine teachings is visible from an example in the stories. At first, people may know only that God came down on Mount Sinai and gave Moses the tablets on which the Ten Commandments were written, that Moses broke them, and that God wrote the same commandments on other tablets [Exodus 19:20; 31:18; 32:19; 34:1, 28]. When they enjoy this simply as a story, they are living a life of shallow truth, a life that is distant from divine teachings.

Later they start to take pleasure in the actual commandments mentioned there, to be affected by them, and to live by them, and then they are living a life of truth, although it is still distant from real, divine teachings. A life in accord with the Commandments is merely a moral life, and everyone living in human society knows the requirements of such a life from public life itself and the laws governing that life. For instance, we have to worship a divine being, honor our parents, and not commit murder, adultery, or theft.

[4] People who are regenerating, on the other hand, are led step by step away from this relatively distant, moral life to a life that is closer

to divine teachings—that is, to a spiritual life. When this happens, they start to wonder why commandments of this kind were handed down from heaven under such miraculous circumstances and written on tablets by the finger of God. After all, every population knows them, and people who have never heard any part of the Word write them into their laws. When people's thinking reaches this stage, then if they are among those who can be reborn, the Lord brings them into an even deeper state, in which they realize that deeper mysteries as yet unknown to them lie hidden there. When they read the Word under these conditions, they find throughout the Prophets and more particularly in the Gospels that everything there contains commandments of a more heavenly nature.

[5] Take the precept that we are to honor our parents. This contains the idea that when we are being born anew—when we are regenerating— we receive a new Father and become his children, and this is the parent we are to honor. So this concept is what lies within the commandment. Gradually we go on to learn that our new Father is the Lord, that the way to honor him is to worship him, and that we worship him when we love him. When people who are being reborn subscribe to this truth and live by it, they possess divine teaching and an angel's frame of mind. From this vantage point they view their previous concepts as building on one another in order, or as emanating from the Divine step by step up a ladder that has Jehovah, or the Lord, standing at the top, and his angels going up and down the steps. So they regard the ideas that used to delight them as being a number of steps further removed from themselves.

The same holds true with the rest of the Ten Commandments; see §2609.

This reveals what a life that is more distant from divine teachings is, as symbolized by *Jacob went out from Beer-sheba.*

3691   *And went to Haran* means to goodness and truth on that level. This can be seen from the symbolism of *Haran* as superficial goodness and truth. Haran symbolizes what is superficial, and Laban, who lived in Haran, symbolizes goodness and truth, so in this verse Haran symbolizes superficial goodness and truth. (For this symbolism of Haran, see §§1430, 3612.) In an inner sense, then, *Jacob went out from Beer-sheba and went to Haran* plainly means that he moved further away from divine teachings, turning to superficial goodness and truth.

[2] The reason for speaking of goodness and truth *on that level* is that different levels fully distinguish the different kinds of goodness and truth

from each other. The deeper kinds are at a higher level, and the shallower kinds are at a lower level. Goodness and truth belonging to the rational dimension are on a higher level, while goodness and truth belonging to the earthly dimension are on a lower level. Goodness and truth belonging to the physical senses are on the lowest level of all.

Deeper, higher-level goodness and truth flow into shallower, lower-level goodness and truth, creating an image of themselves there, in almost the same way that our deeper feelings reveal themselves in changes of our facial expression.

This shows that inner goodness and truth are entirely separate from outer, or higher from lower. They are so entirely separate that inner, higher kinds can exist without outer, lower kinds.

People who do not have a clear notion of the different levels cannot have a clear notion of inner and outer kinds of goodness, nor can they see how matters stand in the other world with the human soul—the human spirit and body—or with the heavens. [3] There are three heavens, as people know, and one is more inward than another, the third being the inmost. These heavens are clearly distinguished from each other by level. Inhabitants of the third and inmost heaven are closer to the Lord. Inhabitants of the second, intermediate heaven are more distant, and those of the first or outer heaven are still farther away. The only contact possible among these heavens resembles that between a person's inmost and outer levels. An individual who loves the Lord and treats her or his neighbor with charity is essentially a miniature heaven, an image corresponding to the three heavens. Out of the three heavens, from the Lord, goodness and truth flow into that person on the same three levels.

The relationship of these levels to each other can be seen from the two examples cited above in §§3688 and 3690.

[4] People who truly love the Lord, to the point where they feel that love, have the highest level of goodness and truth. They are in the third and inmost heaven, nearer the Lord, and are called heavenly angels. People who show charity toward their neighbor, to the point where they feel charity (more than they feel love for the Lord), have a lower level of goodness and truth. They are in the second, intermediate heaven, farther from the Lord, and are called spiritual angels. Some people, though, show charity toward their neighbor only because truth appeals to them, to the point where they do not feel any real charity for their neighbor except on account of the truth to which they are drawn. They have a still lower level of goodness and truth, inhabit the first or

outer heaven, are still more distant from the Lord, and are called good spirits.

[5] To some extent this illuminates the following fact about the different levels: Attributes at a higher level present an image of themselves within attributes on the next lower level. Love for the Lord contains the closest image of the Lord, which is called a likeness, so people who love the Lord are called his likenesses. Charity also contains an image of the Lord—although a more distant one—because the Lord is present in genuine charity. So people with charity are called his images (see §§50, 51, 1013). People who feel drawn to truth and therefore have a type of charity for their neighbor are also the Lord's image but even more distantly so.

These are the levels that the three heavens are divided into and that determine how the Lord flows in with divine goodness and truth, with wisdom and understanding, and with heavenly joy and happiness.

3692   *And he happened on a place* symbolizes a state, as is evident from the symbolism of a *place* as a state (discussed in §§1273, 1274, 1275, 1377, 2625, 2837, 3356, 3387).

3693   *And spent the night there because the sun went down* symbolizes life in a dim situation, as can be seen from the following: *Night* symbolizes shadowy conditions, as noted in §1712, so *spending the night* means living in those conditions. And the *sun's going down* means in a dim situation because it happens at evening time, which symbolizes what is dim; see §3056.

The dimness meant here is a dim understanding of truth and faint wisdom about what is good. The light the Lord sheds on angels contains understanding and wisdom and emanates from understanding and wisdom (§§1521, 1524, 1529, 1530, 3138, 3167, 3195, 3339, 3341, 3636, 3637, 3643). So the more light angels have, the more understanding and wisdom they also have; and the less light they have, or the more shadow they have, the less understanding and wisdom (§§2776, 3190, 3337).

That is why people refer to intellectual matters as matters of light, even in casual conversation. They do not recognize the underlying cause, so they presume it is just a metaphorical way of speaking. In addition to this figure of speech, we also acquire many others from a perception of the kinds of things that exist in the other world, where our spirit lives. We embrace them in our conversation because deep inside we acknowledge them, even though they are obliterated by the bodily concerns that blot out the perceptions our inner self enjoys.

[2] In the Word, *sunset* symbolizes the falsity and evil to which people lacking charity and faith are devoted, so it also symbolizes the church's final days; see §1837. In addition it symbolizes dim sight of that which is good and true, like the sight of people who are on a level relatively distant from divine teachings (§3690). The following Scripture passages demonstrate these meanings of sunset, or of "the sun went down." In Micah:

> You will have night instead of visions, and you will have darkness instead of divination. And *the sun will set on the prophets,* and over them the day will blacken. (Micah 3:6)

"The sun will set on the prophets" means that they will no longer know or understand truth. The prophets stand for people who teach doctrinal truth (§2534). In Amos:

> It will happen on that day that *I will make the sun set at noon* and overshadow the earth on a day of light and turn your feasts into mourning and all your songs into a lament. (Amos 8:9, 10)

Making the sun set at noon stands for a dim sight of truth in people who know what is good and true. Noon means a state of light, or knowledge of truth; see §§1458, 3195 at the beginning. [3] In Isaiah:

> *No longer will your sun set,* and your moon will not withdraw, because Jehovah will become an eternal light to you. (Isaiah 60:20)

This is about the Lord's kingdom. "No longer will the sun set" means that people will display goodness in their lives, and wisdom, because they have the Lord's heavenly love and light. "The moon will not withdraw" means that they will have truthful lives, and understanding, because they have the Lord's spiritual love and light. In the next life, the Lord is the sun to heavenly angels and the moon to spiritual ones, and this is the source of their wisdom and understanding; see §§1053, 1521, 1529, 1530, 1531, 2441, 2495, 3636, 3643. This shows what sunrise and sunset mean in the Word's inner sense. [4] In David:

> Jehovah my God, you are very great; glory and honor you have put on. [You are he] who covers himself with the light as clothing; stretches out the heavens like a tent curtain. He made the moon for appointed feasts; the *sun,* [which] knows *its going down.* You arrange the darkness; and may night fall! (Psalms 104:1, 2, 19, 20)

Here too the moon stands for understanding, and the sun, for wisdom, granted by the Lord. The sun's going down stands for the dimness of both. Arranging the darkness so that night may fall stands for regulating the state of dimness. The conditions angels experience range between a peak of light and a relatively small amount, or between a peak of wisdom and a relatively small amount. These differing conditions resemble morning with its sunrise, midday when the sun is at its height, evening when it sets, and then a return of morning, as I will say elsewhere, by the Lord's divine mercy. [5] In Joshua:

> From the desert and Lebanon all the way to the great river, the river Euphrates, the whole land of the Hittites, and even to the Great Sea— the *sunset*—will be your border. (Joshua 1:4)

This verse describes the extent of the land of Canaan, which in an inner sense means the Lord's kingdom; see §§1607, 3038, 3481. The river Euphrates means one of its borders: that of spiritual and heavenly qualities (§1866). The Great Sea and the sunset mean the other border, representing the furthest limit, which is relatively dim. (All the boundaries of Canaan and all places in it represent something; see §1585.) [6] In Moses:

> If you go so far as to take your companion's garment as collateral, *before the sun sets* you shall restore it to him, because it alone is his covering; it is his garment used as a hide, in which he must lie down. (Exodus 22:26, 27)

And in another place:

> If a man is poor, you shall not lie down on his collateral; you shall make sure to restore the collateral to him *before the sun sets,* and may he bless you, and you will possess justice in the eyes of Jehovah your God. (Deuteronomy 24:12, 13)

Like all the other laws, this one contains a representation and symbol of divine law, which is the law of goodness and truth in the Lord's kingdom and which gives rise to this law of Moses', as its particulars show. The divine law lying within and giving rise to Moses' is that we are not to cheat our companions of their superficial truth—in other words, of the doctrines they live by and their ritual. A garment means this kind of truth; see §§297, 1073, 2576. Restoring it before the sun sets means doing so before truth dies in them. Since that truth lies on the surface, it is called a garment used as a hide, in which the person must lie down. [7] In the same author:

> Souls that touch anything unclean shall be unclean up till the evening and shall not eat any of the sacred items; but when they wash their flesh with water, and the *sun sets,* they shall be clean. And afterward they shall eat of the sacred items. (Leviticus 22:6, 7)

And in another place:

> Those who are not clean shall wash themselves toward evening with water, and *when the sun sets,* they shall enter into the middle of the camp. (Deuteronomy 23:10, 11)

This law also traces its origin to laws in the Lord's kingdom concerning goodness and truth, or concerning the divine plan, as is clear. Otherwise it would not have been commanded that people be unclean up till the evening, wash themselves with water, and be clean after the sun set. The law that lays out the divine plan in the Lord's kingdom and gives rise to the law in Moses is this: When good, angelic spirits sink into a state of self-love and so into a state of falsity, for a short while they are let back into their earthly condition (a lower condition) and filled with knowledge of goodness and truth in regard to the matter at hand. This is what washing oneself with water at evening symbolizes. (On the point that washing with water means being purified of falsity, see §§3147, 3148; and that water means knowledge of truth, §§28, 680, 739, 2702, 3058.) After they have experienced the dim state symbolized by sunset, they return to their previous state, as symbolized by "they shall be clean" and "they shall enter into the middle of the camp." I will say more about my experiences with this elsewhere, the Lord in his divine mercy willing.

These remarks now show that sunset in the Word symbolizes a state in good people of dimness concerning truth, and in evil people, of falsity.

And he took one of the stones of the place symbolizes truth in that state. **3694** This can be seen from the symbolism of *stones* as lower truth, like that known to a person whose attention is on the earthly plane (discussed in §§643, 1298).

And put it as his headrest symbolizes the most general possible com- **3695** munication with the Divine. This can be seen from the symbolism of a *headrest* or pillows for the neck as communication with what lies on the surface and therefore as the most general communication possible. A neck means communication and therefore union of the inner depths with the outer surface or (to put the same thing another way) of what is higher with what is lower; see §§3542, 3603. So supports under the neck symbolize contact between the inmost, divine core and the outermost shell, this contact being the most general possible. Anything superficial is relatively general, and what is most superficial is the most general of all. The detail of the inner depths appears as a single, generalized whole on the outer surface.

This is also what is represented and symbolized by the ladder resting on the earth whose head reached the sky, on which God's angels went up and down, as discussed below.

3696   *And lay down in that place* symbolizes the calmness of the state, as can be seen from the fact that *lying down* means being in a calm state, since that is exactly what lying down and sleeping is. That it is the inner-level symbolism of *lying down* can be seen from other passages in the Word dealt with just below.

This is how the case stands with people who are to be reborn—the people spoken of in an inner, representative sense here: At the very beginning they enjoy a state of calm, or of outward peace. (Outward peace, or peace on the surface, is called calm.) The state is produced by a state of divine peace deep within that reveals itself on the outer surface in the removal of cravings and falsities—these being the elements that cause all disquiet.

As babies, we always start our life in a state of serenity, but the further we go in life, or the more we mature, the further from that state we move. We surrender to worldly cares and consequently to anxiety brought on by the cravings of self-love and materialism and by the falsities they spawn.

[2] Almost the same thing happens in our new life when we are being reborn. At first we experience a tranquil state, but as we enter into our new life, we also enter a disquieted state. The evil and falsity we previously absorbed emerge into the open and agitate us. In fact, we eventually suffer trials and harassment inflicted by the Devil's crew, which constantly strives to destroy our new life. Nonetheless there is a state of peace at our center. If there were not, we would not fight. In the struggles we go through, we keep our eye on that state as the goal, and if we did not have it to aim for, we would never have the strength or power to fight. It is also owing to this vision that we conquer. Since it is our goal,

it is also the state we enter after our struggles or trials. It is like a state of spring taking over after states of fall and winter. It is like a state of dawn taking over after evening and night. (A state of spiritual peace resembles earthly spring and dawn; see §§1726, 2780. Goodness and truth yield peace, while evil and falsity yield strife; §3170.)

[3] The following passages show that in the Word, *lying down* symbolizes a calm state. In Moses:

> If you walk in my statutes and observe my commandments and do them, *I will put peace on the earth,* and you will *lie down*—and no one [will be] causing terror. And I will bring an end to the evil wild animal on the earth, and the sword will not pass through your land. (Leviticus 26:3, 6)

The lying down obviously has to do with peaceful, calm conditions. The evil wild animal stands for evil cravings (§§45, 46, 908), which will end. The sword stands for falsity fighting truth (§2799), which will not pass through. From this it is also plain that peace and a peaceful calm result from goodness and truth and that their destruction results from evil and falsity. [4] In Isaiah:

> The wolf will stay with the lamb, and the leopard will *lie down* with the kid, and the calf and the young lion [will live] together, and a little child will lead them. And the heifer and bear will pasture; *together their offspring will lie down.* (Isaiah 11:6, 7)

This is about the Lord and the state of peace in his kingdom. "They will lie down together" means that they cannot be molested by any evil or falsity. In Hosea:

> I will strike a pact with them on that day—with the wild animal of the field, and with the bird in the heavens and the creeping animal of the earth. And bow and sword and war I will break off from the earth, *and I will make them lie down securely.* (Hosea 2:18)

Lying down again stands for a state of calm upon the removal of falsity and evil, which create disquiet. [5] In David:

> I will *lie down and sleep* and wake up, because Jehovah sustains me. I will not be afraid of myriads of people who place themselves all around against me. (Psalms 3:5, 6)

Lying down and sleeping stands for a state of calm and safety. In the same author:

> *In peace I will both lie down and sleep,* because you, Jehovah, alone make me dwell securely. (Psalms 4:8)

In the same author:

> *He will make me lie down in grassy pastures;* he will lead me to *quiet waters.* He will restore my soul. (Psalms 23:2, 3)

These passages show that lying down depicts a state of peace and calm, and that *lying down in that place* symbolizes the calmness of the state, since in an inner sense a *place* means a state (§3692).

3697   Genesis 28:12, 13, 14, 15. *And he dreamed. And look: a ladder resting on the earth, and its head reaching the sky, and look: God's angels going up and going down on it! And look: Jehovah standing above it; and he said, "I am Jehovah, God of Abraham your father and God of Isaac; the land that you are lying on, to you I will give it and to your seed. And your seed will be like the dust of the earth, and you will burst out toward the sea and toward the east and toward the north and toward the south. And in you all the clans of the ground will be blessed, and in your seed. And look: I am with you and will guard you in every [place] where you go and will bring you back to this ground, because I will not abandon you until I have done what I spoke to you."*

He dreamed symbolizes foresight. *And look: a ladder resting on the earth* symbolizes communication of the lowest truth and the goodness from that truth. *And its head reaching the sky* means with the Divine. *And look: God's angels going up and going down on it* symbolizes infinite and eternal communication, and resulting union; it also symbolizes an apparent climb from the lowest level and then, when the pattern reverses, a descent. *And look: Jehovah standing above it* symbolizes the Lord at the top. *And he said, "I am Jehovah, God of Abraham your father,"* symbolizes the Lord, the source of that goodness. *And God of Isaac* symbolizes the Lord in his divine humanity. *The land that you are lying on, to you I will give it* means that he himself would be the source of the goodness he had. *And to your seed* means the truth too. *And your seed will be like the dust of the earth* means that divine earthly truth would resemble earthly goodness. *And you will burst out toward the sea and toward the east* symbolizes the infinite reach of goodness; *and toward the north and toward the south* symbolizes the infinite reach of truth; and therefore all states of goodness and truth.

And in you all the clans of the ground will be blessed means that all doctrinal truth relating to goodness will unite with goodness. *And in your seed* means and with truth. *And look: I am with you* means that it is divine. *And will guard you in every [place] where you go* symbolizes divine providence. *And will bring you back to this ground* means internalizing divine teachings. *Because I will not abandon you until I have done what I spoke to you* means that nothing needed for putting the teachings into action will be lacking.

He dreamed symbolizes foresight. This can be seen from the symbolism of *dreaming* on an inner level as predicting the future. The dreams of the prophets, which were divine, predicted future events, as the prophetical dreams described in the Word show (§§1975, 1976).

3698

Since dreams and dreaming have this symbolism on an inner level, on the highest level, which is about the Lord, they symbolize foresight. It is from the Lord's divine foresight that predictions come. There is no other source for predictions about events that do not follow the usual, earthly pattern and cannot be foreseen that way, as shown in Scripture, including these words in Moses:

> When a prophet spoke in Jehovah's name but the word did not happen, and that word did not come about, Jehovah had not spoken; with arrogance the prophet spoke it. (Deuteronomy 18:22)

[2] Predictions of events that did happen sometimes came from evil people and devotees of another god. In the same author:

> If prophets or dreamers of dreams rise in your midst and give you a sign or else a portent, and there is a fulfillment of the sign and portent that they spoke to you, saying, "Let's walk after other gods whom you do not know, and serve them," you shall not obey the words of those prophets or the *dreamers of* those *dreams,* because Jehovah is testing you. (Deuteronomy 13:1, 2, 3)

This shows that nevertheless the prediction itself is from the Divine, even though the enticement to worship other gods was the prophet's own idea. The prophet was permitted to advance the idea so that the people could be tested, as the passage says.

It was for this reason and others that people long ago who worshiped baals and other gods also prophesied, saw visions, and dreamed dreams on many occasions. What they said came to pass, too, and they frequently led others astray. They are spoken of in Jeremiah 23. This is in addition to the people called diviners, fortune-tellers, sorcerers, and mediums, who were among those studying earthly magic. Magic was unable to predict anything divine, only what opposed the Divine—that is, what opposed the Lord, good done out of love for him, and the truth taught by faith in him. This is magic, whatever it may look like in its outward appearance.

3699   *And look: a ladder resting on the earth* symbolizes communication of the lowest truth and the goodness from that truth. This can be seen from the symbolism of a *ladder* as communication (dealt with below) and from that of the *earth* as the lowest part, since the text says next that its head reached the sky, meaning the highest part. This makes it clear that a ladder between the earth and the sky, or between the lowest and highest parts, means communication. Communication of the lowest truth and the goodness from that truth is plainly what the ladder resting on the earth symbolizes because the inner meaning is currently focusing on that level's truth and consequent goodness, as represented by Jacob.

In the original language, the word for ladder comes from one that means a path or road, which has to do with truth (see §§627, 2333). When angels are talking about truth, it is represented visually in the world of spirits as paths; see §§189, 3477. This clarifies the symbolism of a ladder of which one end rests on the earth and the other end reaches the sky; it symbolizes the communication of truth on the lowest level with truth on the highest level. This communication will be discussed later. On the point that there is such a thing as lowest truth and goodness and highest truth and goodness, separated by steps resembling those of a ladder, see §3691.

3700   *And its head reaching the sky* means with the Divine—that is, communication with the Divine. This can be seen from the symbolism of the *head of a ladder* or its top as its highest point and from that of the *sky* as the Divine. In the highest sense, which has to do with the Lord, the sky means divinity itself. In a representative sense, which has to do with a person being reborn, it means the inmost goodness and consequent truth that come from the Lord—goodness and truth of the kind that exist in heaven and of which heaven itself is made. This too is called divine, because it comes from the Lord. The Lord—in other words, what is divine (which comes from the Lord alone)—is the all-in-all of heaven. Anything there that does not come from the Divine is not part of heaven. That is why it has been said several times already that the Lord is heaven itself and that everyone who is in heaven is in the Lord [§1733].

And look: God's angels going up and going down on it symbolizes infinite **3701**
and eternal communication, and resulting union; it also symbolizes an
apparent climb from the lowest level and then, when the pattern reverses,
a descent. This can be seen from the symbolism of *angels*. When the Word
mentions angels, they mean something divine belonging to the Lord, as
noted in §§1925, 2319, 2821, 3039. You can see that it means divine truth
here, because they are called *God's* angels. God is mentioned when the
inner meaning has to do with truth, while Jehovah is mentioned when it
has to do with goodness; see §§2586, 2769, 2807, 2822. That is why God's
angels are spoken of here, even though Jehovah's name comes up right
afterward in the phrase "Jehovah standing above it"; the focus here is on
truth from which comes goodness, this being what Jacob currently means,
as noted many times before.

In the highest sense, *going up and going down on the ladder* symbolizes infinite and eternal communication, and resulting union. This can be
seen without further explanation. The Lord's divinity itself cannot be said
to communicate and therefore unite with his divine humanity unless the
communication and union are described as infinite and eternal. Everything in the Lord is infinite and eternal—infinite in its existence and eternal in its emergence.

The discussion to this point shows that "a ladder resting on the earth,
and its head reaching the sky, and look: God's angels going up and going
down on it" taken as a whole symbolizes an apparent climb from the lowest level and then, when the pattern reverses, a descent.

[2] How the case stands with this climb and descent can be seen from
remarks and illustrations above in §§3539, 3548, 3556, 3563, 3570, 3576,
3603, 3607, 3610, 3665, 3690. However, since the church knows nothing
about this sequence—a sequence that occurs during human rebirth and
is described in the inner meaning of these and subsequent verses—let me
go a little further in illuminating its nature.

It is known that we are born into the character of our parents, grand-
parents, and great-grandparents going back for eons, so that we are born
into the evil we inherit from all of them. This evil has gradually piled up
so high that so far as a thing is our handiwork, it is purely evil. As a result,
both our intellect and our will are entirely corrupt. On our own we
cannot will anything good, so we cannot understand anything true. Evil
accordingly is what we refer to as goodness and even believe to be good,
and falsity is what we refer to as truth and even believe to be true. Take as
an example the idea of loving ourselves more than others, wishing better

to ourselves than to others, envying what belongs to others, and looking after ourselves alone, not others, unless it can benefit us. Because this is what we want on our own, we call it good and also true. What is more, if people injure this "goodness" and this "truth" in us, or try to, we hate them. We take avid revenge on them, longing and even striving for their ruin, which brings us satisfaction. The more we lock ourselves into our so-called goodness and truth by practice—that is, the more often we act on them—the more we indulge in this behavior.

[3] When we come into the other world with this character, we want the same things there. The very nature we contracted in the world by the deeds of our life remains, and others plainly sense the kind of pleasure we took. As a consequence we cannot enter any heavenly community, where all the inhabitants wish better to others than to themselves. Instead we join a hellish community that enjoys the same things we do.

This character is what needs to be rooted out while we are living in the world. The only way it can be removed is by the Lord's regeneration of us—in other words, by our reception of an entirely new will and so an entirely new intellect, or again by the remaking of both capacities in us.

For this to happen, we first of all have to be reborn as if we were babies again. We have to learn what evil and falsity are and to learn what goodness and truth are. Without such knowledge, we cannot develop any goodness, because on our own we acknowledge nothing but evil as good, nothing but falsity as true. [4] To this end, a kind of knowledge that does not directly refute what we previously knew is instilled into us. For instance, we learn that all love begins with ourselves; that we have to take care of ourselves first and of others second; that we have to help those who seem on the face of things to be the poor and wretched, whatever they may be like inside; the same for widows and orphans by virtue of their status; and the same for our enemies in general, whatever they are like. We also learn that by taking these actions we can earn heaven. Such concepts and others like them belong to the childhood of our new life. Since they draw to some extent on our previous life, or the character of that life, they also draw on the new life we are being introduced to. So they are the kind of concepts that embrace what leads to the formation of a new will and a new intellect.

These are the lowest-level types of goodness and truth, which we start with when we are being reborn. Because they embrace inner truth—truth closer to divine truth—they can serve as means for uprooting the falsity we formerly believed to be true.

[5] People who are being reborn do not learn this truth as bare fact but as a matter of life, because they act on it. They act on it, though, as a result of their budding new will, which the Lord instills without their slightest awareness. The more they accept this new will, the more of the knowledge they receive, put into act, and believe. If they refuse to accept the new will, they can still learn increasing amounts of the knowledge, but they cannot put it into act, because all they care about is learning it, not living it.

[6] This is the stage of childhood and youth in our new life, which eventually replaces our earlier life. At a stage of early and midadulthood in that life, though, we stop paying attention to the way people appear on the outside and look at the kind of goodness they have, first in their public life, then in their moral life, and finally in their spiritual life. Goodness is what we then start to place first and to love; it is for their goodness that we love the people. Finally, when we become still more perfect, we put effort into helping people who are devoted to what is good—and helping them in a way that harmonizes with the kind of goodness they have. In the end, we feel pleasure in benefiting them, because we feel pleasure in goodness; and we find delight in thoughts that confirm it. These confirmatory ideas we acknowledge as truth, and they are the truth of our new intellect, stemming from the goodness in our new will.

[7] The degree to which we enjoy that goodness and take delight in that truth is also the degree to which we sense displeasure in the evil of our former life and distaste in its wrong thinking. The contents of our previous will are consequently separated at this point from those of our new will, and the contents of our previous intellect, from those of our new intellect. They are separated not so far as we desire to know about the new ones but so far as we desire to act on them.

So we now see that the truth we knew in our childhood was relatively upside-down and that little by little it is rearranged. One truth becomes subordinate to another, so that what used to be first is now last. The truths we knew in childhood and youth were the ladder by which God's angels climbed from earth to heaven, but now the truths of our adult years are the ladder by which they descend from heaven to earth.

And look: Jehovah standing above it symbolizes the Lord at the top. This can be seen from the fact that the Old Testament Word calls the   **3702**

Lord Jehovah so many times (see §§1736, 3023, 3035), while the New Testament Word never calls him Jehovah but the Lord instead (§2921). To *stand above it* means to be at the top, as is clear without explanation.

A secret lying hidden in the inner meaning of these words is that everything good and true comes down from the Lord and goes up to him. In other words, he is the First and the Last. Humankind was created so that the Lord's divine qualities could descend through us right to the outermost level of the physical world and climb from the outermost level of the world up to him. In this way humankind would be an intermediary uniting the Divine with the physical world, and the physical world with the Divine. Through humankind as the uniting medium, the very outermost plane of the physical world would be alive with the Divine. This would actually happen, if we lived according to the divine plan.

[2] Evidence that we were created to play this role is the fact that our body is a microcosm, since every secret in the physical world is stored in it. Every secret regarding the ether or modified forms of the ether is stored in the eye, and every secret regarding the air is stored in the ear. Whatever invisible elements float and stir in the air are taken into account and sensed in the organ of smell, and those in water or any other liquid, in the organ of taste. Changes of state are actually stored throughout by the sense of touch. Entities that lie still more deeply hidden would be perceived by our inner organs if our lives were in order. Clearly, then, what is divine would come down through us into the outermost level of the physical world and would go back up from there to the Divine if with faith in our heart, or with love, we would only acknowledge the Lord as our first and final goal.

[3] This was the state of the earliest people (who were heavenly), because whatever they took in with any of their senses they used as material for thoughts about matters involving the Lord and so for thoughts about the Lord and his kingdom. The pleasure they took in worldly and earthly objects came from such thoughts; see §§1409, 2896, 2897, 2995. In fact, when they contemplated the lowest, outermost objects of the physical world, to their eyes the objects seemed alive, because the living force from which they descended was present in the inner sight of their perception. The entities presenting themselves to their eyes were like images of that life—images intrinsically dead but animated in this way for them. That is the kind of perception heavenly angels have about everything in the world, as I have often been allowed to perceive. Little children have the same

kind of perception for the same reason; see §§2297, 2298. This shows the nature of the people through whom the Lord's divine qualities descend to the very outermost level of the physical world and climb from there up to him. These are the people who represent the divine communication and resulting union symbolized on the highest level by the angels going up and going down on the ladder resting on the earth whose head reached the sky, above which stood Jehovah.

And he said, "I am Jehovah, God of Abraham your father," symbolizes the Lord, the source of that goodness. This can be seen from the consideration that *Jehovah* is the core, divine reality of the Lord. He is called *God of Abraham* because of his divine goodness. (*Abraham* represents the Lord's divine goodness; see §§2172, 2198.) Divine goodness is the source of all heavenly and spiritual goodness and so of all truth, and that is why the current verse calls Abraham *father,* and specifically *your father*—Jacob's—even though Isaac was his father.

3703

In an inner sense a *father* means goodness because goodness is the source from which absolutely everything exists, truth being the means by which it emerges. So everything comes from the marriage of goodness and truth. Heaven itself, which consists solely of the divine marriage of goodness and truth, arises from the divine marriage of goodness with truth, and of truth with goodness, in the Lord. [2] Everything throughout the physical world relates to goodness and truth, because the world contains representations of the heavenly and spiritual goodness and truth found in heaven, while heaven contains representations of the divine goodness and truth found in the Lord.

From this it can be seen that goodness is like a father, and truth, like a mother. So on an inner level of the Word, a father symbolizes goodness, and a mother, truth. In fact, they symbolize the goodness and truth from which come lower or secondary forms of goodness and truth, and these are like their daughters and sons. As a result they are called daughters and sons in the Word (§§489, 490, 491, 2362). They also resemble brothers and sisters, grandchildren and great-grandchildren, sons-in-law, mothers-in-law, daughters-in-law; in short, blood relatives and connections on every level. The resemblance is due to the marriage of goodness as father with truth as mother. (Absolutely everything in the heavens depends on the way love for the Lord and faith in him are related to one another—in other words, on the way goodness and truth are related; see §§685, 917, 2739, 3612. For this reason the earliest people compared everything to marriage; §§54, 55. See also §§718, 747, 1432, 2508, 2516, 2524, 2556.)

[3] The meaning in the Word's inner sense of a father as goodness can be seen from many passages, such as the following. In Isaiah:

> Listen to me, you who pursue justice, who seek Jehovah: Look to the rock [from which] you were cut, and to the excavation of the pit [from which] you were dug. Look to *Abraham your father,* and to *Sarah,* [who] bore you, because I have called only him and blessed him and will multiply him. For Jehovah will comfort Zion, he will comfort all its wastelands, and he will make its wilderness like Eden and its desert like a garden of Jehovah. (Isaiah 51:1, 2, 3)

This is about the Lord and his Coming, as the individual elements show. His divine truth is referred to as a rock and a pit, and his divine goodness is referred to as Father Abraham. Abraham and Sarah represent the divine marriage of goodness and truth (see §§1468, 1901, 1965, 1989, 2011, 2063, 2065, 2172, 2173, 2198, 2507, 2833, 2836, 2904, 3245, 3251, 3305 at the end), so the passage speaks of Abraham as a father and says "Sarah bore you." That is why the verses say to look to the rock and the pit and Father Abraham and Sarah. For the same reason it says immediately afterward that Jehovah will comfort Zion, which is a heavenly religion (see §2362), and that he will comfort its wastelands and make its wilderness like Eden, its desert like a garden of Jehovah.

[4] Abraham has the same symbolism in other places in the Word where he is called father. In John, for example:

> Jesus said, "I speak what I have seen at my Father's side; so you also do what you have seen at your father's side." They answered and said to him, "*Abraham is our father.*" Jesus says to them, "If *you were children of Abraham, you would do the deeds of Abraham;* you do the deeds of your father." (John 8:38, 39, [41])

And in Matthew:

> Do not presume to say in yourselves, "*We have Abraham as our father.*" I tell you that God from these stones can raise up *children for Abraham.* Look: the ax lies at the root of the trees; every tree not making good fruit will be cut down and thrown into the fire. (Matthew 3:9, 10)

And in Luke:

> When Lazarus, a poor man, died, he was taken by the angels into *Abraham's embrace.* When the rich man, who also died and was buried, was in hell, lifting his eyes he saw *Abraham* from far away, and Lazarus

in his embrace. And [the rich man] crying out said, "*Father Abraham,* have mercy on me! I ask you, *father,* to send [Lazarus] to my father's house." (Luke 16:19–end)

In these passages it is plainly not Abraham but the Lord's divine goodness that is meant. Abraham is unknown in heaven, and when the Word mentions him it means the Lord; see §§1834, 1876, 1989, 3305 at the end.

[5] The following places show that in an inner sense a father means goodness. In Moses:

Honor *your father* and *your mother,* so that your days may lengthen on the land that Jehovah your God is giving you. (Exodus 20:12; Deuteronomy 5:16)

Like the rest of the Ten Commandments, this one is true in both [inner and outer] senses, and honoring one's father and mother in an inner sense means loving goodness, truth, and the Lord within goodness and truth (see §§2609, 3690). Days on the land mean the good states one experiences in the Lord's kingdom as a result. This can be seen from the symbolism of days as states (23, 487, 488, 493, 893, 2788) and from that of Canaan—the land referred to here—as the Lord's kingdom (1607, 3038, 3481). Lengthening has to do with goodness (1613).

[6] Because this is the symbolism of father and mother, the representative Jewish religion was given many laws about parents and children. Goodness and truth are symbolized on an inner level of all these laws, and the Lord's divine goodness and truth on the highest level. In Moses, for example:

Those who hit *their father* or *their mother* shall surely die. If any curse *their father* or *their mother,* they shall surely die. (Exodus 21:15, 17)

In the same author:

Any man who curses *his father* or *his mother* shall surely be killed. One who curses *his father* or *his mother*—his blood shall be upon him. (Leviticus 20:9)

A curse on those who dishonor *their father* and *their mother;* and all the people shall say, "Amen!" (Deuteronomy 27:16)

In Ezekiel:

Here, now, the chieftains of Israel—a man according to [the strength of] his arm—have been in you to shed blood; *father* and *mother* they have dishonored in you. (Ezekiel 22:6, 7)

In Moses:

> When a man has a son defiant and rebellious, *never obeying the voice of his father* or *the voice of his mother,* and although they chastise him he still does not obey them, *his father* and *his mother* shall take hold of him and bring him out to the city elders and to the gate of his place, and all the men of his city shall stone him with stones so that he dies. (Deuteronomy 21:18, 19, 21)

[7] In all these places, father and mother in a literal sense mean father and mother; in an inward sense, goodness and truth; and in the highest sense, the Lord's divine goodness and truth. The Lord even teaches this in Matthew:

> Jesus, stretching out his hand over his disciples, said, "Look: *my mother* and my siblings. Whoever does the will of my Father, who is in the heavens, that one is my brother and sister and *mother.*" (Matthew 12:49, 50)

And in the same author:

> Do not use the name Teacher, because one person is your teacher: Christ; you, though, are all siblings. And *you are not to call anyone your father* on earth, because one person is *your Father,* who is in the heavens. (Matthew 23:8, 9)

This does not forbid people to be called teacher or father on earth but bans them from acknowledging any other father in their heart than the Lord. That is, when a teacher or father is mentioned [in the Word], we should take it to be the Lord that is represented in the highest sense. This accords with the remarks just above at §3702 about the earliest people, who were heavenly: whatever they perceived on earth they used as material for thoughts about the Lord.

[8] There is a similar meaning in the Lord's words to one of his disciples, who said:

> "Lord, let me first go and *bury my father.*" Jesus said to him, "Follow me; let the dead bury the dead." (Matthew 8:21, 22)

A father on earth compares to our Father in heaven—the Lord—as a dead person compares to a living one. Likewise even the law about honoring our parents is dead unless it contains honor, worship, and love for the Lord. That law [in the Commandments] descends from this divine one; the actual living element in that law comes from this one, which is why the Lord said, "Follow me; let the dead bury the dead."

Again, Elijah's words to Elisha mean the same thing:

Elijah passed by Elisha and threw his cloak over him, and he left the oxen and ran after Elijah and said, "Please *let me kiss* my *father* and *mother;* then I will come after you." So [Elijah] said to him, "Leave; go back, *for what have I done to you?"* (1 Kings 19:19, 20)

Elijah represented the Lord; see the preface to Genesis 18, and §2762. [9] In Malachi:

Here, I am sending you Elijah the prophet before the day of Jehovah comes, great and fearsome; and he will *turn the heart of the fathers to their children,* and the *heart of the children to their fathers,* to forestall my coming and striking the earth with extermination. (Malachi 4:5, 6)

And in Luke:

To Zechariah concerning his son, John, the angel said, "He will go ahead before the face of the Lord in the spirit and power of Elijah to *turn the hearts of the fathers to their children."* (Luke 1:17)

Clearly the fathers and children do not mean fathers and children but goodness and truth in religion, which the Lord will restore. [10] In Malachi:

May Jehovah be exalted from above the border of Israel! *Children will honor their father,* and slaves their master. Because if *I am father,* where is my honor? If I am master, where is the fear of me? (Malachi 1:[5,] 6)

The children stand for people dedicated to what the church values as good, and the slaves for those dedicated to what the church values as true. The father plainly stands for the Lord's divine goodness, and the master, for his divine truth. [11] In David:

My father and *my mother* have deserted me, and Jehovah gathers me up. (Psalms 27:10)

The father and mother stand for goodness and truth, which are said to desert us when we realize we cannot do anything good or know anything good on our own. Obviously it does not mean that David's father and mother deserted him. [12] In the same author:

Far more beautiful are you than the children of humankind. All glorious is the *king's daughter* within [the palace]; her clothing is made of gold braid. *In place of your fathers will be your children;* you will make them chieftains in all the earth. (Psalms 45:2, 13, 16)

This is about the Lord. "In place of your fathers will be your children" means that divine truth will resemble divine goodness. The king's daughter stands for a love of truth. Clothing of gold braid stands for the quality of truth that results from goodness. The subject here is the Lord and his divine humanity, as the whole psalm and everything in it makes clear, so naturally all the details in it have the same kind of application: The king's daughter does not mean a king's daughter. Her clothing of gold braid does not mean that, nor does "in place of your fathers will be your children," nor does the children's status as chieftains in all the earth. No, divinely heavenlike and spiritual qualities are what each of them signifies. A daughter means desire, or love (see §§490, 491, 2362). A king means divine truth (1672, 1728, 2015, 2069, 3009). Gold means what is good (113, 1551, 1552). Its being braided relates to earthly fact (2831), so in this case it relates to divine earthly truth. Clothing means the kind of truth that enrobes goodness (297, 2576). Children in place of fathers means the truth that comes of goodness, and in this case it means divine truth resembling divine goodness (264, 489, 491, 533, 1147, 1729, 1733, 2159, 2623, 2803, 2813). Chieftains in all the earth mean the most important aspects of the Lord's kingdom and church, chieftains being that which is most important (1482, 2089), and the earth being the Lord's kingdom and church (1413, 1607, 1733, 1850, 2117, 2118 at the end, 3355). [13] In Moses:

> Jehovah delighted in *your fathers,* to love them, and he chose their seed after them: you, out of all the peoples, as is the case this day. So circumcise the foreskin of your heart; and do not harden your neck any longer. (Deuteronomy 10:15, 16)

The fathers in an inner sense stand for the ancient and earliest churches. Their adherents were called fathers for the love they bore toward goodness and truth—love of goodness in the earliest people, who were heavenly, and love of truth in the ancients, who were spiritual. The goodness and truth of people in the church are what are being called the seed that God chose. Clearly it is not Abraham, Isaac, Jacob, and his twelve sons that are the fathers here, or the people of Israel and Judah that are the seed. These words are said of them and to them in order to wrap the inner meaning in an outer layer intelligible to human beings. [14] In Isaiah:

> They will vaunt themselves, youth against elder, and the contemptible against the honored, because a man will take hold of his brother in *his*

father's house: "You have a garment! You will be chieftain to us." He will say, "In my house there is no bread and no clothing. Do not make me chief of the people." (Isaiah 3:[5, 6,] 7)

In an inner sense this deals with the corrupt state of the church, when people no longer acknowledge truth as true or know what is good. "A man will take hold of his brother in his father's house" stands for acknowledging anything at all as good; the garment, for truth (§§1073, 2576); the chief, for the main teaching of that truth (1482, 2089). No bread and no clothing in the house stands for no goodness or truth, bread meaning goodness (276, 680, 3478) and clothes meaning truth (297, 2576).

[15] Representations of goodness and truth by a father and mother and by daughters and sons gave rise to many laws in representative religions— laws that took their divinity from such representations. The following are examples:

> The *daughter of a priest,* if she profaned herself by whoring, was profaning *her father;* she would be burned with fire. (Leviticus 21:9)

The priest's daughter stands for a desire for goodness; the father, for the goodness from which that desire comes; whoring, for profaning what is good. For the meaning of whoring, see §§2466, 2729, 3399; and for that of profaning, §§1008, 1010, 1059, 2051, 3398, 3399. Another example:

> If the daughter of a priest becomes widowed or divorced and she has no seed, she shall return to *her father's house* as in her youth; *of her father's bread she shall eat.* No stranger shall eat of it. (Leviticus 22:13)

[16] Take this law, too:

> If you see in captivity a wife of beautiful form and want her, to take her as your woman, you shall bring her into the middle of your house, and she shall shave her head and trim her nails and take the clothing of her captivity off her and sit in your house and *cry for her father and her mother* a month of days, and afterward you shall go in to her and know her, and she will become your woman. (Deuteronomy 21:11, 12, 13)

Every part of this law is representative of earthly truth, which is adopted by goodness after it has been purified of falsity. A wife beautiful of form in captivity symbolizes earthly truth. Being brought into the middle of the house, shaving her head, trimming her nails, taking off the clothing of her captivity, and crying for her father and mother means being purified of falsity. Going in to her afterward, knowing her, and taking her as a woman means adopting that truth.

[17] The laws for marriage stating that the people were to marry within their tribe and clan, and the inheritance laws stating that an inheritance was not to pass from tribe to tribe, which are detailed in the Word, also derived from the same source. That is, they derived from the heavenly and spiritual marriage in the Lord's kingdom, or the marriage of goodness and truth, symbolized by a father and mother. Likewise the laws laid down concerning the degrees of allowable and forbidden relations. Each of these laws in the Word inwardly relates to the law governing the alliance and union of goodness and truth in heaven—and to alliances of evil and falsity in hell, which are a separate matter. Concerning the degrees of allowable and forbidden relations, see Leviticus 20; for the idea that inheritances were not to pass from tribe to tribe, and that marriage was to be contracted within the tribe, see Numbers 27:7, 8, 9, and elsewhere. On the point that everything in the heavens interrelates according to the blood ties and connections between goodness and truth, see §§685, 917, 2739, 3612.

[18] Since the Israelite people represented the Lord's kingdom in the heavens and consequently the heavenly way things are arranged there, it was also commanded that they be divided by *tribe,* by *clan,* and *by their fathers' households;* see Numbers 26:1–end. The same arrangement determined the pattern in which they camped around the meeting tent and in which they set out to travel. Moses describes it in these words: "A man under his banner, with his insignia, *according to their fathers' house* the children of Israel shall camp, opposite [and] around the meeting tent"; and that is also how they set out (Numbers 2:2, 34). So when Balaam saw Israel dwelling by its tribes, the spirit of God came over him and he uttered a pronouncement, saying, "How good are your tents, Jacob; your dwellings, Israel! They are planted as valleys are, as gardens beside the river," and so on (Numbers 24:2, 5, 6, and following verses). Neither Jacob nor Israel is meant in this prophecy. Instead the Lord's kingdom in the heavens and his church on earth are what are represented by the pattern in which he then saw them arranged, as the individual words there reveal.

[19] This also shows what is symbolized on an inner level of the Word by orphans, or the fatherless—namely, people in a state of innocence and of love for their neighbor who want to know and do what is good

but cannot. This is especially the condition of people outside the church, whom the Lord takes care of and adopts as his children in the next life. Since these are the people symbolized by orphans, most Scripture passages mentioning them also speak of immigrants and widows. Immigrants symbolize people learning about goodness and truth (§1463), and widows symbolize those at a stage where they have either more goodness than truth or more truth than goodness but want to have both. Because these three—orphans, immigrants, and widows—symbolize almost the same thing, one after the other, they are spoken of together in most passages, as noted. See Deuteronomy 14:29; 16:[11,] 14; 24:17, 19; Jeremiah 7:6; 22:3; Ezekiel 22:6, 7; Zechariah 7:10; Psalms 94:6; 146:9.

From the above it is now possible to see what a father symbolizes in a positive sense: goodness and, on the highest level, the Lord.

[20] Like most things in the Word, however, a father also has a negative meaning, in which it symbolizes evil, just as a mother symbolizes truth in a positive sense and falsity in a negative sense. The following passages show that this is so. In David:

> The *wickedness of their fathers* will be recalled to Jehovah, and the *sin of their mother* will not be erased. (Psalms 109:14)

In the same author:

> They regressed and committed treachery *like their fathers;* they veered like an untrue bow. (Psalms 78:57)

In Moses:

> . . . until those left among you waste away in their wickedness in the lands of your foes, and also in the *wickedness of their fathers;* along with them they will waste away. (Leviticus 26:39)

In Isaiah:

> Prepare slaughter for *his children, because of the wickedness of their fathers;* and may they not rise again and take possession of the land and fill the face of the land with cities! (Isaiah 14:21)

In the same author:

> I will repay your wickedness and the *wickedness of your fathers* at the same time. (Isaiah 65:7)

[21] In Jeremiah:

> The house of Israel have been shamed—they, their monarchs, their chieftains, and their priests and their prophets, saying to wood, *"You are my father,"* and to stone, *"You gave birth to me,"* because they turned me their neck, not their faces. (Jeremiah 2:26, 27)

In the same author:

> I am putting stumbling blocks before this people, and *fathers* and *children* will stumble over them together, neighbors and their companions; and they will perish. (Jeremiah 6:21)

In the same author:

> The *children* gather wood, and the *fathers* light the fire, and the women are kneading dough to make cakes for Melecheth. (Jeremiah 7:18)

In Ezekiel:

> I will do in you what I have not done and what I will never do the like of again, because of your abominations; therefore *fathers will eat their children, and children will eat their fathers,* and I will carry out judgments on you and scatter all your survivors to every wind. (Ezekiel 5:9, 10)

This is about the profanation of what is holy. In the same author:

> This is what the Lord Jehovah has said to Jerusalem: "Your trading and your generations are from the land of the Canaanite; *your father* is an Amorite and *your mother* a Hittite." (Ezekiel 16:3)

[22] In Matthew:

> Brother will hand brother over to death; and *the father, the son;* and *children* will rise up *against their parents* and put them to death. And moreover you will be hated by everyone because of my name. I came to pit a person *against that person's father* and a *son against his mother,* and a daughter-in-law against her mother-in-law. And people's foes will be their housemates. Whoever loves *father* and *mother* above me is not worthy of me, and whoever loves *son* and *daughter* above me is not worthy of me. (Matthew 10:21, 22, 35, 36, 37; Luke 12:49, 52, 53)

In the same author:

> All who leave behind houses or brothers or sisters or *father* or *mother* or wife or children or fields for my name will receive a hundredfold; eternal life they will inherit. (Matthew 19:29; Luke 18:29, 30; Mark 10:29, 30)

In Luke:

> If any come to me and do not *hate their father* and *their mother* and wife
> and children and brothers and sisters and in fact even their own soul,
> they cannot be my disciples. (Luke 14:26)

[23] In Mark:

> Brother will hand brother over to death, and *a father his children,* and
> *children* will rise up *against their parents* and kill them, because you will
> be hated by all because of my name. (Mark 13:12, 13; Luke 21:16, 17)

This treatment of the close of the age depicts the condition of goodness
and truth in a corrupt religion; evil will rise up against truth, and falsity
against goodness.

The quotations just above show that in a negative sense a father symbolizes evil, as this passage in John also shows:

> Jesus said, "If God were *your Father,* you would love me, because I issued
> and come from God. You are from your *father, the Devil,* and *your father's*
> *desire* you wish to do; he was a murderer from the start and did not stand
> on truth, because there is no truth in him. When he tells a lie, he is talk-
> ing on his own, because he is a liar and *the father of [a lie].*" (John 8:38,
> 39, 41, 42, 44)

And God of Isaac symbolizes the Lord in his divine humanity. This
can be seen from the representation of *Isaac* as the Lord's divine rationality. Since rationality is the starting point of humanity (§2194) and therefore is the source of and path to humanity, *God of Isaac* here symbolizes
the Lord's divine humanity.

Each and every thing in heaven, in us, and in fact in the whole of
creation relates to what is good and true, so the Lord's divinity is also
distinguished into divine goodness and divine truth, his divine goodness
being called the Father, and his divine truth, the Son. The Lord's divinity
is nothing but goodness and in fact is goodness itself, but divine truth is
the Lord's divine goodness made visible to angels in heaven. The sun provides a parallel, in that it is essentially nothing but fire. The light we see it
shed is not *in* the sun but comes *from* the sun. The sun represents the
Lord's divine goodness, which in the other life is the sun of all heaven (see
§§1053, 1521, 1529, 1530, 1531, 2495, 3636, 3643). Light represents the Lord's
divine truth, which in the other life is the light of all heaven (§§1053, 1521,
1529, 1530, 2776, 3138, 3195, 3222, 3223, 3339, 3341, 3636, 3643). [2] So in

his essence the Lord is nothing but divine goodness, in regard to both his divinity itself and his divine humanity. Divine truth does not exist in divine goodness but comes from it, because that is the form in which divine goodness appears in heaven, as noted above. Since divine goodness appears as divine truth, the Lord's divinity is distinguished into divine goodness and divine truth to enable us to grasp it. Divine goodness is what the Word calls the Father, and divine truth is what it calls the Son.

This is the secret that lies hidden in the fact that the Lord himself so often speaks of his Father as separate and seemingly different from himself, while in other places he speaks of his Father as being one with him.

Just above at §3703 it was shown that in an inner sense a father means goodness, and in the highest sense, the Lord's divine goodness. It was shown in §§1729, 1733, 2159, 2803, 2813 that a son means truth and that the Son of God and Son of Humankind mean the Lord's divine truth. The same meanings can be seen from all the passages in which the Lord mentions his Father and refers to himself as the Son.

[3] The Lord is who is called Jehovah in the Old Testament Word (see §§1343, 1736, 2921), but he is also called a father there, as the following passages show. In Isaiah:

> A child has been born for us, a son has been given to us, and sovereignty will be on his shoulder, and his name will be called Miraculous, Counselor, God, Hero, *Eternal Father,* Prince of Peace. (Isaiah 9:6)

Obviously the child born for us and the son given to us is the Lord, who accordingly is the one called Eternal Father. In Jeremiah:

> I will be *as a father to Israel,* and Ephraim is my firstborn. (Jeremiah 31:9)

This is about the Lord, who is the God of Israel and the Holy One of Israel; see §3305. Here he is a father to Israel. In Malachi:

> Do we not all have *one Father?* Did not one God create us? (Malachi 2:10)

Creating stands in an inner sense for regenerating here as in other Scripture passages (see §§16, 88, 472), and since the Lord is the only Regenerator and Redeemer, he is the one being called Father and God, as he also is in Isaiah:

> *You are our Father,* because Abraham does not know us and Israel does not acknowledge us. *You are Jehovah our Father,* our *Redeemer;* your name is from eternity. (Isaiah 63:16)

[4] In the same author:

> I will dress him in your tunic, and with your belt I will brace him, and your ruling power I will give into his hand, *so that he may be a father to the resident of Jerusalem* and *to the house of Judah.* And I will put the key of David's house on his shoulder, and he will open, and there will be no one closing; and he will close, and there will be no one opening. And I will drive him as a nail in a dependable position, so that he may become the glorious throne of his father, on which to hang *all the glory of his father's house,* of the children and grandchildren—all the small vessels, from vessels that are bowls to all the vessels that are nablia. (Isaiah 22:21, 22, 23, 24)

Plainly the Lord is the one being represented and symbolized on an inner level and being called a father to the resident of Jerusalem and to the house of Judah. He is the one with the key of David's house on his shoulder; who opens, and no one closes; who closes, and no one opens (see the preface to Genesis 22). He is also the one with the glorious throne of his father, on whom and from whom hangs everything holy, here called vessels. Things that are holy and heavenly are called vessels that are bowls, and those that are holy and spiritual are called vessels that are nablia.

[5] Monarchs and priests represented the Lord, monarchs through the royalty attached to them representing his divine truth, and priests representing his divine goodness (§3670). As a result, priests were called fathers, as can be seen in Judges:

> Micah said to the Levite, "Stay with me and serve as a *father* and *priest* to me." (Judges 17:10)

The children of Dan said the same to him:

> Quiet! Put your hand on your mouth and go with us and serve *as a father* and *priest* to us. (Judges 18:19)

Even monarchs called priests "father." In 2 Kings:

> The king of Israel said to Elisha, "Shall I strike, *my father?*" He said, "You shall not strike." (2 Kings 6:21, 22)

And when Elisha was about to die, King Joash addressed him:

> Joash the king wept before his face and said, "*My father! My father!* The chariots of Israel, and its horsemen!" (2 Kings 13:14)

The reason monarchs used that name was that they represented the Lord's divine truth, and priests represented his divine goodness, and truth relates to goodness as children to their father, because truth derives from goodness.

[6] This is very well known in the other life, so heaven's inhabitants do not call anyone but the Lord their father, and when the Word according to the Gospels mentions the Father, they do not take it to mean anyone else; see §§15, 1729. When children in heaven are being introduced into a loving goodness and the truth that goes with it, they are always taught to acknowledge the Lord alone as their father. Newcomers to heaven are also taught with scrupulous care that God is one, and those who had been part of the [Christian] church learn that the whole Trinity is in the Lord. Almost all from the Christian world bring with them the notion of three Gods, even though they had said with their lips that there was only one. It is not in human nature to think of one God when the mind has already admitted an image of three, each of them called God, each differing from the others in attributes and functions, and each being worshiped individually. Consequently the worship of three Gods occupies the heart; the worship of one rests merely on the lips.

[7] Christians know that the whole Trinity exists in the Lord, but in the next life they think about the Lord very little. In fact, his human nature is an impediment for many because they separate his humanity from his divinity and do not consider it divine. People say they themselves have been made righteous and in this way have become pure and almost holy, but they do not think that the Lord was glorified—that his human side was made divine—even though he was conceived by Jehovah himself. What is more, no one can be made righteous, let alone holy, except by a divine force and in fact by the Lord's divine humanity. This is represented and symbolized in the Holy Supper by the fact, explicitly stated, that the bread is the Lord's body, and the wine, his blood.

[8] The Word makes it quite plain that the Lord is one with the Father, that he has existed from eternity, that he governs the universe, and consequently that he is divine goodness and truth itself.

The Lord is one with the Father. In John:

> God has never been seen by anyone [except] the only-born Son, *who is in the Father's embrace.* (John 1:18)

In the same author:

> The Jews sought to kill Jesus because he had said God was his Father, *making himself equal to God.* Jesus answered and said, "Truly, truly, I say to you: The Son cannot do anything on his own, except what he sees the Father doing; that is, what [the Father] does, this the Son likewise does. Just as the Father revives the dead and gives them life, so also the Son gives life to whom he wishes. And the Father does not judge anyone but has given all judgment to the Son so that all may honor the Son as they honor the Father. *Just as the Father has life in himself, so he has also granted the Son to have life* in himself. The Father who sent me, he has testified of me; you have never heard his voice or seen his form. Examine the Scriptures; they are what testify of me." (John 5:1–end)

The Father, as already noted, means divine goodness, and the Son, divine truth—both of them in the Lord. Divine goodness, the Father, can produce or send out only what is divine, and what it produces or sends out is divine truth, the Son. [9] In the same author:

> *Everyone who hears from the Father and learns comes to me*—not that anyone has seen the Father, except the one who is with the Father; this one has seen the Father. (John 6:44–48)

In the same author:

> They said to him, "Where is your father?" Jesus answered, "You know neither me nor my Father; *if you knew me, you would also know my Father."* (John 8:18, 19)

In the same author:

> *I and the Father are one.* Even if you do not believe me, believe my deeds, so that *you may know and believe that the Father is in me and I am in the Father.* (John 10:30, 38)

In the same author:

> Jesus said, "Whoever believes in me believes not in me but in him who sent me, *and whoever sees me sees him who sent me.* I have come into the world as the light, so that no one who believes in me should stay in the dark." (John 12:44, 45, 46)

In an inner sense, the Father's *sending* him means that he emanates from the Father. The meaning applies here and in other passages where the Lord says the Father sent him. Light means divine truth; see above. [10] In the same author:

> "I am the way and the truth and life; no one comes to the Father except through me. *If you know me, you also know my Father;* and from now on you know him and have *seen him."* Philip says, "Lord, show us the Father." Jesus said, "So much time I've spent with you, and you do not know me, Philip? *Whoever has seen me has seen the Father.* How then can you say, 'Show us the Father'? *Don't you believe that I am in the Father and the Father is in me?* The words that I speak to you I do not speak from myself; the Father who dwells in me, he does the works. Believe me *that I am in the Father and the Father is in me.* Whatever you ask in my name, that I will do, so that the Father may be glorified in the Son." (John 14:6–11, [13])

In the same author:

> Whoever has my commandments and does them, that is the person who loves me; but those who love me will be loved by my Father, and I will love them and reveal myself to them. If any love me, they will keep my word, and my Father will love them, and we will come to them and make a home in them. (John 14:21, 23)

[11] Those who have the commandments and do them are people who know divine truth. Those who love are people with divine goodness, which is why the passage says, "They will be loved by the Father, and we will come to them and make a home with them"—"we" being divine goodness and divine truth. As a result the same author says, "On that day you will know *that I am in my Father* and *you are in me"* (John 14:20). And in another place, "Holy Father, preserve them in your name *so that they can be one as we are"* (John 17:11). This shows that the Lord uses the term Father for the divine goodness he has, and Son for the divine truth that springs from divine goodness. They are not two, then, but one.

The Lord spoke this way so that the Word would be accepted both on earth and in heaven. He also spoke this way because until he was glorified, he was divine truth rising out of divine goodness. After his glorification he was divine goodness itself in regard to both [his divine and his human] natures, this goodness being the source of everything—what is divinely good and what is divinely true.

[12] *The Lord has existed from eternity.* The Lord is the one who spoke through the prophets. Because of this, and because divine truth had its source in him, he was called the Word, concerning which John says this:

> *In the beginning there was the Word.* And the Word was with God, and the Word was God. *This was with God in the beginning.* Everything was made by him, and nothing that was made was made without him. In him was life, and the life was the *light of humankind.* And the Word became flesh and resided among us, and we saw his glory: glory like that of the Only-Born of the Father. (John 1:1, 2, 3, 4, 14)

The Word stands for all truth in the heavens and on earth that comes from the Divine.

[13] He teaches plainly in other passages in John that he has existed from eternity:

> John said, "This was the one who, coming later than I, *existed before me, because he was earlier than I.* Central among you stands he whom you do not know. He it is who will come after me, who *existed before me."* (John 1:15, [26,] 27, 30)

In the same author:

> [What] if you see the Son of Humankind going up where he was before? (John 6:62)

In the same author:

> Jesus said, "Truly, truly, I say to you: *before Abraham existed, I am."* (John 8:58)

In the same author:

> He knew that from *God he came* and to God he would go. (John 13:3)

In the same author:

> The Father himself loves you because you have loved me and believed that *I came from God. I came from the Father and have come into the world;* again I leave the world and go to the Father. (John 16:27, 28)

In the same author:

> I have glorified you on earth; I have completed the work that you gave me to do. Now therefore glorify me, Father, in yourself, with the glory *that I had in you before the world existed;* so that they can see my glory, which you gave me because you loved me *before the foundation of the world.* (John 17:[4,] 5, 24)

In Isaiah:

> A child has been born for us, a son has been given to us, and his name will be called Miraculous, Counselor, God, Hero, *Eternal Father,* Prince of Peace. (Isaiah 9:6)

[14] *The Lord governs the universe.* This can be seen in Matthew:

> Everything has been turned over to me by my Father. (Matthew 11:27)

In the same author:

> Jesus said to his disciples, "All power in heaven and on earth has been given to me." (Matthew 28:18)

In John:

> The Father has given everything into the Son's hand; those who believe in the Son have eternal life. (John 3:35, 36)

> The Father does not judge anyone but has given all judgment to the Son. (John 5:22)

In the same author:

> Jesus knew that the Father had given everything into his hands. (John 13:3)

In the same author:

> Everything whatever that the Father has is mine. (John 16:15)

In the same author:

> Jesus said, "Glorify your Son so that your Son may also glorify you, just as you have given him power over all flesh." (John 17:1, 2)

In the same author:

> Everything of mine is yours and of yours is mine, but I am glorified in
> them; I am no longer in the world, because I am coming to you. (John
> 17:10, 11)

In Luke:

> Everything has been turned over to me by my Father. (Luke 10:22)

[15] The above evidence now shows that divine goodness is what is
called the Father, and divine truth, what is called the Son, and that from
divine goodness by means of divine truth the Lord governs absolutely
everything in the universe.

In view of this, and considering how clear-cut the idea is in the Word,
it is amazing that the Christian world does not acknowledge and revere
the Lord alone and therefore one God, as heaven does. After all, Christians
know and teach that the whole Trinity exists in the Lord.

The Holy Spirit, which is also worshiped as a separate God from the
Son and the Father, is the holy operation of the spirit. In other words, it
is the holy influence exerted by the Lord through spirits, or angels—that
is, by the Lord's divine goodness through his divine truth. This will be
clarified elsewhere, by the Lord's divine mercy.

The land that you are lying on, to you I will give it means that he
himself would be the source of the goodness he had, as can be seen from
the following. The *land* symbolizes earthly goodness, as discussed below.
That you are lying on means that he possessed. And *giving it to you* means
being the source, as also discussed below.

The *land* symbolizes the earthly goodness that Jacob will come to
represent because the land of Canaan symbolizes the Lord's kingdom
(§§1413, 1437, 1585, 1607, 1866), and since it symbolizes the Lord's kingdom, in the highest sense it also symbolizes the Lord (3038). The Lord is
the all-in-all of his kingdom, and anything in it that does not come from
him and focus on him as the goal is not part of his kingdom. The Lord's
kingdom is also symbolized in the Word by heaven and earth (1733, 1850,
2117, 2118 at the end), but heaven then symbolizes his inner kingdom,
and the earth, [or land,] his outer kingdom (82, 1411, 1733, 3355 at the
end). So in the highest sense, heaven symbolizes the Lord's divine rationality, and the land, his earthly divinity. In the current verse, then, *the
land where you are lying* symbolizes the earthly goodness he had, which

3705

Jacob represented. I have said many times already that Jacob means the Lord's earthly divinity.

[2] What is more, the symbolism of land varies; see §§620, 636, 1066, 2571, 3368, 3379. Why? Canaan, which is called the Holy Land, symbolizes the Lord's kingdom in general. When heaven is mentioned along with the land, heaven symbolizes the Lord's inner kingdom, and the land his outer kingdom, as noted. So the latter also symbolizes his kingdom on earth, which is his church. As a result it symbolizes a person who *is* a kingdom of the Lord or a church. People like this have heaven inside and the land outside—that is, they have rationality as their heaven, and an earthly level as their land, because rationality is inside people, and earthliness, outside them. Since the land symbolizes these things, it also symbolizes the factor that makes a person a kingdom of the Lord: a loving goodness that comes from the Divine. From this you can see how the scriptural symbolism of the land varies.

[3] *I will give you* means that he himself would be the source, as can be seen from the symbolism of *giving* in the Word when it applies to the Lord. As shown directly above, the Lord is divine goodness and also divine truth, the former being called the Father, and the latter, the Son. Since divine goodness is his own, it follows that when Jehovah is said to "give you" something, and the phrase applies to the Lord, it means that he himself is the source.

This shows the inner-level significance of the fact that the Lord so often said the Father had given something to him—that is, to himself—as in John:

> Father, glorify your Son so that your Son may also glorify you, *just as you have given him* power over all flesh, so that to all *that you have given him* he may give eternal life. I have glorified you on earth; I have completed the work *that you gave me* to do. I have manifested your name to the people *whom you gave me* out of the world. Yours they were, and *to me you gave them.* Now they know that everything *that you have given me* is from you, because the words *that you gave me* I have given them. I pray for those *whom you have given me,* because they were yours. For *everything of mine is yours and of yours is mine.* (John 17:1, 2, 4, 6–10)

When this passage says that the Father gave something, it means that it came from the divine goodness the Lord had, so that he himself was the source.

[4] This shows what immense secrets lie hidden in the individual words the Lord spoke. It also shows how much at variance the literal meaning is with the inner meaning, not to mention the highest meaning. The reason the Lord spoke this way was to give humankind the chance to grasp and therefore accept his words in its own way, although people at that time knew absolutely no divine truth. It also gave angels the chance to grasp and accept it in *their* own way, since they knew that Jehovah and the Lord were one, and that the Father was divine goodness. As a consequence they also knew that when the Lord said that the Father had given him something, that meant he had given it to himself, so that he himself was the source.

And to your seed means [he himself would be the source of] the truth too. This is established by the symbolism of *seed* as religious truth, a symbolism discussed in §§255, 880, 1025, 1447, 1610, 2848, 3038, 3310, 3373. | **3706**

Your seed will be like the dust of the earth means that divine earthly truth would resemble earthly goodness, as is established by the following: *Seed* symbolizes truth, as dealt with just above in §3706, so *your* seed—Jacob's—means divine truth on the earthly level. (Jacob represents the Lord's earthly divinity, as shown above.) And the *dust of the earth* symbolizes goodness, as dealt with in §1610. So in an inner sense, *your seed will be like the dust of the earth* means that divine truth on the earthly level will resemble divine goodness on the earthly level. | **3707**

The reason the *dust of the earth* symbolizes goodness is that the earth, [or land,] symbolizes the Lord's kingdom and therefore goodness, as shown just above in §3705. The dust of that land, then, means goodness, but earthly goodness, since the land symbolizes what is lowest in the Lord's kingdom, as also shown in that section. So it symbolizes the earthly level whenever heaven (if it too is mentioned) symbolizes an inner, rational level.

That is why the increased fruitfulness of goodness and the multiplying of truth is expressed here and there in the Word as a promise that "your seed will be like the stars of the heavens and like the dust of the earth." The stars of the heavens symbolize rational traits, and the dust of the earth symbolizes earthly traits, which will proliferate in this manner.

What it means to say that earthly truth will resemble earthly goodness will be explained later, with the Lord's divine mercy.

And you will burst out toward the sea and toward the east symbolizes the infinite reach of goodness; *and toward the north and toward the south* | **3708** symbolizes the infinite reach of truth; and therefore all states of goodness and truth. This can be seen from the following: *Bursting out* means a reach—in this case an infinite reach, since it is ascribed to the Lord. The *sea,* or west, symbolizes goodness that is still dim and therefore goodness that is just beginning. The *east* symbolizes goodness that shines brightly and therefore goodness that is complete. The *north* symbolizes truth that is still dim. And the *south* symbolizes truth in the light.

[2] Many Scripture passages mention the sea (or west), east, north, and south, but no one has yet realized that like everything else they have an inner sense in which they mean not the literal, worldly phenomena but spiritual and heavenly qualities, and in the highest sense, the divine qualities of the Lord himself. So people could not help thinking that west, east, north, and south in the Word mean simply the four quarters of the world, and that bursting out in those directions means multiplying. However, all passages in the Word (especially the Prophets) that mention the directions can be used to demonstrate that they do not mean those quarters nor the multiplication of a people but the states and reach of goodness and truth.

The inhabitants of heaven have no idea what west, east, north, and south are. Heaven's sun, which is the Lord, is not like the world's sun, rising and setting, creating noon at its zenith and night at its nadir. Instead the appearance of the sun is unchanging—although it depends on the states of the people receiving light from it. The light contains wisdom and understanding (see §§1619–1632, 2776, 3138, 3167, 3190, 3195, 3222, 3223, 3339, 3341, 3485, 3636, 3643), so the sun's appearance depends on the state of wisdom and understanding in the individual. To people with goodness and truth it seems warm and bright (with a heavenly and spiritual warmth and light), like the sun at dawn and noon. To people without goodness and truth it resembles the sun at sunset and night. East, south, west, and north on the Word's inner level, then, plainly symbolize states of goodness and truth.

[3] It needs to be known that the Word depicts states of goodness and truth not only as the directions currently under discussion but also as seasons or states of the year (spring, summer, fall, and winter) and as times or states of the day (morning, noon, evening, and night). The reason in each case is the same. However, when the theme is the *extent* of what is good and true, it is depicted by the four quarters.

The specific symbolism of each direction can be seen from passages in the Word mentioning them. The symbolism of the east as the Lord and as a loving, charitable goodness received from the Lord was demonstrated earlier, in §§101, 1250, 3249; and that of the south as truth in the light, in §§1458, 3195 at the beginning. [4] The positive and negative symbolisms of west and north will become clear from the following passages. In Isaiah:

> Don't be afraid, because I am with you; from the *east* will I bring your seed, and from the *west* will I gather it. I will say to the *north,* "Hand them over!" and to the *south,* "Do not hinder them! Bring my sons from far away and my daughters from the end of the earth." (Isaiah 43:5, 6)

This is about a new spiritual religion, which is represented here by Jacob and Israel [Isaiah 43:1]. Bringing seed from the east and gathering it from the west stands for people with goodness. Saying "Hand them over!" to the north and "Do not hinder them!" to the south stands for people with truth. [5] In David:

> [So] will say Jehovah's redeemed, whom he redeemed from the hand of the foe; and from the lands he gathered them—from *sunrise* and from *sunset,* from the *north* and from the *sea.* They wandered in the wilderness, in a desert path; a habitable city they did not find. (Psalms 107:2, 3, 4)

This passage concerns people who do not know about goodness or truth. "From sunrise and from sunset" stands for those lacking knowledge of goodness; "from the north and from the sea," for those lacking knowledge of truth. People without knowledge of goodness are being said to wander in the wilderness; those without knowledge of truth, in a desert path. Concerning ignorance of both kinds it says that they did not find a habitable city—a city meaning a true doctrine (§§402, 2449, 2943, 3216) and habitation relating to goodness (§§2268, 2451, 2712). [6] In Isaiah:

> Look: these will come from far off! And look: those will come *from the north* and *from the west;* and those, from the land of Sinim! (Isaiah 49:12)

The north stands for people with a dim sight of truth; the west, for people with a dim sight of goodness. They are said to come from far off because they are remote from the light the Lord sheds. [7] In Amos:

> Watch! The days will come in which I send famine into the land, and they will wander *from sea to sea;* and from *the north all the way to the*

east they will dash about to seek Jehovah's Word and will not find it. (Amos 8:11, 12)

The famine stands for a scarcity and lack of religious knowledge (§§1460, 3364). Wandering from sea to sea stands for trying to find out where the knowledge is, seas meaning knowledge in general (§§28, 2850). Dashing about from the north all the way to the east means dashing from a dim to a radiant sight of that knowledge. Obviously the object is knowledge, because it says they dash about to seek Jehovah's Word and will not find it. [8] In Jeremiah:

> Shout these words *toward the north* and say, "Come back, rebellious Israel! I will not make my face fall regarding you, because I am merciful." In those days the house of Judah will go toward the house of Israel, and they will come as one from the *land of the north* onto the land that I made your ancestors inherit. (Jeremiah 3:12, 18)

This passage is about rejuvenating the church with people from outside it. The north stands for people who do not know the truth but live a good life. The passage is clearly not talking about the north and the land of the north, because Israel no longer existed at that time. In the same author:

> As Jehovah lives, who brought the children of Israel up *from the land of the north!* (Jeremiah 16:15)

Again the north stands for ignorance of truth. [9] In the same author:

> Watch: I am bringing them *from the land of the north,* and I will assemble them *from the flanks of the land;* among them are the blind and the lame. (Jeremiah 31:8)

The land of the north stands for ignorance of goodness resulting from ignorance of truth. Canaan represented the Lord's kingdom and therefore represented what is good (see §3705 above), and its central points, such as Zion and Jerusalem, represented inmost goodness, to which truth has been united. So the more remote parts represented a dim sight of goodness and truth. All goodness and truth lying in the semidark is called the land of the north and the flanks of the land. [10] In addition, since everything good that flows in from the Lord with light ends up in our murky minds, the north is also called a place of assembly, as in Isaiah:

> You have said in your heart, "I will scale the heavens; I will raise my throne above the stars of God and sit on the *mountain of assembly,* on the *flanks of the north.*" (Isaiah 14:13)

In the same author:

> Wail, you gate! Shout, you city! Philistia, the whole of you has dissolved, because *from the north* comes smoke, and [there will not be] one single person *in the assemblies*. (Isaiah 14:31)

In David:

> Great is Jehovah, and highly praised in the city of our God, his holy mountain; the joy of the whole earth is Mount Zion, the *flanks of the north,* the city of the great king. (Psalms 48:1, 2)

Further in the same author:

> Yours are the heavens; yours also the earth. The world and its abundance you founded; the *north* and the right-hand side you created. (Psalms 89:11, 12)

The north stands for people who are fairly distant from the light of goodness and truth; the right-hand side, for those who are closer. The latter are on the Lord's right hand; see §§1274, 1276. [11] In Zechariah:

> [Zechariah] saw four chariots going out between two bronze mountains. [The chariots] had horses that were chestnut, black, white, and hail-spotted, sturdy. The angel said, *"These are the four winds of the heavens* going out from where they stand by the Lord of the whole earth"—the black horses going out *into the land of the north;* and the white went out after them, and the hail-spotted went out into the *land of the south.* "Those going out *to the land of the north* bring my spirit to rest *in the land of the north."* (Zechariah 6:1–8)

Chariots going out between two bronze mountains stand for doctrines teaching what is good. The meaning of chariots as doctrines will become clear elsewhere. A mountain means love (see §§795, 1430, 2722), so two mountains mean two kinds of love: heavenly love, or love for the Lord, and spiritual love, or love for one's neighbor. Bronze means goodness on the earthly level resulting from this love (425, 1551). Horses mean intellectual matters and therefore an understanding of teachings about goodness (2760, 2761, 2762, 3217). The land of the south stands for people with a knowledge of what is good and true (1458, 3195). The land of the north stands for people who lack a knowledge of what is good and true but live a good life, as upright non-Christians do. When a new religion starts up among them, the spirit of God is said to rest there. [12] In Jeremiah:

> . . . Jehovah, who summoned up and who brought back the seed of the house of Israel *from the land to the north* and from all the lands to which I drove them, so that they could live on their land. (Jeremiah 23:8)

"From the land to the north" means from a dark place of ignorance concerning goodness and truth. In the same author:

> Will iron be broken—iron *from the north*—and bronze? (Jeremiah 15:12)

Iron stands for earthly truth (§§425, 426); bronze, for earthly goodness (§§425, 1551). They are said to come from the north because they come from the earthly level, where there is relative darkness and an outer limit. The meaning in this prophetic utterance is not that iron and bronze come from the north, as is obvious without explanation. If that were the meaning, what divinity would the passage have? In fact, how would it connect with the verses before and after it? [13] In Matthew:

> I tell you that many will come *all the way from the east and from the west* and recline at [the table] with Abraham, Isaac, and Jacob. (Matthew 8:11; Luke 13:29)

Many all the way from the east and from the west stands for people who know and live by what is good, and for people encumbered by darkness and ignorance—in other words, people inside and outside the church. As noted above, east and west symbolize states of goodness. Reclining with Abraham, Isaac, and Jacob means being with the Lord; see §3305 at the end.

The Prophets say the same thing: that from east and west will come the people who will live with the Lord in his kingdom, or his church. In Isaiah, for example:

> *From the east* will I bring your seed, and *from the west* will I gather you. (Isaiah 43:5)

In another place:

> They will fear Jehovah's name *from the west,* and his glory *from the east.* (Isaiah 59:19)

In another place:

> They will know *from sunrise* and *from sunset* that there is none besides me; I am Jehovah, and there is no one else. (Isaiah 45:6)

And in another place:

> I will rouse one *from the north* who will come; *from the rising of the sun,* that one will call on my name. (Isaiah 41:25)

[14] The same symbolism of east, west, south, and north can also be plainly seen from the construction of the tabernacle; the way in which the children of Israel camped and set out to travel; the description of the land of Canaan; and the description of the new temple, the new Jerusalem, and the new earth.

The construction of the tabernacle: Everything in the tabernacle was arranged according to the compass directions (see Exodus 38), which determined, for instance, what went on the eastern and western sides and what went on the southern and northern ones (Exodus 26:18, 20, 22, 27; 27:9, 12, [13]). The lampstand stood opposite the table [of show-bread] on the side of the dwelling place *toward the south,* but the table, *on the north side* (Exodus 26:35; 40:22).

[15] *The way the children of Israel camped and set out to travel:* This too was determined by the quarters. The people camped around the meeting tent—the tribe of Judah, the tribe of Issachar, and the tribe of Zebulun *toward the east;* the tribes of Reuben, Simeon, and Gad *toward the south;* those of Ephraim, Manasseh, and Benjamin *toward the west;* and those of Dan, Asher, and Naphtali *toward the north* (Numbers 2:1–end). Of the Levites, the Gershonites were *toward the west;* the Kohathites, *toward the south;* the Merarites, *toward the north;* and Moses, Aaron, and their off-spring, in front of the dwelling place *toward the east* (Numbers 3:23–38). These positions represented the heavenly pattern displayed in the Lord's kingdom as determined by the states of goodness and truth there. The people would trumpet an alert *toward the south* for setting out on their journeys (Numbers 10:6), and they set out in the same order in which they camped (Numbers 2:34).

[16] *The description of the land of Canaan:* Moses first described the land in terms of its borders all around—*on the southern side, western side, northern side,* and *eastern side* (Numbers 34:2–12). This was repeated later when Canaan was assigned to the tribes by lot (Joshua 15, 16, 17, 18, 19). As a result, and because of the earliest people (who lived in Canaan), all locations there developed a representation and symbolism according to their placement, distance, and directional borders (§§1607, 1866).

[17] *The description of the new temple, the new Jerusalem, and the new earth:* Ezekiel too speaks in terms of quarters; for instance, in saying that the

structure of the city was *on the south,* and in speaking of a gate to the building as having its face *toward the east, toward the north,* or *toward the south* (Ezekiel 40:2, 6, 19, 20–46). He speaks of the measurement of the temple and of its doorway *toward the north* and *south* (Ezekiel 41:11); of the courtyard toward the *north, east, south,* and *west* (Ezekiel 42:1, 4, 11, [16,] 17, 18, 19); of the glory of Jehovah, Israel's God, entering by *way of the east* (Ezekiel 43:1, 2, 4); of the gates to the courtyard (Ezekiel [44]:1, 2, 4; [46]:1, 9, 10, 19, 20); of the Holy Land's borders toward the *north* (Ezekiel 47:15, 16, 17), toward the *east* (Ezekiel 47:18), toward the *south* (Ezekiel 47:19), and toward the *west* (Ezekiel 47:20); and of each tribe's territorial inheritance in terms of the four quarters (Ezekiel 48). And gates to the holy Jerusalem are spoken of as being *on the east, north, south,* and *west* (Revelation 21:13).

What is meant in an inner sense by the four quarters of the world in which such holy objects—or objects representing something holy—were arranged? Clearly they do not mean the four quarters but states of goodness and truth in the Lord's kingdom.

[18] The negative symbolism of *north* and *west* as something false and evil is clear from the following passages. In Jeremiah:

> The word of Jehovah came to me a second time, saying, "What are you seeing?" I said, "An open pot I am seeing, and *its face is toward the north.*" And Jehovah said, "From the *north, evil will open* over all the inhabitants of the land. Watch! I am calling *all the clans of the north* to come." (Jeremiah 1:13, 14, 15)

In the same author:

> Raise a signal toward Zion! Assemble; do not stand there, because *I am bringing evil from the north,* and great wreckage. (Jeremiah 4:6)

In the same author:

> The sound of a din! Look: it is coming, and great commotion *from the land of the north,* to reduce the cities of Judah [to] a wasteland. (Jeremiah 10:22)

In the same author:

> In Tekoa, blow a horn, because *evil looks out from the north,* and great wreckage. Here comes a people coming *from the land of the north,* and a large nation will be stirred up *from the flanks of the land.* (Jeremiah 6:1, 22)

In the same author:

> I took the goblet from Jehovah's hand and gave a drink to all the nations—
> Jerusalem and the cities of Judah and its monarchs; Pharaoh, monarch of
> Egypt, and *all the western horde;* all the monarchs of Arabia and *all the*
> *monarchs of the west* living in the wilderness and all the *monarchs of the*
> *north* near and far. (Jeremiah 25:17–26)

[19] In the same author:

> The swift will not flee nor the mighty escape; *toward the north* along the
> shore of the river Euphrates they have stumbled and fallen. Who is this
> who rises like the river? Egypt rises like the river, for it said, "I will go up; I
> will blanket the land; I will destroy the city and those living in it." But that
> day belongs to the Lord Jehovih Sabaoth—a day of vengeance—because
> there will be sacrifice to the Lord Jehovih *in the land of the north* along the
> river Euphrates. A very beautiful heifer is Egypt; *destruction comes from the*
> *north.* The daughter of Egypt has been shamed, has been delivered *into*
> *the hand of the people of the north.* (Jeremiah 46:6, 7, 8, 10, 20, 24)

In the same author:

> This is what Jehovah has said: "Look! Water *climbing from the north;*
> and it is like a flooding river, and will flood the earth and its abun-
> dance, the city and those living in it." (Jeremiah 47:2)

[20] In the same author:

> Jehovah has spoken against Babylon: "A *nation from the north* will come
> up against them; it will make their land a desolation so that nothing
> can live in it." (Jeremiah 50:[1,] 3)

In the same author:

> Look: I am stirring and bringing up against Babylon an assembly of
> great nations *from the land of the north,* and they will draw up their
> ranks against it; from there it will be seized. Look: *a people coming from*
> *the north,* and a large nation; and many monarchs will be stirred up
> *from the flanks of the land.* (Jeremiah 50:9, 41)

In the same author:

> Then the heavens and the earth and all that is in them will sing over Bab-
> ylon, because *from the north* destroyers will come to it. (Jeremiah 51:48)

In Ezekiel:

> Tell Gog, "You will come from your place, *from the flanks of the north,* and many peoples with you; you will come up against my people Israel like a cloud to blanket the land." (Ezekiel 38:14, 15, 16)

In the same author:

> Here, now, I am against you, Gog, you chief; I will make you return, destroy a sixth of you, and bring you down *from the flanks of the north* and lead you onto Israel's mountains. On Israel's mountains you will fall; on the face of the field you will fall. (Ezekiel 39:1, 2, 4, 5)

In Zechariah:

> "Oh, flee *from the land of the north!*" says Jehovah, "for I will spread you out like the four winds of the heavens. Oh, Zion, escape—you who live with the daughter of Babylon!" (Zechariah 2:6, 7)

[21] These passages show what the north symbolizes in an opposite sense: falsity that produces evil, and falsity that comes from evil. Falsity that produces evil rises out of shallow reasoning about and against divine qualities on the basis of facts known to our earthly self, so it is said to be a people of the north from Egypt. (Egypt means facts of this type; see §§1164, 1165, 2588 at the end.) Falsity that comes from evil rises out of superficial worship that is seemingly devout but inwardly profane, so it is called a nation of the north from Babylon. (Babylon means this kind of worship; see §§1182, 1283, 1295, 1304, 1306, 1307, 1308, 1321, 1322, 1326. Babylon also means the force that causes spiritual devastation, §1327.) Both the falsity that produces evil and the falsity that comes from evil are said to hail from Gog, because Gog means an outward show of worship without any inward content. Accordingly it means idolatry of the kind in which Jews engaged in every era. (For this symbolism of Gog, see §1151.)

[22] Out of the semidark in our earthly self, either truth dawns or falsity rises. When we allow ourselves to receive light from the Lord through the Word, the gloom we live in brightens. An inner path opens, enabling the Lord to flow in and communicate with us through heaven. When we do not allow ourselves to receive light from the Lord through the Word but only through our own intellect, the gloom we live in deepens into darkness, or falsity. The inner path closes, preventing the Lord from flowing in or communicating with us through heaven. The only inflow and communication that remains is the kind preserving the outward appearance of a

human being who thinks and speaks, though solely at the inspiration of evil and falsity. Consequently in people who allow themselves to receive light, the north symbolizes truth, and in those who do not, it symbolizes falsity. The former rise out of the semidark, soaring into the light; the latter sink farther down from the semidark, recoiling from the light. The former go to the south; the latter, to Tartarus.

[23] The meaning of the north as the pitch black of falsity and of the south as the light of truth is obvious in passages in Daniel about the ram and the buck of the goats and about the kings of the south and north. Concerning the ram and the buck of the goats:

> The ram butted *toward the west* and *toward the north* and *toward the south,* so that no animals could stand before it. The buck of the goats came *from the west* onto all the face of the earth, and from one of its horns went out a horn that grew immensely toward the *south* and toward the *sunrise* and toward the ornament [of Israel]. (Daniel 8:4, 5, 9)

Concerning the kings of the south and north, the king of the south symbolizing people with a knowledge of truth, and the king of the north symbolizing people with falsity:

> At the end of years they will become allies, so that the daughter of the *king of the south* will come to the *king of the north* to do what is right, but her arm will not gain strength. From her lineage will rise one who will come into the stronghold of the *king of the north* and prevail. And he will take captives away *into Egypt.* The *king of the south* will come into the kingdom and fight with the *king of the north.* The *king of the north* will return and marshal a great throng—more than before. Many will stand against the *king of the south.* The *king of the north* will come and seize a fortified city and destroy much. The *king of the south* will engage in war with a large army but will not stand, because [people] will plan plans against him. Later he will come back but will not be as before. The people who know their God will grow strong. Finally, at the time of the end, the *king of the south* will clash with [the king of the north]; therefore the *king of the north* will storm onto him with chariot and riders. In the beautiful land, many will be overthrown. But rumors will scare him *from the sunrise* and *from the north,* so that he goes out with great anger. He shall come to his end, and none will be helping him. (Daniel 11:1–end)

The king of the south means people who live in the light of truth, and the king of the north means those who live first in the shadow, then in the pitch black of falsity, as the details of the passage show. So the verses depict conditions in the church and the way they gradually deteriorate. The two kinds of people are called kings of the south and north because on the Word's inner level kings symbolize truth and, in a negative sense, falsity (§§1672, 2015, 2069). Kingdoms symbolize aspects of truth and, in a negative sense, aspects of falsity (§§1672, 2547).

3709　　*In you all the clans of the ground will be blessed* means that all doctrinal truth relating to goodness will unite with goodness, as is established by the following: Being *blessed* means uniting, as noted in §§3504, 3514, 3530, 3565, 3584. *Clans* symbolize what is good and also truth concerning what is good, as noted in §§1159, 1261. And the *ground* symbolizes that which belongs to the church, so it symbolizes teachings about goodness and truth in the earthly or outer self—currently represented by Jacob—as noted in §§268, 566, 990, 3671. Clearly, then, *in you all the clans of the ground will be blessed* means that all doctrinal truth relating to goodness will unite with goodness.

Doctrinal truth relating to goodness consists of teachings pertaining to love for the Lord and charity toward our neighbor. They are said to unite with goodness in our earthly self when we find pleasure and joy in knowing them for the sake of putting them into practice.

3710　　*And in your seed* means and with truth—that is, [doctrinal truth rising out of goodness] also unites with truth. This is established by the symbolism of *seed* as truth (discussed in §§29, 1025, 1447, 1610, 2848, 3373).

3711　　*Look: I am with you* means that it is divine. *And will guard you in every [place] where you go* symbolizes divine providence. This can be seen from the fact that *I* refers to Jehovah and so to the Lord's divine nature, and from the symbolism of *guarding you in every [place] where you go* as providential care based on what is divine. Since the Lord is the subject, it symbolizes divine providence.

In speaking of divinity and the divine providence here, I mean that the Lord made even his earthly level divine.

3712　　*And will bring you back to this ground* means internalizing divine teachings. This can be seen from the symbolism of *bringing back* as reuniting, or internalizing again, and from that of the *ground* as teachings about goodness and truth in the earthly self (discussed in §§268, 566, 990). In this case the ground symbolizes divine teachings, because Jacob's stay with Laban represents the transitional means by which the Lord made his earthly level divine. Jacob's return to the land of Canaan represents the end of the transition, when he had finished making his earthly level divine. So *I will bring you back to this ground* means internalizing divine teachings.

[2] Divine teachings are divine truth, and divine truth is the Lord's whole Word. Real divine teachings consist of the Word's very highest meaning, which deals exclusively with the Lord. As a result, it also consists of the inner meaning, which deals with the Lord's kingdom in the heavens and on earth, and of the literal meaning, which deals with things seen in the world and on earth. The literal meaning contains the inner meaning, which contains the highest, with which it fully corresponds through representation and symbolism, so even the teaching culled from the literal level is divine.

Because Jacob represents the Lord's earthly divinity, he also represents the Word's literal meaning. After all, the Lord is the Word, which is to say that he is all divine truth, as people recognize. [3] The Word's earthly level is exactly the same as its literal meaning, which is essentially a cloud (see the preface to Genesis 18). Its rational or deeper spiritual level is the same as the inner meaning, and so far as the Lord is the Word, it can be said that the inner meaning is represented by Isaac, and the highest meaning by Abraham.

This shows what it is to internalize divine teachings, when the Lord's earthly divinity (represented by Jacob) is said to do so.

However, the situation is not the same with the Lord himself. Everything in him is divine goodness, not divine truth, let alone divine truth on the earthly level. Divine truth is divine goodness appearing to the angels in heaven and to us on earth. Although it is an appearance, it is still divine truth, because it comes from divine goodness, just as light belongs to the sun, because it comes from the sun (see §3704).

Because I will not abandon you until I have done what I spoke to you **3713** means that nothing needed for putting the teachings into action will be lacking. This is clear without explanation.

Genesis 28:16, 17. *And Jacob woke from his sleep and said, "Surely* **3714** *Jehovah is in this place and I didn't know." And he was afraid and said, "How frightening this place is! This is nothing but the house of God, and this is the gate of heaven."*

Jacob woke from his sleep symbolizes enlightenment. *And said, "Surely Jehovah is in this place,"* symbolizes divinity in that state. *And I didn't know* means being in shadow. *And he was afraid* symbolizes a sacred change. *And said, "How frightening this place is!"* symbolizes a holy state. *This is nothing but the house of God* symbolizes the Lord's kingdom on the outermost level of the divine design. *And this is the gate of heaven* symbolizes the outermost level on which the divine design rests, which appears to provide a point of entry from the physical world.

3715   *Jacob woke from his sleep* symbolizes enlightenment. This can be seen from the symbolism of *sleep,* which means a dim state, compared to consciousness, which is a bright state. So in a spiritual sense, *waking from sleep* means being enlightened.

3716   *And said, "Surely Jehovah is in this place,"* symbolizes divinity in that state. This can be seen from the symbolism in scriptural narrative of *saying* as perceiving (dealt with many times before) and from that of a *place* as a state (dealt with in §§1273, 1274, 1275, 1377, 2625, 2837, 3356, 3387). *Jehovah,* of course, means divinity. From this it is plain that *he said, "Surely Jehovah is in this place,"* symbolizes a perception that there was divinity in that state.

3717   *And I didn't know* means being in shadow, as is clear without explanation, since not knowing is being in the dark about the objects of intellectual sight.

The equivalence of not knowing with being in the dark, and of waking from sleep with being enlightened, shows what the inner meaning is and how it works. The literal meaning holds the kinds of things that present themselves to our physical sight or to some other sense, and we grasp them in terms of those senses. The inner meaning holds the kinds of things that present themselves to our inner sight or to some other inner sense. So the contents of the literal meaning, which we grasp with our outer senses, in terms of worldly phenomena or worldly thinking, are perceived by angels with their inner senses, in terms of heavenly phenomena or heavenly thinking.

The former compare to the latter as the objects of the world's light compare to objects of heaven's light. Objects of the world's light are dead, compared to those of heaven's light. Heavenly light contains wisdom and understanding radiating from the Lord (§§3636, 3643). So when objects of worldly light are obliterated or erased, objects of heavenly light remain. That which is heavenly replaces that which is earthly, and that which is spiritual replaces that which is physical. For example, as noted above, lack of knowledge equals a state of darkness concerning goodness and truth, and waking from sleep equals being enlightened. Likewise with everything else.

3718   *And he was afraid* symbolizes a sacred change. This can be seen from the symbolism of *fear* as a sacred change, which in turn can be seen from the words that follow immediately afterward. Jacob says, "How frightening this place is! This is nothing but the house of God, and this is the gate of heaven"—words that clearly express a sacred change.

For the inner meaning of fear, see §2826. In general, there are two kinds: fear without reverence and fear with reverence. Fear without reverence is the fear evil people have; fear with reverence is the fear good people have. The fear good people have is called holy fear and comes from a feeling of awe for the Divine and from love. Love without holy fear is insipid, like food devoid of salt and therefore of flavor, but love containing fear is like salted food that does not taste of salt. The fear that goes with love is the fear of hurting the Lord or one's neighbor in any way, so it is the fear of hurting what is good and true in any way, of hurting holy love and holy faith, of hurting sacred worship. This fear comes in many forms, different in one person than in another. As a rule, the more we love what is good and true, the more we dread violating goodness and truth, and yet the less the emotion looks like fear. The less we love what is good and true, the less we fear for them, and the more the emotion looks like fear rather than love; and what we are afraid of is hell. When we completely lack any love for goodness and truth, we lack all holy fear. The only thing we are afraid of is losing status, wealth, and the prestige these give us, and of incurring punishment or death. This fear is shallow, mainly affecting our body, our earthly self, and our earthly thoughts. Holy fear, though, mainly touches our spirit or inner self and its conscience.

And said, "How frightening this place is!" symbolizes a holy state, as can be seen from this: Fear symbolizes a sacred change, as explained just above in §3718, and because the word *frightening* in the original language is derived from the same word *fear* comes from, holiness is what it symbolizes. Since on an inner level fear symbolizes something holy, as just mentioned, the same word in the original language means veneration and reverence, which is also a holy fear. And a *place* symbolizes a state, as noted just above in §3716.

3719

This is nothing but the house of God symbolizes the Lord's kingdom on the outermost level of the divine design, as can be seen from the symbolism of the *house of God.*

3720

Many passages in the Word mention *the house of God,* which superficially or literally means a building for sacred worship; in an inner sense, the church; in a broader sense, heaven; in the broadest sense, the Lord's whole kingdom; and in the highest sense, the Lord himself in his divine humanity. The Word calls it the House of God in one place but the Temple in another, both meaning the same thing, with one difference: it speaks of the House of God where the topic is goodness, but of the

Temple where the topic is truth. Clearly, then, the House of God symbolizes the Lord's heavenly church; in a broader sense, the heaven of heavenly angels; in the broadest sense, the Lord's heavenly kingdom; and in the highest sense, the Lord's divine goodness. The Temple just as clearly symbolizes the Lord's spiritual church; in a broader sense, the heaven of spiritual angels; in the broadest sense, the Lord's spiritual kingdom; and in the highest sense, the Lord's divine truth. (See §2048.)

The reason the House of God symbolizes heavenliness, which has to do with goodness, while the Temple symbolizes spirituality, which has to do with truth, is this: In the Word a house symbolizes what is good (see §§710, 2233, 2559, 3128, 3652), and the earliest people built their houses out of wood, because wood symbolized goodness (§§643, 1110, 2784, 2812). The Temple symbolizes truth, because it was built of stone, and stones mean truth (see §§643, 1296, 1298).

[2] This symbolism of wood and stone can be seen not only from places in the Word that mention them but also from representations in the other world. People who think their good deeds make them deserving of salvation appear to themselves to chop wood. Those who think the truth they had makes them deserving of salvation, believing they knew more truth than others, even though they lived evil lives, appear to themselves to split stone. This I have often seen, and it has demonstrated to me the symbolism of wood and stone—of wood as goodness and of stone as truth. Another piece of evidence was that when I saw a wooden house, the idea of goodness immediately came to my mind, and when I saw a stone house, the idea of truth did. Angels have also taught me about this.

That is why angels think of goodness when the Word mentions the House of God—the kind of goodness being dealt with in the given context. When it mentions the Temple, they think of truth—the kind of truth being dealt with in the context.

From the same evidence one can conclude how deeply and inwardly secrets of heaven must lie hidden in the Word.

[3] The reason the house of God now symbolizes the Lord's kingdom on the outermost level of the divine design is that the focus is on Jacob, who represents the Lord's earthly divinity, as shown many times already. The earthly dimension lies on the outermost level of the divine design because all things inward rest on it and are present together in it. Since all things inward are present together in it, and their numerous components are accordingly seen as an undifferentiated whole, conditions are relatively dim there. This dimness has also been discussed several times already [§§3693, 3708, 3717].

And this is the gate of heaven symbolizes the outermost level on which   3721
the divine design rests, which appears to provide a kind of entry point
from the physical world. This can be seen from the symbolism of a *gate*
as that which provides exit and entry. In the current verse it means the
outermost level on which the divine design rests because the theme is the
earthly level represented by Jacob. The meaning of a gate can be seen from
the remarks and explanations at §§2851, 3187; and the fact that the earthly
dimension is the outermost level of the divine design, from the material in
§§775, 2181, 2987–3002, 3020, 3147, 3167, 3483, 3489, 3513, 3570, 3576, 3671.

The reason this outermost level appears to provide a kind of entry
point from the physical world is that a person's earthly mind is the route
by which the attributes of heaven—that is, of the Lord—flow down
into the physical world, and the attributes of the physical world rise
back up (see §3702). But it only *appears* to be an entry from the physical world through the earthly mind into deeper levels, as statements
and demonstrations in various earlier sections show. [2] It seems to us
that the objects of the world enter through our physical or outward
senses and affect our inner reaches. So it looks as though there is a way
to enter from the outermost level of the divine design into interior levels. This is an appearance and illusion, however, as is clear from the
universal rule that what comes later cannot flow into what comes earlier, or what comes lower cannot flow into what comes higher, or what
is on the outside cannot flow into what is on the inside, or what belongs
to the world and nature cannot flow into what belongs to heaven and
the spirit. The former are cruder; the latter, purer. Those cruder elements belonging to the outer, earthly self owe their whole existence to
elements of the inner, rational self and cannot affect the purer elements
but rather are affected by them.

With the Lord's divine mercy, the way this inflow works will be told
later, where spiritual inflow is the subject, since a deceptive appearance
urges us to believe the exact opposite.

This, then, is the reason for saying that the outermost level on which
the divine design rests appears to provide a kind of entry point from the
physical world.

Genesis 28:18, 19. *And Jacob got up early in the morning and took the*   3722
stone that he had put as his headrest and put it as a pillar and poured oil
on its head. And he called the name of that place Bethel. And certainly Luz
had been the name of the city earlier.

Jacob got up early in the morning means an enlightened state. *And*
took the stone symbolizes the truth. *That he had put as his headrest* means

through which he had communication with his divine side. *And put it as a pillar* symbolizes a sacred boundary. *And poured oil on its head* symbolizes sacred goodness, the source. *And he called the name of that place Bethel* symbolizes the nature of the state. *And certainly Luz had been the name of the city earlier* symbolizes the nature of the previous state.

3723   *Jacob got up early in the morning* means an enlightened state. This can be seen from the symbolism of *getting up early in the morning* as an enlightened state (discussed in §3458). Where the Word speaks of *getting up,* it involves some kind of elevation (§§2401, 2785, 2912, 2927, 3171), and the *morning* symbolizes the arrival of heavenly light. Here the phrase symbolizes elevation from gloom into light, so it symbolizes an enlightened state.

3724   *And took the stone* symbolizes the truth. This is established by the symbolism of a *stone* as truth (discussed in §§1296, 1298, 3720).

3725   *That he had put as his headrest* means through which he had communication with his divine side. This is established by the symbolism of a *headrest* or support for the neck as the most general communication possible (discussed above in §3695).

3726   *And put it as a pillar* symbolizes a sacred boundary, as can be seen from the symbolism of a *pillar,* discussed below.

How the case stands in this can be seen from the discussion so far, which focuses on the pattern the Lord followed in making his earthly level divine and, in a representative sense, on the way he renews or regenerates a human being's earthly level. Several earlier sections describe and illustrate the pattern, showing that it turns upside down when we are being reborn and truth comes first, but that the pattern is righted again when we have finished being reborn. Goodness then takes first place, and truth, last. On this subject, see §§3325, 3330, 3332, 3336, 3539, 3548, 3556, 3563, 3570, 3576, 3603, 3688.

This situation was represented by the ladder on which the angels went up and down, where the text says first that they went up and then that they went down (§3701). Their ascent from the outermost level of the divine design (discussed just above in §§3720, 3721) is being dealt with currently. This particular verse says that truth is the outermost level of the divine design. The outermost level is what is being called a sacred boundary, as symbolized by the stone Jacob took and put as a pillar.

You can see that truth is the outermost level of the divine design by considering that the outer boundary of goodness is formed not of goodness but of truth, because truth is designed to contain goodness (§§2261, 2434, 3049, 3068, 3180, 3318, 3387, 3470, 3570). [2] Any goodness in us that lacks truth, or that lacks a bond with truth, is the kind that exists in little children, who as yet have no wisdom because they have no understanding. As they grow up, the more truth they glean from what is good—or the more truth unites with what is good in them—the more human they become. Plainly, then, goodness is first in the divine design and truth is last.

As a consequence, we have to start with secular facts (the truth known to our earthly self) and then with religious teachings (truth for our spiritual self known to our earthly self), in order to be initiated into the understanding that comes of wisdom—that is, in order to take up the spiritual life that makes us human (§3504). For example, if we want to love our neighbor in our capacity as spiritual people, we first have to learn what spiritual love or charity is and who our neighbor is. Admittedly, we can practice neighborly love before we know these things, but only as people limited to the earthly plane, not as spiritual people—in other words, from earthly rather than spiritual goodness in ourselves (see §§3470, 3471). After we learn them, the Lord can graft spiritual goodness onto our knowledge of the subject. The same applies to anything else called religious knowledge, or teachings, or (to put it broadly) truth.

[3] As mentioned, the Lord can graft spiritual goodness onto our religious knowledge, and truth is designed to contain goodness. Some people view knowledge and truth strictly as abstractions (as most consider thoughts to be), and they cannot possibly grasp what it means to say that goodness is grafted onto knowledge, or that truth is a container for goodness. It needs to be known that knowledge and truth are no more detached from the finest substances of our inner self (our spirit) than sight is detached from its organ, the eye, or than hearing is detached from its organ, the ear. Finer substances—real substances—are what they emerge from; and changes in the form of these substances, stimulated and directed by inflowing life from the Lord, make the knowledge and truth perceptible. Concord and harmony among the changing forms—whether they occur one after the other or simultaneously—are what touch the heart, creating what we call beauty, appeal, and pleasure.

[4] Spirits themselves are forms, or consist of a seamless series of forms, just as people on earth do, but the forms are too refined to be seen by the physical eye. Since these forms or substances are invisible to the physical

eye, people today are thoroughly convinced that concepts and thoughts are abstractions. This error leads to the modern insanity of denying we have a spirit that will live on after bodily death. In reality, a spirit is a substance much more real than the substance of its material body. In fact, believe it or not, after it has sloughed off physical elements the spirit is the actual purified body that many say they will receive at the time of the Last Judgment, when they believe they will first rise again.

As the lessons of experience I have reported on at such length show plainly, spirits—or souls, to put it another way—are provided with a body, see each other in broad daylight, talk together, listen to each other, and enjoy much keener sensations than when they inhabited a body in the world.

3727   The reason a *pillar* symbolizes a sacred boundary and therefore the outermost level of the divine design is that in earliest times, people marking off one individual's property or inheritance from another's put stones where their borders ran. The stones served as a sign and witness that the boundaries were in such and such a place. The earliest people, for whom every object and every statute called to mind something heavenly and spiritual (§§1977, 2995), were reminded of humankind's outermost dimension by these stones they set up. So they were reminded of the outermost level of the divine design, which is truth in a person's earthly self.

These earliest people, who lived before the Flood, passed the practice on to the ancients, who lived after the Flood (§§920, 1409, 2179, 2896, 2897). The ancients started to view the stones themselves set up on borders as sacred, the reason being that the stones symbolized holy truth on the outermost level of the divine design, as noted [§3726], and they referred to the stones as pillars. That is how pillars came to be used for worship. The ancients erected them where they had their groves and later where they had their temples. They also anointed them with oil, as discussed directly below [§3728]. The worship of the ancient church consisted of the perceptions and symbolisms of the earliest, pre-Flood people, as the sections just cited show.

The earliest people talked and interacted with angels while still on earth, so they learned from heaven that stones symbolized truth and wood symbolized goodness (see just above in §3720). That is why pillars symbolize a holy boundary and therefore the truth that constitutes the outermost level of the divine design in a person. Goodness, which flows in from the Lord through our inner self, comes to rest in our outer self and in the truth there. Our thoughts, words, and deeds, which are the outermost elements of the divine design, are simply the truths resulting from that goodness, because they are images or forms of that goodness. They belong to our intellectual side, but the goodness within them that is their source belongs to our volitional side.

[2] Other passages in the Word can demonstrate that pillars were raised as a sign and witness and also for worship, and that on an inner level they symbolize a sacred boundary, or truth on our earthly plane, which is the outermost level of the divine design. Take the following verses, which speak of the pact between Laban and Jacob:

> "Now, come, let's strike a pact, I and you, and let it be *for a witness* between me and you." And Jacob took a *stone* and *set it up as a pillar.* Laban said to Jacob, "Look: this heap; and *look: the pillar* that I have set up between me and you. This heap is *a witness* and *the pillar is a witness* that I will not cross this heap to you and that you will not cross this heap or *this pillar* to me for evil." (Genesis 31:44, 45, 51, 52)

The symbolism of the pillar as truth will be seen in the explanation of this passage [§§4190, 4205]. [3] In Isaiah:

> On that day there will be five cities in the land of Egypt speaking the tongues of Canaan and swearing to Jehovah Sabaoth. On that day there will be an *altar to Jehovah* in the middle of the land of Egypt and a *pillar* to Jehovah *by its border.* And it will serve *as a sign* and *as a witness* to Jehovah Sabaoth in the land of Egypt. (Isaiah 19:18, 19, 20)

Egypt stands for facts, which belong to our earthly self. The altar stands for worship of God in general, because the altar became the main representative object in the worship of the second ancient church, a church started by Eber (§§921, 1343, 2777, 2811). The middle of the land of Egypt stands for the deepest, most important facets of worship (§§2940, 2973, 3436). The pillar stands for the truth that is the outermost level of the divine design, on the earthly plane. This truth stands on the border as a sign and witness, as you can see. [4] In Moses:

> Moses wrote all Jehovah's words and got up in the morning and built an *altar* by Mount Sinai and *twelve pillars* for the twelve tribes of Israel. (Exodus 24:4)

This altar too represented all worship and specifically the goodness in worship. The twelve pillars represented truth rising out of goodness in worship—twelve meaning all truth taken as a whole; see §§577, 2089, 2129 at the end, 2130 at the end, 3272. The twelve tribes likewise mean all truth in the church, as the following chapter, by the Lord's divine mercy, will show [§3858].

[5] Altars represented everything good in worship. The Jewish religion was established to represent the heavenly church, which acknowledged no truth except the truth that comes of goodness, called heavenly truth. The people of the heavenly church refused to separate truth from goodness in the least—so much so that they refused to say a word about faith (truth) unless they were thinking about goodness and doing so under the inspiration of goodness. (See §§202, 337, 2069, 2715, 2718, 3246.) Because of all these considerations, truth was represented [in the Jewish religion] by the altar stones, and to represent it by pillars was forbidden. Otherwise the people might have split truth from goodness and offered their representative worship to truth instead of goodness. This is the reason Moses says:

> You shall not plant yourself a grove of any tree whatever beside the *altar of Jehovah* your God that you shall make for yourself, and *you shall not set up for yourself a pillar,* which Jehovah your God hates. (Deuteronomy 16:21, 22)

Worshiping truth in isolation from goodness, or faith in isolation from neighborly love, goes against the Divine because it goes against the ordained plan. That is what is meant by "You shall not set up for yourself a pillar, which Jehovah [your] God hates." [6] The people raised pillars anyway, though, and in doing so represented what violates the divine plan. This is clear in Hosea:

> In proportion to the multiplying of its fruit, Israel *multiplies altars;* in proportion to the goodness of their land, they *make good pillars.* But [Jehovah] will overturn *their altars;* he will devastate *their pillars.* (Hosea 10:1, 2)

In 1 Kings:

> Judah did evil in Jehovah's eyes, and they built themselves high places and *pillars* and groves on every tall hill and under every green tree. (1 Kings 14:[22,] 23)

In 2 Kings:

> The children of Israel *raised themselves pillars* and groves on every tall hill and under every green tree. (2 Kings 17:10)

In the same book:

> Hezekiah took away the high places and *smashed the pillars* and cut down the grove and crushed the bronze snake that Moses had made, because people were burning incense to it. (2 Kings 18:4)

[7] The surrounding nations also inherited the tradition of using altars and pillars to represent sacred worship, but they lived in evil and falsity, so their altars symbolize evil in worship, and their pillars, falsity. That is the reason for the command that they be destroyed. In Moses:

> *The altars of the nations you shall overturn* and *their pillars you shall smash* and their groves you shall cut down. (Exodus 34:13; Deuteronomy 7:5; 12:3)

In the same author:

> You shall not bow down to the gods of the nations and shall not worship them and shall not do according to their deeds, because you shall utterly destroy them and utterly *smash their pillars*. (Exodus 23:24)

The gods of the nations stand for falsity; their deeds, for evil. Smashing their pillars stands for destroying worship inspired by falsity. [8] In Jeremiah:

> Nebuchadnezzar king of Babylon will smash the *pillars of the house of the sun* in the land of Egypt; and the houses of Egypt's gods he will burn with fire. (Jeremiah 43:13)

In Ezekiel:

> With the hooves of his horses Nebuchadnezzar king of Babylon will trample all your streets, the people he will kill with a sword, and *your strong pillars* he will bring down to the earth. (Ezekiel 26:11)

This is about Tyre. Nebuchadnezzar king of Babylon stands for a destructive force (§1327 at the end). The horses' hooves stand for the lowest components of the intellect, such as the things we learn from our senses alone. Hooves mean what is lowliest, as will be demonstrated elsewhere, with the Lord's divine mercy [7729]; and horses stand for matters of intellect (2760, 2761, 2762). Streets stand for truth and, in a negative sense, for falsity (2336), and trampling them means destroying the knowledge of truth, a knowledge symbolized by Tyre. For the symbolism of Tyre, the subject of the verse, as the knowledge of truth, see §1201. Killing the people with a sword stands for destroying truth by means of falsity. "People" has to do with truth (1259, 1260, 3295, 3581), and a sword means falsity engaged in battle (2799). This explanation clarifies what bringing strong pillars down to the earth means. Strength has to do with truth and falsity, which also becomes clear from the Word.

3728   *And poured oil on its head* symbolizes sacred goodness. This can be seen from the symbolism of *oil* as the heavenly quality of love, or goodness (discussed in §§886, 3009), and from that of the *head* as what is higher— in other words, inward. Goodness is higher or inward, and truth is lower or outward, as shown in many places. This reveals what the ancient custom of pouring oil on the head of a pillar symbolized: that there is no truth without goodness, only *from* goodness, so that goodness dominates, just as the head dominates the body. Without goodness, truth is not true; it is babble devoid of life and breaks down spontaneously. In the other world this happens in people who knew more truth than others, or more religious teachings (including teachings about love), if they did not live a good life and so if goodness did not enable them to retain the truth. [2] A church is a church, then, not on account of truth detached from goodness, and therefore not on account of faith detached from neighborly love, but on account of truth originating in goodness, or of faith originating in neighborly love.

The same thing is meant by the Lord's words to Jacob: "I am the God of Bethel, *where you anointed a pillar,* where you vowed me a vow" (Genesis 31:13); and also by the second occasion on which Jacob "*raised a pillar, a pillar of stone,* and offered a drink offering on it and *poured oil on it*" (Genesis 35:14). Offering a drink offering on a pillar symbolizes what is divinely good within faith, and pouring oil on it symbolizes what is divinely good within love.

Pouring oil on stone would be an absurd, idolatrous act if it had no heavenly and spiritual significance, as anyone can see.

3729   *And he called the name of the place Bethel* symbolizes the nature of the state. This can be seen from the symbolism of a name and *calling a name* as its nature (discussed in §§144, 145, 1754, 1896, 2009, 2724, 3006, 3421) and from that of a *place* as a state (discussed in §§2625, 2837, 3356, 3387). The nature of the state is what *Bethel* symbolizes. In the original language, *Bethel* means "the house of God," which symbolizes goodness on the outermost level of the divine design; see §3720.

3730   *And certainly Luz had been the name of the city earlier* symbolizes the nature of the previous state. This is established by the symbolism of a *name* as the nature (discussed just above in §3729) and from that of a *city* as doctrinal truth (discussed in §§402, 2268, 2449, 2712, 2943, 3216).

In the original language, *Luz* means a parting and therefore disconnection, which occurs when we put truth-filled doctrine or truth first and ignore goodness—that is, when there is only truth on the outermost level of the design. (When truth coexists with goodness on that level, there is no parting or disconnection but closeness and union.)

That is the nature of the state symbolized by Luz.

Genesis 28:20, 21, 22. *And Jacob vowed a vow, saying, "If God is with me and guards me on this way that I am walking and gives me bread to eat and clothing to wear, and I return in peace to the house of my father, Jehovah will become my God. And this stone that I have put as a pillar will be the house of God, and everything that you give me, I will make sure to tithe it to you."* **3731**

Jacob vowed a vow, saying, symbolizes a state of providence. *If God is with me and guards me on this way that I am walking* symbolizes a constant divine presence. *And gives me bread to eat* means to the point of uniting with divine goodness. *And clothing to wear* means uniting with divine truth. *And I return in peace to the house of my father* means to the point of complete union. *Jehovah will become my God* means that even his earthly divinity will be Jehovah. *And this stone that I have put as a pillar* symbolizes truth on the outermost level. *Will be the house of God* here as before symbolizes the Lord's kingdom on the outermost level of the divine design, which houses higher levels. *And everything that you give me, I will make sure to tithe it to you* means that the Lord did absolutely everything by his own divine power.

Jacob vowed a vow, saying, symbolizes a state of providence. This can be seen from the symbolism on an inner level of *vowing a vow* as wanting the Lord to provide, and consequently on the highest level, which deals with the Lord, as a state of providence. **3732**

The inner-level meaning of *vowing a vow* as wanting the Lord to provide comes from the presence in vows of a longing and desire for a wished-for event to occur and accordingly for the Lord to provide.

[When we make vows,] there is a setting of conditions and also some obligation on our part—something we undertake to do if we receive our wish. Jacob, for instance, promised that Jehovah would become his God, the stone he put as a pillar would be the house of God, and he would tithe everything given to him, if Jehovah guarded him on the way and gave him bread to eat and clothing to wear and he returned in peace to the house of his father.

This shows that vows in those days were specific promises people made, mostly to acknowledge God as their God if he provided their desires, and to repay him with some offering if he provided.

[2] This reveals plainly what the ancestors of the Jewish nation were like. At the current point, for instance, Jacob did not yet acknowledge Jehovah and was still choosing whether to acknowledge him or another as his God. This was a unique trait that that nation possessed all the way back to their forebears: the members each wanted to have their own god. If any of them worshiped Jehovah, it was only because they were worshiping some god called Jehovah, distinguished by this name from the gods of other nations. So their worship even under those circumstances was idolatrous. The adulation of a name alone, even if it is Jehovah's, is nothing but idolatry (§1094). People who call themselves Christians, for instance, and say they worship Christ but do not live by his commandments worship him in an idolatrous way because they worship only his name. It is a false Christ they worship, as said in Matthew 24:23, 24 (§3010).

3733   *If God is with me and guards me on this way that I am walking* symbolizes a constant divine presence. This can be seen from the symbolism of *God's being with* people and *guarding them on the way that they walk* as a constant divine presence. The clause has to do with the Lord; and the true, core essence of the Lord's life was Jehovah. So throughout his life, from infancy to the end, divinity was constantly present, right until his human nature became completely one with his divine nature.

3734   *And gives me bread to eat* means to the point of uniting with divine goodness, as established by the following: *Bread* symbolizes all heavenly and spiritual goodness received from the Lord and, in the highest sense, the Lord himself in regard to his divine goodness, as discussed in §§276, 680, 1798, 2165, 2177, 3464, 3478. And *eating* means being communicated, adopted, and united, as noted in §§2187, 2343, 3168, 3513 at the end, 3596.

3735   *And clothing to wear* means uniting with divine truth. This can be seen from the symbolism of *clothing* as truth (discussed in §§1073, 2576)—divine truth, in this case, since the focus is on the Lord—and from the symbolism of *wearing* it as making it his own and internalizing it.

The nature of the Word's inner meaning can be seen from this context and from the rest of the Word. Sometimes the literal meaning speaks of bread and clothing, occasionally as part of a story, as it does here in saying, "If God gives me bread to eat and clothing to wear." When it does, the angels with a person [reading it] do not think about bread but about a loving goodness, and in the highest sense about the Lord's divine goodness. They do not think about clothing but about truth, and in the highest sense about the Lord's divine truth. For them the kinds of things found in the literal meaning are merely springboards to thought about heavenly and divine subjects. The literal images are vessels on the outermost level of the divine design.

[2] So when we are in a reverent mood and think about bread, such as the bread in the Holy Supper or the daily bread mentioned in the Lord's Prayer, our thoughts about it serve the angels with us as a stimulus for thinking about a loving goodness received from the Lord. Angels pick up none of our thoughts about bread but think about goodness instead. That is what correspondence is like. Again, when we are in a reverent mood and think about clothing, angels think about truth. The same occurs with everything else in the Word.

This shows what kind of bond heaven and earth have through the Word: a bond that closely ties us to heaven by means of these correspondences and through heaven to the Lord. It occurs when we are reverently reading the Word, even though we are thinking only about the contents of its literal meaning. The reverence we feel actually results from the inflow of heavenly and spiritual thoughts and feelings as they exist with the angels.

[3] The Lord established the Holy Supper to create this kind of inflow and in the process unite us to himself. The passage describing it says in plain language that the bread and wine are the Lord. The Lord's body means his divine love and a reciprocal love in humankind, like that felt by heavenly angels. His blood also means his divine love and a reciprocal love in humankind, but the kind that exists in spiritual angels.

This shows how much divinity there is in each word of Scripture, even though people have no idea what it is or what it is like. Those who lived good lives when they were in the world, though, come into the knowledge and perception of all these things after death, because they then shed what is earthly and worldly and take on what is heavenly, including the spiritual and heavenly way of thinking that angels have.

And I return in peace to the house of my father means to the point of **3736** complete union. This can be seen from the fact that, applied to the Lord, his *father's house* means the divinity itself he had from the moment of conception. *Returning to* that house means returning to divine goodness itself, which is called the *Father*. (For this meaning of a father, see §3704.) Returning to that house obviously means being united.

The Lord meant the same thing when he said that he came from the Father and came into the world and that he was going back to the

Father. Coming from the Father meant that the Divine itself adopted a human nature. Coming into the world meant that he was like other people. Going to the Father meant that he had united his human nature with his divine nature.

That is the meaning of these words the Lord spoke in John:

> [What] if you see the Son of Humankind going up where he was before? (John 6:62)

In the same author:

> Jesus knew that the Father had given everything into his hands and that from God he had come and to God he would go. "Children, a short time yet I am with you; where I am going, you cannot come." (John 13:3, 33)

In the same author:

> "Now I go to him who sent me, but none of you asks me, 'Where are you going?' It profits you that I go, because if I did not go, the Paraclete would not come to you; but if I go, I will send him to you. There will be a little while when you will not see me and again a little while when you will see me, [because I go to the Father." Some of his disciples said to each other, "What is this that he is saying to us—'there will be a little while when you will not see me and again a little while when you will see me'] and 'because I go to the Father'?" (John 16:5, 7, 10, 16, 17)

In the same author:

> I came from the Father and have come into the world; again I leave the world and go to the Father. (John 16:28)

In these passages, going to the Father means uniting his human nature to his divine nature.

3737
Jehovah will become my God means that even his earthly divinity will be Jehovah. This can be seen from the sequence of ideas in the highest inner meaning, which deals with the uniting of the Lord's human side with his divine side. To see this meaning, you have to turn your thoughts away from Jacob's story and train them on the Lord's divine humanity— at this point on his earthly divinity, represented by Jacob.

True humanity, as stated several times before, consists of rationality (which is the same as the inner self) and earthliness (the outer self) [§§1940, 2106, 2183, 2194, 2625]. It also includes the body, which serves the earthly level as a means or outermost organ for living in the world. Through the earthly level it serves the rational level, and through this, the divine level.

The Lord came into the world to make everything human in himself divine, and to do so according to the divine plan. Jacob represents the Lord's earthly level; and in the highest sense Jacob's life as an immigrant represents the way the Lord made his earthly level divine. So the words *if I return in peace to my father's house, Jehovah will become my God* symbolize the uniting of the Lord's human side with his divine side. They also mean that even his earthly divinity would be Jehovah, because of the union of his divine with his human nature, and of his human with his divine.

By their oneness is not meant the oneness that exists between two distinct individuals joined only by love, like the union between parent and child, in which the parent loves the child and the child loves the parent, or like that between siblings or friends. It is a real merging into one, so that they are not two but one, as the Lord teaches in many places. Since they are one, everything human in the Lord is also the divine essence, or Jehovah; see §§1343, 1736, 2156, 2329, 2447, 2921, 3023, 3035.

And this stone that I have put as a pillar symbolizes truth on the outermost level, as established by the discussion above in §§3724, 3726, where the same words occur.

3738

Will be the house of God symbolizes the Lord's kingdom on the outermost level of the divine design, which houses higher levels. This too can be seen from the discussion above where the same words occur, at §3720, and also from remarks in §3721.

3739

Here is how the outermost level of the divine design provides a kind of home for higher levels: The Lord has set up a design in which higher levels flow into lower ones and present a general image of themselves there. So higher levels coexist on lower levels in a general form, arranged in order from the highest (which is the Lord) down. Consequently the inmost heaven is the most direct image of the Lord. This heaven is the heaven of innocence and peace, where the heavenly live, and since it is closest to the Lord, it is called his likeness.

The second heaven—the one that comes on the next, lower level— is the Lord's image because the attributes of the higher heaven present themselves there in a more general form.

The outermost heaven, which comes after the second, bears the same relation to it, because the particular qualities and the smallest details of each quality in the next higher heaven flow into the outermost heaven and present themselves there in a general, corresponding form.

[2] It is the same in us, because we were created and formed as a copy of the three heavens. What is inmost in us likewise flows into what is lower, which in turn flows into what is lowest or outermost. Our earthly or bodily level consists of this kind of inflow and confluence into lower elements and finally into the outermost. The result is a connection of outermost elements with that which is first. Without the connection, the outermost level of the divine design would not survive for even the smallest moment.

This shows what is meant by the statement that the outermost level of the divine design provides a kind of home for higher levels.

It is all the same whether you say higher and lower or inner and outer, because what is inward appears higher to human beings. That is why we put heaven up high, when it is actually within.

3740   *And everything that you give me, I will make sure to tithe it to you* means that the Lord did absolutely everything by his own divine power, as can be seen from the following: When mentioned in connection with the Lord, *giving* means that he gave to himself, as noted at the end of §3705; so it means that something came from his own power. And *tithing* and tithes symbolize good desires and true thoughts stored up by the Lord in our inner depths. This goodness is called a remnant, as discussed in §§576, 1738, 2280. In relation to the Lord, a remnant is divine goodness and divine truth that he acquired for himself by his own power; see §§1738, 1906.

The Universal Human
and What Corresponds to It (Continued)

3741   THE kingdom of heaven is like a single person because its individual parts correspond to the Lord alone, the only human, and specifically to his divine humanity (§§49, 288, 565, 1894). Because heaven corresponds with him and is his image and likeness, it is called a universal human. All the heavenly qualities of goodness and all the spiritual qualities of truth in heaven come from the Lord's divinity. All the angels there are forms—in other words, are substances shaped by their reception of divine traits from the Lord. What are called heavenly and spiritual qualities are the Lord's divine attributes received by angels when divine life and therefore divine light exist and change form in the angels who receive them.

[2] As a result, forms and substances in us that consist of matter share this characteristic but to a lesser degree, because they are less refined and more composite. They too are forms designed to receive heavenly and spiritual qualities, as is obvious from unmistakable signs. Take thought, for instance, which acts on the organic forms of the tongue to produce speech; or the moods of the lower mind, which reveal themselves in the face; or the will, which flows through the forms of the muscles into action; and so on. Thought and will, which produce these effects, are spiritual and heavenly qualities, but the forms or substances that receive them and put them into act are made of matter. Clearly the latter are formed exclusively for the reception of the former, so plainly they stem from the former, and if they did not, they could not possibly exist.

There is only one life force, which comes from the Lord alone, and angels, spirits, and people merely receive it. This I have learned from such plentiful experience that not a shadow of doubt remains. Heaven itself perceives that it is so. In fact, angels plainly sense *that* life flows in, *how* it flows in, and how much and what kind they receive. When they are receiving life to the full, they are happy and at peace. The rest of the time they are uneasy and somewhat anxious.

3742

Nevertheless they adopt the Lord's life so implicitly that they feel as though they live on their own, even though they know they do not. The ability to make the Lord's life their own comes from his love and mercy toward the whole human race. He wants to give himself and what is his to everyone, and actually does so to the extent that human beings receive him—that is, to the extent that they become his likenesses and images by living lives of goodness and truth. Because the Lord is constantly making this divine effort, people adopt his life as their own, as just mentioned.

People who do not love the Lord or their neighbor and consequently do not live good, true lives cannot acknowledge that there is only one life force, which flows in. Still less can they acknowledge that this life comes from the Lord. They always resent and in fact reject it when told they do not live on their own. Self-love is what causes this effect. In the other life they are shown and convinced by personal experience that they do not live on their own, and at that point they admit it is true. Amazingly, though, they afterward persist in their opinion, imagining

3743

that if they lived from another rather than themselves, all pleasure would disappear from their lives. They do not realize that the reality is just the opposite.

This is why the evil adopt evil as their own, because they do not believe it comes from hell, and why they cannot adopt goodness, because they believe goodness comes from themselves rather than from the Lord.

Still, the evil and even the hellish are forms that receive life from the Lord, but they are the kind of forms that reject, smother, or corrupt what is good and true. So in them, the goodness and truth springing from the Lord's life become evil and false. The situation resembles that with sunlight. Even though sunlight is uniformly white, it changes as it moves through various forms, or flows into them, producing both lovely, pleasant colors and ugly, unpleasant ones.

3744   This shows what heaven is like and why it is called a universal human; but the variations on a life of goodness and truth there are beyond number, reflecting different ways life is received from the Lord. The variations bear the exact same relationship to each other as the organs, limbs, and viscera in a person, which are formed in an endless variety of ways to receive life from the person's soul, or rather through the soul from the Lord. Yet although they vary so much, they still make up one individual.

3745   The amount and type of variety [in heaven] can be seen from the variety in the human body. People realize that one organ or limb is not like another. For example, they know that the organ of sight is not like the organ of hearing, and also not like the organ of smell, the organ of taste, or the organ of touch (which permeates the whole body). The same holds true for different limbs, like the arms, hands, hips, legs, and feet; for different internal organs, like those in the head (the cerebrum, cerebellum, medulla oblongata, and spinal medulla), together with all the component parts of the organs and viscera and the blood vessels and nerve fibers that make them up; for the organs of the body below the head, like the heart, lungs, stomach, liver, pancreas, spleen, intestines, mesentery, and kidneys; and for reproductive organs in both sexes. It is recognized that these all differ from each other in form and function to such a degree that they are completely unalike. The same is true of the forms within the forms, which also display such variety that not one form or part of a form resembles another precisely enough to be substituted for it without some kind of adjustment, however small.

All these body parts correspond to the heavens, but what is physical and matter-based in a person is heavenly and spiritual in the heavens. The correspondence is such that what is physical and material emerges into lasting existence from what is heavenly and spiritual.

Speaking generally, the variations mentioned above [§3744] are divided into those relating to features of the head, the chest, the abdomen, and the reproductive organs. They are also divided into those that are internal and those that are external, throughout the body.

3746

Several times I talked to spirits about the scholars of our day, saying, "They know nothing but the difference between the inner and the outer person, and this they know not from reflecting on their own inner thoughts and feelings but from the Lord's Word. Even so they do not know what the inner self is, and what is more, many of them doubt or deny it exists. That is because they do not live the life of the inner self but the life of the outer self. What leads them badly astray is the fact that brute animals appear to have the same organs, viscera, senses, appetites, and emotions they do.

3747

"Scholars know less about this than the uneducated do but seem to themselves to know much more. They argue about the interaction of the soul and body and even about the nature of the soul. But the uneducated know that their soul is their inner self, that their spirit is what will live on after physical death, and that this is the real self inside their body.

[2] "The educated are more likely than the uneducated to consider themselves the same as animals, to ascribe everything to nature and hardly anything to the Divine. They do not reflect on the fact that unlike heedless animals people can think about heaven and God, which lifts them out of themselves. They do not see that this enables them to unite with the Lord in love, so that they cannot help living forever after death.

"They are especially ignorant that everything in us is dependent through heaven on the Lord, that heaven is an all-encompassing person, and that everything in us and everything in the material world corresponds to this universal human.

"When they hear or read this, they may find it so puzzling that they reject it as a fabrication, if they cannot confirm it from experience. Likewise when they hear that we have three planes of life in us, just as there are three planes of life in heaven, or three heavens; or that we correspond to the three heavens in such a way that we are a kind of miniature portrait of heaven, when we live lives of goodness and truth; or that this life makes us an image of the Lord."

[3] I have been taught about these planes of life and learned that the outermost plane of life is the one called the outer or earthly self. This

self provides us with a similarity to animals in regard to our cravings and imaginings. The second level is the one called the inner or rational self, which raises us above animals. It enables us to think and will what is good and true and to control our earthly self. This we do by reining in and even rejecting our cravings and the delusions they produce, and by meditating on heaven and the Divine, which unthinking animals absolutely cannot do.

There is a third plane of life, of which humankind is deeply ignorant, but this is the plane through which the Lord acts on our rational mind, giving us the faculty of human thought, conscience, and a perception of what is good and true. Through this plane he also lifts us to himself.

These concepts, though, are remote from the thinking of modern scholars, who only dispute whether this is the way matters stand, all the while unable to tell whether it is, let alone what it means.

3748   There was a spirit, famous among the educated crowd when he lived in the world, whose talents were well honed when it came to proving what was false but quite dull when it came to proving what was good and true. He imagined he knew all there was to know, just as he had imagined earlier, in the world. People like him consider themselves very wise, believing that nothing escapes them; and they are the same in the next life as they were during bodily life. Every aspect of our lives—everything we love and yearn for—follows us and lodges in us as a soul lodges in its body, because we formed the character of our soul from it.

Now he was a spirit, and he came and talked with me. Considering his character, I asked who understands more, a person who knows a great deal of falsity or one who knows a little truth. He answered, "One who knows a little truth"—thinking that the falsity he knew was truth and that he was therefore wise.

[2] Then he wanted to debate about the universal human and its influence on everything in a person, but since he understood nothing about it, I said, "How do you see thought, which is spiritual, as manipulating the whole face to express itself there? How does it move all the organs of speech in specific response to a spiritual perception of that thought? How does the will move the muscles of the whole body and the thousands of nerve fibers scattered throughout it to a single action, when the moving force is spiritual but the thing being moved is physical?" He did not know what to answer.

Then I asked about impetus. "Do you know that impetus produces activity and motion? And that impetus clothes itself in activity and motion in order to come into being and last?" He said no.

"Then how can you want to debate," I asked, "when you do not even know the first thing about it? Debating is then like strewing dust that cannot hold together, and falsity scatters it so thoroughly that you end up knowing nothing and therefore believing nothing."

A spirit came to me unexpectedly, affecting my head—and spirits can be identified by their influence on various parts of the body. I asked who he was and where he came from. He kept quiet, but after a little while the angels with me said that he was delegated from the spirits accompanying a certain learned person alive in the world today who had sought greater fame as a scholar than others. I was then granted the opportunity to share in that person's thought through the spirit as an intermediary.

3749

I asked the spirit what picture the scholar could have of the universal human, its inflow, and the resulting correspondence [with the human body]. He said the scholar could not have any picture. I then asked what picture he had of heaven. The spirit said none, only disparaging concepts, such as the idea that the inhabitants would play songs of praise on musical instruments of the kind country folk use for making a sound.

And yet people esteem this man above others! They think he knows what spiritual inflow is, what the soul is, and how it interacts with the body. Maybe they even believe he knows best what heaven is.

This shows what people who teach others are like today. [Their teachings] consist of mere obstacles to belief in what faith teaches as good and true, even though they proclaim otherwise.

I received vivid demonstration of the way people picture heaven, even when they are believed to be in touch with heaven and influenced by it more than anyone else.

3750

Spirits who appear overhead are those who wanted to be worshiped as gods in the world, whose love for themselves was raised to its highest pitch by their increasing power and the license they believed this power gave them. Such people also hide themselves deceitfully under a guise of innocence and love for the Lord. They appear high overhead from fantasizing about their own loftiness, but in reality they live underfoot in hell.

[2] One of them lowered himself to me, and I heard from others that he had been a pope in the world. He talked with me ever so politely, speaking first of Peter and his keys, which he believed he himself possessed. When asked about his power to let anyone he wanted into heaven, his idea of heaven was so primitive that he portrayed it as a door providing entry. "I open it freely to the poor," he said, "but the rich were assessed, and the money they paid was holy."

"Do you think the people you let in there stay?"

"I don't know. If not, they leave."

"You cannot see their inner depths and tell whether they are deserving. Maybe they are robbers who ought to be in hell."

"I don't care. If they are not worthy, they can be thrown out," he said.

However, I taught him that Peter's keys mean the faith that comes of love and charity. Since only the Lord gives this faith, he alone is the one who lets people into heaven. No one comes into Peter's presence. "You are just an ordinary spirit," I said, "with no more authority than anyone else."

His only opinion about the Lord was that he ought to worship the Lord so long as the Lord gave him that authority. Otherwise (I sensed him thinking) he no longer needed to worship the Lord.

When I talked with him about the inner self, his mind had a filthy image of it.

[3] What free, full, satisfied breaths he drew as he sat on his throne in the consistory, believing his words to be inspired by the Holy Spirit—this was shown to me in a living way. He returned to the state he had experienced in the consistory (in the other life anyone can easily be brought back into a state he or she went through in the world, because the states of our life await each of us after death), and his breathing was communicated to me in the form it had then taken. It was pleasantly free, slow, regular, and deep, filling the chest. When he was contradicted, his breathing continued but produced a rolling, creeping sensation in his belly. When he thought his pronouncements divine, he perceived this from a type of breathing which was quieter and which assented, so to speak.

[4] Then I was shown who governs pontiffs of this kind; it was a horde of sirens overhead who had adopted a character and life devoted to worming their way into all kinds of emotions. Their urge was to dominate and control others, destroying all others for their own benefit. To them, holiness and innocence are simply a means. They are fearful and act cautiously, but given the opportunity they plunge into cruelty for selfish purposes, completely devoid of mercy.

Genesis 29

[Matthew 24:19–22]

A T the beginning of the previous chapter, Genesis 28, I explained the **3751** Lord's predictions in Matthew 24:15, 16, 17, 18 concerning the last days of the church [§§3650–3655]. To continue the pattern I will introduce this chapter by explaining the next verses, Matthew 24:19, 20, 21, 22, containing these words:

> But alas to those who are pregnant or nursing in those days! Pray, though, that your flight not happen in winter or on the Sabbath. For there will then be great affliction such as there has not been from the beginning of the world until now and will not come to be. And if those days were not shortened, no flesh would be rescued. Yet for the sake of the chosen, those days will be shortened. (Matthew 24:19, 20, 21, 22)

No one can possibly understand what these words mean without the **3752** light shed by the inner meaning. They do not refer to the destruction of Jerusalem, as is apparent from much of the chapter. Take these words: "If those days were not shortened, no flesh would be rescued, yet for the sake of the chosen, those days will be shortened." Consider later verses, too: "After the affliction of those days, the sun will go dark, and the moon will not shed its light; and the stars will fall down from the sky, and the powers of the heavens will be shaken. And then will appear the sign of the Son of Humankind, and they will see the Son of Humankind coming in the clouds of heaven with strength and glory" [Matthew 24:29, 30]. There are other examples as well.

The verses above also do not refer to the end of the world, and many parts of the same chapter make this clear, too, such as these words earlier on: "Those then on top of the house should not go down to take anything from their house, and those in the field should not turn back behind to take their clothes" [Matthew 24:20]. From the verses just now quoted: "Pray that your flight not happen in winter or on the Sabbath." And from what follows: "Two will then be in the field; one will be taken, the other left. Two grinding; one will be taken, the other left" [Matthew 24:40, 41].

Clearly the passage is about the last days of the church, or its devastation. The church is said to be devastated when it no longer has any neighborly love.

3753 Anyone who thinks reverently about the Lord, believing that he possessed divinity and spoke from the Divine, can see and believe that these words apply to the whole human race rather than one nation, and to its spiritual rather than a worldly condition. The same is true of everything else he taught and said. The Lord's words covered what has to do with his kingdom and the church, because these are divine and eternal.

People who believe this conclude that "Alas to those who are pregnant or nursing in those days" is not about people who are pregnant or nursing. They figure out that "Pray that your flight not happen in winter or on the Sabbath" is not about any flight from worldly foes; and so on.

3754 The previous verses spoke of three stages in the corruption of goodness and truth in the church. The current passage speaks of a fourth and final stage. In the first stage, people started to forget what was good and true and quarreled about it, which gave rise to falsity; see §3354. In the second, people despised and opposed what is good and true, and faith in the Lord gradually died out as neighborly love came to an end; see §§3487, 3488. In the third, the church was ruined in regard to its goodness and truth; see §§3651, 3652. The current verses accordingly focus on a fourth stage, in which goodness and truth are profaned. The fact that such a stage is depicted here can be seen from the inner meaning of the individual words, which is as follows.

3755 *But alas to those who are pregnant and nursing in those days* symbolizes people steeped in goodness that comes of love for the Lord and goodness that comes of innocence. "Alas" is a term symbolizing the danger of eternal damnation. Being pregnant means conceiving a goodness associated with heavenly love. Nursing means also conceiving a state of innocence. "Those days" symbolize states the church is in.

[2] *Pray, though, that your flight not happen in winter or on the Sabbath* means withdrawal from such things and prayer that this not happen too suddenly in a state of excessive cold or excessive heat. Flight means withdrawal from a state marked by goodness that comes of love and of innocence, mentioned just above. Flight in winter means withdrawal from those things in a state of excessive cold, the cold being a distaste for them generated by different kinds of self-love. Flight on the Sabbath means withdrawal from them in a state of excessive heat, the heat being a

sanctity that appears on the outside when self-love and materialism lie inside.

[3] *For there will then be great affliction such as there has not been from the beginning of the world until now and will not come to be* means corrupting and destroying goodness and truth in the church to the utmost, which is profanation. Profanation of what is holy brings on eternal death in a form much worse than that incurred by any other state of evil. The deeper the goodness and truth being profaned, the worse the death. The Christian church has been explicitly aware of these deeper levels of goodness and truth and has profaned them, so the text says, "Then there will be great affliction such as there has not been from the beginning of the world until now and will not come to be."

[4] *And if those days were not shortened, no flesh would be rescued; yet for the sake of the chosen, those days will be shortened* means drawing people in the church away from deeper levels of goodness and truth to shallower levels so that those who live good, true lives can still be saved. The shortening of the days symbolizes the condition of being drawn away. No flesh being rescued means that otherwise no one could be saved. The chosen symbolize people who live good, true lives.

It would be possible to demonstrate convincingly that this is the inner meaning of the words—that pregnant women symbolize people who at first adopt goodness; that women nursing babies symbolize those who adopt a state of innocence; that flight symbolizes withdrawal from such things; that winter symbolizes a distaste for those types of goodness, rising out of deeply ingrained self-love; and that flight on the Sabbath symbolizes profanation, which occurs when sanctity appears on the outside but self-love and materialism lurk within. However, since the same words and phrases come up from time to time in later chapters, it will be shown there that this is their symbolism, the Lord in his divine mercy willing. **3756**

Few know what the profanation of holy things is, but it can be seen from previous discussions and explanations of the subject, which you are invited to consider: People who know, acknowledge, and absorb what is good and true are capable of committing profanation; not so those who do not acknowledge, let alone those who do not know (593, 1008, 1010, 1059, 3398); consequently, people in the church are capable of profaning what is holy, but those who are outside it are not (2051). Those who are part of a heavenly religion are able to profane sacred **3757** goodness; those who are part of a spiritual religion are able to profane sacred truth (3399); so inner truth was not disclosed to the Jews, to prevent them from profaning it (3398); non-Christians are the least capable of all of committing profanation (2051); profanation is an intermingling and binding-together of goodness and evil, truth and falsity (1001, 1003, 2426); profanation was symbolized by the eating of blood, which was strictly forbidden in the Jewish religion (1003); accordingly, people are kept as far as possible from acknowledging and believing in goodness and truth unless they can hold on to them permanently (3398, 3402); for this reason they are kept in ignorance (301, 302, 303); for the same reason their worship turns shallow (1327, 1328). Deep truth is not revealed until the church has been devastated, because then goodness and truth can no longer be profaned (3398, 3399); so that is when the Lord first came into the world (3398); how dangerous it is to profane what is holy or to desecrate the Word (571, 582).

Genesis 29

1. And Jacob lifted his feet and went to the land of the children of the east.

2. And he looked, and here, a well in the field! And look: three droves of the flock there lying by it, because from that well they watered the droves. And a big stone was on the mouth of the well.

3. And all the droves would gather there, and they would roll the stone off the mouth of the well and water the flock and return the stone onto the mouth of the well to its place.

4. And Jacob said to them, "My brothers, where are you from?" And they said, "We are from Haran."

5. And he said to them, "Do you know Laban, the son of Nahor?" And they said, "We know him."

6. And he said to them, "Does he have peace?" And they said, "Peace; and look! Rachel his daughter comes with the flock."

7. And he said, "Here, now, the day is still at its height; it is not time for the livestock to be gathered. Water the flock and go, pasture it."

8. And they said, "We cannot, until all the droves are gathered and they roll the stone off the mouth of the well; and [then] we will water the flock."

9. He was still speaking with them when Rachel came with the flock that belonged to her father, because she was a shepherd.

10. And it happened as Jacob saw Rachel, the daughter of Laban, his mother's brother, and the flock of Laban, his mother's brother, that Jacob came up and rolled the stone off the mouth of the well and watered the flock of Laban, his mother's brother.

11. And Jacob kissed Rachel and lifted his voice and wept.

12. And Jacob told Rachel that he was her father's brother and that he was Rebekah's son. And she ran and told her father.

13. And it happened as Laban heard the report concerning Jacob, his sister's son, that he ran to meet him and hugged him and kissed him and brought him to his house, and [Jacob] told Laban all these words.

14. And Laban said to him, "Surely you are my bone and my flesh!" And [Jacob] resided with him a month of days.

15. And Laban said to Jacob, "Because you are my brother, should you also serve me for free? Tell me what your wages are."

16. And Laban had two daughters, the name of the older being Leah, and the name of the younger, Rachel.

17. And Leah's eyes were weak; and Rachel was beautiful in form and beautiful in appearance.

18. And Jacob loved Rachel and said, "I will serve you seven years for Rachel your younger daughter."

19. And Laban said, "It is better that I give her to you than give her to another man; stay with me."

20. And Jacob served for Rachel seven years, and they were in his eyes like several days, in his loving her.

21. And Jacob said to Laban, "Give me my woman, since my days have been fulfilled, and I will come to her."

22. And Laban gathered all the men of the place and made a banquet.

23. And it happened in the evening that he took Leah his daughter and brought her to [Jacob], and he came to her.

24. And Laban gave Zilpah his slave to her—to Leah his daughter for a slave.

25. And it happened in the morning that look: she was Leah! And [Jacob] said to Laban, "What is this you have done to me? Didn't I serve with you for Rachel? Then why have you cheated me?"

26. And Laban said, "It is not done this way in our region—to give the younger-born before the firstborn.

27. Fulfill this week and we will give you her as well, for the service that you serve with me yet another seven years."

28. And Jacob did so and fulfilled this week, and [Laban] gave him Rachel his daughter as his woman.

29. And Laban gave Bilhah his slave to Rachel his daughter as her slave.

30. And [Jacob] also came to Rachel and loved Rachel too, more than Leah, and served with [Laban] yet another seven years.

31. And Jehovah saw that Leah was hated and opened her womb; and Rachel was infertile.

32. And Leah conceived and bore a son and called his name Reuben, because she said, "Jehovah has seen my affliction, because now my husband will love me."

33. And she conceived again and bore a son and said, "Because Jehovah heard that I was hated and gave me this one too," and called his name Simeon.

34. And she conceived again and bore a son and said, "Now this time my husband will cling to me, because I have borne him three sons"; therefore she called his name Levi.

35. And she conceived again and bore a son and said, "This time I will acclaim Jehovah"; therefore she called his name Judah, and she stopped giving birth.

Summary

3758 IN the figure of Jacob, this chapter deals in its inner meaning with the Lord's earthly level and the way goodness-from-truth on that level united with a related form of goodness that had a divine origin—this goodness being meant by Laban. First they were united by a desire for outer truth (Leah) and then by a desire for inner truth (Rachel).

3759 The birth of four sons to Jacob by Leah later in the chapter in its highest sense depicts the climb from outer truth to inner goodness. In a representative sense it depicts the state of the church, which is such that it does not acknowledge or accept the inner but only the outer truth in the Word. That being the case, the church climbs to more inward levels in this order: First it acquires the truth called religious truth. Then it carries out that truth. From this it develops neighborly love. Last of all it receives heavenly love. These four planes are symbolized by Jacob's four sons with Leah: Reuben, Simeon, Levi, and Judah.

Inner Meaning

GENESIS 29:1. *And Jacob lifted his feet and went to the land of the children of the east.* **3760**

Jacob lifted his feet symbolizes elevation of the earthly level. *And went to the land of the children of the east* means toward the truth that comes of love.

Jacob lifted his feet symbolizes elevation of the earthly level. This can **3761** be seen from the symbolism of *lifting* as elevating and from that of *feet* as the earthly level (discussed below). The elevation symbolized here is what the chapter is focusing on: the climb from outer truth to inner goodness. In the highest sense it is telling how the Lord raised his earthly level all the way to divinity in accord with the ordained plan, climbing step by step from outer truth to inner goodness. In a representative sense it is telling how the Lord renews our earthly part when he regenerates us in accord with the same plan.

People who are being reborn as adults follow the process described in the inner meaning of the current chapter and the chapters that follow, but not many know this. One reason they do not know is that few reflect on it. Another is that few today are capable of rebirth, because these are the church's final hours, when there is no longer any neighborly love or consequently any faith. As a result, people do not even know what faith is (despite the lip service everyone pays to the idea that faith saves us), let alone what neighborly love is. When people know only the terms for these concepts and not the real nature of them, the result is the one just mentioned: few can reflect on the process we follow in being renewed or reborn, and few can be reborn.

[2] Since the current theme is the earthly level, and Jacob represents it, the text says not that he *got up* and went to the land of the children of the east but that he lifted his feet. Both symbolize elevation. (For this

symbolism of getting up, [or rising,] see §§2401, 2785, 2912, 2927, 3171.)
The use of *lifting the feet* here has to do with the earthly plane, because *feet*
symbolize that plane (see §§2162, 3147). Feet symbolize the earthly plane
and its contents because of correspondence with the universal human,
which is currently being discussed at the ends of the chapters. Individuals in the universal human who belong to the region of the lower leg are
those who enjoy earthly light but not much spiritual light. As a result,
the parts at the bottom of the lower leg, such as the foot and the heel,
symbolize the very lowest contents of the earthly plane (see §259). So a
shoe, which the Word also mentions several times, symbolizes the earthly,
bodily level, which is the outermost level (§1748).

3762   *And went to the land of the children of the east* means toward the truth
that comes of love, namely, elevation toward it, as can be seen from the
symbolism of the *land of the children of the east*. Aram (Syria) plainly was
called the land of the children of the east, because Aram was where Jacob
fled; see also §3249. Broadly speaking, Syria symbolizes knowledge of what
is good (as shown in §§1232, 1234), but in specific, Aram-naharaim, or
"Syria of the Rivers," symbolizes knowledge of truth (§§3051, 3664). The
current verse refers to the place Jacob went as the land of the children of
the east rather than Aram or Syria in order to symbolize what this whole
chapter is about: climbing to the truth that comes of love.

"Truth that comes of love" is a term for the truth I have referred
to elsewhere as heavenly truth [§§1465–1474, 1494–1497, 1545, 2069,
3688]; it consists of knowledge about charity toward our neighbor and
about love for the Lord. In the highest sense, which treats of the Lord,
it means the truth that comes of divine love. [2] This truth about charity toward our neighbor and love for the Lord is truth we have to learn
before we can be reborn. We also have to acknowledge and believe it.
The more we acknowledge and believe it and absorb it into our lives,
the more we regenerate and find it implanted in our earthly part, which
acts as soil for it. It is planted there first by instruction from our parents and teachers, then by instruction from the Lord's Word, and then
by personal reflection on what we have learned. However, these things
simply store the truth in our earthly memory among the religious concepts there. We do not acknowledge, believe, or absorb it unless we
live by it. When we do, it starts to affect us, and the more it affects us
because of the way we live, the more it is implanted in the soil of our
earthly level. Truth that is not implanted this way does stay with us,

but only as some secondhand knowledge in our memory. It is useless except as something for us to talk about, something to help us build a reputation in order to gain wealth and position. It has not yet been implanted.

[3] The symbolism of the *land of the children of the east* as the truth that comes of love—that is, a knowledge of truth that moves in the direction of goodness—can be seen from the following: *Children,* [or sons,] symbolize truth, as discussed in §§489, 491, 533, 1147, 2623, and the *east* symbolizes love, as discussed in §§101, 1250, 3249. Their *land* means the soil in which the truth is planted.

There are also other scriptural passages showing that *children of the east* means people with a knowledge of truth and goodness and consequently with the truth that comes of love. One such passage occurs in 1 Kings:

> Solomon's wisdom multiplied *beyond the wisdom of all the children of the east* and beyond all the wisdom of the Egyptians. (1 Kings 4:30)

The wisdom of the children of the east symbolizes deep knowledge of truth and goodness and therefore people with this knowledge. The wisdom of the Egyptians, on the other hand, symbolizes the study of that knowledge as a set of facts, which is a step lower. Egyptians symbolize factual knowledge in general; see §§1164, 1165, 1462. [4] In Jeremiah:

> This is what Jehovah has said: "Rise, go up against Kedar; lay waste to the *children of the east.* [Others] will take their tents and flocks; [others] will take their tent curtains and all their vessels and their camels." (Jeremiah 49:28, 29)

The meaning of children of the east as people with a knowledge of goodness and truth can be seen, for example, from the statement that [others] would take their tents and flocks, their tent curtains, all their vessels, and their camels. Tents symbolize sacred goodness (§§414, 1102, 2145, 2152, 3312). Flocks symbolize good done out of neighborly love (343, 2566). Tent curtains symbolize holy truth (2576, 3478). Vessels symbolize both religious truth and secular facts (3068, 3079). And camels symbolize facts in general (3048, 3071, 3143, 3145). So the children of the east mean people who possess these entities—in other words, people with a knowledge of what is good and true.

[5] The sages from eastern parts who came to Jesus when he was born hailed from the people called the children of the east, as can be seen from

the consideration that they knew the Lord would be born; and from a star that appeared to them in the east they learned of his Coming. Matthew says this about them:

> When Jesus was born in Bethlehem of Judea—here, *sages from eastern parts* came into Jerusalem, saying, "Where is the one born king of the Jews? Because we have seen his star in the east and have come to worship him." (Matthew 2:1, 2)

The children of the east, who were from Syria, had received this prophecy long before, as Balaam's prophecy in Moses about the Lord's Coming shows:

> I see him, but not now; I view him, but he is not near. *A star will rise* out of Jacob, and a scepter will spring up from Israel. (Numbers 24:17)

The following words in Moses make it clear that Balaam was from the land of the children of the east, or Syria:

> Balaam uttered his pronouncement and said, "*From Syria* has Balak brought me—from the *mountains of the east.*" (Numbers 23:7)

The sages who came to Jesus when he was born are called magi, or magicians, but that is what the wise were called in those days, as is indicated in many passages, such as Genesis 41:8; Exodus 7:11; Daniel 2:27; 4:6, 7; 1 Kings 4:30; and in various places in the Prophets.

[6] In an opposite sense, the children of the east symbolize a knowledge of evil and falsity and therefore people with that knowledge, as can be seen in Isaiah:

> Ephraim's envy will withdraw, and Judah's foes will be cut off. They will fly against the shoulder of the Philistines toward the sea, and together they will plunder the *children of the east.* (Isaiah 11:[13,] 14)

In Ezekiel:

> Against the children of Ammon: Look: I have handed you over to the *children of the east* as an inheritance, and they will place their rows [of tents] in you. (Ezekiel 25:4, 10)

In Judges:

> When Israel sowed, Midian also went up, as did Amalek and the *children of the east,* and they went up over him. (Judges 6:3)

Midian stands for people who are immersed in falsity because they do not live good lives (§3242). Amalek stands for people immersed in a falsity that they use in attacking truth (§1679). The children of the east stand for people with a knowledge of falsity.

Genesis 29:2, 3. *And he looked, and here, a well in the field! And look: three droves of the flock there lying by it, because from that well they watered the droves; and a big stone was on the mouth of the well. And all the droves would gather there, and they would roll the stone off the mouth of the well and water the flock and return the stone onto the mouth of the well to its place.* **3763**

He looked symbolizes a perception. *Here, a well* symbolizes the Word. *In the field* means for the churches. *And look: three droves of the flock there lying by it* symbolizes what is holy in the churches and in their teachings. *Because from that well they watered the droves* means that from it comes knowledge. *And a big stone was on the mouth of the well* means that it was closed up. *And all the droves would gather there* means it is the source of all the churches and their teachings. *And they would roll the stone off the mouth of the well* means that they opened it. *And water the flock* means that it yielded doctrine. *And return the stone onto the mouth of the well to its place* means that it was closed in the meantime.

He looked symbolizes a perception. This is established by the symbolism of *looking* [or seeing] as perceiving, which will be discussed later on in this chapter, at verse 32, in the treatment of Reuben, whose name came from [a word for] seeing. **3764**

Here, a well symbolizes the Word. This can be seen from the symbolism of a *well* as the Word and also as doctrine from the Word (discussed in §§2702, 3096, 3424). The Word is called a well here because the topic of discussion is the earthly plane, which, viewed on its own, grasps the Word only according to its literal meaning. The Word is instead called a spring when the topic is the rational mind, which enables us to perceive the Word according to its inner meaning. **3765**

In the field means for the churches. This is established by the symbolism of a *field* as a church's goodness (discussed in §2971). In the Word, a church is symbolized by the land, the ground, and a field, but in different ways. A field means a church because the church resembles a field in receiving seeds of goodness and truth. After all, the church has the Word, which gives it existence. Because of this, anything *in* a field— sowing, harvest, a crop, wheat, barley, and so on—also symbolizes some facet of a church, again with differences. **3766**

3767   *And look: three droves of the flock there lying by it* symbolizes what is holy in the churches and in their teachings. This can be seen from the symbolism of *three* as something holy (discussed in §§720, 901) and from the symbolism of *droves of the flock* as that which characterizes the church and therefore as doctrinal teachings. Narrowly speaking, a flock symbolizes people in the church, who learn about and absorb the good done out of neighborly love and the truth taught by faith. The shepherd, [or pastor,] is then the one who teaches about these things. Broadly speaking, though, a flock symbolizes everyone devoted to goodness, so it symbolizes people belonging to the Lord's church throughout the world. And since religious teachings are what lead them all to goodness and truth, a flock also symbolizes such teachings.

A given word in its inner sense means both that which gives people such and such a character and the people who have that character. The kind of person we are is viewed in terms of that which makes us so. [2] That is why I say from time to time that names symbolize attributes and also people who have those attributes. For instance, Tyre and Sidon symbolize a knowledge of what is good and true, and also the people who have that knowledge [§§2576, 3448]. Egypt symbolizes secular learning [§1462], and Assyria, the ability to reason, but they also mean people with that learning or this ability. And so on. However, angels in heaven talk in terms of attributes without picturing individuals, so they speak in universal terms. One reason is that this enables them to express countless things at once. More importantly, though, they ascribe everything good and true to the Lord and none of it to themselves, so the thoughts behind their words focus on the Lord alone.

This explains why a flock is said to symbolize the churches and their teachings as well.

The droves of the flock are described as *lying by the well* because doctrinal teachings come from the Word. A well means the Word, as noted just above at §3765.

3768   *Because from that well they watered the droves* means that from it (the Word) comes knowledge. This is established by the symbolism of a *well* as the Word (discussed just above in §3765), by that of *watering* or giving a drink to as teaching (discussed in §3069), and by that of *droves* as a knowledge of doctrine (also discussed just above, in §3767). This shows that *from the well they watered the droves* means that from the Word comes knowledge about the doctrines concerning goodness and truth.

In the next part of Jacob's story, the highest meaning deals with the Lord and the way he made his earthly level divine, the current chapter describing the start of the process. The inner, representative meaning deals with people who are being reborn and the way the Lord renews their earthly self, the current chapter describing the start of the process. So this verse talks about the Word and the doctrine that comes from it, because it is through doctrine from the Word that we start to regenerate.

Since such things are symbolized by the well and the three droves of the flock, these details make part of the story. If they did not have the symbolism described, they would not rate any mention in the Word of God. What they enfold is evident: that all knowledge of and doctrine concerning goodness and truth comes from the Word.

[2] The earthly self, admittedly, can learn and even perceive what is good and true, but only on the physical and civic plane, not on a spiritual plane. The latter has to come from revelation and therefore from the Word. For example, the rationality we all have can show us that we ought to love our neighbor and worship God, but we cannot learn *how* to love our neighbor or worship God except from the Word. So we have no other way of knowing what is spiritually good and true. Take the concept that goodness itself is our neighbor, that people with goodness are consequently our neighbor, and that they are our neighbor according to the goodness they have. Goodness, then, is our neighbor, because the Lord is present in it, and we love the Lord by loving what is good.

[3] Again, people who do not have the Word cannot know that all goodness comes from the Lord, that it flows into us and creates a desire for goodness, or that this desire is called charity. People who do not have the Word also cannot know who the God of the universe is—that he is the Lord. This is hidden from them; and yet the feeling called charity at its deepest level has to center on the Lord, with the result that goodness at its deepest level has to center on him. This shows what spiritual goodness is, which can be known only from the Word.

As for non-Christians, they lack this knowledge as long as they are in the world, but if they live among each other in mutual kindness, they develop the ability to be taught such things in the other world and to accept and absorb them readily. See §§2589–2604.

And a big stone was on the mouth of the well means that it (the Word) **3769** was closed up, as can be seen without explanation.

The Word is said to be closed up when people take it in a purely literal sense and accept everything they find there as doctrine. It is still more tightly closed when they acknowledge as doctrine what panders to the cravings of self-love and materialism, because this in particular rolls a big stone onto the mouth of the well—in other words, closes the

Word. Then they do not know and do not want to know that the Word has any inner meaning, even though they can see it from a large number of passages explaining the literal meaning in terms of its inner meaning. They can see the same thing from the fact that they use various interpretations to relate the Word's whole literal meaning to the church's accepted doctrines.

[2] What it means to say the Word is closed is especially clear to see from Jews, who interpret absolutely everything in a literal way, which leads them to believe they were chosen above everyone else in the whole world. They believe that the Messiah will come to lead them into the land of Canaan and raise them up above all other nations and peoples of the lands. They are steeped in earthly, bodily kinds of love, which by their very nature completely close off the inner depths of the Word. As a result they do not yet know whether there is a heavenly kingdom, whether they will live on after death, what the inner self is, not even that a spiritual dimension exists, let alone that the Messiah has come to save people's souls. It is also fairly plain to see that the Word is closed to them from their failure to accept any Christian doctrine despite the fact that they live among Christians. As Isaiah says:

> "You are to tell this people, 'Listen—listen!—and do not understand; and see—see!—and do not know.' Make the heart of this people fat and make their ears heavy and smear their eyes." And I said, "How long, Lord?" and he said, "Until the cities have been devastated (till there is not a resident), and the houses (till there is not a [single] person), and the ground has been devastated to become a desert." (Isaiah 6:9, 10, 11; Matthew 13:14, 15; John 12:40, 41)

[3] The more we wallow in love for ourselves and love of worldly gain and in the cravings they produce, the more the Word is closed to us. These kinds of love make personal interest the goal, and this goal kindles the flame of earthly illumination while it douses the flame of heavenly light. It gives us sharp vision into everything connected with our personal and material advantage and no vision at all into anything connected with the Lord and his kingdom. Under those circumstances people can still read the Word, but only with the aim of amassing influence and wealth, with the intent of being seen, from custom and therefore habit, or out of devotion, but not for the purpose of reforming their life.

The Word is closed to them in different ways. Some of them have no desire to see anything but what their doctrines teach, whatever that may be. [4] For instance, if you tell them that the power to open and close heaven was given not to Peter but to the faith that is born of love (which is what Peter's keys symbolize), they cannot possibly acknowledge it, because self-love and greed prevent them. If you say people should not worship saints, only the Lord, they do not accept it. If you say that the bread and wine in the Holy Supper mean the Lord's love for the whole human race and the love we return to him, they do not believe it. If you say that faith accomplishes nothing unless it is put into action—that is, unless it becomes neighborly love—they turn it upside down. And so on.

People like this cannot see a single truth in the Word, and do not want to, but stubbornly cling to their creed. They are unwilling even to hear that there is an inner meaning containing the Word's holiness and glory. In fact, when they hear it exists, the mere mention is so repellent to them that it turns their stomach.

Consequently the Word is closed off to them, even though in reality it offers access all the way to heaven and through heaven to the Lord. It is closed to people only in the degree that they make the evils of self-love and materialism their life goals and as a result adopt false principles.

This shows what is meant by the statement that a big stone was on the mouth of the well.

And all the droves would gather there means it is the source of all the churches and their teachings. This can be seen from the symbolism of *droves* as the churches and the churches' doctrines (discussed above in §§3767, 3768). Their *gathering there* means that they come from the Word. **3770**

And they would roll the stone off the mouth of the well means that they opened it. This can be seen from remarks just above at §3769 about the big stone on the mouth of the well as meaning that the Word was closed up. Clearly, then, *they would roll the stone off the mouth of the well* means that they opened it. **3771**

And water the flock means that it yielded doctrine. This can be seen from the symbolism of *watering* or giving a drink as teaching (discussed in §§3069, 3768) and from that of a *flock* as people with the goodness and truth belonging to faith (discussed in §§343, 3767). Watering it, then, means teaching them from the Word and therefore means doctrine. **3772**

3773   *And return the stone onto the mouth of the well to its place* means that it was closed in the meantime. This is evident from remarks at §§3769, 3771 about the stone on the mouth of the well.

A word about the fact that the Word was opened to the churches and then closed: When a church is first being established, the people in it initially find the Word closed. Then the Lord in his providence opens it up to them and from it they learn that all doctrine is founded on two commandments: to love the Lord above all and to love their neighbor as themselves. When they make these two commandments their goals, the Word opens up, because all the Law and all the Prophets—the whole Word—depend on them. In fact, everything comes from them and therefore relates back to them. Since people then hold truth and goodness as their principles, they are enlightened regarding everything they see in the Word. The Lord is then present with them through his angels, teaches them (though they do not know it), and leads them to a life of truth and goodness.

[2] This phenomenon is visible in all the churches. In their infancy they have been as described: the people in them worshiped the Lord with love and loved their neighbor with all their heart.

As time passes, though, they move away from these two precepts and turn from a loving and charitable goodness to considerations that are said to compose faith. So they turn from life to doctrine, and the more they do so, the more the Word closes.

That is the inner-level symbolism of the words *Here, a well in the field! And look: three droves of the flock there lying by it, because from that well they watered the droves; and a big stone was on the mouth of the well. And all the droves would gather there, and they would roll the stone off the mouth of the well and water the flock and return the stone onto the mouth of the well to its place.*

3774   Genesis 29:4, 5, 6. *And Jacob said to them, "My brothers, where are you from?" And they said, "We are from Haran." And he said to them, "Do you know Laban, the son of Nahor?" And they said, "We know him." And he said to them, "Does he have peace?" And they said, "Peace; and look! Rachel his daughter comes with the flock."*

Jacob said to them symbolizes truth that comes of goodness. *My brothers, where are you from?* means, what was the source of the neighborly love there? *And they said, "We are from Haran,"* means it was from goodness of the same stock. *And he said to them, "Do you know Laban, the son of Nahor?"* means, did they have goodness from that stock? *And they said, "We know him,"* means yes. *And he said to them, "Does he have peace?"* means, did it not come from the Lord's kingdom? *And they said, "Peace,"* means yes. *And look! Rachel his daughter* symbolizes a desire for inner truth. *Comes with the flock* symbolizes deeper teachings.

Jacob said to them symbolizes truth that comes of goodness. This can be seen from the representation of *Jacob* as the Lord's earthly divinity, discussed earlier.

Since absolutely everything everywhere relates to goodness and truth (§§3166, 3513, 3519), so do the contents of the earthly level. When we are being reborn, goodness and truth on our earthly level is in a different state at the beginning than in the middle of the process or at the end. So Jacob's representation of truth and goodness on the earthly plane depends on the stage. Here he represents the truth that comes of goodness on that plane.

Individually explaining all the variations wherever they occur would cast darkness over the whole subject, especially in people who see no clear distinction between truth and goodness, let alone the truth that leads to goodness and the truth that emerges from goodness.

My brothers, where are you from? means, what was the source of the neighborly love there? This can be seen from the symbolism of *brothers* as people with goodness, and therefore as goodness itself, and therefore as love for others (discussed in §§367, 2360, 3303, 3459); and from the meaning of *where are you from?* as what is the source?

This provides fresh evidence that when the literal meaning contains a question addressed to specific individuals, the idea expressed in the inner meaning is not narrowed down to anyone. When the narrative details of the literal meaning leave us and pass into heaven, they fade into nothing among the angels there. This shows that Jacob's question to the men of Haran, "My brothers, where are you from?" means, what was the source of the neighborly love there?

[2] Here is the situation: Love for others that looks like love on the outside is not always love on the inside. Its ultimate purpose reveals its character and source. Neighborly love that has personal interest and worldly advantage as its purpose is not love, viewed inwardly. It should not even be called love. In contrast, neighborly love that has one's fellow humans, the common good, heaven, and therefore the Lord as its purpose is neighborly love itself. It harbors a heartfelt desire to do good, so it contains life's highest pleasure, which in the next world becomes a blessedness.

It is tremendously important for us to learn this, so that we see what the Lord's kingdom in us is.

An inquiry into this neighborly love, or this goodness, is the theme of the current verses. The first question concerns the source of the love there [on the earthly plane], as symbolized by "My brothers, where are you from?"

3777   *And they said, "We are from Haran,"* means it was from goodness of the same stock. This can be seen from the symbolism of *Haran* as goodness branching off from the same stock (dealt with in §3612).

3778   *And he said to them, "Do you know Laban, the son of Nahor?"* means, did they have goodness from that stock? This can be seen from the representation of *Laban* as goodness branching off from the same stock (discussed in §§3612, 3665) and from that of *Nahor* as the shared stock from which the goodness meant by Laban grew. *Knowing* in an inner sense means having that origin, as the thread of the meaning shows.

A few words should be said about the representation of Nahor, Bethuel, and Laban as a side branch of goodness. Terah, the father of three sons, Abram, Nahor, and Haran (Genesis 11:27), represents a common trunk from which various religions grew. Terah himself was an idolater, it must be said, but representations do not relate to a figure's personality, only to some spiritual quality (see §1361). The representative Jewish religion started with Abraham and was established among the descendants he had through Jacob, so Terah and his three sons took on the representation of [other] religions. Abram took on that of a genuine religion, as it exists with people who have the Word. His brother Nahor, however, took on that of religion as it exists among nations that do not have the Word. The Lord's church is spread all over the globe, and exists among non-Christians who live in charity, as discussions about them throughout this work have shown.

[2] That is why Nahor, his son Bethuel, and Bethuel's son Laban represent goodness branching off to the side from the same trunk, or the goodness in people who make up the Lord's church among non-Christians.

This goodness differs from goodness growing directly out of the same stock in that the truth attached to it is not genuine. Most of this truth consists of superficial appearances called illusions of the senses, because non-Christians do not have the Word to enlighten them. In its essence goodness is uniform, admittedly, but it takes its character from the truth implanted in it and in the process becomes differentiated.

The truth that appears true to non-Christians includes the following generalities: They worship a God, from whom they seek what seems good to them and to whom they attribute this goodness. During life in the world they do not know that this God is the Lord. To this God, in the form of various images (which they consider holy), they offer their devotions. Not to mention many other things. These notions do not prevent them from being saved just as Christians are, as long as they live lives of love for their God and love for their neighbor. Doing so gives them the ability to accept deeper truth in the other world; see §§932, 1032, 1059, 2049, 2051, 2284, 2589–2604, 2861, 2863, 3263.

This shows what goodness branching off from the same stock means. Nahor represents people outside the church whose goodness makes them part of the fellowship (see §§2863, 2866, 2868). Bethuel represents goodness among people outside the church who belong to a first category (§§2865, 3665). Laban represents a desire for superficial, tactile goodness, and strictly speaking, represents goodness that branches off from a shared stock (§§3612, 3665).

[3] The very first thing this kind of goodness does is to serve as a means for us to acquire spiritual goodness. It is a shallow, tactile kind of goodness deriving from superficial appearances, which are actually illusions of the senses, and in our youth we do not acknowledge anything else as true or good. Even if we are taught what inner goodness and truth are, we do not have any other notion of them than a physical one. Since our first notions are physical, this kind of goodness and truth is an initial means for introducing deeper truth and goodness. This is the secret represented here by Jacob and Laban.

And they said, "We know him," means yes, as is clear without explanation.

3779

And he said to them, "Does he have peace?" means, did it (the goodness) not come from the Lord's kingdom? This can be seen from the symbolism of *peace,* dealt with below.

3780

On the story level, it is Laban's peace that is being inquired after, but on an inner level it is the peace belonging to the goodness represented by Laban. Laban means goodness branching off from a shared stock—in other words, goodness as it exists among nations in the broader church, or the Lord's kingdom (see just above at §3778). Clearly, then, the question means, did it not come from the Lord's kingdom?

[2] As for *peace,* on the highest level it symbolizes the Lord himself, so on an inward level it symbolizes his kingdom. Peace is the Lord's divine nature intimately affecting the goodness of the people in his kingdom.

This symbolism of peace can be seen from many passages in the Word, such as the following one in Isaiah:

> A child has been born for us, a son has been given to us, on whose shoulder will be sovereignty; and his name will be called Miraculous, Counselor, God, Hero, Eternal Father, *Prince of Peace.* Of the increase of [his] sovereignty and *peace* there will not be an end, on the throne of David and on his kingdom. (Isaiah 9:6, 7)

Obviously the Prince of Peace stands for the Lord. The increase of [his] sovereignty and peace stands for attributes of his kingdom and accordingly for the kingdom itself. In the same author:

> The work of justice will be *peace,* and the labor of justice will be *rest* and *safety* forever. And my people will live *in a dwelling of peace.* (Isaiah 32:17, 18)

This is about the Lord's kingdom, in which peace, rest, and safety come one after the other. A dwelling of peace stands for heaven. [3] In the same author:

> The *angels of peace* weep bitterly. The paths have been devastated; the traveler on the way has ceased. (Isaiah 33:7, 8)

The angels of peace stand for inhabitants of the Lord's kingdom, consequently for the kingdom itself, and in the highest sense for the Lord. "The paths have been devastated, and the traveler on the way has ceased" means that there is no longer any truth anywhere. For the meaning of paths and ways as truth, see §§627, 2333. In the same author:

> How gratifying on the mountains are the feet of the one who brings good news, *who lets people hear about peace,* who says to Zion, "Your monarch reigns!" (Isaiah 52:7)

Bringing good news and letting people hear about peace means [telling about] the Lord's kingdom. In the same author:

> The mountains will withdraw and the hills recede, but my mercy will not withdraw from you, and *my compact of peace* will not recede. (Isaiah 54:10)

In the same author:

> The *way of peace* they do not know. Nor is there judgment in their course. (Isaiah 59:8)

In Jeremiah:

> "I will *gather my peace away* from this people," says Jehovah; "[I will gather away] compassion and mercy." (Jeremiah 16:5)

[4] In the same author:

> The *peaceful sheepfolds* have been laid waste because of Jehovah's burning heat. (Jeremiah 25:37)

In the same author:

> The prophet who *prophesies of peace*—when Jehovah's word comes [to pass], that prophet will be recognized, that Jehovah sent him. (Jeremiah 28:9)

In the same author:

> "I know the plans that I am planning for you," says Jehovah; "*plans of peace.*" (Jeremiah 29:11)

In Haggai:

> Greater will the glory of this later house be than that of the earlier, because in this place I will *put peace.* (Haggai 2:9)

In Zechariah:

> *The seed of peace they will be.* The grapevine will yield its fruit, and the earth will yield its produce, and the heavens will yield their dew. (Zechariah 8:12)

In David:

> Guard uprightness and see what is correct, because *a man's final possession is peace.* (Psalms 37:37)

In Luke:

> Jesus said to his disciples, "Whatever house you enter, first say, '*Peace to this house,*' and if a *child of peace* is there, *your peace* will rest on it. But if not, it will return upon you." (Luke 10:5, 6)

In John:

> *Peace* I leave to you; *my peace* I give to you. Not as the world gives do I give to you. (John 14:27)

In the same author:

> Jesus said, "I have said these things to you so that *in me you may have peace.*" (John 16:33)

[5] In the highest sense of all these passages, peace symbolizes the Lord, and in a representative sense it symbolizes his kingdom and the goodness he bestows on it. So it symbolizes the divine quality that flows into what is good, or into good emotions, which causes joy and happiness to well up from deep within.

This clarifies what is meant by these words of blessing in Numbers 6:26: "Jehovah will lift his face toward you and *give you peace.*" It also clarifies the meaning of the ancient traditional greeting *Peace to you!*—the same greeting the Lord spoke to his apostles in John 20:19, 21, 26. See further remarks on peace in §§92, 93, 1726, 2780, 3170, 3696.

3781 *And they said, "Peace,"* means yes, as is evident without explanation, since it is an affirmative answer.

3782 *And look! Rachel his daughter* symbolizes a desire for inner truth. This can be seen from the representation of *Rachel* as a desire for inner truth and from that of Leah as a desire for outer truth, which are treated of in what follows.

3783 *Comes with the flock* symbolizes deeper teachings. This can be seen from the symbolism of a *flock* as the church and also as its teachings (discussed in §§3767, 3768, 3772), and in this case as deeper teachings since Rachel is the one said to be coming with the flock.

3784 Genesis 29:7, 8. *And he said, "Here, now, the day is still at its height; it is not time for the livestock to be gathered. Water the flock and go, pasture it." And they said, "We cannot, until all the droves are gathered and they roll the stone off the mouth of the well, and [then] we will water the flock."*

He said, "Here, now, the day is still at its height," means that this state was now progressing. *It is not time for the livestock to be gathered* means that the goodness and truth in the churches and in their teachings had not yet formed a single whole. *Water the flock and go, pasture it* means that a few would be taught from [the Word] anyway. *And they said, "We cannot, until all the droves are gathered,"* means that they ought to come together. *And they roll the stone off the mouth of the well* means that this brings the Word's contents out in the open. *And we will water the flock* means that they are then instructed.

3785 *He said, "Here, now, the day is still at its height,"* means that this state was now progressing. This can be seen from the symbolism of a *day* as a state (discussed in §§23, 487, 488, 493, 893, 2788, 3462). *Here, now, it is still at its height* means that it was now progressing, as the series of ideas shows.

It is not time for the livestock to be gathered means that the goodness and truth in the churches and in their teachings had not yet formed a single whole. This can be seen from the general symbolism of *time* as a state (discussed in §§2625, 2788, 2837, 3254, 3356), from the symbolism of being *gathered* as forming a single whole, and from the general symbolism of *livestock* as the goodness and truth of the churches and their teachings. The reason livestock symbolize these in a general way is that in the rituals of the representative religion, and in the Word, animals mean different kinds of desire for goodness and truth, as is shown by the explanations in §§45, 46, 142, 143, 246, 714, 715, 776, 1823, 2179, 2180, 2781, 3218, 3519. Since goodness and truth are religious, doctrinal matters and are the focus of the inner meaning, "It is not time for the livestock to be gathered" clearly means that goodness and truth in the churches and in their teachings have not yet formed a single whole.

Here is how matters stand in regard to the representative meaning of these words: People who are being reborn have to shed their old state and take on a new one. Before this can happen, they have to learn about and absorb the goodness and truth taught by the church and its doctrines. After all, religious concepts and a desire for them are the vessels that receive new life. That is why we can be reborn only by growing up and reaching a state of completeness; see what was shown at §§677, 679, 711, 1555, 2046, 2063, 2636, 2679, 2697, 2979, 3203, 3502, 3508, 3510, 3665, 3690, 3701.

[2] The case is the same with the church at large when it is being established: the doctrines concerning goodness and truth first have to be brought into a unified whole, because they are the foundation on which the church is built. What is more, the doctrines interconnect and refer to one another, so unless they first come together as one, the whole will necessarily be defective. Anything missing would have to be supplied by human rationality, and I have already demonstrated in many places the extent to which human rationality blinds and deludes itself regarding spiritual and divine concerns when it draws its own conclusions.

This is why the church has been given the Word, which contains all the doctrines concerning goodness and truth.

In this regard, the church on a large scale resembles a regenerating individual on a small scale, because the latter is a church on a small scale. In an individual, the church's doctrines concerning goodness and truth first have to come together before rebirth can happen, as mentioned above. This is the inner-level symbolism of the words *here, now, the day is still at its height; it is not time for the livestock to be gathered.*

3787   *Water the flock and go, pasture it* means that a few would be taught from [the Word] anyway. This can be seen from the symbolism of *watering the flock* as offering instruction from the Word (discussed in §3772) and from that of *go, pasture it* as the fact that the Word is the source of life and doctrine. *Going* means life (see §§3335, 3690), and *pasturing* means doctrine (§343 and below [§3795]).

The secret lying hidden in this is that nevertheless there are a few who reach a complete state (described in §2636) and who can accordingly be reborn.

3788   *And they said, "We cannot, until all the droves are gathered,"* means that they ought to come together. This can be seen from the symbolism of being *gathered* as forming a single whole, or coming together (as noted above in §3786), and from that of *droves* as doctrines (discussed in §§3767, 3768). What ideas these words involve can be seen from the discussion just above in §§3786, 3787.

3789   *And they roll the stone off the mouth of the well* means that this brings the Word's contents out in the open. This can be seen from the symbolism of *rolling the stone off* as being brought out in the open (discussed in §§3769, 3771, 3773) and from that of a *well* as the Word (discussed in §§3424, 3765).

3790   *And we will water the flock* means that they are then instructed. This can be seen from the symbolism of *watering the flock* as teaching (discussed in §§3772, 3787). This too is evident from the preceding remarks.

3791   Genesis 29:9, 10, 11. *He was still speaking with them when Rachel came with the flock that belonged to her father, because she was a shepherd. And it happened as Jacob saw Rachel, the daughter of Laban, his mother's brother, and the flock of Laban, his mother's brother, that Jacob came up and rolled the stone off the mouth of the well and watered the flock of Laban, his mother's brother. And Jacob kissed Rachel and lifted his voice and wept.*

He was still speaking with them symbolizes [the Lord's] thinking at that point. *When Rachel came with the flock* symbolizes a desire for inner truth within the church's teachings. *That belonged to her father* means having its source in goodness. *Because she was a shepherd* means that the desire for the Word's inner truth is a teacher. *And it happened as Jacob saw Rachel, the daughter of Laban, his mother's brother,* symbolizes a recognition of the source from which the desire for that truth comes. *And the flock of Laban, his mother's brother,* symbolizes the church and its teachings, from the same source. *That Jacob came up and rolled the stone off the mouth of the well* means that the Lord uncovered the Word's inner depths by the power of earthly goodness. *And watered the flock of Laban, his mother's brother,* symbolizes instruction. *And Jacob kissed Rachel* symbolizes love for inner truth. *And lifted his voice and wept* symbolizes intense love.

He was still speaking with them symbolizes [the Lord's] thinking at that point. This can be seen from the symbolism in the scriptural narrative of *speaking* as thinking (discussed in §§2271, 2287, 2619). It was obviously "at that point," because Rachel came at just the moment when Jacob was speaking with the men—that is, when he was "still speaking with them."

3792

When Rachel came with the flock symbolizes a desire for inner truth within the church's teachings. This can be seen from the representation of *Rachel* as a desire for inner truth and from the symbolism of a *flock* as the church and its doctrine (discussed in §§3767, 3768, 3783).

3793

To show what is involved in Rachel's representation as a desire for inner truth, and Leah's as a desire for outer truth, I must say a few words.

The earthly level, which Jacob represents, consists of goodness and truth, and the two need to be married on that level, just as they need to be married in *every* facet of a human being. In fact, they need to be married everywhere in earthly creation. Nothing is produced without the marriage of goodness and truth. From that marriage comes every object and every result ever produced.

Goodness and truth are not wedded on our earthly level when we are born, because we are the only creatures not born into the divine pattern. Innocent, charitable goodness does flow into us from the Lord when we are babies, but there is no truth for it to join with. As we grow, this goodness that the Lord instills in us during our childhood withdraws to a deeper spot, where it is held in keeping by the Lord to mitigate the stages of life we pass through later. As a result, we would be worse and wilder than any wild animal without the goodness of our childhood and early youth. When this childish goodness withdraws, evil enters and replaces it on our earthly plane. Falsity joins with the evil, creating a bond or marriage, so to speak, between evil and falsity in us. If we are to be saved, then, we have to be reborn. Evil needs to be moved aside and goodness from the Lord needs to be instilled. As we accept goodness, truth is instilled, so that a joining or marriage of the two takes place.

[2] This is what Jacob and his two wives, Rachel and Leah, represent. Jacob, therefore, has now put on the representation of earthly goodness, and Rachel, of truth, but since all union of truth with goodness happens through desire, a desire to join truth with goodness is what Rachel represents. In addition, inner and outer dimensions exist on the earthly level, just as they do on the rational level, and Rachel represents a desire for inner truth, while Leah represents a desire for outer truth.

Laban, their father, represents goodness that comes from a shared stock but branches off to the side, as noted [§3778]—a parallel line of goodness corresponding to truth on a rational plane, or Rebekah (§§3012, 3013, 3077). So the daughters of that goodness represent desires on the earthly plane, because these desires are like daughters to that goodness as their father. These desires need to join with earthly goodness, so they represent desire for truth, one of them representing the desire for inner truth, and the other, for outer truth.

[3] Matters stand exactly the same with the rebirth of a person's earthly level as they do with Jacob and the two daughters of Laban, Rachel and Leah. People capable of seeing and grasping the Word's inner meaning here see this secret laid bare. The only people who can see it, though, are those endowed with goodness and truth. No matter how perceptive others are in matters of moral and public life, no matter how insightful they seem, they cannot see enough of the secret to acknowledge it, because they do not know what goodness and truth are. They consider evil good and falsity true, so the instant you say "goodness," an image of evil presents itself, and when you say "truth," an image of falsity presents itself. That is why they perceive none of the ideas contained in the inner meaning. The moment they hear it, darkness rises and snuffs out the light.

3794 *That belonged to her father* means having its source in goodness. This is established by the representation of Laban, the *father* here, as goodness branching off from the same stock (discussed in §§3612, 3665, 3778) and also from the symbolism of a *father* as goodness (discussed in §3703).

3795 *Because she was a shepherd,* or one who feeds a flock, means that the desire for the Word's inner truth is a teacher. This can be seen from the symbolism of a *shepherd,* or one who feeds a flock, as a person who leads and teaches (discussed in §343) and from the representation of Rachel— *she*—as a desire for inner truth (treated of just above in §3793). (The truth desired is from the Word because Rachel took her flock to the well, and a well means the Word; see §3765.) Besides, a desire for inner truth is what teaches people, because it is what makes a religion a religion and is what makes a pastor a shepherd.

A shepherd in the Word symbolizes people who lead and teach, because a flock symbolizes people who are led and taught, as a result of which it symbolizes churches and also a church's doctrines (§§3767, 3768, 3783). The Christian world knows this perfectly well, because that is what it calls people who teach and people who learn. There is no need, then, to offer supporting evidence from the Word.

And it happened as Jacob saw Rachel, the daughter of Laban, his mother's brother, symbolizes a recognition of the source from which the desire for that truth comes. This can be seen from the symbolism here of *seeing* as recognizing (as is clear from the thread of the story) and from the representation of *Rachel* as a desire for inner truth (discussed above in §3793). *The daughter of Laban, his mother's brother,* involves the idea of its source: a side branch of goodness, which had a brother's close connection with the rational truth represented by Rebekah, Jacob's mother.

[2] To take up the topic of desire for truth and goodness: Any genuine desire we feel for truth and goodness comes from a divine origin, because it comes from the Lord. On its way down, though, it flows off into various different channels, where it forms new sources for itself. As it flows into desires for truth and goodness that are feigned rather than genuine and into desires for evil and falsity, it changes accordingly. The outward appearance it presents is often the same as that of genuine desire, but this is what its inner form is like. One sign by which we may recognize it is the aim. If the aim of desire is personal power or worldly advantages, the desire is not genuine. If on the other hand the aim is the good of our neighbor, society at large, and the country, and particularly if it is the good of the church and the Lord's kingdom, it is genuine. The aim is then the Lord, because the Lord is present in that goodness.

[3] It takes wisdom, though, to know what our own aims are. Sometimes our goal seems selfish when it is not, because out of custom and habit we naturally ponder what something means for us at every step. However, if you want to know what your ultimate goal is, simply notice the kind of pleasure you feel when given praise and glory and the kind of pleasure you feel in useful activity apart from personal benefit. If you enjoy the latter, your desire is genuine.

We ought to pay attention to the various states we pass through, because the states themselves usually affect our perception. This is something we can examine in ourselves but not in others, because the Lord alone knows the aim of every desire. That is why the Lord said, "Don't judge anyone, or you will be judged; don't condemn anyone, or you will be condemned" (Luke 6:37). A thousand people can seem to have the same desire for truth and goodness when in reality each has a desire with a different origin, or a different aim.

[4] The reason the aim determines whether a desire is real, feigned, or deceitful is that our purpose is our very life. What we live for—in other words, what we love—is what we hold as our goal. When the welfare of our neighbor, the larger community, the church, and the Lord's kingdom forms our goal, our soul dwells in the Lord's kingdom and therefore in the Lord. The Lord's kingdom is nothing other than a kingdom of purposes and usefulness seeking the good of the whole human race (§3645). Even the angels who attend us concern themselves only with our goals. So far as our ultimate goal matches that of the Lord's kingdom, the angels delight in us and bind themselves to us as their sisters or brothers. So far as we make ourselves the ultimate goal, though, the angels withdraw and evil spirits from hell move closer. The people in hell have no other goal.

This shows how important it is to examine and discover the origin of our desires, which we can determine only from our purpose.

3797 *And the flock of Laban, his mother's brother,* symbolizes the church and its teachings, from the same source. This is established by the symbolism of a *flock* as the church and its teachings (discussed in §§3767, 3768, 3783).

Here too Laban is called the brother of Jacob's mother because again it symbolizes a recognition of the source, as just above.

3798 *That Jacob came up and rolled the stone off the mouth of the well* means that the Lord uncovered the Word's inner depths by the power of earthly goodness, as the following shows: *Jacob* represents the Lord's earthly divinity, as dealt with before, and here he represents goodness on that plane. And *rolling the stone off the mouth of the well* means uncovering the Word's inner depths, as discussed in §§3769, 3771, 3773, 3789.

The reason this clause in its highest inner sense means the Lord's use of earthly goodness to uncover the Word's inner depths is that Jacob now represents goodness on the earthly plane. He has come to represent goodness because goodness was now destined to have truth attached to it by means of the desire that Rachel represents (see just above at §§3775, 3793). On the point that goodness uncovers the inner depths of the Word, see §3773. Obviously it is goodness that has the power to do so, because the love we feel enables each of us to see the implications of that love. What we see we refer to as truth, because it conforms with what we love. The love we each feel contains within it the light of our life, because love resembles a blaze that gives off light. Whatever the love (or fire) is like, that is what the light of truth is like for us. People who love what is good can see what that love implies, so they can see the truth the Word holds. The greater the quantity and quality of their love for goodness, the more truth they see, because the light of understanding then streams in from heaven, or rather through heaven from the Lord. That is why no one (as was said before [§3793]) can see or acknowledge the Word's inner depths except the person who lives a good life.

And watered the flock of Laban, his mother's brother, symbolizes instruc- **3799** tion. This can be seen from the symbolism of *watering a flock* as teaching (discussed in §3772).

For the third time Laban is called the brother of Jacob's mother, in order to indicate the origins of the flock and of Rachel, or of the doctrine and the desire for inner truth.

And Jacob kissed Rachel symbolizes love for inner truth, as the follow- **3800** ing shows: *Kissing* symbolizes oneness and union resulting from desire, as discussed in §§3573, 3574, so it symbolizes love, because viewed in itself, love is oneness and union resulting from desire. And *Rachel* represents a desire for inner truth, as noted in §3793. This shows that *Jacob kissed Rachel* symbolizes love for inner truth.

And lifted his voice and wept symbolizes intense love. This can be seen **3801** from the symbolism of *lifting one's voice and weeping* as intense love. Tears are a sign of sadness and of love and mark the highest degree of both.

Genesis 29:12, 13. *And Jacob told Rachel that he was her father's brother* **3802** *and that he was Rebekah's son. And she ran and told her father. And it hap- pened as Laban heard the report concerning Jacob, his sister's son, that he ran to meet him and hugged him and kissed him and brought him to his house, and [Jacob] told Laban all these words.*

Jacob told Rachel that he was her father's brother symbolizes kinship between the goodness that is Jacob and the goodness that is Laban. *And that he was Rebekah's son* symbolizes the connection between the kin. *And she ran and told her father* symbolizes recognition through inner truth. *And it happened as Laban heard the report concerning Jacob, his sister's son,* symbolizes the recognition of related goodness. *That he ran to meet him* symbolizes compatibility. *And hugged him* symbolizes affection. *And kissed him* symbolizes initiation. *And brought him to his house* means into union. *And he told Laban all these words* means as a result of truth.

3803　　*Jacob told Rachel that he was her father's brother* symbolizes kinship between the goodness that is Jacob and the goodness that is Laban, as can be seen from the following: *Telling* means informing. *Jacob* represents goodness, as discussed before. *Rachel,* who received the information, represents a desire for inner truth, as discussed in §3793. A *brother,* who is Jacob in this case, symbolizes goodness, as noted in §§367, 2360, 3303, 3459. And a *father,* who is Laban in this case, also symbolizes goodness, as noted in §3703. This explanation and the overall context shows that *Jacob told Rachel that he was her father's brother* symbolizes kinship between the goodness that is Jacob and the goodness that is Laban.

To explain the kinship and the way the two are united by the desire for inner truth that Rachel represents would be to cast darkness over the whole subject. After all, few know what goodness on the earthly level is, or that it is something different from goodness on the rational level. Few know what goodness branching off from the same stock is, or what a desire for inner truth is. People who have not acquired any idea of these things by their own investigation gain little or no idea from the description, because we accept from others only as much as we see on our own, or else only as much as we acquire by pondering the subject inside ourselves. The rest falls to the side. It is enough to know that there are countless ties of kinship between goodness and truth and that the communities of heaven are arranged in accord with those ties (see §§685, 917, 2739, 3612).

[2] The reason Jacob calls himself Laban's brother, even though he was the son of Laban's sister, is that goodness makes everyone a brother and a sister. Laban in turn calls Jacob *his* brother for the same reason (verse 15). Goodness creates family ties and brings people together, because goodness comes of love, and love is spiritual union. That is why people in the ancient churches called everyone with goodness their sister or brother. People in the Jewish religion did the same, but since they despised everyone else and considered themselves alone to be the chosen, it was only native Jews they called their brothers and sisters. The rest they referred to as companions or strangers.

The people of the early Christian church also addressed everyone governed by goodness as their brother or sister, but later they restricted the term to those in their own congregation. As goodness vanished among Christians, the term disappeared, and when truth took the place of goodness, or faith took the place of charity, they could no longer call each other sister or brother on account of goodness but used the name neighbor instead. Doctrine focusing on faith, without a life of charity, also brings with it the attitude that it is beneath us to be a sister or brother to those who are lowlier than we. In this case brother- or sisterhood traces its origin not to the Lord and therefore to goodness but to self-interest and therefore to position and wealth.

[3] *And that he was Rebekah's son* symbolizes the connection between the kin, as can be seen without explanation; Rebekah—Jacob's mother and Laban's sister—provided the connection.

And she ran and told her father symbolizes recognition through inner truth. This can be seen from the symbolism of *running and telling* as the desire to inform, inspired here by recognition, and from the symbolism of *her father* as the goodness that Laban stands for. Inner truth was the means, and this is represented by Rachel, the desire for inner truth. In consequence, the clause symbolizes recognition through inner truth.

3804

Here is the situation: People recognize and acknowledge the existence of the goodness that Jacob represents (goodness on the earthly level), as they recognize that of all goodness in general, but they do not see its nature except through truth. Goodness takes its character from truth, so it is known and recognized through truth. It does not become the kind of goodness called charity until truth is planted in it, and the quality of the truth planted in it determines the quality of the goodness. [2] That is why one person's goodness is not like another's, even if it looks exactly the same. Goodness differs in each and every person in the entire world.

It is the same as the human face, in which an emotion is usually making itself known: in the entire human race, no two faces are ever identical. Truth itself makes a kind of face for goodness. The beauty of that face comes from the shaping of truth, but what affects the observer is the goodness. That is what all angel forms are like, and that is what we would be like if our inner life moved us to love the Lord and show charity to our neighbor. We have been created to be such forms, because we have been created as God's likeness and image. People whose spirits have been reborn are forms of this kind, no matter what their bodies look like.

From this you can see what it means to say that goodness is recognized through inner truth.

3805   *And it happened as Laban heard the report concerning Jacob, his sister's son,* symbolizes the recognition of related goodness. This too can be seen from the consequences of the sentence's symbolism on an inner level. A reciprocal recognition is what is being depicted.

The passage speaks to the choosing of goodness, of course, and this choice precedes the marriage of goodness and truth.

3806   *That he ran to meet him* symbolizes compatibility. This can be seen from the symbolism of *running to meet* as compatibility, because it anticipates the union discussed below [§3809]. It is generally recognized that compatibility, or similarity, unites people.

3807   *And hugged him* symbolizes affection. This can be seen from the symbolism of *hugging* as affection. A hug is the gesture by which inner affection expresses itself. Every emotion has physical gestures corresponding to it, and affection in general has hugging, as is known.

3808   *And kissed him* symbolizes initiation. This is established by the symbolism of *kissing* as union resulting from desire (discussed in §§3573, 3574, 3800). Here it symbolizes initiation into that union, since initiation precedes union.

3809   *And brought him to his house* means into union. This can be seen from the symbolism of *bringing to the house* as bringing to himself; in an inner sense the actual person is called a house (see §§3128, 3142, 3538) because of the goodness that a house properly stands for (§§2233, 3652, 3720). Here, then, it means to the goodness that Laban represents; so *bringing him to his house* symbolizes union.

The inner meaning here fully describes the process by which the earthly goodness that is Jacob is united with the side branch of goodness that is Laban. These are the five steps that constitute that process—mutual recognition, compatibility, affection, initiation, and union. Mutual recognition was symbolized by Rachel's running and telling her father and by Laban's hearing the report concerning Jacob, his sister's son (spoken of in §§3804, 3805); compatibility, by Laban's running to meet him (spoken of in §3806); affection, by Laban's hugging him (spoken of in §3807); initiation, by Laban's kissing him (spoken of in §3808); and union, by Laban's bringing him to his house (spoken of here).

3810   *And he told Laban all these words* means as a result of truth (the result being recognition, compatibility, affection, initiation, and union). This can be seen from the logical progression and also from the explanation of the words according to their inner meaning, to which this forms the conclusion. See the remarks just above at §3804.

Genesis 29:14, 15. *And Laban said to him, "Surely you are my bone and*   3811
my flesh!" And [Jacob] resided with him a month of days. And Laban said to
Jacob, "Because you are my brother, must you also serve me for free? Tell me
what your wages are."

Laban said to him, "Surely you are my bone and my flesh!" means that
they were united in regard to truth and goodness. *And he resided with him*
a month of days symbolizes a new state of life. *And Laban said to Jacob,*
"Because you are my brother," means because goodness made them relatives. *Must you also serve me for free? Tell me what your wages are* means it
had to lead to union.

Laban said to him, "Surely you are my bone and my flesh!" means that   3812
they were united in regard to truth and goodness. This can be seen from
the symbolism of *you are my bone and my flesh* as union. It was standard
for the ancients to speak of people in the same household or clan or in
some relationship with them as "my bone and my flesh" (see §157). That
is why these words symbolize union.

The union extended to both truth and goodness because all spiritual
union depends on them, and all earthly union relates to them. In addition,
bone and flesh symbolize human autonomy—*bone,* autonomy of intellect,
and *flesh,* autonomy of will. So bone symbolizes autonomy in regard to
truth, truth being a matter of the intellect, while flesh symbolizes autonomy
in regard to goodness, goodness being a matter of the will (see §§148, 149).

[2] Regarding autonomy in general, there are two kinds. One is hellish; the other, heavenly. We receive the hellish kind from hell and the
heavenly kind from heaven, or rather through heaven from the Lord.
All evil and consequent falsity flows in from hell, but all goodness and
consequent truth, from the Lord.

People know this because faith teaches it, but scarcely one in a mil-
lion believes it, which explains why people adopt the evil that flows into
them from hell, or make it their own. It also explains why the goodness
that comes from the Lord does not move them and is therefore not cred-
ited to them.

The reason we do not believe that evil flows in from hell and goodness from the Lord is that we love ourselves. Self-love carries this disbelief
with it—so much so that we become outraged when told that everything
comes to us from elsewhere. The result is that our whole sense of self is
pure evil; see §§210, 215, 694, 731, 874, 875, 876, 987, 1023, 1044, 1047. If
we do believe that evil comes from hell and goodness from the Lord, it
is because we love our neighbor and the Lord rather than ourselves. This

love carries such a belief with it, enabling us to receive a heavenly sense of self from the Lord. Heavenly autonomy is discussed in §§155, 164, 731, 1023, 1044, 1937, 1947, 2882, 2883, 2891.

[3] Bone and flesh symbolize autonomy in both senses. Accordingly, bones in the Word symbolize truth, and in a negative sense, falsity. Flesh symbolizes goodness, and in a negative sense, evil. This symbolism of *bones* can be seen from the following passages. In Isaiah:

> Jehovah will guide you always and satisfy your soul in the barrens and *make your bones ready* so that you may be like a well-watered garden. (Isaiah 58:11)

Making someone's bones ready stands for bringing a person's intellectual autonomy to life, or shedding the light of understanding in a person's mind. That is why the verse says, "So that you may be like a well-watered garden"—a garden meaning understanding (see §§100, 108, 1588). In the same author:

> Then you will see, and your heart will rejoice, and *your bones will sprout like grass.* (Isaiah 66:14)

Bones sprouting like grass have a similar meaning. [4] In Jeremiah:

> The Nazirites were whiter than snow; they were whiter than milk. *Their bones were redder than jewels;* their polish was sapphire. Darker than black was their form; they are not recognized on the streets. *Their skin clung to their bone;* it dried out; it became like wood. (Lamentations 4:7, 8)

A Nazirite stands for a heavenly person (§3301). Being whiter than snow and whiter than milk stands for knowing heavenly truth. Heavenly truth develops out of a love for what is good, so the passage says that their bones were redder than jewels. White is mentioned in connection with truth (3301); red, in connection with goodness (3300); and jewels, in connection with truth that develops out of goodness (114). "Their skin clung to their bone" depicts a change in regard to the heavenly qualities of love that leaves bone without flesh, or without goodness anymore. Under those conditions, all truth is like skin that clings to bone, dries out, and becomes like wood. [5] In Ezekiel:

> Utter a parable against the house of rebellion and say to them, "This is what the Lord Jehovih has said: 'Put the pot on, put it on, and also pour water into it, gathering *its pieces* into it, every *good piece,* thigh and shoulder. *With the choice of the bones fill it,* taking the choice of the

flock; and a *burning-pile of bones* should also go under it. And let them *cook the bones* within it.'" (Ezekiel 24:3, 4, 5, 10)

The pot stands for violence inflicted on goodness and truth, for which reason verse 6 of the same chapter calls the pot a blood-soaked city. The pieces and the good piece, thigh and shoulder, gathered into the pot, are pieces of flesh, which mean different kinds of goodness. The choice of the bones with which the pot was filled stands for truth. The burning-pile of bones stands for a desire for truth. "Let them cook the bones within it" stands for violence inflicted on truth. Anyone can see that this parable hides a secret, divine meaning, and that the meaning can never be known until one knows the inner-level symbolism of the pot, the pieces, thigh and shoulder, the choice of the bones, the burning-pile of bones, and the cooking. In Micah:

Is it not your part to know judgment?—you who hate goodness and love evil, who strip people's skin off them, and *their flesh* off *their bones,* who have eaten the *flesh of my people* and torn their skin off them and *splintered their bones* and split them up as into a *pot* and as *flesh* into the midst of a cauldron. (Micah 3:[1,] 2, 3)

The meaning is similar. [6] In Ezekiel:

He brought me out in the spirit of Jehovah and put me in the middle of the valley, which was *full of bones.* He said to me, "Will *these bones* live?" He said to me, "Prophesy *over these bones* and say to them, '*Dry bones,* listen to the word of *Jehovah.* This is what the Lord Jehovih has said *to these bones:* "See? I am bringing breath into you so that you may live. I will put tendons on you and bring *flesh* up over you and draw skin over you and put breath in you so that you may live."'" I prophesied, and the *bones assembled, bone to* its *bone.* I looked, when there!— tendons on them; and *flesh* came up and skin was drawn over them on top, and there was no breath in them. And breath came into them and they came back to life and stood on their feet. (Ezekiel 37:1 and following verses)

The general subject of this passage is the establishment of religion among people outside the church; the specific subject is an individual's rebirth. Dry bones stand for intellectual autonomy, which is lifeless until it receives from the Lord the life force belonging to goodness; this life animates it, or brings it to life. The flesh the Lord brings up over the bones is autonomy of will, which is called heavenly autonomy and therefore consists of goodness. Breath is the Lord's life. When this life flows into the goodness that we

seem to will and do on our own, the goodness comes alive and brings truth
to life, and out of dry bones a human being is formed. [7] In David:

> All my bones have come apart; my heart has become like wax; I can
> count all my bones. They divided my garments for themselves, and over
> my clothing they cast lots. (Psalms 22:14, 17, 18)

This is about the Lord's trials in regard both to divine truth, which belonged
to him and is therefore called "my bones," and to divine goodness, which
belonged to him and is therefore called "my heart." A heart means goodness (see §§3313, 3635). Bones symbolize divine truth, and counting them
means wanting to dispel that truth through sophistry and distortion. As a
consequence the text immediately adds that they divided his garments and
cast lots over his clothing, since clothes also mean truth, but outer truth
(§§297, 1073, 2576). Dividing his garments and casting lots over his clothing involves much the same meaning, as it also does in Matthew 27:35. In
the same author:

> My soul rejoices in Jehovah; it is glad in his salvation. Let all my bones
> say, "Who is like you?" (Psalms 35:9, 10)

The bones clearly have the spiritual meaning of a person's own intellect.
In the same author:

> You will make me hear joy and gladness; the bones you crushed will
> rejoice. (Psalms 51:8)

"The bones you crushed will rejoice" stands for being renewed by truth
after we have been tested.

[8] Since a bone symbolized one's own proper intellect, or autonomy
in regard to truth—and in the highest sense divine truth proper to the
Lord—one of the statutes for Passover required the people not to break a
bone of the Passover lamb. Moses says this about it:

> In a single house it shall be eaten; you shall not take any of the flesh out-
> side the house, and not a bone shall you break in it. (Exodus 12:46)

And in another place:

> They shall not leave any of it till morning, and not a bone of it shall they
> break. (Numbers 9:12)

In the highest sense, not breaking a bone stands for not violating divine
truth. In a representative sense it stands for not violating the truth belonging

to any type of goodness, because truth gives goodness its quality and provides it with a form. It also is a framework for goodness, just as bones are a framework for flesh.

[9] The Word, which consists in truth that is genuinely divine, brings the dead to life, and this was represented by the man in 2 Kings 13:21 who was thrown into Elisha's grave, *touched his bones,* came back to life, and got up on his feet. Elisha represented the Lord in regard to divine truth, or the Lord as the Word; see §2762.

The negative symbolism of bones as the falsity produced by human autonomy is evident in the following places. In Jeremiah:

> At that time they will bring out the *bones of Judah's monarchs and the bones of its chieftains and the bones of the priests and the bones of the prophets and the bones of Jerusalem's residents* from their graves and spread them out before the sun and the moon and the whole army of the heavens, [bones] that they loved and that they served. (Jeremiah 8:1, 2)

In Ezekiel:

> I will put the corpses of the children of Israel before their idols and *scatter your bones* around your altars. (Ezekiel 6:5)

In Moses:

> God, who brought them out of Egypt (he has strength like that of a unicorn), will consume the nations, his foes; and *their bones he will break* and their arrows he will crush. (Numbers 24:8)

In 2 Kings:

> King Josiah shattered the pillars and cut down the groves and filled their place with *human bones.* He took the bones out of the graves and burned them on the altar to defile it. All the priests of the high places who were there he sacrificed on the altars, and *human bones he burned on them.* (2 Kings 23:14, 16, 20)

In Moses:

> The soul who has [gone] on the open field [and] touched one stabbed by a sword, or a dead body, or a *human bone,* or a grave will be unclean seven days. (Numbers 19:16, 18)

[10] Bones symbolize falsity, and graves symbolize the evil containing that falsity. Hypocrites have a kind of evil that looks good on the outside

but is polluted within by falsity and profanation, which is why the Lord says this in Matthew:

> Doom to you, scribes and Pharisees—*hypocrites!* Because you make your-selves like *whitewashed tombs* that do look beautiful outside but inside *are full of the bones of the dead* and every kind of uncleanness. Likewise, yes, on the outside you also look righteous to people, but inside you are full of hypocrisy and wickedness. (Matthew 23:27, 28)

These quotations now show that bones symbolize a person's own proper intellect in regard to both truth and falsity.

3813   As for *flesh,* in the highest sense it symbolizes the property distinctive to the Lord's divine humanity, which is divine goodness. In a second-ary sense it symbolizes the property distinctive to the human will when this has been brought to life by divine humanity's distinctive property—in other words, by the Lord's divine goodness. This property is what is called heavenly autonomy. In itself it belongs to the Lord alone but is adopted by people who are devoted to goodness and therefore to truth. It is the type of autonomy enjoyed by angels in heaven and by people whose inner dimension (or spirit) is in the Lord's kingdom. In a negative sense, however, flesh symbolizes human autonomy of will that in itself is sheer evil. Since this autonomy has not been brought to life by the Lord, it is called dead, so the person who has it is also said to be dead.

[2] The Lord's words in John show that in the highest sense flesh means the property unique to the Lord's divine humanity and therefore his divine goodness:

> Jesus said, "I am the living bread who came down from heaven; if any-one eats of this bread, that person will live forever. The bread that I will give *is my flesh,* which I will give for the world's life." The Jews fought with each other, saying, "How can he give his *flesh* to eat?" So Jesus said to them, "Truly, truly, I say to you: unless you eat the *flesh of the Son of Humankind* and drink his blood you will not have life in yourselves. Whoever eats my flesh and drinks my blood has eternal life, and I will revive that person on the last day, *because my flesh is truly food,* and my blood is truly drink; those who eat *my flesh* and drink my blood remain in me, and I in them. This is the bread that came down from heaven." (John 6:51–58)

It is quite plain in this passage that flesh means the property unique to the Lord's divine humanity—divine goodness. The flesh is what is called the body in the Holy Supper, where the body (or flesh) means divine goodness and the blood means divine truth; see §§1798, 2165, 2177, 3464, 3735. Bread and wine have the same symbolism as flesh and blood, bread symbolizing the Lord's divine goodness, and wine, his divine truth, and that is why bread and wine were commanded in place of his body and blood. Accordingly the Lord says, "I am the living bread; the bread that I will give is my flesh; those who eat my flesh and drink my blood remain in me, and I in them; this is the bread that came down from heaven." Eating means being communicated, united, and adopted; see §§2187, 2343, 3168, 3513 at the end, 3596.

[3] The same thing was represented in the Jewish religion by the fact that the flesh of the sacrifices was eaten by Aaron, by his sons, by the people offering the sacrifice, and by others who were clean, and that this was a sacred act. See Exodus 12:7, 8, 9; 29:30–34; Leviticus 7:15–21; 8:31; Deuteronomy 12:27; 16:4. Consequently, if people who were unclean ate of that flesh, they would be cut off from their people (Leviticus 7:21). The sacrifices were called bread (see §2165). The flesh was called holy flesh (Jeremiah 11:15; Haggai 2:12) and the flesh of the offering on the tables in the Lord's kingdom (Ezekiel 40:43, which describes the new temple). Clearly this symbolizes different ways of worshiping the Lord in his kingdom.

[4] The secondary meaning of flesh as human autonomy of will, brought to life by the Lord's divine goodness, can be seen from the following places. In Ezekiel:

> I will give them one heart. And a new spirit I will put in their midst, and I will remove the heart of stone *from their flesh* and give them a *heart of flesh*. (Ezekiel 11:19; 36:26)

The heart of stone removed from their flesh stands for a will and autonomy that have not been brought to life. The heart of flesh stands for a will and autonomy that *have* been brought to life. A heart represents the goodness in a person's will; see §§2930, 3313, 3635. In David:

> God, you are my God; I seek you by morning. My soul thirsts for you; *my flesh* longs for you in a land of drought, and I am faint without water. (Psalms 63:1)

In the same author:

> My soul yearns for Jehovah's courts; my heart and *my flesh* shout for joy to the living God. (Psalms 84:2)

[5] In Job:

> I know my Redeemer; he is alive and in the end will rise upon the dust. And afterward all this will be wrapped in my skin, and from *my flesh I will see God,* whom I will see for myself; and my eyes will see, and no other will. (Job 19:25, 26, 27)

Being wrapped in skin stands for being wrapped in the kind of earthly element that we take with us after death, as described in §3539. Seeing God from one's flesh stands for seeing him from a selfhood that has been brought to life, which is why Job says, "Whom I will see for myself; and my eyes will see, and no other will." The [ancient] churches knew that flesh symbolized a sense of self, [or autonomy,] and Job is a book of the ancient church (§3540 at the end), so he spoke symbolically on these and many other topics, in keeping with the custom of that time. People who conclude from this passage that our actual corpse will be gathered from the four winds and rise again do not know the Word's inner meaning. People who do know it know that they will go to the other world with a body, but a purer one, because bodies there are purer. People there see each other, talk together, and enjoy every sensation they enjoyed in the body but more keenly. The body we carry around on earth is designed for use here, so it consists of bones and flesh. The body a spirit carries around in the other life is for use there, so it consists not of bones and flesh but of what corresponds to bones and flesh. See §3726.

[6] The opposite symbolism of flesh as human autonomy of will that in itself is sheer evil is clear from the following passages. In Isaiah:

> A man will eat the *flesh of his own arm.* (Isaiah 9:20)

In the same author:

> I will feed your oppressors with *their own flesh,* and they will become drunk on their blood as on new wine. (Isaiah 49:26)

In Jeremiah:

> I will feed you with the *flesh of their sons* and the *flesh of their daughters,* and a man will eat the *flesh of his companion.* (Jeremiah 19:9)

In Zechariah:

> The survivors will eat *each other's flesh.* (Zechariah 11:9)

In Moses:

> I will castigate you six times harder for your sins. And may you eat the *flesh of your sons;* and the *flesh of your daughters* you will eat. (Leviticus 26:28, 29)

These passages portray autonomy of will—in other words, human nature. Eating the flesh of one's arm, the flesh of one's sons and daughters, and each other's flesh actually symbolizes evil and the falsity it spawns and therefore hatred of truth and goodness. [7] In John:

> I saw one angel standing in the sun, who shouted in a loud voice, saying to all the birds flying in midair, "Come and gather to the supper of the great God, so that you can eat the *flesh of monarchs* and the *flesh of commanders,* and the *flesh of the mighty,* and the *flesh of horses* and of the people sitting on them, and the *flesh of all, free people* and slaves, both small and great." (Revelation 19:17, 18; Ezekiel 39:17, 18, 19, 20)

Anyone can see that the flesh of monarchs, commanders, the mighty, horses and their riders, and free people and slaves does not mean actual flesh, so it means something else, something so far unknown. What it symbolizes (as the details indicate) is evil that grows out of falsity, and evil that gives rise to falsity, which have their source in human autonomy of will.

[8] Since blood in an inner sense means falsity that springs from a person's own intellect, and flesh means evil that springs from a person's own will, the Lord says this about people who are being reborn:

> As many as did accept him, to them he gave the power to be God's children, to those believing in his name, *who* had their birth *not from blood or from the will of the flesh* or from a man's will but from God. (John 1:12, 13)

That is why flesh in general means every person (see §§574, 1050 at the end); it is all the same whether you speak of a person or the person's sense of self.

[9] The symbolism of flesh on the highest level as the Lord's divine humanity is illustrated by the quotation above and also by this one in John:

> *The Word became flesh* and resided among us, and we saw his glory: glory like that of the Only-Born of the Father. (John 1:14)

This flesh gives life to all flesh; that is, we all receive life from the Lord's divine humanity. We do so by making his love our own, and this appropriation is symbolized by eating the flesh of the Son of Humankind (John 6:51–58) and by eating the bread of the Holy Supper. The bread means his body, or flesh (Matthew 26:26, 27).

3814   *And he resided with him a month of days* symbolizes a new state of life. This can be seen from the symbolism of *residing* as life (discussed in §§1293, 3384, 3613) and from that of a *month of days* as a new state. All periods of time mean states (see §§1274, 1382, 2625, 2788, 2837, 3254, 3356, 3404), so years, months, and days have this meaning. What specific state they symbolize can be seen from the numbers attached to them, but when a single year, month, or day is mentioned, it symbolizes an entire state. So it symbolizes the end of the previous state and the start of the next. This too has been explained and demonstrated in various places. The month here, then, means the end of the previous state and the start of the next, so it symbolizes a new state. The symbolism is the same elsewhere in the Word, as in Isaiah:

> "Eventually it will happen, *from one month* to the *next,* and from Sabbath to Sabbath, that all flesh will come to bow down before me," Jehovah has said. (Isaiah 66:23)

In John:

> He showed me a pure river of the water of life, brilliant as crystal, going out from the throne of God and the Lamb. In the middle of its street and of the river, on this side and that, was the tree of life, making twelve fruits, *offering up its fruit each month.* (Revelation 22:1, 2)

"Offering up its fruit each month" means always a new state of receiving and therefore exercising goodness. [2] In Moses:

> Register the sons of Levi according to the house of their father and according to their clans, every male; *from the son of a month* and above you shall register them. Register every firstborn, the male of the children of Israel, from the *son of a month* and above, and take up the number of their names. (Numbers 3:15, 40)

Since a month symbolized the end of a previous state and the start of the next, or a new state, the command was to register them from the son of a month and above. In the same author:

> If you see in captivity a woman beautiful of form and want her, to take her as your wife, she shall take the clothing of her captivity off her and

sit in your house and cry for her father and her mother a *month of days;*
afterward you shall go in to her and know her, and she will become
your wife. (Deuteronomy 21:11, 13)

Obviously the month of days stands for the end of a prior state and the
start of a next, new state.

And Laban said to Jacob, "Because you are my brother," means because
goodness made them relatives. This can be seen from the representation
of *Laban* as goodness branching off from a shared stock, and that of
Jacob as goodness on the earthly plane, both of which are discussed
above; and from the symbolism of a *brother* as goodness (discussed in
§3803). In this case a brother symbolizes something related, because
Laban addresses Jacob as his brother; that is, goodness addresses goodness this way. All kinship traces its origin to goodness, because goodness
is a matter of love. What I am describing as something related is the next
level of love in a descending line, and that is what is meant by a brother
in the strict sense.

In the spiritual world, or heaven, no other blood ties or family connections exist than those of love for the Lord and love for one's neighbor—in
other words, those of goodness. I was able to see this by observing that all
the countless communities making up heaven are precisely distinguished
from each other by different levels and types of love and therefore of
faith; see §§685, 917, 2739, 3612. Another piece of evidence was that the
inhabitants there acknowledge each other not from any kinship they had
in bodily life but only from their goodness and the truth it leads to. A
parent does not acknowledge a daughter or son as such; a sibling does not
acknowledge a sibling; not even a husband acknowledges his wife unless
they had the same kind of goodness. When they first go to the other
world, they meet but break off with one another, because goodness itself,
or love and charity, directs and assigns them each to their own community. For every individual, relatedness starts in the community where she
or he lives, and various kinds of connection fan out from there to the
circumference.

Should you also serve me for free? Tell me what your wages are means it
had to lead to union. This can be seen from the symbolism of *serving for
free* as doing so without obligation, and from that of *wages* as a means of
union. The Word speaks of wages several times, and in the inner meaning of those passages it actually symbolizes a means of union. The reason
this is its only meaning is that angels refuse to listen to the idea that they
are rewarded for anything in them; in fact, they absolutely oppose the

3815

3816

thought of a reward for any good or well-done deed. They realize that anything in us of our very own is unqualified evil, so whatever we do by ourselves, under our own power, carries with it the opposite of a reward. Everything good comes from the Lord and flows into us out of pure mercy, not on our own account as a result of our hope for reward. Even what is good ceases to be so when we think of being rewarded for it, because selfish aims immediately attach themselves. The more they attach themselves, the more they persuade us to deny that goodness comes from the Lord and his mercy. They increasingly cut us off from his inflow and alienate us from heaven and its blessings, which lodge within goodness and the desire for goodness. A desire for goodness, or love for the Lord and love for our neighbor, contains blessings and happiness, which dwell in the actual desire and love. To do a deed because of this desire and its blessings and at the same time for the sake of a reward is completely self-contradictory. That is why the mention of wages in the Word produces no thought of reward in angels' minds, only the thought of what the Lord gives them freely in his mercy.

[2] However, rewards serve as a means of union for people who have not yet been initiated into goodness and the desire for goodness—that is, who have not yet been fully reborn. They cannot help thinking about a reward, because they do good not out of a desire for goodness but out of a desire for their own blessings and happiness and out of a fear of hell. When they regenerate, this mindset flips and turns into a desire for goodness, at which point they no longer look for a reward.

[3] The situation can be illustrated by the experiences of public life. Those who love their country so much that serving it out of pure goodwill is a pleasure for them would grieve if the opportunity were denied them and would beg to have it restored. Benefiting their country is central to their desires, so it is central to their pleasure and bliss. People like this also accept high rank and promotion because they use it as a means of serving their country, even though it is called a reward. People who do not love their country, on the other hand, but only themselves and their material advantage do what they do for the sake of position and riches, which they look to as their goals. People like this put themselves ahead of their country, or their own good ahead of the common good. They are quite base but want others to see them as acting out of sincere love. When they think about it privately, they deny that anyone acts sincerely and marvel that anyone can.

People who adopt these attitudes toward their country or the public during physical life have the same attitude toward the Lord's kingdom when they reach it. Our desire or love stays with each of us, because desire or love is everyone's life.

Genesis 29:16, 17. *And Laban had two daughters, the name of the older being Leah, and the name of the younger, Rachel, and Leah's eyes were weak; and Rachel was beautiful in form and beautiful in appearance.* **3817**

Laban had two daughters symbolizes two kinds of desire for truth, stemming from goodness of a shared stock. *The name of the older being Leah* symbolizes the desire for outer truth, and its quality; *and the name of the younger, Rachel* symbolizes the desire for inner truth, and its quality. *And Leah's eyes were weak* means that this was the nature of the desire for outer truth, so far as understanding it went. *And Rachel was beautiful in form and beautiful in appearance* means that this was the nature of the desire for inner truth, so far as its spiritual aspect went.

Laban had two daughters symbolizes two kinds of desire for truth, stemming from goodness of a shared stock. This is established by the representation of *Laban* as goodness from the same stock but branching off to the side (dealt with in §§3612, 3665, 3778) and from the symbolism of *daughters* as desire (dealt with in §2362). Here they symbolize a desire for truth, stemming from the goodness that is Laban (see §3793). **3818**

The name of the older being Leah symbolizes the desire for outer truth, and its quality; *and the name of the younger, Rachel* symbolizes the desire for inner truth, and its quality, as the following establishes: *Leah* represents a desire for outer truth, and *Rachel* represents a desire for inner truth, as noted at §3793. And a *name* symbolizes a quality, as discussed at §§144, 145, 1754, 1896, 2009, 2724, 3006. Leah is called the *older* because we learn outer truth first. Rachel is called the *younger* because we learn inner truth afterward. To put the same thing another way, we are affected by outer truth first and inner truth afterward. Outer truth forms a matrix for inner truth, because general concepts are what specific concepts are instilled in. If we lack any notion of some general subject, we cannot comprehend any specific facet of it. That is why the Word's literal meaning contains general truth, while its inner meaning contains specific truths. The former is being called outer; the latter, inner. **3819**

Truth is not true without desire, because otherwise it has no life, so when I speak of outer and inner truth, I mean a desire for them.

3820

And Leah's eyes were weak means that this was the nature of the desire for outer truth, so far as understanding it went. This can be seen from the representation of *Leah* as a desire for outer truth (discussed at §3793 and just above in §3819), from the symbolism of *eyes* as the power of understanding (discussed in §2701), and from the meaning of *weak* as relatively so.

The desire for outer truth—or a person drawn to that truth—is weak, so far as understanding it goes. This can be seen from superficial, general ideas, which are flimsy and wavering, allowing themselves to by carried off by every gust of wind, or swayed by every viewpoint, until specific ideas shed light on them. Once specific ideas *have* shed light on them, though, the same ideas become firm and consistent. Specific ideas give them the essential and formal elements symbolized by the beauty of form and beauty of appearance possessed by Rachel, who represents the desire for inner truth.

[2] What is outer truth and the desire for it? What is inner truth and the desire for it? How is the former relatively weak of eye, while the latter is beautiful in form and appearance? Take as an example people focused on outer truth who have only the general idea that we ought to do good to the poor. They do not know how to tell exactly who the truly poor are; still less do they realize that by the poor the Word means those who are spiritually so. So they help the evil and the good indiscriminately. They do not see that to help the evil is to harm the good, because in benefiting the evil they give them the means of harming the good. People with this simplistic zeal find themselves plagued by tricksters and swindlers at every turn. People who know inner truth, on the other hand, know just who the poor are and distinguish among them, benefiting each according to the nature of each.

[3] Take as another example people restricted to outer truth who have only the general idea that we ought to love our neighbor. They believe that everyone is our neighbor to the same extent and ought to be embraced with the same love. So they let themselves be led astray. Those who know inner truth, though, will know to what extent others are their neighbor, each in a different way, so they know immeasurably more than the first group. As a result they do not let themselves be fooled by the mere name of neighbor into doing evil under the persuasion that it is good, as the claim of neighborliness would lead them to believe.

[4] Take as yet another example people with nothing more than outer truth who think that the educated will shine like stars in the other world and that anyone who labors in the Lord's vineyard will receive a

greater reward than others. But people who possess inner truth know that by the educated, wise, and intelligent are meant people with goodness, even if they have no human wisdom or understanding. These are the ones who will shine like stars. They also know that those who labor in the vineyard will each obtain a reward matching the desire for goodness and truth that inspires them. The ones who labor for themselves and the world—for preeminence and riches—are rewarded during physical life, but in the other life they find their lot to be among the evil there (Matthew 7:22, 23).

This shows how weak people's comprehension is when they know only outer truth. It also shows that inner truth gives outer truth its essence and form and gives people's goodness its character.

Nonetheless, people with outer truth who also possess simple goodness during life in the world receive inner truth and its accompanying wisdom in the other life. Simple goodness brings them into a state in which they can accept these things.

And Rachel was beautiful in form and beautiful in appearance means **3821** that this was the nature of the desire for inner truth, so far as its spiritual aspect went. This is established by the remarks just above. *Form* symbolizes essence, and *appearance* symbolizes the resulting beauty.

Genesis 29:18, 19, 20. *And Jacob loved Rachel and said, "I will serve you* **3822** *seven years for Rachel your younger daughter." And Laban said, "It is better that I give her to you than that I give her to another man; stay with me." And Jacob served for Rachel seven years, and they were in his eyes like several days, in his loving her.*

Jacob loved Rachel symbolizes the love that goodness bore for inner truth. *And said, "I will serve you seven years for Rachel your younger daughter,"* means studying to unite with inner truth, and the sacred conditions then. *And Laban said, "It is better that I give her to you than that I give her to another man; stay with me,"* symbolizes a means of union with that goodness through inner truth. *And Jacob served for Rachel seven years* symbolizes fulfillment. *And they were in his eyes like several days, in his loving her* symbolizes a state of love.

Jacob loved Rachel symbolizes the love that goodness bore for inner **3823** truth. This can be seen from the representation of *Jacob* as goodness on the earthly level (discussed in §§3599, 3659, 3775) and from that of *Rachel* as the desire for inner truth (discussed in §§3793, 3819). Here she represents inner truth looking to union with goodness on the earthly level—a union that [earthly goodness] loved.

3824   *And said, "I will serve you seven years for Rachel your younger daugh-ter,"* means studying to unite with inner truth, and the sacred conditions then. This can be seen from the symbolism of *serving* as study; from that of *seven* as something holy (discussed in §§395, 433, 716, 881); and from that of *years* as a state (discussed in §§487, 488, 493, 893). Obviously the goal was union. This shows that *I will serve you seven years for Rachel your younger daughter* means studying to unite with inner truth, and the sacred conditions then.

Inner truth is said to unite with or be internalized by our earthly plane when we learn, acknowledge, and believe it. Our earthly plane and its memory contain both outer and inner truth in the form of doctrinal facts, but they do not unite with them until we desire them for use in our life, or love them for their effect on our life. When we do, goodness joins with doctrinal facts, enabling them to be united to our rational plane and so to our inner self.

This is the path by which life from the Lord flows into those facts.

3825   *And Laban said, "It is better that I give her to you than that I give her to another man; stay with me,"* symbolizes a means of union with that goodness through inner truth. This can be seen from the symbolism of *wages*—what Laban is talking about and agreeing to—as a means of union (discussed above in §3816). Rachel *(her)* means inner truth, and Jacob *(you)* means goodness, as already shown.

The union of the goodness that is Jacob with the goodness that is Laban through the inner truth that is Rachel is a mystery that cannot easily be explained in an intelligible way. One first needs to be able to picture clearly both kinds of goodness and the desire for inner truth. Our understanding of a subject always depends on our idea of it. If we have no idea, we have no understanding; if we have a vague idea, we have a vague understanding; if we have a twisted idea, we have a twisted understanding; and if we have a clear idea, we have a clear understanding. Our understanding of it also depends on our feelings, which can affect even a clear picture.

Still, despite the difficulty, a few words need to be said on the topic. In everyone being reborn, the earthly goodness being represented by Jacob first unites with the goodness being represented by Laban through the desire for inner truth being represented by Rachel. Later it unites with goodness on the rational plane and the truth connected with this goodness, meant by Isaac and Rebekah. The first of these two unions brings us into a condition in which we accept inner or spiritual truth, which is the means to union between the earthly and rational levels, or our outer and inner selves.

And Jacob served for Rachel seven years symbolizes fulfillment. This is established by the symbolism of these words as studying to unite with inner truth, and the sacred conditions then (treated of above in §3824). Plainly this is the fulfillment of the plan.

§3826

And they were in his eyes like several days, in his loving her symbolizes a state of love—in other words, a lack of tedium. This is established by the meaning of *being in his eyes* as so appearing, and from that of *days* as states (discussed in §§893, 2788, 3462, 3785). So *like several days in his loving her* means a state of love. When we are in a state of heavenly love or emotion, we are in an angelic state. If there is no impatience in our mood we seem to step outside of time. Impatience is a bodily emotion, and the more we succumb to it, the more we are trapped in time; but the freer we are of impatience, the freer we are of time.

§3827

The pleasures and happiness brought by an emotion or feeling of love illustrate this fact, in that time disappears when we are enjoying the pleasure and happiness, because our inner self then comes to the fore. The emotions involved in real love draw us out of our bodily and worldly concerns, lifting our mind toward heaven and freeing us from the restraints of time. Time is an appearance we fall into when we reflect on things we do not feel moved by or love—in other words, things that are tedious.

This demonstrates the meaning of the statement that *the seven years were in his eyes like several days, in his loving her.*

Genesis 29:21, 22, 23, 24. *And Jacob said to Laban, "Give me my woman, since my days have been fulfilled, and I will come to her." And Laban gathered all the men of the place and made a banquet. And it happened in the evening that he took Leah his daughter and brought her to [Jacob], and he came to her. And Laban gave Zilpah his slave to her—to Leah his daughter for a slave.*

§3828

Jacob said to Laban, "Give me my woman," means that generalized goodness would now form a bond with the desire for inner truth. *Since my days have been fulfilled, so that I can come to her* means that this was the right stage. *And Laban gathered all the men of the place* symbolizes all the truth in that state. *And made a banquet* symbolizes initiation. *And it happened in the evening* symbolizes a phase that was still dim. *That he took Leah his daughter and brought her to [Jacob], and he came to her* means that as yet the bond was only with a desire for outer truth. *And Laban gave Zilpah his slave to her—to Leah his daughter for a slave* symbolizes shallow desires, or outward restraints, serving as means.

3829   *Jacob said to Laban, "Give me my woman,"* means that generalized goodness would now form a bond with the desire for inner truth. This can be seen from the representation of *Jacob* as goodness on the earthly level (discussed earlier). Here he represents generalized goodness, because the traits of the earthly level are relatively general. There are countless elements in our inner self that flow into our earthly or outer self and appear there as a single, general whole, especially when we have not yet acquired the particular elements that make up the general ones. Such is the situation here. That is why the goodness that Jacob represents is now being called generalized goodness.

The bond is plainly with the desire for inner truth because Rachel—*my woman*—represents that desire, as shown above.

3830   *Since my days have been fulfilled, so that I can come to her* means that this was the right state. This can be seen from the symbolism of *days* as states (discussed in §§23, 487, 488, 493, 893, 2788, 3462, 3785). No explanation is needed to show that *my days have been fulfilled, so that I can come to her* means that this was now the state for it.

3831   *And Laban gathered all the men of the place* symbolizes all the truth in that state. This can be seen from the symbolism of *men* as truth (discussed in §3134) and from that of a *place* as a state (discussed in §§2625, 2837, 3356, 3387).

3832   *And made a banquet* symbolizes initiation. This can be seen from the symbolism of a *banquet* as adoption and union (discussed in §3596). Here it symbolizes initiation, since initiation comes before union and promises and testifies to union.

Banquets in ancient times, held among people who used symbolism and representation, always stood for initiation into the mutual love that marks charity. Wedding feasts symbolized initiation into marriage love, and holy feasts, initiation into spiritual and heavenly love. This symbolism resulted from that of feasting, or eating and drinking, as adopting and uniting (shown in §3734). Because it symbolized these things, the Lord said in the same sense that "many will come all the way from the east and from the west and *recline at [the table]* with Abraham, Isaac, and Jacob in the kingdom of the heavens" (Matthew 8:11). In another place he said to his disciples, ". . . *so that you may eat and drink at my table* in my kingdom" (Luke 22:30). And when he established the Holy Supper, he said, "I say to you that from now on I will not *drink* any of this produce of the grapevine until that day *when I drink it anew with you in my Father's kingdom"* (Matthew 26:29). Anyone can see that reclining at the table, eating, and drinking in the Lord's kingdom does not mean reclining, eating, and drinking but the kind of activity that does occur there: adopting a loving goodness and religious truth. So it is talking about that which is called spiritual and heavenly food. These quotations also show plainly that what the Lord said contains an inner meaning. Without a concept of that meaning we cannot tell what it means to recline at the table with Abraham, Isaac, and Jacob; to eat and drink at the table in the Lord's kingdom; or to drink any of the produce of this grapevine with anyone in the Father's kingdom. Nor can we tell what it means to eat bread and drink wine in the Holy Supper.

And it happened in the evening symbolizes a phase that was still dim, as can be seen from the symbolism of *evening* as a dim state (discussed in §3056). Among the ancients, whose customs were in harmony [with the inner meaning], banquets took place in the evening, at supper time, so what they actually meant was the state of initiation that comes before union. This phase is somewhat dark by comparison with a state of oneness. **3833**

When we are being initiated into truth and then into goodness, everything we learn is dim to us, but when we internalize goodness and view truth from the standpoint of goodness, it becomes clear to us—increasingly so. We no longer wonder whether such and such exists or such and such is so but *know* that it exists and is so. [2] In this phase we start to acquire vast knowledge. From a center point of goodness and truth that we believe in and perceive, we move out toward the edges, and the further we go, the better we see what lies all around. Our view constantly broadens, because we are always expanding and widening the outer limit. Moreover, we also start from each point within the circle as a new center and expand new boundaries from there, and so on. The light of truth radiating from goodness consequently grows beyond measure and becomes a kind of perpetual flame, because we are then bathed in heavenly light from the Lord.

When people doubt and examine whether such and such exists and whether such and such is true, they see none of this vast and even boundless knowledge. Every bit of it is completely dark. They reduce it all to a single whole, which they view not as an established fact but as an uncertain possibility. Such is the current state of human wisdom and understanding that the ability to argue cleverly over whether a thing exists is the mark of a sage, and to argue that it does not is the mark of an even greater sage!

[3] For example, take the question of whether the Word has an inner meaning, which people call a mystical meaning. Until they believe it exists, they cannot know a single one of the myriad concepts of the inner meaning, which are so numerous that they fill the whole of heaven with infinite variety.

Take as another example people who argue about divine providence, asking whether it is only universal and is unconcerned with the small details. They cannot learn the multitudinous secrets of providence, which are as numerous as the contingencies of every person's life from start to finish and from the creation of the world to its end and beyond to eternity.

Take as yet another example people who debate whether anyone can have goodness, since the human will is rotten to the core. They can never learn any of the numerous secrets concerning rebirth, not even the fact that the Lord implants a new will in people, or the secrets associated with this will. And so on with all other subjects.

From this you can see what kind of gloom such people live in, and that they cannot even see the near side of the threshold to wisdom, let alone touch it.

3834   *That he took Leah his daughter and brought her to [Jacob], and he came to her* means that as yet the bond was only with a desire for outer truth. This can be seen from the representation of *Leah* as the desire for outer truth (discussed in §§3793, 3819). *Bringing her to him* obviously symbolizes a marriagelike bond.

Here is the situation: People who long for inner truth—people with a desire to learn the deeper secrets of the Lord's kingdom—do not internalize that truth at first, although they know it and sometimes acknowledge and even seem to believe it. Worldly and bodily desires are still present in them, leading them to accept and seemingly to believe inner truth, yes; but as long as these desires remain in them, they cannot internalize such truth. Only two kinds of desire—a desire for truth inspired by goodness and a desire for goodness itself—spur us to apply truth to ourselves. The more these desires motivate us, the more we internalize inner truth. After all, truth is a vessel designed to receive goodness. [2] The Lord watches to prevent heavenly and spiritual truth (which all inner truth is) from uniting with any nongenuine desire. That is why the first thing that develops is a general desire for truth inspired by goodness, and why the truth instilled at this stage is merely general truth. Different stages of truth go hand in

hand with different stages of goodness; stages of faith go with the state
of neighborly love. The evil, for instance, can learn that the Lord rules
all of heaven, that heaven consists in mutual love and love for the Lord,
and that this love produces union with the Lord, which produces angels'
wisdom and happiness. In fact, they can persuade themselves that this is
so. However, evil people do not internalize religious truth, let alone a loving goodness. Whether they have internalized it can be known from the
way they live, just as a tree is known by its fruit. The situation resembles
seedless grapes, which rot and decay when put in the ground, no matter
how fertile it is. It also resembles swamp light at night, which disappears
the instant the sun rises.

More will be said on this subject later, by the Lord's divine mercy
[§3843].

And Laban gave Zilpah his slave to her—to Leah his daughter for a slave **3835**
symbolizes shallow desires, or outward restraints, serving as means. This can
be seen from the symbolism of a female *slave* as shallow desires (discussed
in §§1895, 2567). *Laban gave* means that they develop out of goodness that
branches off from a shared stock (since that is the source of such desires).

They are called outward restraints because all emotions are restraints
(see §§1077, 1080, 1835, 1944). Nothing shackles us but our feelings. Our
own personal emotions do not seem like restraints to us, but that is still the
proper name for them, because they control us and keep us on their leash.
Deeper desires are called inward restraints; desires for what is true and
good, for instance, are called the bonds of conscience. Outward restraints,
or superficial desires, correspond to them, because everything inside has
something on the outside that corresponds to it.

Since what is external introduces regenerating people to the inner
dimension, and introduction is the stage under discussion here, this verse
mentions that Laban's slave was given to his daughter Leah as a slave,
meaning that such desires serve as means. They are utterly superficial
(like the effects called bodily desires), which is evident from the fact that
Leah represents desires for outer truth.

More will be said on this subject elsewhere, the Lord in his divine
mercy willing [§3849].

Genesis 29:25, 26. *And it happened in the morning that look: she was* **3836**
Leah! And [Jacob] said to Laban, "What is this you have done to me? Didn't
I serve with you for Rachel? Then why have you cheated me?" And Laban
said, "It is not done this way in our region—to give the younger before the
firstborn."

It happened in the morning symbolizes enlightenment in that state. *That look: she was Leah!* means that there was a bond with outer truth. *And he said to Laban, "What is this you have done to me?"* symbolizes outrage. *Didn't I serve with you for Rachel?* means that the goal of the studying was the desire for inner truth. *Then why have you cheated me?* symbolizes greater outrage. *And Laban said, "It is not done this way in our region,"* means that this was not the right state. *To give the younger before the firstborn* means for a desire for inner truth to precede a desire for outer truth.

3837   *It happened in the morning* symbolizes enlightenment in that state. This is established by the symbolism of *morning* as enlightenment (discussed in §§3458, 3723). Since all time symbolizes a state (§§2625, 2788, 2837, 3356), morning time does too.

The enlightenment relates to what comes next, which is the acknowledgment that the union was only with outer truth.

3838   *That look: Leah!* means that there was a bond with outer truth. This is established by the representation of *Leah* as a desire for outer truth (discussed in §§3793, 3819). Clearly the meaning is that there was a bond with this desire, because she instead of Rachel was given [to Jacob] as his woman. The meaning involved can be seen from the discussion above at §3834 about the bond formed with outer truth before any bond with inner truth can be formed, and from the discussion below at §3843.

3839   *And he said to Laban, "What is this you have done to me?"* symbolizes outrage, as can be seen from the emotion in these words and those that follow. Obviously the emotion is outrage, and it is being expressed this way to accord with the story.

There are two components to the Word's inner meaning: emotions and subject matter. The emotions hidden in the expressions of the Word are not apparent to us but lie stored away deep inside it. They *cannot* reveal themselves to us, because while we are living in our bodies we experience worldly and bodily emotions, which have nothing in common with the emotions contained in the Word's inner meaning. The emotions in the Word embody spiritual and heavenly love, which are all the harder for us to perceive because few of us experience them. Of the few who do, most are unsophisticated, incapable of reflecting on the emotions. The rest of us do not even know what genuine emotion is. These feelings belong to charity for our neighbor and love for God, and people who lack charity and love do not believe in their existence, although such feelings completely fill heaven, and do so with inexpressible variety.

These emotions in all their diversity are what lie hidden in the Word's inner meaning. They are found not only in every sentence but also in every word and in fact in every jot. To angels' eyes, they glow—again, in endlessly varied ways—whenever the Word is being read by people of simple goodness and of innocence.

[2] There are two main kinds of desire shining out of the Word for angels to see: desires for truth and desires for goodness. Desires for truth display themselves to spiritual angels, and desires for goodness, to heavenly angels. The latter—desires for goodness—which spring from love for the Lord, are absolutely indescribable to people on earth, so they are also incomprehensible. Desires for truth, though, which spring from mutual love, can be grasped to some extent in their broadest forms, but only by people who feel true mutual love. These individuals rely on a certain inner perception, but one that is quite vague.

[3] Take, for example, the emotion of outrage under discussion here. People who do not know what the emotion of neighborly love is because they have never felt it cannot help picturing this outrage as the emotion most of us feel when someone wrongs us. This is an angry outrage, which does not exist among angels. Their outrage is entirely different, being marked not by anger but by zeal. It is free of evil and stands as far from hatred, revenge, or the payback of evil for evil as heaven stands from hell, because it wells up out of goodness. Yet, as mentioned before, there is no way to express its nature in words.

The case is similar for other desires that rise out of goodness and truth and that seek goodness and truth.

[4] The same thing can be seen from the fact that angels care only about final purposes and about the realization of those purposes (§§1317, 1645, 3645). Purposes are actually different kinds of love or desire (§§1317, 1568, 1571, 1909, 3425, 3796), because what people love they set as their goal. Since angels focus on purpose, they respond emotionally to the Word's contents, and these responses vary widely, according to different angels' desires. This makes it fairly clear how holy the Word is, since holiness resides in divine love (love received from the Divine) and therefore in the Word's contents.

Didn't I serve with you for Rachel? means that the goal of the studying was the desire for inner truth. This can be seen from the representation of *Rachel* as a desire for inner truth (discussed in §§3758, 3782, 3793, 3819) and from the symbolism of *serving* as studying (discussed in §3824).

3840

3841   *Then why have you cheated me?* symbolizes greater outrage, as can be seen from the discussion just above in §3839.

3842   *And Laban said, "It is not done this way in our region,"* means that this was not the right state. This can be seen from the symbolism of a *region* or place as a state (discussed in §§1273, 1274, 1275, 1377, 2625, 2837, 3356, 3387). *It is not done this way in our region,* then, means that this was not the right state.

3843   *To give the younger before the firstborn* means for a desire for inner truth to precede a desire for outer truth. This is established by the representation of Rachel, the *younger,* as a desire for inner truth (dealt with in §§3758, 3782, 3793, 3819) and from that of Leah, the *firstborn,* as a desire for outer truth (dealt with in §§3793, 3819). *To give the younger before the firstborn,* then, plainly means for a desire for inner truth to precede a desire for outer truth.

The situation in all this was explained briefly at §3834 and is further explained by the following: People who do not know the human condition might think we can internalize not only outer but also inner truth as long as we know both kinds, or have them in our memory. We do not internalize them, though, until we live by them, because the way we live shows whether they are internalized. [2] The case is the same with every idea implanted in us from our youth on: it does not become our own until we act on it, and do so voluntarily. When we do this, it permeates our will. We no longer put the idea into act because we know or were taught about it but because it gives us subconscious pleasure and seems to come from our character or nature. We each develop our character by frequent practice, or habit, and what we practice is the ideas we have learned.

This second nature cannot develop, though, until the lessons we learn through doctrine shift from our outer self to our inner self. When they are fixed in our inner self, we no longer obey them from memory but by nature, until in the end they seem to flow spontaneously into act. By then they have been written on the memory of our inner self, and anything that proceeds from this memory appears to be inborn. Take as illustration the languages a person absorbs in youth, or the ability to reason, or conscience.

Clearly, then, we do not internalize theological truth, including its deeper forms, until we make it part of our life. But by the Lord's divine mercy, more will be said on this elsewhere.

3844   Genesis 29:27, 28, 29, 30. *"Fulfill this week and we will give you her as well, for the service that you serve with me yet another seven years." And*

Jacob did so and fulfilled this week, and [Laban] gave him Rachel his daughter as his woman. And Laban gave Bilhah his slave to Rachel his daughter as her slave. And [Jacob] also came to Rachel and loved Rachel too, more than Leah, and served with [Laban] yet another seven years.

Fulfill this week symbolizes developments in this study. *And we will give her as well, for the service that you serve with me yet another seven years* means that by then the studying phase would be complete. *And Jacob did so and fulfilled this week* symbolizes the outcome. *And he gave him Rachel his daughter as his woman* symbolizes union at that point between goodness and the desire for inner truth. *And Laban gave Bilhah his slave to Rachel his daughter as her slave* symbolizes fairly shallow desires that serve as restraints, or means. *And he also came to Rachel* symbolizes union with the desire for inner truth. *And loved Rachel too, more than Leah* symbolizes love for inner truth over outer truth. *And served with him yet another seven years* symbolizes holy study.

Fulfill this week symbolizes further developments in this study. This **3845** can be seen from the meaning of *fulfilling* here as serving—fulfilling a requirement by serving—and therefore as studying (discussed in §3824), and from the symbolism of a *week* as a state and a whole time span (discussed in §§728, 2044). In this case a week symbolizes the next stage of that state and time, so it symbolizes developments in it.

When mentioned in the singular, a *week* (like a month, as mentioned in §3814) symbolizes the end of a previous state and the start of the next, so it symbolizes a new state. *Fulfilling* that state means going from the beginning to the end of it.

The reason a week means a state and also a whole time span, as every specific block of time does, is that all states have their spans; they all begin, develop, and end. In the other world they are not perceived as time periods but as states and as the cycles of these states.

The current verse shows plainly what the ancients meant by a week, in its proper sense; they meant any span of time divided in seven, whether it was days, years, or centuries, and consequently whether the time was long or short. Obviously the span is seven years here. Since to them seven symbolized something holy (§§84–87, 395, 433, 716, 881), a week symbolized a holy period and the holiness of that period.

And we will give you her as well, for the service that you serve with me **3846** *yet another seven years* means that by then the studying phase would be complete. This is established by the symbolism of *service* and *serving* as study (discussed in §3824) and from that of *seven years,* which is the same as a week: a state and a whole time span (as just above in §3845) and therefore a completed phase, which is also holy (as in §3824). *We will give you her as well* means that union with the desire for inner truth will then take place.

Serving means study, in an inner sense, because toil by the outer self is equivalent to study by the inner self. That is why studying is called mental work.

3847   *And Jacob did so and fulfilled this week* symbolizes the outcome. This is established by the symbolism of *fulfilling a week* as developments in the study (as above in §3845). Here, of course, it means the outcome of the study.

3848   *And he gave him Rachel his daughter as his woman* symbolizes union at that point between goodness and the desire for inner truth. This can be seen from the representation of Jacob as goodness on the earthly plane (dealt with before) and from that of *Rachel* as a desire for inner truth (also dealt with before). *Giving her as his woman* means union, as is evident.

Since at first all union of goodness with truth seems to progress from outer levels to inner levels in sequence and finally to the inmost levels, I speak here of a desire for inner truth. The desire itself stems from goodness.

Goodness first unites with a desire for inner truth when earthly goodness unites with rational truth, and through rational truth with rational goodness. This union is represented by Jacob's return to his mother and father's house after the birth of his twelve sons, which will be addressed later on [§§4108, 4563, 4610–4621].

3849   *And Laban gave Bilhah his slave to Rachel his daughter as her slave* symbolizes fairly shallow desires that serve as restraints, or means, as can be seen from the discussion above at §3835.

Bilhah, [Rachel's] slave, symbolizes desires that are fairly shallow, while Zilpah, Leah's slave, symbolizes those that are truly shallow, because Rachel represents the desire for inner truth while Leah symbolizes the desire for outer truth. Relatively shallow desires are desires on the earthly level that serve inner desires.

Relatively shallow desires serve as means for uniting truth with goodness because only through desire can any trace of religious or even of secular knowledge enter us. Desires have life in them, but religious and secular truth separated from desire does not. This is patently obvious. Without feelings we cannot even think, or say a single word. Anyone who pays attention will notice that speech without feeling is like a mechanical voice—sound alone, without any life—and that the amount and kind of life in it depends on the amount and kind of feeling in it. From this fact it is plain what truth is when it lacks goodness, and that truth receives its emotion from goodness. [2] Anyone can see the same thing from the fact that our intellect is nothing unless our will is in it. The life of our intellect comes from our will. This too makes it plain what truth is when it lacks goodness. Without goodness it is nothing, and it draws its life from goodness, because truth belongs to our intellectual side, and goodness to our volitional side. From this anyone can judge the nature of faith (which has to do with truth) when it lacks charity (which has to do with goodness): faith's truth is dead without charity's goodness. As noted, the amount and kind of life it contains depends on the amount and kind of feeling it contains.

Truth can still look animate, even when neighborly kindness is lacking, because of the desires that go with self-love and materialism. The only life these desires contain is the life called death, in a spiritual sense, which is hellish life.

I speak of desire, by which I mean an extension of love.

[3] All these remarks now show that desires serve as means for uniting truth with goodness, that they introduce truth, and that they arrange truth in a pattern. Genuine desires, which come of love for the Lord and for our neighbor, arrange truth in a heavenly pattern. Evil desires, which come of love for ourselves and for worldly advantages, arrange it in a hellish pattern—the opposite of the heavenly pattern.

[4] The shallowest desires are those tied to the body and are called appetites and sensual pleasures. The next deeper kind belong to the lower mind and are called earthly desires. The inner kind belong to the rational mind and are called spiritual desires. Doctrinal truth is introduced to the spiritual desires of the higher mind through the two shallower levels of desire—earthly and bodily. The latter kinds of desire therefore serve as means and are symbolized by the slaves that Laban gave to Rachel and Leah.

They are called Laban's slaves, which means that they trace their origin to the goodness represented by Laban—a goodness that has already been described. The truth we learn first cannot initially be instilled through any other kind of desire. Genuine desires come with time, and only when we act from goodness.

3850   *And he also came to Rachel* symbolizes union with the desire for inner truth. This can be seen from the symbolism of *coming to* as uniting with, and from the representation of *Rachel* as the desire for inner truth (treated of before).

3851   *And loved Rachel too, more than Leah* symbolizes love for inner truth over outer truth. This can be seen from the representation of both—of *Rachel* as inner truth, and of *Leah* as outer truth. For what inner and outer truth are, see §3820.

3852   *And served with him yet another seven years* symbolizes holy study. This is established by the symbolism of *serving* as study (discussed in §§3824, 3846) and from that of *seven* as something holy (discussed in §§395, 433, 716, 881, 3824). "Holy study" refers to study leading to a union of deep truth with goodness. Deep truth focuses exclusively on the Lord and unites [with goodness] through love for him. This love is the holy element.

3853   *Genesis 29:31. And Jehovah saw that Leah was hated and opened her womb; and Rachel was infertile.*

Jehovah saw symbolizes the Lord's foresight and providence. *That Leah was hated* means that the desire for outer truth was not loved as tenderly, because it was further from divinity. *And opened her womb* means that it is the source of different churches' doctrines. *And Rachel was infertile* means that inner truth was not accepted.

3854   *Jehovah saw* symbolizes the Lord's foresight and providence. This can be seen from the symbolism of *seeing,* when the Lord is said to do it, as foresight and providence. This will be discussed at the next verse, which is about Reuben, whose name comes from a word for seeing. On the point that *Jehovah* is the Lord, see §§1343, 1736, 1793, 2156, 2329, 2921, 3023, 3035.

[2] Concerning foresight and providence in general: What we view as foresight, the Lord views as providence. The Lord foresaw from eternity what the human race and every member of it would be like, and he foresaw that evil would constantly grow until at last humankind would voluntarily plunge into hell. So not only did he provide the means by which we could be turned from hell and led to heaven; in his providence he is constantly turning and leading us, too.

He also foresaw that nothing good would ever take root in us unless we were free, since what takes root when we are not free dissolves as soon as evil approaches or we are tested. This the Lord foresaw, along with the fact that on our own, in our freedom, we would head for the deepest hell. So he provides that if we do not let ourselves be led freely to heaven, he will divert us to a milder hell, but that if we allow ourselves to be led freely toward goodness, he will take us to heaven.

This shows what foresight and providence are, and that what is foreseen is provided for.

[3] You can see, then, how mistaken people are when they disbelieve that the Lord has foreseen and now sees the tiniest details of our life, and that he provides for and guides us in each of those details. The reality is that the Lord's foresight and providence concerns itself with the smallest possible aspects in human affairs—so small that we cannot in any way comprehend one out of millions. Every split second of our life carries with it a series of consequences that continues forever. Each moment is like a new starting point for another series, and this is true for each and every moment of life in both our intellect and our will. Since the Lord foresaw from eternity what we would be like now and forever, his providence must obviously be present in the smallest facets, governing us and (again) bending us in this direction by continually moderating our freedom.

More will be said on this topic below, however, by the Lord's divine mercy.

That Leah was hated means that the desire for outer truth was not loved as tenderly, because it was further from divinity. This can be seen from the meaning of *hated* as not loved and from the representation of Leah as a desire for outer truth (discussed before [§§3793, 3819]).

3855

Surface truth is more distant from divinity than inner truth, of course, since it emerges from inner truth. Outer truths, each of which seems single, are images and forms put together from thousands and thousands of inner truths. As a result, they are further from divinity, since the divine level is above our inmost level, at the highest height. From that highest plane the Lord acts on our inmost levels and through these on our intermediate levels and through these in turn on our outer levels. So he acts on our outer levels indirectly, and directly as well.

Since the outer plane is further from divinity, it is also more disorganized, by comparison, and does not permit itself to be reduced to order as readily as the inner plane. It is like a seed, which is more perfect on the inside than on the outside. The inside is so perfect that it can produce an entire plant or an entire tree according to plan with all its leaves and fruit. The outer forms of a seed are wide open to all kinds of injury, but not so much its inner or inmost forms, which have a deeper, more perfect nature. The case is the same with a human being's inner and outer forms, so when we are regenerating, our rational dimension is reborn before our earthly dimension (§3493). The rebirth of our earthly dimension is both slower and harder because more of it is disorganized and it is exposed to harm from the body and the world.

This being so, the outer dimension is described as less well loved. However, it is capable of harmonizing with the inner dimension, encouraging this dimension within itself to come alive and be seen, and helping us regenerate; and the more it does these things, the more tenderly it is loved.

3856   *And opened her womb* means that it is the source of different churches' doctrines. This can be seen from the symbolism of *opening a womb,* or conceiving and giving birth, as becoming a church. Since a church comes into existence through doctrine, the opening of a womb symbolizes different churches' doctrines.

Conceptions and births mentioned in the Word symbolize spiritual conceptions and births, as experienced by people being born anew; see §§1145, 1255, 1330, 2584. What is involved will become clear from the discussion just below.

3857   *And Rachel was infertile* means that inner truth was not accepted. This can be seen from the representation of *Rachel* as a desire for inner truth (discussed earlier) and from the symbolism of *infertile* as something that does not yield doctrine and therefore does not produce churches. These words, you see, contrast with those regarding Leah: that Jehovah opened her womb, meaning that different churches' doctrines came from there.

The reason inner truth was not accepted is that it transcends human belief; it is not accessible to our thoughts and does not agree with outward appearances, or sensory illusions. We all let ourselves be led by appearances and refuse to believe anything unless it matches up with them in some way.

[2] For instance, it is inwardly true that there is no time and space in the other world but state instead. While we are living on earth, we live in time and space and base all our thinking on them. In fact, we cannot think without them (§3404). So unless the states of the next life were depicted to us in terms of time and space, or in terms of objects and events shaped by time and space, we would not understand at all and thus would not believe. As a consequence, we would not accept them, the doctrine would be sterile, and no religion would come of it.

[3] For another example, if heavenly and spiritual desires were not depicted in terms of the objects of worldly and bodily desire, we would not comprehend them at all. We are immersed in the latter, from which we can acquire an idea of the former, even though they are as different or as distant from each other as heaven is from earth (§3839). Take heaven's glory, or the glory of angels in heaven. If we did not form a picture of heavenly glory to match our idea of worldly glory, we would not grasp it and so would not acknowledge it. The same holds true for all other inner truth. [4] That is why the Lord in the Word spoke on a level people could understand and in keeping with the appearances they saw. Such is the Word's literal meaning; but it still holds an inner meaning that contains deep truth.

This now explains why the text says that Jehovah opened Leah's womb and Rachel was infertile. To repeat, Leah represents a desire for outer truth, while Rachel represents a desire for inner truth. All the same, since outer truth is the first truth we learn, the Lord provided for it to be capable of introducing us to inner truth. That is what is symbolized in Genesis 30:22 by God's finally remembering Rachel, listening to her, and opening her womb.

[5] This situation can be seen from the religions existing in ancient times and from their doctrines, since their doctrines consisted of outward truth. It can also be seen from the ancient church that followed the Flood, whose doctrines consisted mainly of outward representations and symbols concealing inner truth within them. It was when they were engaged in the outward signs that most of the people were in a state of reverent worship. If anyone had told them at the outset that what was essential to worshiping God was not representations and symbols but the spiritual and heavenly qualities these things represented and symbolized, they would have flatly rejected it. The church would have dissolved.

The same holds even truer for the Jewish religion. If anyone had told the Jewish people that their rituals derived their holiness from the Lord's divine qualities embodied in the rituals, they absolutely would not have acknowledged it.

[6] That is also what humankind was like when the Lord came into the world, though people were even more body-centered then, especially those in the church. The fact is quite plain from the disciples themselves, who spent all their time with the Lord and heard so much about his kingdom but were not yet able to perceive inner truth. The only view of

the Lord they could form was the same one held today by Jews in regard to the Messiah they are awaiting: that he would raise the Jewish people to a position of power and glory over all the nations in the entire world. After listening to all the Lord said about his heavenly kingdom, they still could not help thinking that the heavenly kingdom would resemble an earthly one. They pictured God the Father as the highest in that kingdom, followed by the Son, and then the twelve of them, governing in this order. That is why James and John sought to sit one on his right and the other on his left (Mark 10:35, 36, 37) and why the rest of the disciples were outraged that these two wanted to be greater than they (Mark 10:41; Matthew 20:24). So after the Lord taught them what it was to be greatest in heaven (Matthew 20:25, 26, 27, 28; Mark 10:42, 43, 44, 45), he still spoke in terms they could grasp, saying that they would sit on twelve thrones and judge the twelve tribes of Israel (Luke 22:24, 30; Matthew 19:28). [7] They were not told that "disciples" meant not them but everyone with the goodness that comes of love and faith (§§3354, 3488); that there are no thrones in the Lord's kingdom, or the kinds of sovereignty and autocratic power found in the world; or that they were incapable of passing even the most limited judgment on a single person (§§2129, 2553). If they had been told, they would have spurned the news and each gone back to his own business, leaving the Lord behind. He spoke this way so that they would accept it and be introduced by it to inner truth. Hidden within the outer truth the Lord spoke lay inner truth, which comes out in the open with time, and once it comes out, the external words disappear, serving only as a stimulus or springboard for thought about inner ideas.

From this it can now be seen what is meant by the fact that Jehovah opened Leah's womb first, that she bore Jacob children, and that Rachel bore later.

3858   Since the next verses have to do with Jacob's twelve sons, and they are the ancestors for whom the twelve tribes of Israel were named, I need to start by saying what the tribes symbolize and why there were twelve of them. No one knows the secret hidden in this yet, because people have considered the stories of the Word to be bald history. They have not seen anything divine in the material except that it can serve as illustration when they are discussing religion. So they have believed that the twelve tribes only meant the division of the Israelite people into twelve different nations or general clans. In reality, the meaning involves something divine—the division of faith and love into so many broad categories—and consequently something pertaining to the Lord's kingdom in the heavens and on earth. In fact, each tribe means something universal. What it means will become clear from the discussion directly below focusing on the sons of Jacob for whom the tribes were named.

As a group the twelve tribes symbolized everything involved in the doctrines concerning truth and goodness, or faith and love. After all, truth and goodness, or faith and love, make up the Lord's kingdom. What relates to truth or faith is the all-in-all of the thinking there, and what relates to goodness or love is the all-in-all of the feelings there. Since the Jewish religion was established to represent the Lord's kingdom, these elements are what the division of that people into twelve tribes symbolized. This is a secret that has never been revealed before.

[2] *Twelve* symbolizes everything in general, as demonstrated before in §§577, 2089, 2129, 2130 at the end, 3272. *Tribes* symbolize different facets of truth and goodness, or of faith and love, so the twelve tribes symbolize all facets of them. Let me confirm this from the Word before turning to each tribe in particular. In John:

> . . . the holy city New Jerusalem, having *twelve* gates and on the gates *twelve* angels and names written, which are those of the *twelve tribes of the children of Israel.* The wall of the city had *twelve* foundations and on them the names of the *Lamb's twelve apostles.* He measured the city with the reed at *twelve thousand* stadia, and he measured its wall at a *hundred forty-four* cubits, which is the measure of a human, that is, of an angel. The *twelve* gates were *twelve* pearls. (Revelation 21:12, 14, 16, 17, 21)

Every word of this passage makes it clear that the holy city, New Jerusalem, is the Lord's new church. The preceding verses discuss what the [current] church's condition will be just before it ends, and these verses talk about a new church. As a result, the gates, wall, and foundations are actually aspects of the church, which are aspects of charity and faith (since charity and faith compose the church). [3] Anyone can see, then, that the number twelve (repeated so many times in the quotation), the tribes, and the apostles do not mean twelve or tribes or apostles. No, twelve means everything as a whole, as shown before (see §§577, 2089, 2129, 2130 at the end, 3272). So does a hundred forty-four, because this is twelve times twelve. Since twelve symbolizes everything, clearly the twelve tribes symbolize every attribute of the church, these attributes being truth and goodness, or faith and love, as noted above. Likewise the twelve apostles. On the point that the apostles too represented everything in the church, or everything of faith and love, see §§2129, 3354, 3488, 3857. That is why the number is called "the measure of a human, that is, of an angel," which means states of truth and goodness. A measure means a state (see §3104). A human means some aspect of religion (as is evident from the remarks at §§478, 479, 565, 768, 1871, 1894 about the symbolism of a human). Consider also that the Lord's kingdom is called a universal human and that it is called this because of its goodness and truth, which come from the Lord (as discussed at chapter ends in §§3624–3649, 3741–3750). An angel has the same meaning (§§1705, 1754, 1925, 2821, 3039).

[4] Like John, the Old Testament prophets describe a new Jerusalem that also symbolizes the Lord's new church. Examples are Isaiah 65:18, 19, and following verses; Zechariah 14; and especially Ezekiel 40, 41, 42, 43, 44, 45, 46, 47, 48, where the new Jerusalem, the new temple, and the new land in an inner sense depict the Lord's kingdom in the heavens and his kingdom on the earth, which is the church. The content of those passages illustrates more clearly than that of any others what the *earth, Jerusalem,* the *temple,* and everything in it symbolize. It also shows what the *twelve tribes* symbolize, because it speaks about dividing up the land and their *inheriting it according to their tribes.* It speaks about the *city* and its *walls, foundation,* and *gates,* and about all the furnishings the *temple* in that city will contain. Let me quote just the parts about the tribes.

> The Lord Jehovih said, "This is the border to which you will inherit the *land* in accord with the *twelve tribes of Israel:* You shall divide this land according to the *tribes of Israel.* But it will happen that you shall divide it by lot as an inheritance [for yourselves] and for the immigrants residing in your midst; along with you they shall cast a lot for an inheritance in the *middle of the tribes of Israel.*" (Ezekiel 47:13, 21, 22, 23)

> In regard to the *land,* it will belong to the chieftain as a possession in Israel, and chieftains will no longer afflict my people, and they will *give the land* to the house of Israel according to *their tribes.* (Ezekiel 45:8)

To learn how the inheritances were assigned to each of the tribes, which are named individually there, see Ezekiel 48:1 and following verses. Concerning the city *gates* that were according to the *names of Israel's tribes,* see Ezekiel 48:31–34. [5] It is obvious that the tribes in this passage do not mean tribes, because by then ten tribes had been scattered to the four corners of the earth. They never returned and cannot ever return, because they became gentile. Yet the text names each, tells how it will inherit the land, and describes its borders—the border for the tribe of Dan in verse 1; the border for the tribe of Asher in verse 2; for those of Naphtali, Manasseh, Ephraim, Reuben, and Judah; the Levites' inheritance; the border for the tribe of Benjamin; for that of Simeon; for those of Issachar, Zebulun, and Gad—all in Ezekiel 48:3–29. The text goes on to say that the city had twelve gates according to the names of Israel's tribes: three gates to the north for Reuben, Judah, and Levi; three gates to the east for Joseph, Benjamin, and Dan; three gates to the south for Simeon, Issachar and Zebulun; three gates to the west for Gad, Asher, and Naphtali (Ezekiel 48:31, 32, 33, 34). This shows that the twelve tribes symbolize all the qualities of the Lord's kingdom and accordingly that they mean all aspects of faith and love, since these constitute the Lord's kingdom, as noted above.

[6] Since the twelve tribes symbolized everything in the Lord's kingdom, they represented the same thing by the way they camped and set out to travel, as described in Moses, who says that they *camped around the meeting tent according to their tribes.* Toward the east were Judah, Issachar, and Zebulun; toward the south, Reuben, Simeon, and Gad; toward the west, Ephraim, Manasseh, and Benjamin; toward the north, Dan, Asher, and Naphtali; and as they camped, so they set out (Numbers 2:1–end). In doing so, they represented the Lord's kingdom, as is quite plain in Balaam's prophecy:

> When Balaam raised his eyes and saw Israel *dwelling by tribes,* the spirit of God came over him and he uttered his pronouncement and said, "How good are your tents, Jacob; your dwellings, Israel! They are planted as valleys are, as gardens beside the river; like sandalwoods has Jehovah planted them, like cedars beside the water." (Numbers 24:2, 3, 5, 6)

These words of Balaam's came from Jehovah, as plainly said in Numbers 22:8, 18, 19, 35, 38; 23:5, 12, 16, 26; 24:2, 13.

[7] These considerations also show what the tribe-by-tribe inheritance of the land of Canaan represented, concerning which Moses said that he would "take the total of the assembly of the children of Israel according to

the house of their ancestors, from a son of twenty years; *everyone going out into Israel's army* [would be counted]." The land would be distributed by lot; "*according to the names of the tribes of their ancestors they shall inherit*" (Numbers 26:2, 7–56; 33:54; 34:19–29). Joshua divided the land "by lot *according to the tribes*" (Joshua 13, [14,] 15, 16, 17, 18, 19). Again, the Lord's kingdom is what was being represented, as the details indicate. After all, the land of Canaan symbolized that kingdom (see §§1585, 1607, 3038, 3481, 3705).

[8] The people are called armies and are said to have camped according to their armies and set out to travel according to their armies (Numbers 2:4, 6, 8, 11, 13, 15, 19, 21, 22, 23, 26, 28, 30, [34]). The reason for this wording is that an army symbolized the same thing [as the tribes]: truth and goodness (see §3448). The Lord was called Jehovah Sabaoth, or Jehovah of Armies (§3448). So the people were called Jehovah's army when they left Egypt, as in Moses:

> It happened at the end of four hundred thirty years—it happened on that very day—that *all the armies of Jehovah went out* from the land of Egypt. (Exodus 12:41)

Anyone can see that people who behaved the way these tribes did in Egypt and afterward in the wilderness were called Jehovah's army only in a representative sense. They had no goodness or truth and were the worst nation of all.

[9] This also shows clearly what was symbolized by the names of the twelve tribes on Aaron's breastplate (called the Urim and Thummim). Moses speaks of it this way:

> There shall be four rows there; twelve stones. These stones shall be *according to the names of the sons of Israel*—twelve, according to their names. The engravings of a signet shall be on each, over its name, for the *twelve tribes.* (Exodus 28:[17,] 21; 39:14)

Aaron represented the Lord's divine work as priest, so everything Aaron wore symbolized divinely heavenlike and divinely spiritual qualities. The specific symbolism will become clear where his garments are discussed, by the Lord's divine mercy. Since the breastplate was holiest, on it were representations of everything involved in love for and faith in the Lord—that is, the Urim and Thummim. Why were the names engraved on these precious stones? Stones in general symbolize truth (§§1298, 3720), and precious stones symbolize truth that is translucent with goodness (§114). The name of each tribe symbolized some quality, so each tribe was assigned its own unique stone (Exodus 28:17, 18, 19, 20, [21]; 39:10, 11, 12, 13, [14]), and this stone by its color and brilliance expressed the quality symbolized by that tribe. That is why Jehovah (the Lord) gave answers through the Urim and Thummim.

[10] The two shoham stones on the two shoulders of the ephod represented the same thing but on a smaller scale than the twelve stones on the breastplate. Shoulders symbolized all a person's might, so they symbolized the Lord's omnipotence (§1085). The breast, or the heart and lungs, symbolized divinely heavenlike and spiritual love—the heart, divinely heavenlike love, and the lungs, divinely spiritual love (see §3635 and the end of the current chapter, where the universal human and its correspondence with the realms of the heart and lungs is discussed). Here is what Moses says about the two stones on the shoulders of the ephod:

> You shall take two shoham stones and engrave on them the *names of Israel's sons,* six of the names on one stone and the other six names on the other stone, according to their generations. You shall put the two stones on the shoulders of the ephod, stones of remembrance for *Israel's sons.* (Exodus 28:9, 10, 11, [12]; 39:6, 7)

[11] Again, the tribes symbolized aspects of truth and goodness, or of faith and love, and each tribe symbolized some universal aspect. The tribe of Levi symbolized love, as the explanation at verse 34 of this chapter will show [§§3875–3877]. From this you can see the symbolism of the staffs that the people would put in the meeting tent, one for each tribe, and of the fact that only Levi's staff blossomed with almonds, as Moses describes in these words: He would take *twelve staffs*—one staff for the head of [each] house of their ancestors—which would be left in the meeting tent, and he would write Aaron's name on *Levi's staff.*

> Aaron's staff was put in the midst of them. The next day, look! *Aaron's staff* budded for *Levi's tribe;* it put out a flower to bloom a bloom and bear almonds. (Numbers 17:2–8)

This meant that love was the first, most important thing of all in the Lord's kingdom, the source of all fruitfulness. Aaron's name was on it because he represented the Lord's divine role as priest. The Lord's priestliness means the divine goodness of his love and mercy, while his kingliness means the divine truth that comes of divine goodness; see §§1728, 2015 at the end, 3670.

[12] These quotations now show what "tribes" and "twelve tribes" symbolize in the following passages. In John, for instance:

> I heard the number of those sealed: a *hundred forty-four thousand* sealed from *every tribe of Israel.* From the *tribe of Judah, twelve* thousand sealed. From the *tribe of Reuben, twelve* thousand sealed. From *the tribe of Gad, twelve* thousand sealed. From *the tribe of Asher, twelve* thousand sealed. From *the tribe of Naphtali, twelve* thousand sealed. From *the tribe of Manasseh, twelve* thousand sealed. From *the tribe of Simeon, twelve* thousand sealed. From *the tribe of Levi, twelve* thousand sealed. From *the tribe of Issachar, twelve* thousand sealed. From *the tribe of Zebulun, twelve* thousand sealed. From *the tribe of Joseph, twelve* thousand sealed. From *the tribe of Benjamin, twelve* thousand sealed. (Revelation 7:4, 5, 6, 7, 8)

In Moses:

> Remember the days of old, understand the years of generation after generation, when the Highest One gave an inheritance to the nations; when he divided the children of humankind, he set the boundaries of the peoples *according to the number of the children of Israel.* (Deuteronomy 32:7, 8)

In David:

> Jerusalem has been built as a city that clings together with itself, to which *tribes* go up, the *tribes of Jah,* as testimony to Israel, to acclaim Jehovah's name. (Psalms 122:3, 4)

[13] In Joshua:

> When the ark of the covenant of the Lord of the whole earth crosses before you into the Jordan, take *twelve men of Israel's tribes,* one man *from a tribe.* It will happen, when the soles of the feet of the priests carrying the ark of Jehovah—Lord of the whole earth—rest in the Jordan's waters, that the Jordan's waters will be cut off; they will stand in one heap. (Joshua 3:11–17)

Further:

> "Take from the middle of the Jordan, from the standing place of the priests' feet, and prepare, *twelve stones* that you will carry across with

you; and a man [will carry] one stone on his shoulder, *according to the number of Israel's tribes,* to be as a sign that the Jordan's waters were cut off." Moreover, Joshua set up *twelve stones* in the middle of the Jordan on the standing place of the feet of the priests who carried the ark of the covenant. (Joshua 4:1–9)

Again:

Elijah took *twelve stones, according to the number of tribes of Jacob's sons,* and the word came to him, "Israel will be your name," and he built an altar in Jehovah's name. (1 Kings 18:31, 32)

[14] The meaning of tribes as a loving goodness and religious truth can also be seen from the Lord's words in Matthew:

Then the sign of the Son of Humankind will appear, and *then all the tribes of the earth will mourn,* and they will see the Son of Humankind coming in the clouds of heaven with strength and glory. (Matthew 24:30)

"All the tribes of the earth will mourn" means that people will no longer acknowledge truth or live a good life. The passage is talking about the close of the age. Likewise in John:

Watch: he will come with the clouds, and every eye will see him, as will those who stabbed him; and *all the tribes of the earth* will mourn over him. (Revelation 1:7)

To learn what coming in the clouds of heaven means, see the preface to Genesis 18.

See also what was shown to me about the number twelve in an experience described in §§2129, 2130.

[15] The reason all aspects of faith and love are called tribes is that in the original language the word for a tribe also means a scepter and a staff. A scepter and a staff mean power, as will be shown elsewhere, with the Lord's divine mercy [§§4013, 4876, 4936, 7026]. So the word *tribe* involves the idea that goodness and truth contain all power, imparted by the Lord. For the same reason, angels are called powers and also principalities [Romans 8:38; Ephesians 3:10; 1 Peter 3:22], because princes or chieftains symbolize the main elements of neighborly love and faith, as the twelve chiefs born to Ishmael do (Genesis 25:16; see §2089) and as the chiefs over the tribes do (Numbers 7:1–end; 13:4–16).

[16] From everything said so far about the twelve tribes you can see why the Lord's disciples (later called apostles) numbered twelve. It can also be seen that they represented goodness and truth in the Lord's church, just as the tribes did (§§2129, 3354, 3488, 3857). Peter represented faith; James, neighborly love; and John, acts of neighborly kindness (see the prefaces to Genesis 18 and 22, and §3750), as stands out clearly from what the Lord said about them and to them.

3859   Genesis 29:32. *And Leah conceived and bore a son and called his name Reuben, because she said, "Jehovah has seen my affliction, because now my husband will love me."*

Leah conceived and bore a son symbolizes spiritual conception and birth progressing from outer plane to inner. *And called his name Reuben* symbolizes its nature, which is then delineated. *Because she said, "Jehovah has seen,"* in the highest sense means foresight; in an inward sense, faith; in an intermediate sense, intellect; on the surface, eyesight; in the current case, a faith granted by the Lord. *My affliction* symbolizes a state in which we attain goodness. *Because now my husband will love me* means that the good that comes of truth will result.

3860   *Leah conceived and bore a son* symbolizes spiritual conception and birth progressing from outer plane to inner. This can be seen from the inner-level symbolism of *conceiving and bearing* as regenerating. When we regenerate, we are conceived and born anew, which is why regeneration is called rebirth—spiritual rebirth. Our parents give birth to us as human beings, but we do not become truly human until the Lord gives birth to us again. Spiritual and heavenly life is what makes us human, because it distinguishes us from brute animals. This conception and birth is symbolized by conceptions and births mentioned in the Word, including the statement *Leah conceived and bore a son.* The generations and births are those of faith and love, which is their symbolic meaning; see §§613, 1145, 1255, 2020, 2584, 3856.

The progression of these conceptions and births from outer plane to inner is symbolized by Leah's conceiving and giving birth. Leah represents a desire for outer truth (§§3793, 3819), and Reuben represents religious truth, which is the first requirement for rebirth and is the outer plane on which the process starts.

The whole discussion to come concerning the children Jacob had by Leah and by Rachel will reveal how matters stand with all this.

3861   *And called his name Reuben* symbolizes its nature, which is then delineated. This is established by the symbolism of a name and *calling a name* as the quality (discussed in §§144, 145, 1754, 1896, 2009, 2724, 3006, 3421).

The specific nature is delineated in the words *that Jehovah has seen my affliction, and now my husband will love me,* which is what *Reuben* means.

It has been shown frequently that scriptural names always have symbolic meaning (see §§1224, 1264, 1876, 1888) and that the names given by the ancients symbolized states (§§340, 1946, 2643, 3422). It will be seen that the names of all Jacob's sons symbolize universal qualities in the church. The quality itself was also incorporated into the name of each son, but no one can know just what quality it is without also knowing what the words used for naming each son enfold in an inner sense. For instance, one needs to know the inner meaning of *seeing,* the word used in Reuben's name; that of *hearing,* the word used in Simeon's; that of *clinging to,* used in Levi's; and that of *acclaiming,* used in Judah's. And so on with the words used in the rest of the names.

Section 3858 above showed that the twelve tribes symbolized all facets **3862** of truth and goodness, or of faith and love. The current focus of discussion is the individual sons of Jacob for whom the tribes were named, so I need to reveal another secret here: the meaning that Jacob's sons have.

All heavenly and spiritual warmth, or love and charity, is outwardly perceived in heaven as flames given off by the sun. All heavenly and spiritual light, or faith, outwardly appears in heaven as light radiating from the sun. The heavenly and spiritual warmth contains wisdom, and the resulting light contains understanding, because they come from the Lord, who is the sun there. (See §§1053, 1521–1533, 1619–1632, 2441, 2495, 2776, 3138, 3167, 3190, 3195, 3222, 3223, 3338, 3339, 3341, 3413, 3485, 3636, 3643.) Clearly, then, all goodness comes from the warmth that the Lord gives off as the sun, and all truth comes from the light he sheds. All desires, which relate to love, or goodness, are variations of the heavenly and spiritual warmth given off by the Lord, and from them come changes of state. All thoughts, which relate to faith, or truth, are modifications of the heavenly and spiritual light shed by the Lord, and from them comes understanding.

All of heaven's angels are subject to these influences; their feelings and thoughts have no other source or identity. This fact is clear from their language, which has the same source and therefore consists of variegations or modifications of heavenly light containing heavenly warmth. As a result, their speech is indescribable and displays more variety and fullness than anyone could possibly grasp (§§3342, 3344, 3345).

[2] In order to provide an earthly representation of these concepts, Jacob's sons were each given names symbolizing universal aspects of

goodness and truth, or of love and faith. In consequence, the names symbolized variations of heavenly and spiritual warmth in their universal aspects and modifications of the resulting light in their universal aspects. The pattern of those universal qualities determines what kind of fire and radiance they emit. When the pattern starts with love, anything that genuinely follows it looks fiery. When the pattern starts with faith, anything that genuinely follows it looks brilliant—in all kinds of ways, depending on how the subsequent parts follow the pattern. If they do not truly fit in, it looks dark in all kinds of ways. Variations on the pattern will be discussed below, however, by the Lord's divine mercy. This now is why the Lord gave answers through the Urim and Thummim and why, depending on what the situation was, [the priests] received the answers through flashes of light from the translucent precious stones on which the names of the twelve tribes were engraved. As noted, the names themselves were inscribed with universal aspects of love and faith as they exist in the Lord's kingdom and consequently with universal aspects of fire and light that in heaven represent aspects of love and faith.

[3] Let me start, then, by confirming from the Word that the order in which the tribes are named there varies, depending on the situation under discussion. This will indicate that the answers the Lord gave through the Urim and Thummim were flashes of light whose order was determined by the state of affairs. All light in heaven varies in accord with the situation at hand, and the situation at hand varies in accord with the pattern of goodness and truth. What combination of truth and goodness each pattern symbolizes will become clear from the explanation: Reuben symbolizes a faith imparted by the Lord; Simeon, a faith belonging to the will, imparted by the Lord; Levi, spiritual love, or charity; Judah, divine love and the Lord's heavenly kingdom. The symbolism of the remaining eight will be given in the next chapter.

The pattern depicted here follows their birth order, which runs Reuben, Simeon, Levi, Judah, Dan, Naphtali, Gad, Asher, Issachar, Zebulun, Joseph, and Benjamin. See verses 32, 33, 34, 35 of this chapter; the next chapter, Genesis 30:6, 8, 11, 13, 18, 20, 24; and Genesis 35:18. This order matches the situation being described here, which is a person's rebirth. When we regenerate, we start with faith's truth, meant by Reuben; advance from there to an intent to act on truth, meant by Simeon; from there to charity, meant by Levi; and so to the Lord, meant in the highest sense by Judah. Spiritual conception and birth, or regeneration, progresses from the outer plane to the inner, as noted just above in §3860; that is, it progresses from faith's truth to love's goodness.

[4] Shortly before Jacob came to Isaac his father in Mamre, Kiriath-arba, his sons are named in this order: Reuben, Simeon, Levi, Judah, Issachar, Zebulun, Joseph, Benjamin, Dan, Naphtali, Gad, and Asher (Genesis 35:23, 24, 25, 26). Here the sons of Leah and Rachel come first, and those of the slaves, last, as determined by the situation being treated of.

They are listed in yet another order when they set out and came to Egypt, as described in Genesis 46:9–19; in another when Jacob (who by then was Israel) blessed them before dying (Genesis 49:3–27); and in another when Moses blessed them (Deuteronomy 33:6–24).

When they camped around the meeting tent, they were in this pattern: toward the east, Judah, Issachar, Zebulun; toward the south, Reuben, Simeon, Gad; toward the west, Ephraim, Manasseh, Benjamin; toward the north, Dan, Asher, Naphtali (Numbers 2:1–end).

For the arrangement the tribes stood in on Mount Gerizim to bless the people and on Mount Ebal to curse them, see Deuteronomy 27:12, 13.

When the chief men, one from each tribe, were to be sent to scout out the land, they are listed in this order: Reuben, Simeon, Judah, Issachar, Ephraim, Benjamin, Zebulun, Joseph (that is, Manasseh), Dan, Asher, Naphtali, Gad (Numbers 13:4–16). However, the chiefs who were to give the land as an inheritance are listed in another order (Numbers 34:19–29). For the order in which lots were cast and fell out when the land was given as an inheritance, see Joshua 13–19.

[5] Where Ezekiel deals with the borders of the new, holy land that the tribes were to inherit, they are mentioned in this order: Dan, Asher, Naphtali, Manasseh, Ephraim, Reuben, Judah, Benjamin, Simeon, Issachar, Zebulun, Gad—all reaching from the eastern side to the "sea" side, or western side, except for Gad, which was on the southern side toward the south (Ezekiel 48:1–7, 23–28). Where it deals with the gates of the new, holy city, the tribes are mentioned in this order: to the north, three gates for Reuben, Judah, Levi; to the east, three gates for Joseph, Benjamin, Dan; to the south, three gates for Simeon, Issachar, Zebulun; to the west, three gates for Gad, Asher, Naphtali (Ezekiel 48:31–34).

For the order of the twelve thousand sealed from each tribe, see Revelation 7:5–8.

In all these passages, the list of tribes matches perfectly the situation being spoken of, and the order of the names corresponds to it. The exact nature of the situation becomes clear from the surrounding context.

[6] The Word mentions and describes how the precious stones were arranged in the Urim and Thummim but does not say which tribe each

stone corresponded to. The stones represented every modification of the light given off by heavenly fire—that is, every kind of truth produced by goodness, or every form of faith produced by love. Because that is what they represented, heaven's light itself miraculously shone through them according to the circumstances that the questions and answers were about. It gleamed and shone to affirm what was good and true, and it also varied in color, depending on the different states of goodness and truth, as it does in heaven. In heaven, distinctions among different kinds of light express heavenly and spiritual qualities in a way that is indescribable and completely incomprehensible to people on earth. As has been explained several times, heaven's light contains life from the Lord, so it contains wisdom and understanding [§§3195, 3339, 3636, 3643, 3679]. Different varieties of light contain every facet of the life present in truth—every facet of wisdom and understanding. Different varieties of its fire, gleam, and radiance contain every facet of the life present in goodness and in the truth generated by goodness—every facet of love for the Lord and of the resulting faith. This is what the Urim and Thummim on the breastplate of the ephod over Aaron's heart meant. In further support of this symbolism, *Urim* and *Thummim* mean lights and perfections; and the breastplate they lay on was called the breastplate of judgment because judgment means understanding and wisdom (§2235). It lay on Aaron's heart because the heart symbolizes divine love (3635 and the end of this chapter [3884–3890]). For this reason, the precious stones were set in gold, gold in an inner sense meaning the good that comes of love (113, 1551, 1552), and a precious stone, truth translucent with goodness (114). [7] Here is what Moses says about the Urim and Thummim:

> You shall make a *breastplate of judgment,* a work well designed; like the work of the ephod you shall make it; of gold, blue-violet, and red-violet, and double-dyed scarlet, and interwoven byssus you shall make it. It shall be square when doubled. And you shall set stone-settings in it; four rows of stone there shall be. *Sockets of gold there shall be* for their settings. And *the stones shall be according to the names of the sons of Israel—twelve, according to their names.* The engravings of each signet shall be according to its name *for the twelve tribes.* (Exodus 28:15–21; 39:8–14)

Which stones were in each row is also specified there. To continue:

> The breastplate shall not come off the ephod. And Aaron shall carry the *names of Israel's sons* on the *breastplate of judgment* over *his heart* when he enters the Holy Place, as a memorial before Jehovah continually. And

you shall put the *Urim* and the *Thummim* on the *breastplate of judgment,* and they shall be *over Aaron's heart* in his entering Jehovah's presence. And Aaron shall carry the *judgment of the children of Israel* over *his heart* before Jehovah continually. (Exodus 28:28, 29, 30; Leviticus 8:7, 8)

Jehovah (the Lord) took questions and gave answers through the Urim, as can be seen in Moses:

Jehovah said to Moses, "Take Joshua, son of Nun. You shall put some of your glory on him, so that all the congregation of the children of Israel will obey him. Before Eleazar the priest he shall stand, and [Eleazar] shall *question him in the judgment of the Urim before Jehovah."* (Numbers 27:18, 20, 21)

And in Samuel:

Saul asked Jehovah, and Jehovah did not answer him, whether by dreams or by the *Urim* or by the prophets. (1 Samuel 28:6)

Because she said, "Jehovah has seen" in the highest sense means foresight; in an inward sense, faith; in an intermediate sense, intellect; on the surface, eyesight; in the current case, a faith granted by the Lord. This can be seen from the symbolism of *seeing,* discussed below. **3863**

The foregoing remarks show that the twelve tribes named for Jacob's twelve sons symbolized every form of truth and goodness, or of faith and love, and therefore everything involved in religion. Each tribe symbolized some broad trait. So the twelve tribes symbolized twelve universal traits that embrace as subcategories each and every aspect of the church and (in a universal sense) of the Lord's kingdom. The broad characteristic that Reuben symbolizes is faith. Faith is the first universal characteristic because when we are being reborn, or are becoming a church, we first have to learn and absorb what faith (or spiritual truth) tells us. The teachings of faith (or of truth) get us started. We are not created in such a way that we can see what heavenly goodness is on our own; we have to learn by being taught, and what we are taught is called the teachings of faith. All religious teachings focus on the way we live as their goal, so they focus on goodness, because goodness is a matter of life.

[2] The ancients debated whether the truth that characterizes faith or the goodness that characterizes love was the church's "firstborn." Those who held that it was faith's truth drew their conclusion from the outward appearance, deciding truth was the firstborn because it is and must be

learned first, and because it introduces us to goodness. They did not real-ize that in essence goodness is the firstborn and that the Lord instills it through our inner self so that we can adopt and accept the truth intro-duced by our outer self. Goodness contains life from the Lord. The only life truth contains comes through goodness, so that goodness is the soul of truth. Goodness lays claim to truth and robes itself in truth, as the soul does with the body. Outwardly, then, truth appears to take first place and to be the firstborn when we are regenerating, even though in *essence,* goodness takes first place and is the firstborn. It becomes so in *reality* when our rebirth is complete. To see that this is so, consult §§3539, 3548, 3556, 3563, 3570, 3576, 3603, 3701.

[3] The theme of this chapter and those that come before it is the rebirth of the earthly dimension—at this point, the first stage of its rebirth, in which one is introduced to goodness by truth. That is why Jacob's first son, Reuben, was named for *Jehovah's seeing,* which on an inner plane symbolizes faith granted by the Lord.

Strictly speaking, faith exists in the intellect and in the will. A knowl-edge and understanding of the truth that composes faith is called a faith that belongs to the intellect, but the intent to act on that truth is called a faith that belongs to the will. The former, a faith that belongs to the intel-lect, is what Reuben symbolizes. The latter, a faith that belongs to the will, is what Simeon symbolizes.

Anyone can see that a faith that belongs to the intellect, or an under-standing of truth, comes before a faith that belongs to the will, or an intent to act on truth. When something is unknown to us—as heavenly goodness is—we have to learn that it exists and understand what it is before we can want it.

[4] The idea that on the surface *seeing* means eyesight needs no explanation. The idea that in an intermediate sense it means intellect is also evident. The eye of our inner self is nothing but the intellect, so in everyday language we refer to the intellect as inner sight. We also speak of light in connection with the intellect (just as we speak of it in con-nection with outer vision), calling that light intellectual light.

The inward meaning of seeing as faith granted by the Lord is clear from the fact that the inner intellect deals only with material provided by truth and goodness, the components of faith. We are not as aware of this deeper intellect, or inner eye, which operates on the truth belonging to faith, as we are of that intellect which operates on the truth belong-ing to public and private life, because the former lies within the latter, in heaven's light. Heaven's light is in the dark as long as we live in the world's light. Even so, it reveals itself to people who have been reborn, especially through conscience.

Seeing means foresight in the highest sense, plainly, because the capacity for understanding attributed to the Lord is an infinite capacity, and foresight and infinite understanding are the same.

[5] The inner-level symbolism of seeing—for which Reuben was named—as faith imparted by the Lord becomes clear from many passages in the Word, of which the following could be quoted. In Moses:

> Jehovah said to Moses, "Make yourself a snake and put it on a standard, and it will happen that all who have been bitten and *see it* will live." Moses made a bronze snake and put it on a standard, and it happened that if a snake bit a man and he *laid eyes on* the bronze snake, he lived again. (Numbers 21:8, 9)

The bronze snake represented the Lord's outer, sensory plane, or his earthly dimension; see §197. Bronze means the earthly level (§§425, 1551). The revival of people who saw or laid eyes on the snake represented faith in the Lord, and he himself teaches this in John:

> As Moses lifted up the snake in the wilderness, so must the Son of Humankind be lifted up, *so that anyone who believes in him* will not be destroyed but have eternal life. (John 3:14, 15)

[6] In Isaiah:

> The Lord said, "Go, and tell this people, 'Listen—listen!—but do not understand, and *see—see!*—but do not know.' Make the heart of this people fat and make their ears heavy and *smear their eyes, to prevent them from seeing with their eyes* and hearing with their ears and understanding in their heart." (Isaiah 6:9, 10)

Clearly, seeing—seeing!—and not knowing means understanding that a thing is true without acknowledging it. Smearing their eyes to prevent them from seeing with their eyes means keeping them from understanding truth. The Lord's words in Matthew 13:13, 14, [15] and John 12:36, 37, 39, 40 show that in this passage seeing symbolizes faith in him. [7] In Ezekiel:

> Son of humankind, you are living in the middle of a rebellious house, *who have eyes to see* but *do not see,* who have ears to hear and do not hear. (Ezekiel 12:2)

Having eyes to see but not seeing stands for being able to understand faith's truth but being unwilling to act on it because of evil. Evil is what the rebellious house stands for, and it lends falsity a deceptive light while engulfing truth in darkness, as Isaiah says:

> This is a *rebellious people,* deceptive offspring, offspring [who] did not want to hear the law of Jehovah, who said *to seers, "You are not to see!"* and to those beholding a vision, *"You are not to see accurately for us! Speak flattery to us; see illusions."* (Isaiah 30:9, 10)

In Isaiah:

> This people, walking in darkness, have *seen great light;* those settling in the land of death's shadow—*light has shone on them.* (Isaiah 9:2)

Seeing a great light stands for accepting and believing the truth that faith teaches. People with faith are said to have heavenly light shine on them because the light in heaven is divine truth coming from divine goodness. [8] In the same author:

> Jehovah has poured out a spirit of slumber on you and has *closed your eyes;* the prophets and your heads—*the seers*—he has put hoods over. (Isaiah 29:10)

Closing someone's eyes stands for closing the ability to understand truth. For the symbolism of an eye as the intellect, see §2701. Putting hoods on seers means on people who know and teach religious truth. "Seers" was once the term for prophets, and prophets mean both people who teach and the religious truth they teach; see §2534. In the same author:

> Priest and prophet err through strong drink, they err *among seers,* they stagger in judgment. (Isaiah 28:7)

The meaning is similar. The judgment in which they stagger means religious truth; see §2235. In the same author:

> The *eyes of the seeing* will not blink, and the ears of the hearing will listen closely. (Isaiah 32:3)

The meaning is similar. [9] In the same author:

> Your eyes will regard the king in his beauty; *they will see a land* of great distances. (Isaiah 33:17)

To regard the king in his beauty stands for regarding religious truth that comes from the Lord, which is called beautiful because of its goodness.

To see a land of great distances stands for seeing good done out of love. (A king means religious truth; see §§1672, 2015, 2069, 3009, 3670. A thing is called beautiful because of its goodness; §§553, 3080, 3821. A land is good done out of love; §§620, 636, 3368, 3379.) In Matthew:

> Fortunate are the clean at heart, because they are the ones who *will see God.* (Matthew 5:8)

Seeing God means believing in him, of course, so it means looking on him with faith. People with faith see God from their faith, because God is in their faith, and the part of their faith that is truly faith is God. [10] In the same author:

> If *your eye* makes you stumble, dig it out; it is better for you to enter life *one-eyed* than to be sent into fiery Gehenna *having two eyes.* (Matthew 18:9)

Obviously the eye here is not an eye and is not to be dug out, because it is not our eye that makes us stumble but our understanding of truth, this being what the eye means here (§2701). It is better not to know or grasp faith's truth than to know and grasp it and yet live a life of evil, and this is meant by its being better to enter life one-eyed than to be sent into fiery Gehenna having two eyes. [11] In the same author:

> Your *eyes* are fortunate because they *see,* and your ears because they hear. Truly, I say to you that many prophets and upright people wanted to *see what you see* but *did not see* it. (Matthew 13:13–17; John 12:40)

Seeing stands for knowing and understanding different points of faith in the Lord, so it stands for faith. [The people the Lord was talking to] were fortunate not because they had seen him and his miracles but because they believed. This can be seen from the following words in John:

> I said to you that you *have actually seen me* and *do not believe.* This is the will of him who sent me, that all who *see the Son* and *believe in him* should have eternal life. No one has *seen* the Father, except the one who is with the Father; this one has *seen* the Father. Truly, truly, I say to you: anyone who believes in me has eternal life. (John 6:36, 40, 46, 47)

Seeing and not believing stands for knowing religious truth and not accepting it. Seeing and believing stands for knowing and accepting it. "No one has seen the Father, except the one who is with the Father" means that we cannot acknowledge divine goodness except through divine truth. The Father is divine goodness, and the Son, divine truth (see §3704), which leads to the inner meaning, that no one can have heavenly goodness without acknowledging the Lord. [12] Likewise in the same author:

> *God* has never *been seen by anyone;* the only-born Son, who is in the Father's embrace, is the one who has revealed him. (John 1:18)

And in the same author:

> Jesus said, "*Whoever sees me sees him* who sent me. I have come into the world as the light, so that no one *who believes in me* should stay in the dark." (John 12:45, 46)

This passage plainly says that seeing means believing, or having faith. And in the same author:

> Jesus said, "If you know me, you also know my Father; and from now on you know him and have *seen him; whoever believes in me has seen the Father."* (John 14:7, 9)

In the same author:

> The world cannot accept the Spirit of *Truth,* because it *does not see him* or know him. I will not leave you orphaned; I am coming to you. In a little *while the world will no longer see me, but you will see me;* because I live, you will live too. (John 14:17, 18, 19)

Seeing stands for having faith, since only through faith is the Lord seen. Faith is the eye of love, because we see the Lord from love through faith. Love is the life force within faith, which is why the Lord says, "You will see me; because I live, you will live too." [13] In the same author:

> Jesus said, "For judgment I came into this world, in order that *those who do not see may see* but *those who see become blind."* The Pharisees said, "Are we also *blind?"* Jesus said to them, "If you were *blind* you would have no sin. But now you say, '*We see!*' So your sin remains." (John 9:39, 40, 41)

Those who see stand for people who think they understand more than anyone else does. The text says that they will become blind—in other words, will reject faith. People wallowing in falsity and people who lack knowledge are the ones described as not seeing, or being blind; see §2383. In Luke:

> To you it has been given to know the mysteries of God's kingdom, but to the rest, in parables, so that *seeing, they would not see,* and hearing, they would not hear. (Luke 8:10)

Likewise. In the same author:

> I say to you, there are certain ones of those standing here who will not taste death *until they see God's kingdom.* (Luke 9:27; Mark 9:1)

Seeing God's kingdom stands for believing. In the same author:

> Jesus said to the disciples, "The days will come when you will long *to see one of the days of the Son of Humankind* but will not *see* it." (Luke 17:22)

This is about the close of the age, or the church's last days, when there is no longer any faith. [14] In the same author:

> It happened when Jesus reclined [at table] with them that, taking the bread, he blessed it, and breaking it he handed it to them. *Their eyes, though, were opened,* and they recognized him. (Luke 24:30, 31)

This meant that what is good makes the Lord visible, in a way that truth without goodness does not, bread meaning good that is done out of love (§§276, 680, 2165, 2177, 3478, 3735, 3813). These passages and many others show that in an inner sense seeing means faith granted by the Lord. No genuine faith exists other than faith imparted by the Lord. Faith received from him gives us the ability to see—that is, to believe. By contrast, faith from ourselves, or faith gained by our own independent effort, is not faith. It makes us see falsity as truth, and truth as falsity. If it allows us to see truth as truth, we still do not see it, because we do not believe it, since we see ourselves rather than the Lord in it.

[15] The fact that seeing means having faith in the Lord is plain from frequent earlier remarks about the light of heaven: that because heaven's light comes from the Lord, it brings with it understanding and wisdom and therefore faith in him (since understanding and wisdom enfold faith in the Lord within them). To see by heavenly light as angels do, then, cannot mean anything but faith in the Lord, and the Lord himself is present in that light because it radiates from him. Heaven's light is also the light that shines within the conscience of people who believe in the Lord,

even though they are unaware of the fact as long as they are living in their body, at which time the world's light obscures heaven's light.

3864   *[Jehovah has seen] my affliction* symbolizes a state in which we attain goodness. This can be seen from the symbolism of *affliction* as a time of trial (discussed in §1846). Trials are the means by which we attain goodness, so *my affliction* symbolizes a state in which we leave truth, which is outward, to arrive at goodness, which is within.

3865   *Because now my husband will love me* means that the good that comes of truth will result, as can be seen from the following: *He will love* means that goodness will result. All goodness is a matter of love, so that is what *loving* means here. And a *husband* symbolizes truth, as discussed in §3134.

The good that comes of truth has been defined several times now as a desire to know truth for the sake of living by it [§§3161, 3332, 3539, 3824]. Life is the goodness that is seen as the goal of truth by people who are later reborn. When we do not live by the truth we know, the truth does not unite with goodness, so it does not become part of us.

[2] Anyone observing people who live evil lives and people who live good lives can see this plainly. Those who live evil lives may have known as much about the church's teachings in their youth and early adulthood as anyone, but if you examine their thoughts about the Lord, about faith in him, and about the church's various truths, you will find that they believe none of it. With those who live good lives, you will find that they each have actual faith in the truths they believe to be true.

People (such as church leaders) who teach truth while living badly will say they believe, but at heart they do not believe. [3] Some possess a dogmatic conviction that mimics faith, but in reality this conviction takes the form of superficial fact. They confirm such fact not because it is true but because they have to stand by it publicly if they want to keep their job, prestige, and material advantages. It enters in through their ears no deeper than their memory, from which it issues as words on their lips, rather than entering their heart and issuing from there as a confession of faith.

These considerations show that our lives offer lessons in evaluating our acknowledgment of truth—that is, in evaluating our faith. Faith detached from a good life says that no matter how we live we can be saved by grace. It argues against the teaching that our life awaits each of us after death.

3866   The inner meaning of Leah's speech about Reuben when he was born— "Jehovah has seen my affliction, because now my husband will love me"— reveals the aspect of the church symbolized by Reuben, or by the tribe named after him. Reuben and the tribe of Reuben symbolize the first requirement when a person is regenerating or becoming a church: doctrinal truth through which that person can attain goodness in his or her life.

Genesis 29:33. *And she conceived again and bore a son and said, "Because Jehovah heard that I was hated and gave me this one too," and called his name Simeon.*   **3867**

She conceived again and bore a son as before symbolizes spiritual conception and birth progressing from an outer plane toward more inward ones. *Because Jehovah heard* in the highest sense means providence; in an inward sense, faith's willingness; in an intermediate sense, obedience; on the surface, the sense of hearing; in the current case, a faith that belongs to the will, granted by the Lord alone. *That I was hated* symbolizes the condition of faith when there is no will answering to it. *And gave me this one too* symbolizes what developed. *And called his name Simeon* symbolizes its nature.

She conceived again and bore a son symbolizes spiritual conception and birth progressing from an outer plane toward more inward ones. This is established by the remarks above at §3860, where the same words occur.   **3868**

One is said to progress from an outer plane toward more inward planes when one progresses from factual knowledge in the intellect to the will or, to put it spiritually, from the truth that makes up faith to neighborly love. The intellect comes from the will and reveals the will in a visual form, so to speak, just as faith issues from neighborly love and reveals that love in a form, so to speak. The outward covering of the will, then, is the intellect, and the outward covering of charity is faith. To put the same thing another way, the inner core of the intellect is the will, and the inner core of faith is charity. So advancing from an outward plane to more inward levels means advancing from a faith that belongs to the intellect to a faith that belongs to the will, and therefore from faith to charity. (Charity is represented by Levi, who comes up next.)

It is important to know that when faith is distinguished from charity it means doctrinal truth, the kind of truth found in the creed called the Apostles' Creed. This is how the term is generally understood in the church, since belief in the truth is considered to be the faith that brings salvation. Few know that faith is trust and confidence, and even fewer know that trust and confidence come from love for one's neighbor. It cannot exist in anyone who does not live a life of love for others.

Because Jehovah heard in the highest sense means providence; in an inward sense, faith's willingness; in an intermediate sense, obedience; on the surface, the sense of hearing; in the current case, a faith that belongs   **3869** to the will, granted by the Lord alone. This can be seen from the symbolism of *hearing.*

There is no need to explain that hearing means the sense of hearing. The intermediate meaning of hearing as obedience and its inward meaning as a faith that belongs to the will are clear in many scriptural passages, which follow below. These meanings can also be seen from the nature of hearing as compared to sight. In an intermediate sense sight means the intellect, and in an inward sense, a faith that belongs to the intellect (see §3863), because our inner eye sees things as they really are, enabling us to seize on them with a kind of faith, though only an intellectual kind. As for our ears, information we receive through them also turns into something "visual" when it penetrates to our inner depths. What we hear, we see inside ourselves. Like the power of sight, then, the power of hearing symbolizes matters of intellect and of faith. However, our ears also persuade us that a thing is so, touching not only our intellectual but also our volitional side and leading us to will what we see. That is why hearing symbolizes our intellectual grasp of some matter and obedience to it, and why on the spiritual plane it symbolizes a faith that belongs to the will.

[2] Since obedience and a faith that belongs to the will are implicit in hearing, the everyday language we use for them is *hear, listen,* and *pay attention.* Listening is obeying, and to pay attention to someone is also to obey. The inner reality of a phenomenon is sometimes present this way in the words of human language. The reason for its presence is that our spirit is what thinks and perceives the meaning of verbal language, and our spirit is in some communion with spirits and angels, who pay attention to the fundamental concepts behind words. What is more, this is the standard cycle in us. Whatever enters through our ears and eyes, or through hearing and sight, makes its way to our intellect, then through our intellect to our will, and from our will into act. This includes the truth that goes to make up faith. First it becomes the truth of a faith that is part of our knowledge, then the truth of a faith that belongs to our will, and eventually the truth of faith in action, so it becomes charity. A knowing or intellectual faith is Reuben, as shown earlier [§3863]. A faith that belongs to the will is Simeon. When faith that belongs to the will becomes charity, it is Levi.

[3] The highest meaning of hearing as providence can be deduced from the argument above in §3863 that seeing in the highest sense means foresight. The Lord's foreseeing is his seeing from the eternal past into the

eternal future that a thing is so. His providing is his directing that it be so and his turning our free choice in a good direction, so far as he foresees that we will freely allow ourselves to be turned (see §3854).

[4] In regard to the intermediate symbolism of *Jehovah's hearing* (for which Simeon was named) as obedience, and its inward symbolism as a faith that belongs to the will, granted by the Lord alone, this is evident from numerous passages in the Word, such as those that follow. In Matthew:

> Here, a voice from the cloud saying, "This is my beloved son, in whom I have taken pleasure; *listen to him."* (Matthew 17:5)

Listening to him stands for believing in him and obeying his commandments, so it stands for having a faith that belongs to the will. In John:

> Truly, truly, I say to you that an hour will come when the dead will *hear the voice of the Son of God,* and those who *hear* will *live.* Don't be surprised at this, because an hour is coming in which everyone who is in the tombs will *hear his voice.* (John 5:25, 28)

Hearing the voice of the Son of God stands for believing the Lord's words and intending to act on them. People with a willing faith receive life, so the text says that those who hear will live. [5] In the same author:

> Whoever is entering through the door is the shepherd of the sheep; for this person the doorkeeper opens up, and *the sheep hear this one's voice.* And other sheep I have that are not from this fold; those too I need to bring, and *they will hear my voice,* and there will come to be one flock and one shepherd. My sheep *hear my voice,* and I know them, and they follow me. (John 10:2, 3, 16, 27)

Hearing his voice obviously stands for obeying him with a willing faith. In the same author:

> Everyone who is on the side of truth *hears my voice.* (John 18:37)

Likewise. In Luke:

> Abraham said to him, "They have Moses and the Prophets; *let them listen to them.* If they *don't listen to Moses and the Prophets,* neither will they be persuaded if someone rises from the dead." (Luke 16:29, 31)

Listening to Moses and the Prophets stands for knowing what the Word says and believing in it, so it also means willing or intending to act on what the Word says. Believing without willing is seeing and not hearing, but believing together with willing is seeing and hearing. As a consequence, the Word often speaks simultaneously of seeing and hearing. Seeing has the same symbolism as Reuben, and hearing, the same symbolism as Simeon, since they are united as brother with brother.

[6] The following passages show that seeing and hearing are mentioned jointly. In Matthew:

> Therefore I speak to them in parables, because *seeing, they do not see, and hearing, they do not hear* or understand. And in them is fulfilled the prophecy of Isaiah that says, "*With your hearing you will hear* and not understand, and *seeing you will see* and not discern. Coarsened is the heart of this people, and *with their ears they listened heavily,* and *their eyes they shut,* so that they may not *see with their eyes* and *with their ears hear* and in their heart understand." Your *eyes,* though, are fortunate, *because they see,* and *your ears, because they hear.* Truly, I say to you that many prophets and upright people wanted to *see what you see* but did not see it, and to *hear what you hear* and did not hear it. (Matthew 13:13–17; John 12:40; Isaiah 6:9)

In Mark:

> Jesus said to his disciples, "Why do you deliberate because you do not have bread? Don't you have understanding or understand yet? Do you still have your heart hardened? *Having eyes, don't you see,* and *having ears, don't you hear?*" (Mark 8:17, 18)

[7] In Luke:

> To you it has been given to know the mysteries of God's kingdom, but to the rest, in parables, so that *seeing, they may not see,* and *hearing, they may not hear.* (Luke 8:10)

In Isaiah:

> The *eyes of the blind* will be opened, and the *ears of the deaf* will be opened. (Isaiah 35:5)

In the same author:

> Then on that day the *deaf* will *hear* the words of the book, and out of the darkness and out of the shadows *the eyes of the blind will see.* (Isaiah 29:18)

In the same author:

> *You who are deaf, listen!* And *you who are blind, look and see!* (Isaiah 42:18)

In the same author:

> Lead forth a *blind* people, which will have *eyes,* and the *deaf, who will have ears!* (Isaiah 43:8)

In the same author:

> The *eyes of the seeing* will not blink, and the *ears of the hearing* will listen closely. (Isaiah 32:3)

In the same author:

> Let *your eyes* be *watching* your teachers, and *may your ears hear* a word. (Isaiah 30:20, 21)

In the same author:

> Those who stop up *their ear to keep from hearing* about blood[shed] and shut *their eyes to keep from looking on* evil—these will live on the heights. (Isaiah 33:15, 16)

In Ezekiel:

> Son of humankind, you are living in the middle of a rebellious house, who have *eyes to see* but *do not see,* who have *ears to hear* and *do not hear.* (Ezekiel 12:2)

These passages mention both—both an intellectual faith (seeing) and a willing faith (hearing)—because the one follows the other. Otherwise it would have been enough to mention just one. From this it is clear why one of Jacob's sons was named for seeing, and the next, for hearing.

[8] Seeing symbolizes a knowing or intellectual faith and hearing symbolizes an obedient or willing faith because of correspondences in the other life and the symbolism they give rise to. People who are intellectual and have an intellectual faith belong to the realm of the eye, while those who are obedient and have an obedient faith belong to the realm of the ear. (This will be seen from explanations at the ends of several chapters—the Lord in his divine mercy willing—concerning the universal human and the correspondence of everything in a person's body with that human [§§4403–4421, 4523–4534, 4652–4660].) [9] That is why the *eye* in an inner sense

means the intellect (see §2701). It is also why the *ear* means obedience and, in a spiritual sense, the faith that comes of obedience, or a faith that belongs to the will. The same can be seen from the following passages. In Isaiah:

> *Neither did you hear,* nor did you know, *nor* from then *was your ear open.* (Isaiah 48:8)

In the same author:

> The Lord Jehovih will stir my *ear to listen* as the instructed [listen]. The Lord Jehovih has *opened my ear,* and I have not rebelled. (Isaiah 50:4, 5)

In the same author:

> Pay wholehearted attention to me and eat what is good, so that your soul may revel in the fat. *Bend your ear* and come to me; *listen,* so that your soul may live! (Isaiah 55:2, 3)

In Jeremiah:

> To whom should I speak and testify *so that they hear?* Look, now, *their ear is uncircumcised* and they cannot pay attention. (Jeremiah 6:10)

In the same author:

> This I commanded them, saying, "*Listen to my voice!* Then I will become your God, and you will become my people." And they *did not listen and did not bend their ear.* (Jeremiah 7:23, 24, 26)

In the same author:

> *Listen,* women, to Jehovah's word, and let *your ear* take in the word of his mouth. (Jeremiah 9:20)

In the same author:

> You have not bent *your ear* and have *not obeyed me.* (Jeremiah 35:15)

In Ezekiel:

> Son of humankind, all my words that I have spoken to you *take into your heart* and *listen to with your ears.* (Ezekiel 3:10)

In the same author:

> I will set my zeal against you, and they will deal with you in wrath; your nose and *your ears* they will take off. (Ezekiel 23:25)

Taking off the nose and ears stands for taking away any perception of truth and goodness and any obedience to one's faith. In Zechariah:

> They refused to pay attention and turned a defiant shoulder, and *they made their ears heavy* so as *not to hear,* and they made their heart adamant so that they would *not hear the law.* (Zechariah 7:11, 12)

[10] In Amos:

> This is what Jehovah has said: "As the shepherd rescues from the mouth of the lion two legs or a *piece of an ear,* so will the children of Israel in Samaria be rescued, on the corner of a bed and on the end of a couch." (Amos 3:12)

Rescuing two legs stands for rescuing an intention to do good. Rescuing a piece of an ear stands for rescuing an intention to act on truth. This meaning of a piece of an ear, again, can be seen only from correspondences in the other world and therefore from symbolism governing both the Word's inner meaning and the rituals in the religion of Israel and Judah. That was why the following was commanded among other things when Aaron and his sons were being ordained into the ministry:

> Moses shall take some of the ram's blood and put it *on the lobe of Aaron's ear* and *on the lobe of his sons' ear* and on the thumb of their right hand and on the big toe of their right foot. (Exodus 29:20)

This ritual represented the will or intent involved in faith. As a priest, the candidate was being initiated into this will or intent. Anyone can see that the ritual was holy, because it was commanded of Moses by Jehovah. It was a holy act, then, to put blood on the earlobe; but what was holy about it can be known only from the inner meaning of the Word's contents. The meaning here is this: the holiness that the will lends to faith was to be protected.

[11] The symbolism of the ear as obedience and in an inward sense as the resulting faith can be seen even more clearly from the ritual for a slave who chose not to abandon servitude. The ritual is described this way in Moses: If a male (or female) slave did not want to leave his slavery,

> His master shall bring him to God and bring him to the door or to the doorpost, and *his master shall pierce the ear with an awl,* and [the slave] shall serve him forever. (Exodus 21:6; Deuteronomy 15:17)

Piercing the ear with an awl at the doorpost stands for permanent slavery or obedience. In a spiritual sense it stands for choosing not to understand truth but to intend acting on it out of obedience, which is comparatively nonfree.

[12] Since in an inner sense the ears mean obedience in faith, and hearing or listening means obeying, it is clear what the Lord meant when he said so often, "*Those who have an ear to hear should listen*" (Matthew 13:9, 43; Mark 4:9, 23; 7:16; Luke 8:8; 14:35; Revelation 2:7, 11, 29; 3:13, 22).

[13] The highest meaning of hearing as providence and of seeing as foresight is evident from scriptural passages that ascribe eyes or ears to Jehovah, or the Lord, as in Isaiah:

> *Bend your ear, Jehovah, and listen;* open *your eyes,* Jehovah, and *look.* (Isaiah 37:17)

In Daniel:

> Bend *your ear,* my God, and *listen;* open *your eyes,* Jehovah, and *see* our devastation. (Daniel 9:18)

In David:

> God, bend *your ear* toward me and *hear* my speech. (Psalms 17:6)

In the same author:

> Bend *your ear* toward me and save me! (Psalms 71:2)

In the same author:

> *Turn an ear* toward my prayers because of your truth; answer me because of your justice. (Psalms 143:1)

In Jeremiah:

> Jehovah, you have heard my voice; do not hide *your ear* at my sigh, at my shout. (Lamentations 3:56)

In David:

> Jehovah, do not hide your face from me on the day when I have anguish; bend *your ear* toward me on the day I cry; answer me. (Psalms 102:2)

[14] It is known that Jehovah does not have ears or eyes like ours but some attribute symbolized by an ear and an eye that can be predicated of divinity. That attribute is infinite power of will and infinite power

to understand. Infinite will is providence, and infinite understanding is foresight. That is what an ear and an eye mean in the highest sense when they are ascribed to Jehovah.

All this now shows the meaning on every level of the phrase *Jehovah heard,* for which Simeon was named.

That I was hated symbolizes the condition of faith when there is no will answering to it. This can be seen from the meaning of *hated* as not loved, which describes the situation of faith when there is no will answering to it.

3870

The inner meaning concerns the way human rebirth proceeds from the surface to the core, or from faith's truth to charity's goodness. Faith's truth is on the surface; charity's goodness is at the core.

If the truth that makes up faith is to come alive, it has to be introduced into the will to receive life there. Truth does not receive life from our knowing about it but from our wanting to act on it. The new will the Lord creates in us provides a channel for life from him to flow into us. The first stirrings of life take the form of obedience, obedience being the rudiments of a will. The second kind of life takes the form of a desire for acting on truth—an advanced form of will that exists when we find pleasure and blessing in doing the truth.

If faith does not advance in this way, our truth is not true but is something dissociated from life. Sometimes it confirms falsity, and sometimes it is dogmatic, so it is something filthy. It joins with our evil desires, or our cravings—in other words, with our own, independent will, which opposes neighborly love. Such is the faith that many people these days consider to be faith and to bring salvation by itself without acts of neighborly kindness.

[2] This faith—faith detached from and therefore opposed to charity— is represented later on by Reuben, who lay with Bilhah, his father's concubine (Genesis 35:22). Jacob, who by then was Israel, deplores this faith in the following words:

> Reuben, my firstborn, you are my strength and the beginning of my might. Light as water you are; do not excel! For you climbed onto your father's beds, then you defiled my pallet; he climbed up. (Genesis 49:3, 4)

Associated with this faith—faith separated from charity—is a will and desire opposed to charity, which is depicted by Simeon and Levi in the following words there:

> Simeon and Levi are brothers; weapons of violence are their blades. Into their conspiracy may my soul not come; with their company my

glory is not to unite, because in their fury they killed a man, and in their willfulness they hamstrung an ox. A curse on their fury because it is fierce and on their anger because it is heavy! I will divide them among Jacob and scatter them among Israel. (Genesis 49:5, 6, 7)

These two depict faith separated from charity, as later sections will show, with the Lord's divine mercy.

3871 *And gave me this one too* symbolizes what developed: an obedient or willing faith, which develops out of a knowing or intellectual faith, as shown above [§3869]. That is what *he gave me this one too* symbolizes.

3872 *And called his name Simeon* symbolizes its nature. This can be seen from the symbolism of a name and *calling a name* as the quality (discussed in §§144, 145, 1754, 1896, 2009, 2724, 3006, 3421). The quality itself is contained in the inner meaning of Leah's words, "Jehovah heard that I was hated and gave me this one too." That is the quality symbolized by *Simeon* and by the tribe named for him. It is also the second universal characteristic of the church, or the second stage when a person is being reborn and becoming a church—namely, obedience, or the will to act on the truth that belongs to faith. Into this obedience and this willingness charity is planted, charity being the next development, symbolized by Levi.

3873 Genesis 29:34. *And she conceived again and bore a son and said, "Now this time my husband will cling to me, because I have borne him three sons"; therefore she called his name Levi.*

She conceived again and bore a son as before symbolizes spiritual conception and birth progressing from an outer plane toward an even more inward one. *And said, "Now this time my husband will cling to me,"* in the highest sense means love and mercy; in an inward sense, charity; on the surface, union; in the current case, spiritual love. *Because I have borne him three sons* symbolizes what developed. *Therefore she called his name Levi* symbolizes its nature.

3874 *She conceived again and bore a son* symbolizes spiritual conception and birth progressing from an outer plane toward an even more inward one. This is established by the remarks above at §§3860, 3868, where the same words occur.

3875 *And said, "Now this time my husband will cling to me,"* in the highest sense means love and mercy; in an inward sense, charity; on the surface, union; in the current case, spiritual love. This can be seen from the symbolism of *clinging.*

On the surface, or in its shallowest inner sense, clinging means being united, as is evident without explanation. Its inward meaning as charity can be seen from the fact that charity, or mutual love, is spiritual union. Charity is a union of desires felt by the will and a resulting harmony of thoughts in the intellect, so it is a meeting of minds involving both sides of the mind. The highest-level meaning of clinging as love and mercy follows naturally, because the infinite, eternal quality attributed to charity or spiritual love is mercy, and mercy is God's love for the human race, established as we are in so much misery. We are nothing but evil on our own; nothing exists in us or emanates from us but what is hellish, yet the Lord looks on us with divine love. This being so, the action he takes in lifting us out of the hell we consign ourselves to and liberating us is called mercy. So since mercy originates in divine love, clinging in the highest sense means both love and mercy.

[2] The inward sense of clinging as spiritual love, or charity for our neighbor, can also be seen from other Scripture passages, as in Isaiah:

> It is not to be said by the child of a foreigner *who has clung to Jehovah,* saying, "Jehovah utterly removes me from among his people." The children of a foreigner *who cling to Jehovah,* to wait on him and to *love* Jehovah's name, will become his servants. (Isaiah 56:3, 6)

Clinging to Jehovah stands for keeping his commandments, which is an act of spiritual love, because the only people who keep God's commandments from the heart are those who do the good that charity for their neighbor urges. In Jeremiah:

> In those days Israel's children will come, they and Judah's children; crying along the way they will go, and Jehovah their God they will seek. They will ask about the way to Zion; there their faces [turn]. "Come and let us *cling to Jehovah* in an eternal pact [that] is not forgotten." (Jeremiah 50:4, 5)

Here too clinging to Jehovah stands for keeping his commandments from the heart—in other words, at the urging of neighborly kindness. [3] In Zechariah:

> *Many nations will cling to Jehovah* on that day and will become my people. (Zechariah 2:11)

Likewise. In Isaiah:

> Jehovah will have mercy on Jacob and choose Israel anew and put them on their land; and *immigrants will cling to them* and attach themselves to the house of Jacob. (Isaiah 14:1)

Clinging to them as an immigrant stands for keeping the law the same way they do. Attaching oneself to the house of Jacob stands for doing good out of neighborly love, which is what the people symbolized by the house of Jacob do. In Matthew:

> No one can serve two masters, because either the person will hate the one and love the other or the person will *cling to one* and despise the other. (Matthew 6:24)

In this verse, the heavenly quality of love is to love, and the spiritual quality of love is to cling. Both are mentioned because they are different from each other; otherwise one would have been enough.

[4] People with spiritual love are therefore called children of Levi, as in Malachi:

> Who can endure the day of his coming, and who will stay standing when he appears? He will sit smelting and purging silver and will purify the *children of Levi* and refine them like gold and like silver. (Malachi 3:2, 3)

In the highest sense Levi means the Lord because of his divine love and mercy toward people who possess spiritual love, as in the same author:

> ". . . so that you may know that I have sent you this commandment: for *my compact* to be *with Levi,*" Jehovah Sabaoth has said. "My compact with him will be one of life and peace. You turned back from the way; you caused many to stumble against the law; you corrupted *Levi's compact*. Therefore I have made you despised." (Malachi 2:4, 5, 8, 9)

Because Levi in the highest sense means the Lord's divine love or mercy, and in an inward sense, spiritual love, the tribe of Levi became priests. In the Word's inner sense, priesthood means nothing but the sacred quality of love, while monarchy means the sacred quality of faith (§§1728, 2015 at the end, 3670).

[5] Since the word for clinging used in Levi's name symbolizes spiritual love, which is the same as mutual love, the same word in the original language means lending and borrowing. In the Jewish religion lending and borrowing represented mutual love, as will be discussed elsewhere, with the Lord's divine mercy [§9174].

Mutual love differs from friendship in this: The object of mutual love is the goodness in a person, and because it is the goodness, its object is also the person who exhibits the goodness. The object of friendship, on the other hand, is the actual person. Friendship is also mutual love when it views the person in terms of goodness or makes goodness the goal, but sometimes it does not. Instead it sets self-interest up as the goal and describes this as good. Under those circumstances friendship is not mutual love but something more like self-love, and the more it approaches self-love, the more it opposes mutual love.

In reality, mutual love is nothing but charity for our neighbor, since in an inner sense a neighbor simply means goodness. In the highest sense it means the Lord, since all goodness comes from him and he is goodness itself. (See §§2425, 3419.) This mutual love, or charity for our neighbor, is what the term spiritual love means and is what Levi symbolizes.

[6] The word *cling* in Scripture's literal meaning also expresses heavenly love and married love, but this is a different word in the original language from that used in Levi's name, and it means an even tighter union, as in the following passages. In Moses:

> Jehovah your God you shall fear, him you shall serve, and *to him you shall cling.* (Deuteronomy 10:20)

> After Jehovah your God you shall walk, and him you shall fear, and his commandments you shall keep, and his voice you shall listen to, and him you shall serve, and *to him you shall cling.* (Deuteronomy 13:4)

> . . . to *love Jehovah your God,* to go in all his ways, and *to cling to him.* (Deuteronomy 11:22)

> . . . to *love Jehovah your God,* to obey his voice, and *to cling to him,* because he is your life. (Deuteronomy 30:20)

In Joshua:

> Be very careful to do the commandment and the law that Moses, servant of Jehovah, commanded you: to *love* Jehovah your God and to walk in all his ways and to keep his commandments and *to cling to him* and to serve him with all your heart and with all your soul. (Joshua 22:5)

In 2 Kings:

> King Hezekiah trusted in Jehovah, God of Israel, *clung to Jehovah,* did not turn back from [walking] after him, and kept his commandments, which Jehovah had commanded Moses. (2 Kings 18:5, 6)

In Jeremiah:

> As a *sash clings to the hips of a man,* so *I caused* the whole house of Israel and the whole house of Judah *to cling to me,* to serve me as a people and as a name and as praise and as beauty. And they did not obey. (Jeremiah 13:11)

[7] The following quotations show that married love is also expressed as clinging:

> Therefore a man will leave his father and his mother and *cling to his wife,* and they will become one flesh. (Genesis 2:24)

> Because of your hardness of heart Moses wrote this commandment; from the beginning of creation, though, God made them male and female. Therefore a person shall leave his father and mother and *cling to his wife,* and the two will become one flesh; what God has *joined together,* then, no human shall separate. (Mark 10:5–9; Matthew 19:5)

> *Shechem's soul clung to Dinah,* Jacob's daughter. He *loved* the young woman and spoke to the young woman's heart. (Genesis 34:3)

> Solomon loved many foreign women; *to these Solomon clung, to love them.* (1 Kings 11:1, 2)

These passages now clarify that *cling* is a word associated with love, as used in ancient times by religions that employed symbolism, and what it actually means in an inner sense is spiritual union, which is charity and love.

3876   *Because I have borne him three sons* symbolizes what developed, as can be seen from the remarks above at §3871. The development symbolized here by the *three sons* is that charity comes at this point in our rebirth, or in our becoming a church. In the first place we have to know and understand what constitutes religious truth. In the second, we have to will and do it. In the third, we are affected by it, and when we are touched by truth—when we sense pleasure and blessing in acting on truth—we possess charity, or mutual love. These are the developments meant by *bearing him three sons.*

3877   *Therefore she called his name Levi* symbolizes its nature. This can be seen from the symbolism of a name and *calling a name* as the quality (discussed above in §3872). The quality is contained in the words, "Now this time my husband will cling to me, because I have borne him three sons," which are explained directly above in §§3875, 3876. That is the quality that *Levi* and the tribe named for him symbolize. It is the third universal characteristic of the church, or the third stage when a person is being reborn or becoming a church—namely, charity.

Charity contains the will to act on truth, through which it contains an understanding of truth; whoever has charity, has the other two. However, before we can come into charity, we have to adopt its outward form: we have to understand truth, intend to do it, and finally desire it, which is charity. When we have charity, we focus on the Lord, who is symbolized on the highest level by Judah, Jacob's fourth son.

Genesis 29:35. *And she conceived again and bore a son and said, "This* **3878** *time I will acclaim Jehovah"; therefore she called his name Judah, and she stopped giving birth.*

She conceived again and bore a son as before symbolizes spiritual conception and birth progressing from an outer plane toward an even more inward one. *And said, "This time I will acclaim Jehovah,"* in the highest sense means the Lord; in an inward sense, the Word; on the surface, doctrine from the Word; in the current case, the divinity of love, and the Lord's heavenly kingdom. *Therefore she called his name Judah* symbolizes its nature. *And she stopped giving birth* symbolizes climbing the ladder from earth all the way to Jehovah, or the Lord.

She conceived again and bore a son symbolizes spiritual conception **3879** and birth progressing from an outer plane toward an even more inward one, as can be seen from the remarks above at §§3860, 3868, where the same words occur.

And said, "This time I will acclaim Jehovah," in the highest sense means **3880** the Lord; in an inward sense, the Word; on the surface, doctrine from the Word; in the current case, the divinity of love, and the Lord's heavenly kingdom. This can be seen from the symbolism of *acclaiming*.

On the surface, or in its shallowest inner sense, acclamation clearly means doctrine from the Word. Even in everyday language acclamation [or confession] is a declaration of faith we make to the Lord, so it comprises our beliefs and consequently the teachings we take as doctrine.

The inward meaning of acclamation as the Word follows logically, because all teachings about faith and charity have to come from the Word. On our own we know nothing of what is heavenly and spiritual, so we learn about them from divine revelation, which is the Word.

In the highest sense acclamation means the Lord because the Lord is the Word and is therefore doctrine drawn from the Word. Moreover, the Word's inner meaning centers on the Lord alone and speaks of his kingdom (§§1871, 2859, 2894, 3245, 3305 at the beginning, 3393, 3432, 3439, 3454). That is why acclamation of Jehovah symbolizes the divinity of love, and the Lord's heavenly kingdom. The Lord is divine love itself; and the inflow of divine love is what makes his kingdom, doing so through the Word that is from him.

I have already shown that Judah, named for the acclamation of Jehovah, symbolizes the divinity of love, and the Lord's heavenly kingdom; see §3654. That is why I say that acclamation has this meaning here.

[2] The meaning of acclaiming and acclamation can be seen from places in the Word that mention them, as in Isaiah:

> You will say on that day, "*I will acclaim you, Jehovah,* because you raged against me, your anger turned back, and you comforted me." And you will say on that day, "*Acclaim Jehovah;* call on his name; make his deeds known among the people. Make mention that his name is exalted." (Isaiah 12:1, 4)

In David:

> *We will acclaim you, God, we will acclaim;* and your name is nearby. They recount your marvels. (Psalms 75:1)

In the same author:

> A psalm *for acclamation:* Shout for joy in Jehovah, all the earth! He made us—his people and the flock of his pasture—and we did not, so we are his, his people and the flock of his pasture. Enter his gates *with acclaim;* his courts, with praise. *Acclaim him;* bless his name, because Jehovah is good, his mercy is forever, and his truth to generation after generation. (Psalms 100:1–5)

Acclaiming and acclamation in these passages plainly means acknowledging Jehovah, or the Lord, and his attributes. This acknowledgment, of course, is doctrine, and it is the Word. [3] In Isaiah:

> Jehovah will comfort Zion, he will comfort all its wastelands. Gladness and joy will be found in it; *acclamation* and the voice of song. (Isaiah 51:3)

In Jeremiah:

> This is what Jehovah has said: "Watch! I am bringing back Jacob's captured tents, and on his dwellings I will have mercy, and the city will

be rebuilt on its own [ruin] mound, and the palace will be inhabited according to its custom, and *acclaim* will come out of them, as will the sound of people at play." (Jeremiah 30:18, 19)

In David:

I will *acclaim Jehovah* according to his justice, and sing the name of Jehovah the Highest. (Psalms 7:17)

In the same author:

. . . when I passed over to the House of God with the voice of song and *acclamation,* with the throng keeping the feast. (Psalms 42:4)

In the same author:

I will *acclaim you* among the nations, Lord; I will make music to you among the peoples, because your mercy is great enough to reach the sky. (Psalms 57:9, 10)

[4] These passages show that acclamation relates to heavenly love, as distinguished from acts relating to spiritual love, because they contain the phrases "acclamation and the voice of song," "acclamation and the sound of people at play," and "I will acclaim you among the nations and make music to you among the peoples." Acclamation and acclaiming are heavenly; the voice of song, the sound of people at play, and making music are spiritual. What is more, acclamation is said to be made among the nations, and music, among the peoples, because nations symbolize those devoted to goodness, and peoples symbolize those devoted to truth (§§1416, 1849, 2928). That is, nations and peoples symbolize those who have heavenly love and those who have spiritual love. In the Word, in the Prophets, terms usually occur in pairs, one term relating to what is heavenly, or good, and the other to what is spiritual, or true. So in every part of the Word there is a divine marriage, a marriage of goodness and truth; see §§683, 793, 801, 2173, 2516, 2712, 3132. This too shows that acclamation involves heavenly love, and that real, heartfelt acclamation comes only of goodness. Acclamation that comes of truth is called the voice of song, the sound of people at play, and music making. [5] The same pairing occurs in the following places. In David:

I will praise the name of God with a song and exalt him with *acclamation.* (Psalms 69:30)

In the same author:

> I will *acclaim you* on the lute; your truth, my God, I will sing to you on the harp, Holy One of Israel. (Psalms 71:22)

Singing with a harp symbolizes something spiritual, as do all other stringed instruments; see §§418, 419, 420. In the same author:

> Enter his gates with *acclaim;* his courts, with praise. *Acclaim him;* bless his name. (Psalms 100:4)

Acclaim and acclaiming result from a love for goodness; praise and blessing, from a love for truth. In the same author:

> Answer Jehovah *with acclamation;* make music to our God on a harp. (Psalms 147:7)

In the same author:

> I will *acclaim you* in the great assembly; among a numerous people I will praise you. (Psalms 35:17, 18)

In the same author:

> I will *acclaim Jehovah* with my mouth, and in the midst of many I will praise him. (Psalms 109:30)

In the same author:

> We are your people, and the flock of your pasture. We will *acclaim you* forever; for generation after generation we will recount your praise. (Psalms 79:13)

In the same author:

> Let them *acclaim to Jehovah* his mercy, and his marvels to the children of humankind; let them *sacrifice the sacrifices of acclamation* and proclaim his deeds with song. (Psalms 107:21, 22)

[6] In these passages, you can see, two expressions are used for one entity. They would seem redundant if one did not involve the heavenly quality of goodness, and the other, the spiritual quality of truth, and so if they did not involve the divine marriage. The Lord's kingdom itself is a divine marriage. This secret duality permeates the whole Word, but it can be discovered only through the inner meaning and so through knowing which

words are in the heavenly category and which in the spiritual. Overall, it is necessary to know what heavenliness and spirituality are, and this has been explained many times already.

[7] Heartfelt acclamation comes from heavenly love and therefore is true acclamation. People who acclaim the Lord from the heart acknowledge that all goodness is from him and all evil from themselves. When they acknowledge this, their attitude is humble, because they are acknowledging that the Lord is everything to them and they are nothing in comparison. When acclamation rises out of this state of mind, it rises out of heavenly love.

[8] Sacrifices of acclamation in the Jewish religion were a way of expressing gratitude. As a group they were called sacrifices of thanksgiving and repayment and were of two kinds: those of acclamation and those in fulfillment of a vow. The role of heavenly love in sacrifices of acclamation can be seen from the regulation establishing them, as recorded in Moses:

> This is the law for the sacrifice of thanksgiving that will be offered to Jehovah: If they *offer it in acclamation,* then they shall offer, besides the sacrifice of *acclamation,* unleavened cakes mixed with oil, and unleavened wafers anointed with oil, and parched flour [made into] cakes mixed with oil; in addition to leavened cakes of bread they shall offer their offering, *besides the sacrifice of acclamation.* (Leviticus 7:11, 12, 13, 15)

Everything mentioned here—unleavened cakes mixed with oil, unleavened wafers anointed with oil, parched flour, leavened cakes of bread—symbolizes heavenly love and faith, acclamation rising out of these, and the need for humility. Flour and cakes made of flour mean the heavenly element in love and the resulting spiritual element in faith, which is charity (see §2177). Lack of leavening means purification from evil and falsity (2342). Oil means heavenly love (886, 3728), as does bread (2165, 2177, 3464, 3478, 3735).

[9] On the face of it, sacrifices fulfilling a vow—the second kind of thanksgiving sacrifice—stood for repayment; in an inner sense, for a wish that the Lord provide; and in the highest sense, for a state of providence; see §3732. That is why both [vows and acclamation] are mentioned in many scriptural passages, as in David:

> *Sacrifice acclamation to God,* and *fulfill your vows to the Highest One. Those sacrificing acclamation* honor me; and to those who set up a path I will show God's salvation. (Psalms 50:14, 23)

In the same author:

> On me, God, are *your vows; I will repay acclamation to you.* (Psalms 56:12)

In the same author:

> *To you I will sacrifice a sacrifice of acclamation,* and on Jehovah's name I will call; *my vows to Jehovah I will fulfill.* (Psalms 116:17, 18)

In Jonah:

> *With a voice of acclaim* I will *sacrifice to you;* what *I vowed I will fulfill.* (Jonah 2:9)

[10] From all this it is now clear what is meant by acclamation, for which Judah was named. In the highest sense it means the Lord and the divinity of love; in an inward sense, the Word and the Lord's heavenly kingdom; and in an outward sense, doctrine from the Word in a heavenly religion. What follows just below will show that these things are what Judah symbolizes in the Word.

3881   *Therefore she called his name Judah* symbolizes its nature. This can be seen from the symbolism of a name and *calling a name* as the quality (discussed in §§144, 145, 1754, 1896, 2009, 2724, 3006, 3421). The quality itself is contained in the inner meaning of Leah's words, "This time I will acclaim Jehovah," discussed just above in §3880: in the highest sense, the Lord and the divinity of his love; in an inward sense, the Word and the Lord's heavenly kingdom; and in an outward sense, doctrine from the Word in a heavenly religion.

So far hardly anyone knows this is what Judah symbolizes in places in the Word that mention him, because people consider the narrative parts mere history and count the prophetic parts among those that have been erased from memory (excepting a few source passages for their creeds). They do not believe in the presence of a spiritual meaning, because the modern age does not know what the Word's spiritual meaning is or even what the spiritual dimension is. The prime reason for this ignorance is that people live earthly lives. When we make earthly life our goal, or when earthly life is all we love, it obliterates both religious knowledge and faith. In fact, if we hear any mention of spiritual life or a spiritual meaning, it seems like a nonentity, or a depressing annoyance—something that nauseates us because it clashes with our earthly life. Since this is the state of the human race at the present day, people glean nothing more from names in the Word—and wish to glean nothing more—than the nations, peoples, individuals, regions, cities, mountains, and rivers named. Yet names have symbolic meaning on the spiritual level.

[2] *Judah's* symbolism on an inward level as the Lord's heavenly church, in a universal sense as his heavenly kingdom, and on the highest level as the Lord himself can be seen from many passages in the Old Testament mentioning Judah, such as the following. In Moses:

> *Judah* you are; your brothers will praise you. Your hand is on your enemies' neck; your father's sons will bow down to you. A lion's cub is Judah; from your prey, my son, you have risen. He crouched; he lay like a lion and like an aging lion. Who will rouse him? The scepter will not withdraw from Judah, nor a lawgiver from between his feet, until Shiloh comes; and to him will be the gathering of the peoples. Tying his young donkey to the grapevine, and his jenny's foal to the choice vine, he will wash his garment in wine and his robe in the blood of grapes. He will be red of eye from wine and white of teeth from milk. (Genesis 49:8–12)

[3] This is an oracular utterance by Jacob (who by then was Israel) concerning Judah, and no one can understand it, or even a single phrase in it, except from the inner meaning. What does it mean to say that his brothers will praise him, and his father's sons will bow down to him? That like a lion's cub he rises from his prey? That like a lion he crouches and lies? What is Shiloh? What is it to tie one's young donkey to a grapevine, and one's jenny's foal to a choice vine? To wash a garment in wine and a robe in the blood of grapes? To be red of eye from wine and to be white of teeth from milk? As I said, no one could possibly understand these images except from the inner meaning. The reality is that each and every item symbolizes something heavenly in the Lord's kingdom, and something divine. Each part predicts that Judah would represent the Lord's heavenly kingdom and, in the highest sense, the Lord himself. All of this will be discussed in the explanations at Genesis 49, the Lord in his divine mercy willing.

[4] The case is the same in other passages, especially where the Prophets mention Judah, as in Ezekiel:

> You, son of humankind: take yourself one stick and write on it, "For Judah and for the children of Israel, his companions"; and take one

stick and write on it, "For Joseph: the stick of Ephraim and of the
whole house of Israel, his companions"; and join them, one to the other
for yourself, into one stick, and they will serve as single sticks in my
hand. I will make them into one nation in the land, on the mountains
of Israel. And one monarch will serve them all as monarch. My servant
David will be monarch over them, and there will be a single shepherd
for them all. And they will walk in my judgments and keep my statutes
and do them and live on the land that I gave to my servant Jacob, on
which your ancestors lived; they will live on it—they and their children
and their children's children—forever. And David my servant will be
chief over them forever, and I will strike a pact of peace with them;
it will be an eternal pact with them. I will give to them and multiply
them and place my sanctuary in their midst forever. So will my dwelling place be among them, and I will become their God, and they will
become my people. (Ezekiel 37:15–28)

People who take Judah to mean Judah, Israel to mean Israel, Joseph to
mean Joseph, Ephraim to mean Ephraim, and David to mean David
believe that all the predictions will literally come true. They think that
Israel will join forces with Judah again, as will the tribe of Ephraim,
that David will rule, that they will accordingly live on the land given to
Jacob forever, that there will then be an eternal pact with them, and that
the Lord's sanctuary will be in their midst forever. As a matter of fact,
though, not one bit of the passage is talking about that nation. It is talking about the Lord's heavenly kingdom (Judah), his spiritual kingdom
(Israel), and the Lord himself (David), so the names obviously refer not
to individuals but to what is heavenly and divine.

[5] The situation is the same with the following from Zechariah:

Many peoples and numerous nations will come to seek Jehovah Sabaoth.
In those days, ten men from all the tongues of the nations will clutch
the wing of a Judean man, saying, "We will go with you, because we
have heard that God is with you." (Zechariah 8:[22,] 23)

People who understand these words literally will say what the Jewish nation
itself still believes: that since the prophecy has not been fulfilled yet, it will
be. So they will return to the land of Canaan (they say), and a large number of people from every nation and tongue will follow them, and they
will clutch the wing of a Judean man and beg him to let him follow him.

God will then be with them—God being the Messiah, who Christians say will be the Lord, to whom [Jews] will first be converted. That would be an accurate interpretation of the words if a Judean man meant a Jewish man, but in reality the passage deals in its inner meaning with a new, spiritual religion among people outside the church. The Judean man symbolizes a saving faith, which develops out of love for the Lord.

[6] The following passages also make it clear that Judah does not mean Judah but, in an inner sense (to repeat), the Lord's heavenly kingdom. The religion established with Judah, or with Jews, represented this kingdom. In Isaiah:

> The Lord, when he lifts up a banner for the nations, will assemble the exiles of Israel; and the scattered elements of Judah he will gather from the four wings of the earth. Then Ephraim's envy will withdraw, and Judah's foes will be cut off. Ephraim will not show envy toward Judah, and Judah will not assail Ephraim. (Isaiah 11:12, 13)

In Jeremiah:

> "Look! The days are coming," says Jehovah, "when I will raise up for David a righteous offshoot who will reign as monarch and prosper and exercise judgment and justice in the land. In his days Judah will be saved and Israel will live in safety. And this is his name that they will call him: Jehovah our Righteousness." (Jeremiah 23:5, 6)

In Joel:

> Then you will know that I, Jehovah your God, am living on Zion, my holy mountain; and Jerusalem will be holiness. And it will happen on that day that the mountains will shower down new wine, and the hills will stream with milk, and all the brooks of Judah will stream with water, and a spring will issue from Jehovah's house and water the river of the sheetim. Judah will abide forever and Jerusalem for generation after generation. (Joel 3:17, 18, 20)

[7] In Zechariah:

> On that day I will strike every horse with bewilderment and its rider with insanity; and on the house of Judah I will open my eyes, and every horse of the peoples I will strike with blindness. And Judah's

rulers will say in their heart, "For my sake I will strengthen the residents of Jerusalem in Jehovah Sabaoth their God." On that day I will make Judah's rulers like a pot of fire among the sticks and like a torch of fire in a sheaf, and on the right and on the left they will consume all the peoples all around. And Jerusalem will still be inhabited in its place—in Jerusalem. And Jehovah will save the tents of Judah first, so that the glory of David's house and the glory of Jerusalem's resident will not lift itself up over Judah. On that day Jehovah will protect the resident of Jerusalem. And the house of David will be like God, like Jehovah's angel before them. And I will pour out on David's house and on Jerusalem's resident a spirit of grace. (Zechariah 12:4–10)

This is about the Lord's heavenly kingdom, in which truth will not dominate goodness but be subordinate to it. David's house and Jerusalem's resident symbolize truth, and Judah symbolizes goodness. This explains why the text first says that the glory of David's house and the glory of Jerusalem's resident will not lift itself up over Judah, and then that David's house will be like God and like Jehovah's angel, and that on it and on Jerusalem's resident a spirit of grace will be poured out. This is what conditions are like when truth is subordinate to goodness, or faith to love.

The horse to be struck with bewilderment and the horse of the peoples to be struck with blindness means our own, self-directed intelligence; see §§2761, 2762, 3217.

[8] In the same author:

On that day, "Holiness to Jehovah" will be on the horses' bells. And there will be pots in Jehovah's house like the bowls before the altar. And every pot in Jerusalem and in Judah will be holiness to Jehovah Sabaoth. (Zechariah 14:20, 21)

This is about the Lord's kingdom. In Malachi:

Watch: I am sending my angel, who will prepare the way before me; and suddenly to his temple will come the Lord, whom you are seeking, and the Angel of the Covenant, whom you desire. Watch: He is coming! Who can endure the day of his coming? Then the minha of Judah and Jerusalem will be sweet to Jehovah, as in the days of old and as in former years. (Malachi 3:1, 2, 4)

Plainly this is about the Lord's Coming. People recognize that the minha of Judah and Jerusalem was not sweet at that time, but sweetness does characterize worship springing from love (Judah's minha) and from the resulting faith (Jerusalem's). [9] In Jeremiah:

> This is what Jehovah Sabaoth has said: "They will again say this word in the land of Judah and in its cities, when [I] turn back their captivity: 'A blessing on you from Jehovah, the dwelling place of justice, the holy mountain!' And on [the mountain] will live Judah and all its cities together. Look! The days are coming," says Jehovah, "on which I will sow the house of Judah with the seed of human and the seed of animal. Look! The days are coming," says Jehovah, "on which I will strike a new pact with the house of Israel and with the house of Judah unlike the pact that I struck with their ancestors." (Jeremiah 31:23, 24, 27, 31, 32)

In David:

> The Lord chose the tribe of Judah—Mount Zion, which he loved—and built his sanctuary like the heights; he founded it forever, like the earth. (Psalms 78:68, 69)

[10] These passages and a large number of others not quoted show what Judah symbolizes in the Word. It does not mean the Jewish nation, because this nation was anything but a heavenly religion, or the Lord's heavenly kingdom. In regard to love for the Lord and charity toward one's neighbor and in regard to faith, it was the worst nation of all, and has been so from its first ancestors (Jacob's sons) right up to modern times. Still, people like this could *represent* the heavenly and spiritual qualities of the Lord's kingdom (see §§3479, 3480, 3481), since representations imply nothing about the person, only about the attribute represented (§§665, 1097 at the end, 1361, 3147, 3670).

[11] On the other hand, when they no longer kept up the rituals commanded by Jehovah (the Lord) but turned from them to different forms of idolatry, they no longer represented heavenly and spiritual qualities. Instead they represented the opposites, or hellish and diabolical qualities, according to the Lord's words in John:

> You are from your father, the Devil, and your father's desires you wish to do. He was a murderer from the start and did not stand on truth. (John 8:44)

This negative symbolism of Judah can be seen from the following in Isaiah:

> Jerusalem has stumbled, and Judah has fallen, because their tongue and their deeds are against Jehovah, to rebel against his glorious eyes. (Isaiah 3:8)

In Malachi:

> Judah committed treachery, and an abominable thing was done in Israel
> and in Jerusalem, and Judah profaned Jehovah's holiness, because he
> loved and took as his bride the daughter of a foreign god. (Malachi 2:11)

There are also the following passages: Isaiah 3:1 and following verses; 8:7,
8; Jeremiah 2:28; 3:7–11; 9:[26]; 11:9, 10, 12; 13:9; 14:2; 17:1; 18:11, 12, 13;
19:7; 32:35; 36:31; 44:12, 14, 26, 28; Hosea 5:5; 8:14; Amos 2:4, 5; Zephaniah
1:4; and many others.

3882   *And she stopped giving birth* symbolizes climbing the ladder from earth
all the way to Jehovah, or the Lord. This can be seen from the symbolism
of *giving birth,* or of the children born, as truth and goodness, because
these are offspring in a spiritual sense. It is through truth and goodness
that we regenerate or are born anew.

Truth and goodness are also what are symbolized by the four children Leah bore: Reuben, Simeon, Levi, and Judah. Reuben symbolizes
the truth that forms the first step of regeneration or rebirth—truth as
fact, or simply knowing truth. Simeon symbolizes truth that forms the
second step of regeneration or rebirth—truth in relation to the will, and
so an intention to act on truth. Levi symbolizes truth that forms the
third step of regeneration or rebirth—truth in relation to desire, and so
a desire for truth, which is the same as charity. And Judah symbolizes
goodness, the fourth step of regeneration or rebirth, which is heavenly
love. When regenerate people, or people born anew, reach this step, the
Lord appears to them. They have climbed all the way from the bottom
step by a kind of ladder to the step where the Lord stands. [2] This is
also the upward path symbolized by the ladder Jacob saw resting on the
earth in his dream, its head reaching the sky, God's angels going up and
down on it, and Jehovah (the Lord) standing above it, as described in
Genesis 28:12. This shows that *she stopped giving birth* has the meaning
given.

On the point that these four mentions of conception and birth symbolized progress from an outer plane to an inner one, or from truth to
goodness, earth to heaven, see §§3860, 3868, 3874, 3879.

A descent follows, since we cannot go down until we have gone up; but
the descent is simply an overview of truth from the vantage point of goodness, as though we are standing on a mountain we have climbed, looking at
what lies below. From such a position we can take in immeasurably more

at one glance than those standing in the valley below, as is obvious to anyone. The situation is exactly the same with people devoted to goodness—to love for the Lord and charity for their neighbor—in relation to those who rely solely on truth, or on faith alone.

The Universal Human
and Correspondence (Continued):
Correspondence with the Heart and Lungs

THE universal human and correspondence with it have already been defined. The universal human is the whole of heaven, which is a composite likeness and image of the Lord. The Lord's divine nature corresponds to the heavenly and spiritual attributes there, which correspond to earthly entities in the world, particularly those belonging to a human being. Through heaven or the universal human, then, the Lord's divine nature corresponds with a human being and with all the parts that make up a human being—so much so that we spring from (in other words, are sustained by) this correspondence. **3883**

The world has no idea that heaven, the universal human, corresponds in detail with a human being, or that we emerge from and live off this correspondence, so anything more that can be said about it will necessarily seem puzzling and incredible. Let me recount some experiences that have confirmed my belief in it. **3884**

Once, when an inner heaven opened up to me and I talked with the angels there, I was able to make the following observations.

It needs to be known that although I was in heaven, I was not outside myself but was in my body. Heaven is within a person, wherever the person is, so when it pleases the Lord, we can be in heaven without leaving our body. Accordingly, I was given the opportunity to perceive the general workings of heaven as plainly as anything I observe with my senses.

There were four types of action I sensed at that time. The first played on my brain at the left temple and had a general effect on my organs of reason—the left part of the brain corresponds to rational or intellectual activity, and the right part to affective or volitional activity.

[2] I sensed the second general type of action as working on the breathing of my lungs, gently controlling it from within, so that I had no need to draw breath or respire by any effort of will. Then I clearly sensed heaven's own breathing, which is deep and therefore imperceptible to people on earth. All the same, through the miracle of correspondence, it flows into their breathing, which is superficial, belonging to the body. If we were deprived of this inflow, we would fall down dead in an instant.

[3] The third type of action I sensed affected my heart's systole and diastole, which was then gentler than at any other time. My pulse was regular, about three beats to a breath, but by nature it synchronized with and therefore controlled the rate of breathing. At the end of every breath I was somehow given the ability to observe the way the heart's rhythm inserted itself into the lungs' rhythm. My pulse was so clearly perceptible that I could count the beats, which were distinct and soft.

[4] The fourth general type of action targeted my kidneys, and this too I was allowed to perceive, but only vaguely.

These observations showed me several things: Heaven, the universal human, has a heartbeat and respiration. The heartbeat of heaven, or the universal human, has a correspondence with the heart and with its systolic and diastolic activity. The respiration of heaven (the universal human) has a correspondence with the lungs and their breathing. We cannot observe either, though, because they are internal and consequently imperceptible.

3885 One time, I was withdrawn from the thinking that rises out of the bodily senses and saw a heavenly light. The light itself took me even further out of those thoughts, because heaven's light contains spiritual life (see §§1524, 2776, 3167, 3195, 3339, 3636, 3643). While I was enjoying this light, bodily and worldly concerns appeared to lie below me. I could still perceive them, but only as something distant and irrelevant to me. At this point my head but not my body seemed to me to be in heaven.

In this condition I was again enabled to observe heaven's shared breathing and the nature of it, which was interior, easy, and free, and aligned with my breaths at a rate of three to one. Likewise I was allowed to observe the back-and-forth of the heartbeats.

Then some angels informed me that we on earth all derive our pulse and respiration from there. The reason ours are not synchronized, they told me, is that both the beating of hearts and the breathing of lungs in the heavens turn into a kind of steady impetus that stimulates the same motions at various rates [in us], depending on each individual's state.

Still, it needs to be known that there are many different pulse and respiration rates in the heavens—as many as there are communities. The rates mirror the states of the inhabitants' thoughts and feelings, which mirror the states of their faith and love. Nevertheless there is an overall heartbeat and respiration as described above.

3886

I also had an opportunity once to observe the heartbeats of angels belonging to the area at the back of the head—the heartbeats of the heavenly angels there separately from those of the spiritual ones. Those of the heavenly were quiet and gentle, but those of the spiritual were strong and pounding. The pulse rate of the heavenly compared to that of the spiritual was five to two. The pulsing of heavenly hearts acts on that of spiritual hearts and in this way branches out and crosses into the realm of the material world.

Surprising to say, spiritual angels cannot hear what heavenly angels say but perceive it in the form of a heartbeat, because the language of heavenly angels is not intelligible to spiritual angels. Heavenly angels speak in terms of love's desires, but spiritual angels in terms of the intellect's thoughts (see §§1647, 1759, 2157, 3343), and the former belong to the region of the heart, but the latter to the region of the lungs.

There are two kingdoms in heaven, or the universal human: one called heavenly and the other called spiritual. The heavenly kingdom consists of angels referred to as heavenly—angels who [in earthly life] loved the Lord and as a result had access to all wisdom. They live in the Lord more than others do, so their state is more peaceful and innocent than that of others. To others they look like little children, because this is the appearance that peace and innocence present. Everything they see seems to be alive, because whatever comes directly from the Lord is living. This is the heavenly kingdom.

3887

The other kingdom, called spiritual, consists of angels referred to as spiritual—angels who treated their neighbor with charity. They find the highest pleasure of their life in being allowed to do good to others without reward—which is reward in itself, for them. The more they long for and seek such an opportunity, the more understanding and happiness they gain, because in the next life the Lord grants each of us understanding and happiness in keeping with the useful function we willingly, eagerly serve. This is the spiritual kingdom.

[2] Everyone in the Lord's heavenly kingdom belongs to the region of the heart, and everyone in the spiritual kingdom belongs to the region of the lungs.

The heavenly kingdom's influence on the spiritual kingdom resembles the effect of the heart on the lungs and the effect of everything related to the heart on everything related to the lungs. The heart governs the whole of the body and all its parts through the blood vessels, and the lungs also govern all parts of the body through respiration. So throughout the body the heart exerts a kind of influence on the lungs, depending on the different structures and their state. This influence gives rise to all sensation and action belonging to the body, as can be seen from fetuses and newborns, who are incapable of physical sensation and voluntary action until their lungs open, enabling the one [the heart] to act on the other [the lungs].

Things are similar in the spiritual world, except that it contains heavenly and spiritual qualities—goodness from love and goodness from faith—rather than physical and earthly objects. So in the inhabitants there the activity of the heart depends on the state of love, and the activity of the lungs depends on the state of faith. The effect of the one on the other gives rise to spiritual sensation and spiritual action.

These ideas cannot help but appear baffling to people on earth because people have no idea that the goodness of love and the truth of faith are more than abstractions devoid of the power to make anything happen. In reality the opposite is true: all perception and sensation, all force and action rise out of love's goodness and faith's truth, even in people on earth.

3888   In our case, these two kingdoms manifest themselves as the two kingdoms within us: the kingdom of the will and the kingdom of the intellect. These two compose our mind; in fact, they compose our real self. The will is what the beating of the heart corresponds to, and the intellect is what the breathing of the lungs corresponds to. That is why we also have two kingdoms in our body—those of the heart and the lungs.

People who know this secret can also see how matters stand with the effect of the will on the intellect, and of the intellect on the will, consequently with the effect of love's goodness on faith's truth, and the reverse. So they can see how matters stand with a person's rebirth.

People whose thinking rises purely out of the body—that is, people with an evil will and a distorted intellect—cannot grasp these ideas. They think about spiritual and heavenly subjects solely in a sensory and bodily way. Their thoughts about matters of heavenly light (faith's truth) originate in the dark, and their thoughts about matters of heavenly fire (love's goodness) originate in the cold. Both the dark and the cold snuff out what is heavenly and spiritual so completely that the latter appear worthless to them.

I needed to learn not only that there is a correspondence between the heavenly aspects of love and the motions of the heart, and between the spiritual aspects of a faith based on love and the motions of the lungs, but also how the correspondence worked. To that end I was granted the opportunity to interact for a remarkably long time with angels demonstrating it experientially.

3889

By flowing in spirals in a marvelous fashion that is beyond the power of words to describe, the angels formed a replica of the heart and a replica of the lungs, with all the interweavings of deep and surface [blood vessels and nerves] that compose them. In doing so, they were spontaneously following the flow of activity in heaven, because an inflow of love from the Lord inspires heaven to strive toward such a form. In this way they were presenting a detailed image of the heart's components and afterward of the close connection between heart and lungs—which they also represented as the marriage of goodness and truth.

This demonstration also made it clear that the heart corresponds to heavenliness, which is a matter of goodness, and the lungs, to spirituality, which is a matter of truth. It showed that the union of the two in a physical object resembles the union of heart and lungs.

I was told that the case is the same with the cardiac elements and the pulmonary elements throughout the body, in each of its limbs, organs, and viscera. Anywhere the two do not work together, each performing its own unique functions, there cannot be any living motion coming from any starting point in the will, or any living sensation coming from any starting point in the intellect.

I have said several times before that heaven or the universal human is divided into countless communities, equaling overall the number of organs and viscera in the body, and that each community relates to one of them (§3745); also that although the communities are numerous and varied, they still act as one, just as all the parts of the body do, despite their differences. The communities that belong to the realm of the heart are heavenly ones and stand in the middle, at the core, while those that belong to the realm of the lungs are spiritual and stand around the edges, on the outside. The Lord acts through the heavenly ones on the spiritual, or through the middle on the edges; he moves through the core

3890

toward the outside. The reason is that he acts through love, or mercy, which is the source of everything heavenly in his kingdom, and what he acts on through love and mercy is the goodness taught by faith, which is the source of everything spiritual in his kingdom. His inflow brings with it indescribable variety, yet the variety results not from his inflow but from its reception.

3891   Not only does the whole of heaven in general breathe like one person, but individual communities that are in contact with each other breathe together, as do any angels and spirits who are in contact with each other. Much personal experience has borne this out for me, so that no doubt remains in my mind. In fact, spirits are amazed that anyone could doubt it.

However, few people picture angels and spirits as anything but disembodied. Most suppose they consist of mere thought, hardly viewing them as substantial, let alone as human beings who enjoy the senses of sight, hearing, and touch. Still less would they believe that such beings breathe and therefore have life as we do (though of a deeper kind, like the life of the spirit in comparison to that of the body). So let me cite still more of my experiences.

Once when I was about to go to sleep I was warned that there was a large group plotting against me, intending to choke me to death; but I paid no attention to the group's threats. The Lord was keeping me safe, so I went to sleep unworried. Waking up in the middle of the night, though, I sensed plainly that I was breathing not under my own power but heaven's. My respiration was not my own, yet I was breathing.

On countless other occasions I was able to sense the respiration or breathing of spirits and also of angels by this device: that they breathed inside me at the same time as I did my own breathing, which was separate from theirs. But no one can experience this except a person whose inner depths are open and who by that means is granted communication with heaven.

3892   The earliest people, who were heavenly and loved the Lord more than others do, informed me that they did not have external breathing as their descendants did but internal breathing. They breathed in rhythm with the angels whose company they kept because they were governed by a heavenly love. I also learned that the state of their breathing matched exactly the state of their love and its resulting faith. On this topic, see what has been told before at §§607, 805, 1118, 1119, 1120.

3893   Some angel choruses were celebrating the Lord together, with gladness of heart. Sometimes their praise sounded like sweet singing, because spirits and angels use audible voices with each other and hear their neighbor as clearly as one person hears another. Human song, though, cannot be compared to theirs for heavenly sweetness and harmony. From variations in the sound I could tell that there were a number of choruses.

The angels with me taught me that the angels in the choruses pertained to the area and functions of the lungs. They sing because singing is a function of the lungs. This too I was allowed to learn by experience. They were permitted to regulate my breathing, which they did so gently and sweetly—and so deep within—that I could hardly tell I was breathing.

I also learned that the angels dedicated to involuntary and voluntary respiration were two different sets. What I heard was that those dedicated to involuntary breathing are present when we sleep, because as soon as we drop off, our voluntary breathing stops and our involuntary breathing starts.

Since the breathing of angels and spirits matches exactly the state of their love and its resulting faith, as noted above in §3892, one community does not breathe in the same way as another. The evil, who love themselves and worldly advantages and whose thinking is therefore distorted, cannot keep company with the good. When they approach the good, they feel as though they cannot breathe, almost as if they are suffocating, and they drop half dead and stonelike into hell. There they regain their breath, which coordinates with the breathing of the inhabitants there. This fact shows that individuals immersed in evil and falsity cannot live in the universal human, or heaven. When their breathing falters as they draw closer, so does all their awareness and thought and all their initiative for doing evil and persuading others of falsity. With the death of their initiative comes the end of any activity or motion that makes them feel alive, so they cannot help hurling themselves down from there headlong.   **3894a**

Because this is so, and because the upright, when they go to the next life, at first return to the life they had in this world (§2119) and so to what they loved and relished during that life, they cannot associate with angels yet, not even in their breathing. First they have to be prepared. In the course of preparation they are introduced to angelic life through synchronized breathing, during which they come to enjoy inner perceptions and heavenly freedom. This usually happens in company, or in choruses, in which each individual resembles the next in respiration, perception, and freedom of action. I was shown how this was done, again through firsthand experience.   **3894b**

In the other life, a dogmatic belief in what is evil and false—and even in what is true, if one is living an evil life—by its very nature seems to suffocate others, including upright spirits before they have been initiated into angelic breathing. For this reason, the Lord removes the dogmatic   **3895** and keeps them in hell, where they cannot hurt one another. After all, one spirit's conviction is almost the same as another's in hell, so their breathing coincides.

Certain dogmatic spirits came to me intending to smother me, which they actually managed to do to some extent, but the Lord rescued me. He then sent a little child, whose presence distressed them so much they could hardly breathe. They were kept in this condition until they were reduced to pleading, at which point they were thrust down into hell.

[2] In people living evil lives, here is what a dogmatic belief in the truth is like: They persuade themselves that the truth is true not for good purposes but for evil ones, since what they are seeking is to gain position, prestige, and wealth. The worst are capable of such strong conviction and even apparent zeal that they damn anyone to hell who does not possess the truth, even if the person does possess goodness. For a discussion of dogmatic belief, see §§2689, 3865.

When people like this first come into the other world, they consider themselves angels, but they cannot go near any angelic community. Their own dogmatism essentially chokes them when they do. They are the ones the Lord spoke of in Matthew:

> Many will say to me on that day, "Lord! Lord! Haven't we prophesied in your name and cast out demons in your name and exercised many powers in your name?" But then I'll proclaim to them, "I do not know you. Leave me, you *evildoers!*" (Matthew 7:22, 23)

3896   More about the universal human and its correspondence appears at the end of the next chapter [§§4039-4055].

Genesis 30

[Matthew 24:23–28]

IN keeping with the set pattern, this chapter will be prefaced by an explanation of the Lord's teachings in Matthew 24 about the Last Judgment, or the church's last days. The preamble to the previous chapter [§§3751–3757] explained the contents of Matthew 24:19–22. Those of Matthew 24:23–28 follow here:

> Then if anyone says to you, "Look: here is the Christ!" or "There!" you are not to believe it. Because false Christs and false prophets will arise and do great signs and portents, to lead astray, if possible, even the chosen. Here, I have told you beforehand. So if they say to you, "Look: he is in the wilderness!" you are not to go out; "Look: he is in the inner rooms!" you are not to believe it. Because as the lightning issues from the east and is seen all the way to the west, so also will be the Coming of the Son of Humankind. For wherever the carcass is, there will the eagles also gather. (Matthew 24:23, 24, 25, 26, 27, 28)

Without the lessons of the inner meaning, no one can know what these words involve. What does it mean, for instance, that false Christs would arise to do signs and portents? That if they said the Christ was in the wilderness, [the disciples] were not to go out? That if they said he was in the inner rooms, they were not to believe it? That the Coming of the Son of Humankind would be like the lightning that issues from the east and is seen all the way to the west? Or that where the carcass is, there the eagles will gather?

These words, like those that come before and after them in Matthew 24, seem to exhibit no logical sequence in their literal meaning, but in their inner meaning they show an exquisite progression. This progression first comes to view when we understand the symbolism of false Christs, signs and portents, the wilderness and inner rooms, the Coming of the Son of Humankind, and a carcass and eagles.

[2] The Lord spoke this way in order to keep people from understanding his words, for fear they would profane them. If they had understood the message when the church was spiritually devastated (as it was among the Jews at that time), they would have profaned it. So for the same reason the Lord also spoke in parables, as he himself teaches in Matthew 13:13, 14, 15; Mark 4:11, 12; Luke 8:10. The Word cannot be profaned by those who do not know its mysteries, only by those who do (see §§301, 302, 303, 593, 1008, 1010, 1059, 1327, 1328, 2051, 3398, 3402). It is profaned more by those who see themselves as scholars than by those who see themselves as nonscholars.

[3] The reason the Word's inner depths are being laid open now is that the church today is devastated. It has been so nearly stripped of faith and love that even though people know and understand [the truth] they do not acknowledge let alone believe it (see §§3398, 3399). The only exceptions are the few living a good life, who are called the chosen. They can now be educated, and a new religion is to be established among them. Only the Lord knows where they are. Not many will come from within the church. It is among people outside the church that new religions have been set up before (see §2986).

3899   The previous verses of Matthew 24 had to do with the cumulative devastation of the church. First, people would start to forget what was good and true and would quarrel over it; then they would despise it; in the third place they would refuse to acknowledge it; and in the fourth they would profane it (see §3754).

Now the text discusses what the condition of the church is like in respect to its theology at that stage, in general and among certain people in particular. These are the people who engage in worship that is outwardly reverent but inwardly profane, who proclaim the Lord in holy adoration with their lips but worship themselves and the world at heart. For them, devotion to the Lord is a means of winning high position and riches. The more they have acknowledged the Lord, the life of heaven, and faith, the more these things are what they profane when they commit profanation.

This is the state of the church currently under discussion, as stands out more clearly from the inner meaning of the Lord's words quoted above. The meaning is this:

3900   *Then if anyone says to you, "Look: here is the Christ!" or "There!" you are not to believe it* symbolizes a warning to watch out for such people's theology. The *Christ* means the Lord in regard to divine truth and therefore in regard to the Word and teachings from it. In this case it obviously means the opposite: divine truth distorted, or false doctrine. (On the point that Jesus means divine goodness, and Christ divine truth, see §§3004, 3005, 3008, 3009.)

[2] *Because false Christs and false prophets will arise* symbolizes the falsities in that theology. *False Christs* are falsified teachings from the Word, or truth that is not godly, as the remarks just above show (and see §§3010, 3732 at the end). *False prophets* are people who teach those falsities (§2534).

The main people teaching falsity in the Christian world are those who make self-aggrandizement and worldly wealth their goal. They twist scriptural truth to promote their own interest, because when love for ourselves and the world forms our goal, we think of nothing else. These are false Christs and false prophets.

[3] And *do great signs and portents* symbolizes proofs and persuasions based on shallow, misleading appearances, which the unsophisticated allow to dupe them. This meaning of *doing signs and portents* will be demonstrated elsewhere, with the Lord's divine mercy [§§6870, 7012, 7273, 7633, 7795].

[4] *To lead astray, if possible, even the chosen* means leading astray people who live a life of goodness and truth and therefore live in the Lord. They are the ones the Word calls *chosen*.

Such people rarely appear in company with those who hide their profane worship under a sanctimonious veil, and if the former do appear with the latter, the former are not recognized. The Lord protects them by concealing them, since until they solidify their thinking, they readily allow outward piety to lead them astray. After they solidify it, they stand fast. The Lord keeps them in the company of angels, unbeknownst to them, and then it is impossible for that unspeakable crowd to rope them in.

[5] *Here, I have told you beforehand* symbolizes encouragement to use caution and watch out, because such people live among false prophets who appear in sheep's clothing but inwardly are ravenous wolves (Matthew 7:15). These false prophets are the "children of this age" who are more prudent (more cunning) than the children of light in their generation (as described in Luke 16:8). Accordingly the Lord encourages them with these words: "Here, I am sending you out as sheep in the midst of wolves. So be shrewd as snakes and simple as doves" (Matthew 10:16).

[6] *So if they say to you, "Look: he is in the wilderness!" you are not to go out; "Look: he is in the inner rooms!" you are not to believe it* means that

no one should believe what they say about truth or about goodness or about many other subjects.

Only people who know the inner meaning can see that this is the symbolism. They can tell that the words hold a secret from the fact that the Lord spoke them. Unless there is another meaning hidden within, these instructions (not to go out if people say the Christ is in the wilderness and not to believe it if they say he is in the inner rooms) are trivial. But a *wilderness* symbolizes truth that has been stripped away, and the *inner rooms* symbolize goodness that has been stripped away. A wilderness symbolizes truth stripped away because when the church has been devastated—when it no longer contains any divine truth, because it no longer holds any goodness, no love for the Lord or charity for one's neighbor—it is said to be a wilderness or in a wilderness. A wilderness means any untamed, uninhabited place (§2708) and that which has little life (§1927), and this describes truth in the church at that stage. Clearly, then, the wilderness means a religion lacking in truth. [7] The inner-level symbolism of inner rooms is goodness in the church, and simply goodness. A church with goodness is called the house of God, and the inner rooms are the goodness and truth in that house. On the house of God meaning divine goodness, and a house in general meaning good done out of love and charity, see §§2233, 2559, 3142, 3652, 3720.

The reason no one should believe what such people say about truth or about goodness is that they call falsity true, and evil good. People whose aims focus only on themselves and the world take truth and goodness to mean nothing but the need for others to worship and serve them. If they inspire others to true devotion, it is for the purpose of being seen in sheep's clothing.

[8] Another point: The Word, which the Lord has spoken, teems with inner content, and "wilderness" has a broad range of meaning (since any untamed, uninhabited place is called a wilderness), while all things within us are called inner rooms. So the wilderness also symbolizes the Old Testament Word (since it has been deemed obsolete) and the inner rooms symbolize the New Testament Word (since it teaches about the inner depths, or the inner self).

Then too the whole Word is called a wilderness when it no longer serves as doctrine. Human customs are called inner rooms, and since they depart from scriptural commands and customs, they turn the Word into a wilderness, as the Christian world knows. People whose outward show of worship is reverent but whose inward worship is profane nullify the Word for the sake of innovations aimed at making them greater and wealthier than anyone else. They even go so far as to forbid others to read the Word.

People whose worship is not so profane may consider the Word holy and allow the common person to have it, but with their interpretations they still bend everything in it to the service of their own doctrines. This practice makes everything else in Scripture—everything that conflicts with their doctrines—a wilderness. Look at people who ascribe salvation to faith alone and brush off acts of neighborly love. They make a wilderness out of everything the Lord himself said about love and charity in the New Testament and so many times in the Old. They make inner rooms out of everything advocated by faith detached from good deeds.

These remarks clarify the meaning of the words *If they say to you, "Look: he is in the wilderness!" you are not to go out; "Look: he is in the inner rooms!" you are not to believe it.*

[9] *Because as the lightning issues from the east and is seen all the way to the west, so also will be the Coming of the Son of Humankind* means that inward worship of the Lord will resemble lightning, which vanishes instantly. *Lightning* symbolizes matters of heavenly light, so it symbolizes attributes of love and faith, since love and faith are matters of heavenly light. In its highest sense, the *east* means the Lord; in an inward sense it means good done as a result of love, charity, or faith received from the Lord (see §§101, 1250, 3249). The *west,* in an inward sense, means that which has set, or ceased to exist, so it means a failure to acknowledge either the Lord or good done as a result of love, charity, or faith. Lightning that issues from the east and is seen all the way to the west, then, means disappearance. The Lord's Coming will not be his literal reappearance in the world but his presence in every individual. This coming takes place every time the gospel is preached, every time someone thinks about something holy.

[10] *For wherever the carcass is, there will the eagles gather* means that arguments supporting falsity will proliferate in the devastated church.

When a church lacks the goodness and therefore the truth promoted by faith—when it has been spiritually devastated—it is described as dead, because goodness and truth are its source of life. When it is dead, it is likened to a *carcass.* Arguments to the effect that goodness and truth are nothing but what the teachers take them to be are *eagles,* and so are the use of those arguments to justify evil and falsity. The next section will demonstrate this. The meaning of the carcass as a religion lacking the vitality of charity and faith becomes clear from the Lord's words in Luke describing the close of the age:

> The disciples said, "Where, Lord?" [referring to the close of the age, or the Last Judgment]. Jesus said to them, "*Where the body is, there will the eagles gather.*" (Luke 17:37)

"The body" replaces "the carcass" because it means a dead body here. It symbolizes the church, because the Judgment is destined to start with the house of God, or the church, as various passages in the Word show.

There you have the symbolism of the Lord's quoted words, explained in their inner meaning. They follow in an exquisite series, even if the sequence does not show in the literal meaning, and one who ponders their interconnections according to the explanation can see that this is so.

3901 The church's final stage is compared to eagles gathering around a carcass or body because eagles symbolize a person's rational dimension. In relation to good people they symbolize true reason, but in relation to evil people they symbolize false reason, or sophistry. Birds in general symbolize a person's thoughts, again in both [positive and negative] senses (§§40, 745, 776, 866, 991, 3219), and each species symbolizes something specific. Eagles fly high and have sharp eyes, so they symbolize rationality.

This symbolism can be seen from many passages in the Word. Let me quote the following ones for confirmation—first, those in which eagles symbolize true reason. In Moses:

> Jehovah found his people in a wilderness land, and in emptiness, lamentation, wastelands. He enveloped them, instructed them, guarded them as the pupil of his eye. *As an eagle stirs its nest,* moves constantly over the chicks, spreads its wings, he takes them, carries them on his wing. (Deuteronomy 32:10, 11)

This passage depicts instruction in religious truth and goodness, using the simile of an eagle. The depiction and the simile cover the whole process to the point where we finally become rational and spiritual. All comparisons in the Word rely on symbolism. This one relies on the symbolism of an eagle as rationality. [2] In the same author:

> Jehovah to Moses: "You yourselves have seen what I did to the Egyptians and *that I carried you on eagles' wings* to bring you to me." (Exodus 19:3, 4)

The meaning is similar. In Isaiah:

> Those waiting for Jehovah will be renewed with strength, *will rise on a strong wing like eagles.* They will run and not grow weary; they will walk and not become tired. (Isaiah 40:31)

Being renewed with strength means being increasingly able to will what is good. Rising on a strong wing like eagles means being increasingly able to understand what is true and consequently increasing in rationality. Here as elsewhere, the matter is expressed in two phrases, one involving goodness in the will, the other involving truth in the intellect. Likewise for running without growing weary and walking without becoming tired. [3] In Ezekiel:

> Utter a parable about the house of Israel and say, "This is what the Lord Jehovih has said: '*A large eagle—long in its feathers, full of plumage,* with embroidery—came upon Lebanon and took a cedar twig, brought it into a land of commerce, put it in a city of perfumers; it sprouted and became a luxuriant grapevine. There was *another large eagle, great of wings and full of plumage,* to which—look!—this grapevine applied its roots. And it sent its branches out to [the eagle, for the eagle] to water it from its planting beds, in a good field, near many waters; but it will be devastated. [Israel's prince] sent his ambassadors to Egypt [demanding] that it give him horses and a large populace.'" (Ezekiel 17:2–9, 15)

The first eagle mentioned stands for reason enlightened by the Divine. The second eagle stands for reason rising out of human selfhood that becomes corrupted by false arguments based on sense impressions and factual knowledge. Egypt stands for facts (§§1164, 1165, 1186, 1462); horses, for an intellect composed of facts (§§2761, 2762, 3217). [4] In Daniel:

> Daniel's vision: four beasts coming up out of the sea, each different from the other. The first was like a lion, but *it had an eagle's wings.* I was looking, until its wings were pulled off and it was lifted from the earth, and it drew up on its feet like a human, and a human heart was given to it. (Daniel 7:3, 4)

The lion with an eagle's wings depicts the first stage of a religion, the eagle wings meaning rationality that rises out of human selfhood. When that rationality is taken away, we receive rationality and a will from the

Divine, and this is symbolized by the beast's rising from the earth, drawing up like a human on its feet, and being given a human heart. [5] In
Ezekiel:

> The likeness of the faces of the four living creatures, or guardian beings:
> the face of a human, and the face of a lion on the right for the four of
> them, and the face of an ox on the left for the four of them, and the *face
> of an eagle* for the four of them. (Ezekiel 1:10)

> Their wheels were called Galgal, and each had four faces; the first face
> was the face of a guardian being, and the second face was the face of a
> human, and the third was the face of a lion, and the fourth face the *face
> of an eagle.* (Ezekiel 10:13, 14)

In John:

> Around the throne were four living creatures full of eyes in front and
> behind; the first living creature like a lion, the second living creature
> like a calf, the third living creature having a face like a human, the
> fourth living creature *like a flying eagle.* (Revelation 4:[6,] 7)

Plainly the living creatures in these visions have some unknown, divine
symbolism, so the likeness of their faces does too. Just what the secret
meaning is cannot be seen unless the inner meaning of a lion, calf, human,
and eagle is known. The eagle's face obviously means watchfulness and
therefore prudence, because the guardian beings (portrayed as animals
in Ezekiel) symbolize the Lord's providence making sure we do not rely
on ourselves and our own rationality in exploring religious mysteries (see
§308). So of course when an eagle is mentioned in reference to a human
being, in an inner sense it means rationality. The reason for an eagle's
symbolism is that it flies high, looking down from above on a wide area
below. [6] In Job:

> Is it owing to your intelligence that a hawk flies, that it spreads its wings
> toward the south? Is it at your word that *an eagle soars* and raises its nest
> aloft? (Job 39:26, 27)

The eagle plainly means reason, which is an aspect of intelligence. That
is what an eagle symbolized in the ancient church—Job being a book of
the ancient church (§3540 at the end). Almost all the books of that era
were symbolic compositions, but over time the symbolism passed into
oblivion. Eventually no one knew even that birds in general symbolize

thoughts, despite frequent mention of them in the Word, where they obviously mean something other than birds.

[7] The negative symbolism of an eagle as rationality that is not true but false is clear from the following passages. In Moses:

> Jehovah will raise over you a nation from far away, from the end of the earth, *as the eagle flies in*—a nation whose tongue you cannot hear, a nation hard of face. (Deuteronomy 28:49, 50)

In Jeremiah:

> Look: a cloud rises! And its chariots are like a windstorm; *swifter than eagles are its horses.* Alas for us, because we have been devastated! (Jeremiah 4:13)

In the same author:

> Your boasting has deceived you, the pride of your heart—you who live in openings of rock, who occupy the height of a hill—because *like an eagle you raise your nest aloft;* from there I will throw you down. Look: *like an eagle he rises and flies* and spreads his wings over Bozrah; and the heart of the powerful of Edom on that day became like the heart of a woman in anguish. (Jeremiah 49:16, 17, 22)

In the same author:

> Swifter were our pursuers *than eagles.* On the mountains they chased us; in the wilderness they lay in wait for us. (Lamentations 4:19)

In Micah:

> Make yourself bald and shave yourself, over the children of your pleasures; broaden your baldness *like the eagle* because they have moved away from you. (Micah 1:16)

In Obadiah:

> If you *exalt yourself like an eagle,* and if you put your nest among the stars, from there I will pull you down. (Obadiah verse 4)

In Habakkuk:

> I am rousing the Chaldeans, a nation bitter and rash, invading the breadth of the land to inherit dwellings that are not theirs. *Its horses are nimbler*

than eagles; its riders will come from a distance; they will fly forward like an *eagle darting in to eat.* (Habakkuk 1:6, 8)

[8] In these passages eagles symbolize falsity introduced by logic that is based on sensory illusions and superficial appearances. In the last quotation from the Prophets, the Chaldeans symbolize people with piety on the outside but falsity inside (see §1368). They, like Babylon, are the ones who devastate the church (1327). The breadth of the land means truth (3433, 3434), and invasion of the breadth of the land symbolizes the stripping away of truth. Horses mean the intellectual prowess of these people, which has the same character they do (2761, 2762, 3217). From this it is apparent why the eagle is darting in to eat: to strip humankind of truth (the ruination of the church being the current topic).

These things are merely compared to eagles, but to repeat, comparisons in the Word rely on symbolism.

This discussion now clarifies the meaning of the comparison with eagles who will gather around the carcass.

Genesis 30

1. And Rachel saw that she was not bearing children to Jacob, and Rachel felt jealous toward her sister, and she said to Jacob, "Give me sons; and if not, I will be dead."

2. And Jacob burned with anger against Rachel and said, "Am I in place of God, who is holding back from you the fruit of the belly?"

3. And she said, "Look—my maid, Bilhah; come to her, and let her give birth on my knees, and I, yes I, will be built up from her."

4. And she gave him Bilhah, her slave, to be his woman, and Jacob came to her.

5. And Bilhah conceived and bore Jacob a son.

6. And Rachel said, "God has judged me and has also heard my voice and given me a son." Therefore she called his name Dan.

7. And Bilhah, Rachel's slave, conceived again and bore a second son to Jacob.

8. And Rachel said, "With the wrestlings of God I have wrestled with my sister and even prevailed." And she called his name Naphtali.

9. And Leah saw that she had stopped giving birth, and she took Zilpah, her slave, and gave her to Jacob to be his woman.

10. And Zilpah, Leah's slave, bore Jacob a son.

11. And Leah said, "A troop comes," and called his name Gad.

12. And Zilpah, Leah's slave, bore a second son to Jacob.

13. And Leah said, "In my good fortune! Because daughters will call me fortunate." And she called his name Asher.

14. And Reuben went in the days of the wheat harvest and found dudaim in a field and brought them to Leah his mother; and Rachel said to Leah, "Please give me some of your son's dudaim."

15. And [Leah] said to her, "Is it a little thing that you have taken my husband, and will you also take my son's dudaim?" And Rachel said, "Then he will lie with you tonight, for your son's dudaim."

16. And Jacob came from the field in the evening, and Leah went out to meet him and said, "You shall come to me, because I have indisputably hired you with my son's dudaim." And he lay with her on that night.

17. And God listened to Leah, and she conceived and bore Jacob a fifth son.

18. And Leah said, "God has given me my reward because I gave my slave to my husband." And she called his name Issachar.

19. And Leah conceived again and bore a sixth son to Jacob.

20. And Leah said, "God has gifted me, me, with a good gift; this time my husband will live with me, because I have borne him six sons." And she called his name Zebulun.

21. And afterward she bore a daughter and called her name Dinah.

22. And God remembered Rachel, and God listened to her and opened her womb.

23. And she conceived and bore a son and said, "God is gathering up my disgrace."

24. And she called his name Joseph, saying, "Jehovah add to me another son!"

❊   ❊   ❊   ❊

25. And it happened when Rachel had borne Joseph that Jacob said to Laban, "Send me and let me go to my place and to my land.

26. Give me my women and my children, because I served you for them, and let me go, because you know my service with which I have served you."

27. And Laban said to him, "Please, if I have found favor in your eyes, . . . I have learned by experience that Jehovah has blessed me because of you."

28. And he said, "Name the wage you claim of me and I will give it."

29. And [Jacob] said to him, "You know how well I have served you and how your property has fared with me.

30. Because what you had previous to me was little, and it has burst into abundance, and Jehovah has blessed you at [every step of] my foot; and now, when shall I also do for my household?"

31. And he said, "What shall I give you?" And Jacob said, "You won't [have to] give me anything if you do this word for me: let me return [and] pasture [and] guard your flock.

32. I will pass through your whole flock today removing from it every speckled and spotted animal, and every black animal among the lambs, and the spotted and speckled one among the she-goats, and it will be my wage.

33. And my righteousness will answer for me on a future day, when you come concerning my wage [that is] before you; all that which is not speckled and spotted among the she-goats and black among the lambs—it is stolen with me."

34. And Laban said, "Here, by all means let it be according to your word!"

35. And on that day he removed the mottled and spotted he-goats, and all the speckled and spotted she-goats, every one in which there was white; and every black one among the lambs; and gave them into the hand of his sons.

36. And he put a journey of three days between himself and Jacob; and Jacob was pasturing Laban's remaining flocks.

37. And Jacob took himself a fresh rod of poplar, and hazel and sycamore, and peeled white peelings on them, a baring of the white that was on the rods.

38. And he stood the rods that he had peeled in the channels, in the water troughs, where the flocks came to drink, opposite the flocks, and they went into heat as they came to drink.

39. And the flocks went into heat at the rods, and the flocks bore mottled, speckled, and spotted [offspring].

40. And Jacob separated the lambs and turned the faces of the flock toward the mottled and [toward] every black one in Laban's flock and gave himself droves for himself alone and did not put them into Laban's flock.

41. And it happened at every onset of heat in the flock (those mating first) that Jacob put rods before the eyes of the flock in the channels, for it to go into heat at the rods.

42. And at the later mating of the flock he did not put [the rods there], and [the offspring] of those mating later were Laban's, and [the offspring] of those mating first were Jacob's.

43. And the man spread out greatly, greatly, and he had many flocks and female slaves and male slaves and camels and donkeys.

Summary

THE previous chapter, using the figures of Jacob's four sons by Leah, dealt with the state of a church (or of a person who becomes a church) in its climb from truth taught by faith to good done out of love. **3902**

This chapter uses the figures of Jacob's sons by Rachel's and Leah's slaves, by Leah, and finally by Rachel to focus on the union of earthly truth with spiritual goodness by means of intermediate steps, following the same order we follow when we are being reborn.

After portraying that union, the text depicts the fruitfulness and multiplying of truth and goodness, symbolized by the flock that Jacob amassed for himself through Laban's flock. **3903**

Inner Meaning

GENESIS 30:1, 2. *And Rachel saw that she was not bearing children to Jacob, and Rachel felt jealous toward her sister, and she said to Jacob, "Give me sons; and if not, I will be dead." And Jacob burned with anger* **3904** *against Rachel and said, "Am I in place of God, who is holding back from you the fruit of the belly?"*

Rachel saw that she was not bearing children to Jacob means that inner truth was not yet acknowledged. *And Rachel felt jealous toward her sister* symbolizes resentment that it was not acknowledged the way outer truth was. *And she said to Jacob, "Give me sons,"* means that there was a desire to acquire inner truth from the goodness associated with earthly truth. *And if not, I will be dead* means that if not, inner truth would not rise again. *And Jacob burned with anger against Rachel* symbolizes resentment on the part of earthly goodness. *And said, "Am I in place of God?"* means that it was impossible for earthly goodness. *Who is holding back from you the fruit of the belly* means that it had to come from inside.

3905   *Rachel saw that she was not bearing children to Jacob* means that inner truth was not yet acknowledged. This is established by the representation of *Rachel* as a desire for inner truth, or as inner truth itself (discussed in §§3758, 3782, 3793, 3819); from the symbolism of *bearing children* as acknowledging in faith and deed (discussed below); and from the representation of *Jacob* as the goodness associated with earthly truth (discussed in §§3669, 3677, 3829, and the whole previous chapter).

Bearing children means acknowledging in faith and deed because births mentioned in the Word symbolize spiritual births (§§1145, 1255, 3860, 3868). Giving spiritual birth means acknowledging and believing what is true and good. Here it means acknowledging the inner truth represented by Rachel in faith and deed. Since we do not acknowledge anything in faith until we live by it, I speak of acknowledgment in faith and deed. Religious truth that is learned not for the sake of action but merely knowledge links up with a desire for what is evil and false, so in the person who learns it, such truth is not religious but inwardly counterreligious.

3906   *And Rachel felt jealous toward her sister* symbolizes resentment that it was not acknowledged the way outer truth was, as can be seen from the following. The meaning of *feeling jealous* has to do with resentment—resentment [by Rachel] that she was not bearing children the way Leah was. *Rachel* represents inner truth, as noted just above in §3905. And her *sister*—Leah—symbolizes outer truth. (For the identification of Leah with outer truth, see §§3793, 3819.)

People who are being reborn learn to see what is inwardly true, but at first they do not acknowledge it with strong enough faith to live by it. Inward truth unites with spiritual desire, which cannot flow in until outward truth comes into correspondence with inward truth. [2] Take for example the inner truth that everything good comes from the Lord, and that what comes from human selfhood is not good. At the beginning of regeneration, we can see this and yet not acknowledge it in faith and deed. Acknowledging it in faith and deed means having a perception that it is so—and a desire and intent that it be so—every time we do something good. It also means having a perception that human-generated goodness cannot help focusing on us, our own advantage at others' expense, contempt for others, and a sense of merit for the good we do. These traits lurk within outer truth before inner truth has united with it. The two kinds of truth cannot unite until we start to give up concentrating on ourselves and feel an interest in our neighbor.

These considerations illustrate what is meant by a resentment that inner truth was not yet acknowledged the way outer truth was.

And she said to Jacob, "Give me sons," means that there was a desire to acquire inner truth from the goodness associated with earthly truth. This is established by the representation of *Jacob* as the goodness that comes of earthly truth (mentioned just above in §3905) and by the symbolism of *sons* as truth (discussed in §§489, 491, 533, 1147, 2623), and in this case as inner truth, since they were to come from Rachel, who represents inner truth (see §§3758, 3782, 3793, 3819).

3907

And if not, I will be dead means that if not, inner truth would not rise again. This can be seen from the symbolism of *dying* as not rising to life again. Wives in ancient times called themselves dead if they did not bear a son or daughter. They also believed they *were* essentially dead, because they left behind no memorial of themselves—none of their "life"—in descendants. Admittedly it was for worldly reasons that they said and believed this, but every cause springs from a cause prior to it, so a cause in the earthly world springs entirely from a cause in the spiritual world. The case is the same here. The cause in the spiritual world resulted from the heavenly marriage of goodness and truth, whose offspring are nothing but religious truths and neighborly kindnesses. These are daughters and sons in the spiritual world and are symbolized by daughters and sons in the Word. Anyone who has failed to give birth to religious truth and neighborly kindness is "dead"—in other words, is counted among the dead who do not rise again to life (heaven).

3908

This shows the symbolism of Rachel's words, *if not, I will be dead.*

And Jacob burned with anger against Rachel symbolizes resentment on the part of earthly goodness. This can be seen from the symbolism of

3909

burning with anger as resenting (discussed below) and from the representation of *Jacob* as goodness on the earthly level (mentioned above [§3905]). The verse says *against Rachel* because the inner truth represented by Rachel could not yet be acknowledged in faith and act by the earthly goodness that is Jacob.

Burning with anger means resenting, in an inner sense, because whenever an earthly emotion climbs toward inner levels, or toward heaven, it softens, eventually turning into a heavenly emotion. What we find in the literal meaning—"burning with anger," in this case—is relatively harsh, because it is earthly and bodily, but it grows milder and gentler as it rises from the bodily, earthly self to the inner or spiritual self. That is why the literal meaning, being suited to the grasp of the earthly self, is rough, but the inner meaning, being suited to the grasp of the spiritual self, is not.

This clarifies that burning with anger means resenting. Real spiritual indignation, and more particularly heavenly indignation, does not draw at all on the anger of the earthly self but on the inner essence of zeal. On the surface, zeal resembles anger, but on the inside it is not anger or even hot resentment. Instead it is a kind of sadness accompanied by a prayerful wish that the situation were otherwise. In its still deeper form it is simply a dark blot imposed on our heavenly pleasure by something that is not good or not true in another person.

3910   *And said, "Am I in place of God?"* means that it was impossible for earthly goodness. This can be seen from the symbolism of *not being in place of God* as being impossible. The Word refers to the Divine as God for his ability or power and as Jehovah for his beingness or essence (see §300), which is why he is called God when the theme is truth, and Jehovah when the theme is goodness (§§2769, 2807, 2822). Ability is assigned to truth, whereas beingness is assigned to goodness. Goodness acquires power through truth, because it is through truth that goodness drives everything that happens.

These remarks show that in an inner sense the words *am I in place of God?* mean that the thing was impossible for earthly goodness.

3911   *Who is holding back from you the fruit of the belly* means that it had to come from inside. This can be seen from the meaning that develops out of the inner sense of the words. On an inner level, the *fruit of the belly* symbolizes the same thing as childbirth—an acknowledgment in faith and deed of all that is true and good (§3905)—and something more, which is the union of the resulting truth and goodness.

This acknowledgment and union cannot come from the outer self, only from the inner. Everything good flows in from the Lord through the inner self into the outer self, adopting truth instilled through the sense impressions of the outer self and bringing us to acknowledge it in faith and deed. It also attaches truth to itself and in this way makes it ours. (The fact that all goodness flows in from the Lord through the inner self into truth gathered up into the outer self's memory has already been demonstrated many times.)

That is what is meant by the explanation of the words—that acknowledgment had to come from inside.

Genesis 30:3, 4, 5. And she said, "Look—my maid, Bilhah; come to her, and let her give birth on my knees, and I, yes I, will be built up from her." And she gave him Bilhah, her slave, to be his woman, and Jacob came to her. And Bilhah conceived and bore Jacob a son. **3912**

She said, "Look—my maid, Bilhah," symbolizes an affirmative middle ground between earthly truth and inner truth. *Come to her* symbolizes an ability to unite with it. *And let her give birth on my knees* symbolizes acknowledgment from a desire for inner truth, which leads to union. *And I, yes I, will be built up from her* means that [inner truth] would receive life as a result. *And she gave him Bilhah, her slave, to be his woman* means connecting with the affirmative middle ground. *And Jacob came to her* means internalizing it. *And Bilhah conceived and bore Jacob a son* symbolizes acceptance and acknowledgment.

She said, "Look—my maid, Bilhah," symbolizes an affirmative middle ground between earthly truth and inner truth, as can be seen from the following: A *maid* or female slave symbolizes a desire for the knowledge suited to the outer self, as discussed in §§1895, 2567, 3835, 3849. This desire is a middle ground uniting inner truth with earthly, outer truth, so the maid symbolizes an affirmative middle ground between them. And *Bilhah* represents the nature of the middle ground. **3913**

On an inner level, the slaves that Rachel and Leah gave to Jacob for his women, to produce offspring, simply represent and symbolize something that serves—in this case, something that serves as a means of union, specifically between inner and outer truth. Rachel represents inner truth, and Leah, outer (§§3793, 3819).

Here where the text speaks of Jacob's twelve sons, it is dealing with the twelve main, key methods by which we are introduced to spiritual and heavenly values when being reborn, or becoming a church. When we are reborn, or become a church, when from being dead we come alive, or from being body-oriented we become heavenly, the Lord leads us through many phases. The general phases are designated by these twelve sons and later by the twelve tribes, so the twelve tribes symbolize everything involved in faith and love (see what was shown in §3858). After all, general categories embrace all the subcategories and individual details, which relate back to the categories.

[2] When we are being reborn, our inner self needs to unite with our outer self, so the goodness and truth of our inner self need to unite with the goodness and truth of our outer self (since it is truth and goodness that make us who we are). These things cannot unite without a middle ground. By its very nature the middle ground draws partly on one side and partly on the other and causes one side to wane as the other waxes in our minds. This middle ground is what the slaves symbolize. Rachel's slaves symbolize middle ground verging toward the inner self, and Leah's slaves, middle ground verging toward the outer self.

[3] Clearly there has to be a means of union, when you consider that the earthly self on its own does not harmonize at all with the spiritual self and in fact clashes with it so strongly as to oppose it altogether. Our earthly self loves and focuses on personal and worldly advantages, but our spiritual self does not regard them except so far as doing so helps promote something useful in the spiritual world. So our spiritual self focuses on the services that personal and worldly advantages can perform and loves them for their usefulness and ultimate purpose.

Our earthly self sees itself as coming to life when it attains high rank and superiority over others, but our spiritual self sees itself as coming to life when it is humble and unimportant. It does not spurn lofty positions so long as they can serve as a means of benefiting our neighbor, society as a whole, and the church. This self considers the station to which we rise not in terms of our own advantage but in terms of the useful activities we look to as our goal.

Our earthly self feels blessed when we are richer than others and possess worldly wealth, but our spiritual self feels blessed when we have lots of knowledge about truth and goodness (which is wealth to the spiritual self), and especially when we do the good that truth teaches. This self does not spurn riches, because they allow us to do good in the world.

[4] These brief remarks show that the states of the earthly and spiritual selves are mutually hostile in their aims. They can still unite, however, when the demands of the outer self are subordinate to the goals of the inner self and serve those goals. If we are to become spiritual, then, everything in our outer self has to be reduced to obedience. We have to shed goals that look to ourselves and the world and clothe ourselves in goals that look to our neighbor and the Lord's kingdom. But we can

never shed the former and put on the latter, we can never join the two together, except through what is intermediate. These intermediaries are symbolized by the slaves, and specifically by the four sons born to them.

[5] The first intermediary is an affirmation of inner truth that says, "Yes, it's true." When we affirm this, we come to the threshold of rebirth. Something good is at work inside us causing us to make the affirmation. Before that affirmation, goodness cannot flow into our negative attitude or even into our doubt. After it, the goodness reveals itself in our emotions, when we find ourselves moved by the truth, or starting to delight in it—at first for the pleasure of knowing it but later for the pleasure of acting on it. For instance, take the idea that the Lord is the salvation of the human race. The lessons we learn about the Lord from the Word or in church reside among the facts in our earthly memory. Unless we affirm that the Lord is our salvation, none of these lessons can be internalized by our inner self; none of them can be united to anything that could form part of our inner faith. So a desire for that truth also fails to move us. It cannot even touch our general thinking on this subject, which is so important to our salvation. When we affirm the idea, on the other hand, countless new thoughts crowd in and fill up with inflowing goodness. Goodness constantly flows in from the Lord, but where affirmation is lacking, it is not received.

Affirmation, then, is the first middle ground and the first dwelling place for the goodness that flows in from the Lord.

The case is the same with all other concepts said to belong to faith.

Come to her symbolizes an ability to unite with it. This can be seen from the fact that when it refers to matrimony, *coming to someone* (having access to her) symbolizes union. In this context it symbolizes an ability to unite with that affirmation, because union has to start with the affirmation "Yes, it's true." **3914**

And let her give birth on my knees symbolizes acknowledgment from a desire for inner truth, which leads to union, as is established by the following: *Giving birth* means acknowledging in faith and deed, as discussed above in §3905. And *knees,* or thighs, symbolize facets of marriage love, as discussed in §3021, so they symbolize what is involved in the union between faith's truth and love's goodness, since this union is the real force for marriage in the Lord's kingdom. *Giving birth on my knees,* then, means acknowledging the inner truth that Rachel represents. **3915**

Among the ancients, sons and daughters were acknowledged as legitimate if they were born to female slaves with a wife's consent. To be acknowledged, the children were born on [the wife's] knees. This practice stemmed from the ancient church, whose worship consisted of rituals representing and symbolizing heavenly and spiritual qualities. In that church, child-bearing symbolized acknowledgment of truth. Knees symbolized marriage love and therefore a voluntary uniting of goodness and truth. That is why such a practice was favored when a wife was infertile, so that she would not represent the dead who do not rise again to life, as described just above in §3908.

[2] On an inner plane, these words symbolize a second level of affirmation or acknowledgment that comes from desire. Desire has to be present in acknowledgment or affirmation if union is to occur. All oneness comes about through desire, because without desire truth has no life. For example, we may know the truth that we should love our neighbor, that charity consists in this love, and that spiritual life consists in charity, but unless we want it, unless we wish it from our heart, it is mere knowledge. Without desire, this truth does not live. No matter how well we know it, we do not love our neighbor but love ourselves instead. We are living an earthly rather than a spiritual life. Earthly desire has the upper hand over spiritual desire, and as long as it has the upper hand, we are called dead, since the life we are living goes contrary to heavenly life. Heavenly life is real life.

3916   *And I, yes I, will be built up from her* means that [inner truth] would receive life as a result. This can be seen from the symbolism of *being built up* as not dying (which is discussed in §3908) and so as rising again, or living.

3917   *And she gave him Bilhah, her slave, to be his woman* means connecting with the affirmative middle ground. This can be seen from the representation of *Bilhah* and the symbolism of a female *slave* as an affirmative middle ground (discussed just above in §3913) and from that of *giving [her] to be his woman* as connecting.

3918   *And Jacob came to her* means internalizing it. This can be seen from the fact that when it has to do with matrimony, *coming to* (having access to) *someone* symbolizes union, as mentioned just above in §3914.

3919   *And Bilhah conceived and bore Jacob a son* symbolizes acceptance and acknowledgment. This can be seen from the symbolism of *conceiving* as acceptance and of *bearing* as acknowledgment (dealt with in §§3860, 3868, 3905, 3911). In a spiritual sense, conceptions and births mean acceptance of truth at the inspiration of goodness, and a resulting acknowledgment.

3920   Genesis 30:6. *And Rachel said, "God has judged me and has also heard my voice and given me a son." And therefore she called his name Dan.*

Rachel said, "God has judged me and has also heard my voice," on the highest level symbolizes justice and mercy; on an inner level, sacred faith; and on an outer level, a good life. *And given me a son* symbolizes acknowledgment of this truth. *Therefore she called his name Dan* symbolizes its nature.

Rachel said, "God has judged me and has also heard my voice," on the highest level symbolizes justice and mercy; on an inner level, sacred faith; and on an outer level, a good life. This can be seen from the symbolism of *God's judging me* and from that of *hearing my voice.* The symbolism of *God's judging me* as the Lord's justice is self-evident, and so is that of *hearing my voice* as mercy. After all, the Lord always judges with justice and listens with mercy. He judges with justice because he judges with divine truth, and he listens with mercy because he listens with divine goodness. He exercises justice on people who do not accept divine goodness, and mercy on those who do. Nevertheless, when he employs justice, he also employs mercy, because all divine justice contains mercy, just as divine truth contains divine goodness. But this is too arcane to express in a few words, so it will be explained more fully at another point, by the Lord's divine mercy.

[2] The reason "God has judged me and has also heard my voice" on an inner level means sacred faith is that faith—associated with truth—corresponds to divine justice, while sacredness—a form of goodness—corresponds to the Lord's divine mercy. What is more, judging or judgment relates to the truth taught by faith (§2235), and since the text says that *God* judged, it means something good, or holy. This shows that sacred faith is symbolized by both clauses. Since the two clauses have this one symbolism, they are connected by *and also.* The reason they mean a good life, on an outer level, is also due to correspondence, because a good life corresponds to sacred faith.

Plainly no one can see the symbolism of "God has judged and also heard me" without the inner meaning, because on the literal plane the words do not cohere closely enough to present a single image to the mind.

[3] This verse and those that follow, up to the mention of Joseph, speak of God, while those that came just before spoke of Jehovah. The reason for the change is that the theme here is the rebirth of a spiritual person, and earlier it was the rebirth of a heavenly person. The text mentions God when it is treating of goodness that grows out of faith, which marks a spiritual person, but it mentions Jehovah when it is treating of goodness that springs from love, which marks a heavenly person (see §§2586, 2769, 2807, 2822).

3921

Judah, with whom the series ended in the previous chapter, represented a
heavenly person (see §3881), but Joseph, with whom the series ends in the
current chapter, represents a spiritual person (as discussed below at verses
23 and 24 [§3969]). See verses 32, 33, 35 of the previous chapter for the mention of Jehovah in the series ending with Judah. See verses 6, 8, 17, 18, 20,
22, 23 of the current chapter for the mention of God in the series ending
with Joseph. After that, the text returns to Jehovah, because it moves from
the spiritual person to the heavenly.

That is the secret stored and hidden in these words. To see it, one
has to rely on the inner meaning and know what a heavenly person and a
spiritual person are.

3922   *And given me a son* symbolizes acknowledgment of this truth. This
can be seen from the symbolism of a *son* as truth (discussed in §§489, 491,
533, 1147) and from that of *giving a son* as giving this truth, which is the
same as our acknowledging it, because all truth that we acknowledge is
given us by the Lord. Giving someone a son also involves the same thing
as giving birth, because giving birth means acknowledging (see §§3905,
3915, 3919).

3923   *Therefore she called his name Dan* symbolizes its nature. This can be
seen from the symbolism of a name and *calling a name* as the quality (discussed in §§144, 145, 1754, 1896, 2009, 2724, 3421). The quality actually
shows up in the name *Dan,* because he was named from the word for judging. Still, although the name given him comes from the word for judging,
it involves the symbolism of Rachel's whole speech, "God has judged me
and has also heard my voice." That is, it involves a good life, sacred faith,
and in the highest sense, the Lord's justice and mercy.

This is the general religious phenomenon symbolized by Dan and represented by the tribe named for Dan.

This general quality is the first thing we need to affirm or acknowledge before we can be reborn or become a church. If we do not affirm
and acknowledge it, we cannot possibly accept any other aspects of faith
or life, so we cannot affirm let alone acknowledge them. Some people
personally affirm only faith, not what is sacred in faith, namely, charity
(since this is what makes faith holy). If they do not affirm it by doing
something good with their lives—that is, by acts of neighborly love—
they are denied any further taste of faith's essence, because they reject it.

Affirmation and acknowledgment are the first general step in a person who is being reborn but the last in a person who has been reborn. So
in a regenerating person, Dan is in first place, and Joseph, in last (Joseph

meaning a fully spiritual person); but in a person who has completed the process, Joseph is first and Dan is last. A person who is being reborn, you see, starts with affirmation that sacred faith and goodness of life exist, but a regenerate person, who is spiritual, possesses real spiritual goodness and therefore views the affirmation of their existence as coming last. Such a person has already confirmed the importance of holiness in faith and goodness in life.

[2] Other scriptural passages mentioning Dan also show that he stands for affirmation, which must come first when we are being reborn. Take the prophecy of Jacob, who by then was Israel, concerning his sons:

> *Dan* will judge his people as one of Israel's tribes. *Dan* will be a snake on the path, an asp on the track, biting the horse's heels, and its rider will fall off the back. Your salvation I await, Jehovah! (Genesis 49:16, 17, 18)

Dan stands for affirmation of truth, which is said to be a snake on the path and an asp on the track when we base our reasoning about truth on our sense impressions. It is said to bite the horse's heels when we consult the very lowest contents of our intellect (secular facts) and draw conclusions from them. We then stray from the truth, as symbolized by the fall of the horse's rider off the back, which is why it says, "Your salvation I await, Jehovah!" A snake means people who argue about divine secrets on the basis of sense impressions and secular facts (see §§195, 196, 197). The path and track mean truth (627, 2333). The horse's heels mean the lowest elements of the intellect, or facts (259), because a horse means the intellect (2761, 2762), whose lowest part is the heel. [3] In a prophecy of Moses about the twelve tribes:

> To *Dan* he said, "*Dan* is a lion's cub; he will pounce from Bashan." (Deuteronomy 33:22)

On the Word's inner level, a lion symbolizes the church's truth because of its great might. Truth is what fights and wins, so a lion cub stands for the first stage of truth, which is affirmation and acknowledgment. It is described as coming from Bashan because it develops out of earthly goodness. In Jeremiah:

> Scrub your heart of iniquity, Jerusalem, in order that you may be saved; how long will you cause thoughts about your wickedness to linger in your midst? For there is a voice of one pointing wickedness out *from Dan* and announcing it from Mount Ephraim. (Jeremiah 4:14, 15)

"From Dan" means from truth that is to be affirmed. "From Mount Ephraim" means from a desire for it. [4] In the same author:

> Look for peace, but there will not be goodness; toward a time of healing, but here, terror! *From Dan* was heard the snorting of its horses; at the voice of the whinnyings of its mighty ones, all the earth trembled, and they came and devoured the earth and its abundance, the city and those residing in it. Because look: I am sending against you cockatrice snakes for which there is no spell, and they will bite you. (Jeremiah 8:15, 16, [17])

The snorting of horses heard from Dan stands for reasoning about truth from a nonaffirmative standpoint. The earth, which trembled, and whose abundance they devoured, stands for the church and everything in the church. People who reason about truth from a nonaffirmative, or negative, standpoint destroy everything that makes up faith. Cockatrice snakes stand for skewed reasoning, as above. [5] In Ezekiel:

> *Dan* and Javan as it arrived sold polished iron in your markets; cassia and calamus made part of your trade. (Ezekiel 27:19)

This is about Tyre, which symbolizes knowledge of truth and goodness (§1201). Dan stands for the first truths to be affirmed. Markets and trade stand for acquisition of truth and goodness (§2967). Polished iron stands for earthly truth, which is the first kind (§§425, 426). Cassia and calamus also stand for earthly truth, but earthly truth as the source of what is good. [6] In Amos:

> On that day the beautiful young women and the young men will faint with thirst. They were swearing on the guilt of Samaria and said, "Your God lives, *Dan,* and the way to Beer-sheba lives"; and they will fall and not rise anymore. (Amos 8:[13,] 14)

"God lives, Dan, and the way to Beer-sheba lives" means that people deny everything that goes to make up faith and its doctrine. A way means truth (§§627, 2333). Beer-sheba means doctrine (2723, 2858, 2859, 3466). A denial of everything that goes to make up faith is meant because Dan was the outermost border of Canaan, and Beer-sheba was the starting point, the middle or center of the land. Canaan represented and symbolized the Lord's kingdom and therefore the church (1607, 3038, 3481), so it represented and symbolized everything involved in love and faith, since these are attributes of the Lord's kingdom and the church. Consequently all parts of Canaan had a representation, depending on their relative distance, location, and borders (1585, 1866, 3686). [7] Before Jerusalem existed, Beer-sheba was the starting point, or the middle or center of the land, because Abraham lived there, as did Isaac, but Dan was the outermost or furthest border. So the words "from Dan all the way to Beer-sheba" served as a symbol for everything as a whole. An example in 2 Samuel:

> . . . to transfer the kingship from the house of Saul, and to raise the throne of David over Israel and over Judah, *from Dan all the way to Beer-sheba*. (2 Samuel 3:10)

In the same author:

> The whole of Israel without exception shall be gathered *from Dan all the way to Beer-sheba*. (2 Samuel 17:11)

In the same author:

> David said to Joab, "Roam through all the tribes of Israel *from Dan all the way to Beer-sheba*." (2 Samuel 24:2, 15)

In 1 Kings:

> Judah and Israel lived in safety, all of them under their own grapevine and under their own fig tree, *from Dan all the way to Beer-sheba*. (1 Kings 4:25)

On a narrative level, the phrase means everything in the land of Canaan, but in an inner sense it means everything in the Lord's kingdom and everything in the church. [8] Dan is the starting point and also the outermost border, as noted earlier, because an affirmation of truth and goodness comes first of all when faith and neighborly love begin to take hold in us, and it comes last of all when neighborly love and therefore faith are ours.

That is why the last lot fell to Dan when Canaan was given as an inheritance (Joshua 19:40 and following verses). Lots were cast in Jehovah's presence, you see (Joshua 18:6), so the outcome was determined by the representation of each tribe. [9] Since Dan's lot did not fall within the inheritance of the other tribes but outside their boundaries (Judges 18:1), John omitted the tribe in Revelation 7:5–8, where he speaks of the twelve thousand sealed [from each tribe]. People who simply affirm truth or even goodness but proceed no further are not in the Lord's kingdom. They are not among the sealed. Even the worst people can see what is true and good and also affirm it, but the way they live indicates what kind of affirmation it is.

[10] Dan is also mentioned as a border in Genesis 14:14 [§1710], which says that Abraham pursued his enemies all the way there, and Dan has the same symbolism in that passage. Of course, the city called Dan had not yet been constructed by Dan's descendants but came later (Joshua 19:47; Judges 18:29). Yet even at the time, people applied the name to the first border encountered on entry into Canaan, or the last encountered on exit from it. They called its center Hebron and later Beer-sheba, and Abraham and Isaac lived there.

3924　Genesis 30:7, 8. *And Bilhah, Rachel's slave, conceived again and bore a second son to Jacob. And Rachel said, "With the wrestlings of God I have wrestled with my sister and even prevailed." And she called his name Naphtali.*

Bilhah, Rachel's slave, conceived again and bore here as before symbolizes acceptance and acknowledgment. *A second son to Jacob* symbolizes a second general truth. *And Rachel said, "With the wrestlings of God I have wrestled with my sister and even prevailed,"* on the highest level symbolizes autonomous power; on an inner level, trials in which one wins; on an outer level, resistance put up by the earthly self. *And she called his name Naphtali* symbolizes its nature.

3925　*Bilhah, Rachel's slave, conceived again and bore* symbolizes acceptance and acknowledgment. This can be seen from the symbolism of *conceiving* as acceptance and *bearing* as acknowledgment (discussed above in §3919) and from that of a female *slave* as something that serves as a middle ground (also discussed above, in §§3913, 3917). This verse focuses on a second general means serving the union of the inner with the outer self.

3926　*A second son to Jacob* symbolizes a second general truth. This is established by the symbolism of a *son* as truth (discussed in §§489, 491, 533, 1147). In this case a son symbolizes a general truth, as can be seen from remarks above about Jacob's twelve sons and the twelve tribes named after them, showing that general qualities in the church and consequently general aspects of faith and love, or of truth and goodness, are what they symbolize and represent [§§3858, 3862, 3913]. In a negative sense they stand for general aspects of nonfaith and nonlove, or everything involved in falsity and evil, as later sections will show.

3927　*And Rachel said, "With the wrestlings of God I have wrestled with my sister and even prevailed,"* on the highest level symbolizes autonomous power; on an inner level, trials in which one wins; on an outer level, resistance put up by the earthly self. This can be seen from the symbolism of the *wrestlings of God* and of *wrestling* as trials. Trials are times when the inner self wrestles with the outer self, or when the spiritual self wrestles with the earthly. Both want to be in control, and when dominance is at stake, a struggle—the wrestling—takes place. *Prevailing* obviously means winning.

[2] In the highest sense these words symbolize autonomous power because when the Lord lived in the world as a human he endured all his crises by his own power and achieved victory in them by his own power. In this he differed from any of us, who never survive or win in any spiritual test by our own strength. It is the Lord who does so in us. But see what has already been said and shown on this subject: The Lord endured trials far more severe than anyone else (1663, 1668, 1690, 1737, 1787, 1789, 1812, 1813, 1815, 1820, 2776, 2786, 2795, 2813, 2816, 3318); he fought and won by his own power (1616, 1692, 1813, [3381,] 3382); and he alone fights within us (1692).

[3] The discussion just above shows that in an inner sense the wrestlings of God and prevailing mean trials in which we win.

The outer sense is that of resistance by the earthly self because spiritual trial is never anything else but these. To repeat, the issue in spiritual challenges is dominance, or which is going to be in charge—the inner or the outer self, which is to say the spiritual or the earthly self, since they oppose one another (§3913). When we are being tested, the Lord governs our inner, spiritual self through angels, and our outer, earthly self through spirits from hell. The struggle between them is what we sense as a crisis.

If we are capable of being reborn in both faith and life, we win in our struggles, but if we are not, we fail.

Resistance by the earthly self is symbolized by the statement that Rachel had wrestled with her sister, because Leah (the sister) symbolizes the desire of the outer self, but Rachel symbolizes the desire of the inner self (§§3793, 3819).

And she called his name Naphtali symbolizes its nature—the nature of a trial in which we win, and the nature of the resistance the earthly self puts up. This stands out from the symbolism of a name and *calling a name* as the quality (discussed in §§144, 145, 1754, 1896, 2009, 2724, 3421). *Naphtali* actually means that quality, because he was named for the act of wrestling. So Naphtali also represents this second general kind of truth in the church. Tribulation is a means of uniting the inner with the outer self, because the two clash with one another but are reduced to harmony and correspondence through spiritual struggle. Certainly the outer self on its own longs only for what is bodily and worldly. These are the core pleasures of its life. By contrast, when the inner self opens up toward heaven and seeks what belongs to heaven (as it does in people who can be

3928

reborn), heavenly pursuits are what please it. These two kinds of pleasure fight with each other when we are being tried. We are unaware of the fight because we do not know what heavenly and hellish gratification are, let alone that their mutual opposition is so fierce. However, the angels of heaven cannot possibly join us in bodily and worldly pleasure until that pleasure is brought under control. We have to stop viewing it as a goal in itself and view it instead as useful and subservient to heavenly pleasure (as shown above in §3913). Once this happens, angels can join us in both kinds of pleasure. At that point pleasure becomes a benefit to us, and eventually, in the other life, a source of happiness.

[2] Those who think that the delight of the earthly self before rebirth is not from hell and that they are not possessed by devilish spirits are much mistaken. They do not know how matters stand with humankind. Before we have been reborn, demons and hellish spirits possess our earthly self, though for all we can see we are no different than anyone else. We think that we are as reverent as others and that we can reason about religious truth and goodness and even believe we are committed to them. If we do not perceive in ourselves any desire for what is just and fair in our occupation, or for what is true and good in company and in life, we can be sure that we have the same kind of pleasure the inhabitants of hell do. The only love that lurks within our pleasure is love for ourselves and worldly advantages. When this kind of love makes up our happiness, it contains no neighborly love and no faith.

Once pleasure of this type has prevailed, there is only one way to weaken and dispel it. We have to affirm and acknowledge the importance of a sacred faith and a good life (which is the first means, symbolized by Dan, as was shown above [§3923]) and then endure times of trial (the second means, symbolized by Naphtali). The second step follows the first because people who do not affirm and acknowledge the goodness and truth that constitute faith and charity cannot enter on any spiritual struggle. They have nothing inside them that fights back against the evil and falsity urged on them by earthly pleasure.

[3] In other Scripture passages mentioning Naphtali, he symbolizes a person's state following times of trial, as in the prophecy of Jacob, who by then was Israel:

Naphtali is a doe let loose, delivering elegant sayings. (Genesis 49:21)

A doe let loose stands for a desire for earthly truth during the state of freedom that emerges after spiritual crises. This state also characterizes the crises themselves (symbolized by Naphtali), because during them, freedom is the issue we struggle over. Likewise in a prophecy by Moses:

> To *Naphtali* he said, "*Naphtali* is brimming with the good pleasure and filled with the blessing of Jehovah; the west and the south he will possess." (Deuteronomy 33:23)

The representation of Jacob's sons and the tribes, you see, depends on the order in which they are listed (§3862). And in the prophecy of Deborah and Barak:

> Zebulun is a people that devoted its soul to dying, as did *Naphtali* on the heights of the field. (Judges 5:18)

The inner sense of this verse also deals with the battles of spiritual struggle. Naphtali is among those who are not afraid of any evil because they possess truth and goodness—which is what being on the heights of the field means.

Genesis 30:9, 10, 11. *And Leah saw that she had stopped giving birth, and she took Zilpah, her slave, and gave her to Jacob to be his woman. And Zilpah, Leah's slave, bore Jacob a son. And Leah said, "A troop comes," and called his name Gad.*   **3929**

Leah saw that she had stopped giving birth means that no further outer truth was acknowledged. *And she took Zilpah, her slave,* symbolizes an affirmative middle ground creating a bond. *And gave her to Jacob to be his woman* means that it created a bond. *And Zilpah, Leah's slave, bore Jacob a son* symbolizes acknowledgment. *And Leah said, "A troop comes,"* on the highest level symbolizes omnipotence and omniscience; on an inner level, the goodness inspired by faith; on an outer level, good deeds. *And called his name Gad* symbolizes its nature.

Leah saw that she had stopped giving birth means that no further outer truth was acknowledged. This is established by the representation of *Leah* as outer truth (discussed in §§3793, 3819) and from the symbolism of *giving birth* as acknowledging in faith and deed (discussed in §§3905, 3915, 3919). On an inner level, then, the fact that Leah *stopped giving birth* means that no further outer truth was acknowledged.   **3930**

And she took Zilpah, her slave, symbolizes an affirmative middle ground creating a bond. This can be seen from the symbolism of a female *slave* as an affirmative middle ground serving the union of the outer self with the inner (dealt with in §§3913, 3917).   **3931**

3932   *And gave her to Jacob to be his woman* means that it created a bond. This can be seen from the symbolism of *giving [her] to be his woman* as uniting (mentioned above in §§3915, 3917).

3933   *And Zilpah, Leah's slave, bore Jacob a son* symbolizes acknowledgment— an acknowledgment of outer truth. This becomes clear from the symbolism of *bearing* as acknowledgment, from that of a female *slave* as an affirmative middle ground that creates a bond, and from that of a *son* as truth (discussed in §§489, 491, 533, 1147).

3934   *And Leah said, "A troop comes,"* on the highest level symbolizes omnipotence and omniscience; on an inner level, the goodness inspired by faith; on an outer level, good deeds, as can be seen from the symbolism of the *troop* mentioned here. On the highest level this troop means omnipotence and omniscience, because it is referring to a multitude, and when a multitude is mentioned in connection with the Lord's divinity, it means an infinite number, which is the same as omnipotence and omniscience. Omnipotence relates to size, and omniscience, to number. Omnipotence also relates to infinite goodness, or divine love, and therefore to the divine will, while omniscience relates to infinite truth, or the divine understanding.

The inner meaning of a troop as goodness inspired by faith comes from correspondence. The Lord's divine omnipotence has its counterpart in goodness, which has to do with neighborly love, and his omniscience has its counterpart in truth, which has to do with faith.

[2] On an outer level a troop means good deeds because good deeds correspond to a goodness inspired by faith. The goodness associated with faith produces deeds because it cannot exist apart from them, just as thinking what is good and wanting what is good cannot exist apart from doing what is good. The former are the core; the latter is the corresponding surface.

To delve more deeply into the nature of good deeds: unless they correspond to a faith-inspired goodness, they are not actions of neighborly love or of faith because they do not stem from something inside them. They are lifeless motions containing nothing good or true. When they do correspond, though, they are actions of either neighborly love or faith. Actions of neighborly love are those that flow from such love as their soul, while actions of faith are those that flow from faith. One who has been reborn acts on neighborly love, while one who has not yet been reborn but is regenerating acts on faith. The two kinds of action resemble the two kinds of desire: a desire for goodness and a desire for truth. A regenerate person does good from a desire for goodness and so from *willing* what is good, but a regenerating person does good from a desire for truth and so from *knowing* what is good. The difference between the two has already been demonstrated many times. These remarks make the nature of good deeds clear.

[3] In addition, faith-inspired goodness relates to good deeds the way our intentions and the thoughts they produce relate to our face. People recognize that our face is the visible image of our soul—of our intentions and resulting thoughts. If our face does not present an image of our will and thought, there is no will or thought behind it, and perhaps there is hypocrisy or deceit, because we present a face other than what we will and think.

The same extends to all our bodily acts in relation to the inner levels of our thought and will. Our inner dimension comes to life in our outer dimension through what we actually do. If what we do does not conform to what is inside us, it indicates one of two things. Either it does not come from something internal but instead is a motion we repeat by custom and habit, or it is a sham like that of hypocrisy or deceit. This consideration too makes clear the nature of good deeds.

It follows that people who champion faith and especially the idea that goodness results from faith but deny the role of good deeds [in salvation] are themselves lacking in faith and even more lacking in charity, particularly if they reject good deeds [as merit seeking].

[4] This definition of deeds that are based on charity or faith, and the fact that we absolutely do not have charity or faith if we are not doing good, explains why the Word mentions deeds so often, as the following passages show. In Jeremiah:

> Your eyes are open to all the ways of humanity's children, to give them each according to their ways and *according to the fruit of their deeds.* (Jeremiah 32:19)

In the same author:

> Turn, each of you from your evil way, and *make your deeds good.* (Jeremiah 35:15)

In the same author:

> I will repay them according to *their deed* and according to the *work of their hands.* (Jeremiah 25:14)

In Hosea:

> I will bring on them the consequences of their ways, and *their deeds I will return on them.* (Hosea 4:9)

In Micah:

> The land will become a desolate place on account of its residents, *because of the fruit of their deeds.* (Micah 7:13)

In Zechariah:

> This is what Jehovah Sabaoth has said: "Turn from your evil ways and *your evil deeds."* Jehovah Sabaoth thought to do to us according to our ways and *according to our deeds;* so has he done to us. (Zechariah 1:4, 6)

In John:

> Fortunate are the dead who die in the Lord from now on—"Yes," says the spirit, "so that they can rest from their labors; *their deeds follow them."* (Revelation 14:13)

[5] In the same author:

> I saw the dead, small and large, standing before God, and books were opened. And another book was opened, which has to do with life, and *the dead were judged* by the things written in the books, *according to their deeds.* The sea gave up those in it who were dead, and death and hell gave up those in them who were dead. *So they were each judged according to their deeds.* (Revelation 20:12, 13)

In the same author:

> Watch! I am coming quickly; my reward is with me, *to give them each according to their work.* (Revelation 22:12)

In the Gospel of John:

> This is the judgment: that the light came into the world, but people loved darkness more than light, *since their deeds were evil.* All those who *do evil* hate the light, and they do not come to the light, for fear that *their deeds* will be exposed. Those who *act on the truth,* however, come to the light to allow *their deeds to be revealed,* because they were done in God. (John 3:19, 20, 21)

In the same author:

> The world cannot hate you, but it does hate me, because I testify of it *that their deeds are evil.* (John 7:7)

In the same author:

> Jesus to the Jews: "If you were children of Abraham, *you would do the deeds of Abraham. You do the deeds of your father.*" (John 8:39, 41)

In the same author:

> If you know these things, you are fortunate *if you do them.* (John 13:17)

[6] In Matthew:

> Shine your light before people, for them to see *your good deeds. Those who do* and teach [the Commandments] will be called great in the kingdom of the heavens. (Matthew 5:16, 19)

In the same author:

> Not everyone saying "Lord! Lord!" to me will enter the kingdom of the heavens, but *the one doing the will of my Father* who is in the heavens. Many will say to me on that day, "Lord! Lord! In your name haven't we prophesied and in your name cast out demons and in your name exercised many powers?" But then I will proclaim to them, "I do not know you. Leave me, you *evildoers!*" (Matthew 7:21, 22, 23)

In Luke:

> The householder answering says to them, "I do not know you, where you are from." Then you will start to say, "We ate in front of you, and drank; in our streets you taught." But he will say, "I tell you I do not know you, where you are from. Leave me, all you *evildoers!*" (Luke 13:25, 26, 27)

In Matthew:

> Everyone who hears my words *and does them* I will compare to a prudent man. But everyone hearing my words and yet *not doing them* will be compared to a stupid man. (Matthew 7:24, 26)

In the same author:

> *The Son of Humankind will come in the glory of his Father, with his angels, and then he will repay every person according to that person's deeds.* (Matthew 16:27)

[7] This evidence shows that our deeds are what save us and what condemn us. Good deeds save us, and evil deeds condemn us, because our will is present in our deeds. People who will what is good, do what

is good. Those who do not do good may protest that they intend what is good, but they do not intend it if they do not do it. It is as if they are saying, "I want it but I don't want it."

Our real will is present in our deeds, and charity is a matter of the will, while faith is a matter of charity. So it is clear what type of will or what type of charity and faith we have when we do not do those deeds, let alone when we do their opposites: evil deeds.

[8] A further point to note is that the Lord's kingdom in us starts when we start on a life of good deeds, because we are then just embarking on rebirth; but when his kingdom is ours, it *culminates* in good deeds, and we have then been reborn. Our inner self is then present in an outer self that corresponds to it. Deeds belong to the outer self, while charity and therefore faith belong to the inner self, so our deeds then constitute charity.

Since the vital force of our inner self finds expression in the actions of our outer self in this way, the Lord lists nothing but deeds in Matthew 25:32–46, where he talks about the Last Judgment. He says that people who have done good deeds will enter eternal life, and those who have done evil deeds will enter damnation.

These comments also indicate the meaning of what we read about John, that he reclined on Jesus' chest in Jesus' embrace, and that Jesus loved him more than he loved the others (John 13:23, 25; 21:20). John represented good deeds (see the prefaces to Genesis 18 and 22).

By the Lord's divine mercy, deeds of faith (which can also be called the fruit of faith, in keeping with appearances) and deeds of neighborly love will be defined more fully elsewhere.

3935   *And called his name Gad* symbolizes its nature. This is established by the symbolism of a name and *calling a name* as the quality (mentioned above [§3928]). Gad symbolizes the actual quality of faith-inspired goodness and of good deeds. By the quality of a thing is meant absolutely everything present in it—in this case, everything present in faith-inspired goodness and good deeds. Such contents are boundless, because the nature of a thing varies with everyone who possesses it. It even turns into its opposite in people who do not have the goodness that grows out of faith and so do not do good deeds. Gad also symbolizes this latter quality, when his name comes up in a negative sense.

Faith-based goodness, which marks the inner self, and good deeds, which characterize the outer self, correspond to each other, as shown above [§3934]. They are the third general intermediate step that needs to be acknowledged in faith and deed before we can enter the Lord's kingdom, or before we can become an individual church through regeneration.

Genesis 30:12, 13. *And Zilpah, Leah's slave, bore a second son to Jacob. And Leah said, "In my good fortune! Because daughters will call me fortunate." And she called his name Asher.* | **3936**

Zilpah, Leah's slave, bore a second son to Jacob symbolizes acknowledgment of the second [general truth]. *And Leah said, "In my good fortune! Because daughters will call me fortunate,"* on the highest level symbolizes eternity; on an inner level, the happiness of eternal life; on an outer level, pleasurable feelings. *And she called his name Asher* symbolizes its nature.

Zilpah, Leah's slave, bore a second son to Jacob symbolizes acknowledgment of the second general truth, as can be seen from the following: *Giving birth* symbolizes acknowledgment, as discussed above in §§3911, 3915, 3919. A female *slave* symbolizes an affirmative middle ground serving the union of the outer self with the inner, as dealt with in §§3913, 3917. A *son* symbolizes truth—here, general truth, as noted above at §3926. And *Jacob, Leah,* and *Zilpah* have the same representation they had earlier. Clearly, then, the inner meaning of these words is acknowledgment of the second general truth that serves as a means of uniting the outer self with the inner. | **3937**

And Leah said, "In my good fortune! Because daughters will call me fortunate," on the highest level symbolizes eternity; on an inner level, the happiness of eternal life; on an outer level, pleasurable feelings. This can be seen from the symbolism of *good fortune* and of *daughters will call me fortunate.* | **3938**

The symbolism of *good fortune* on the highest level as eternity is evident only from correspondence with human characteristics. Divine or infinite attributes cannot be grasped except from finite ones, which we are able to picture. Unless our ideas are formed out of finite material— chiefly involving space and time—we cannot comprehend anything divine, much less infinite. Without a notion of space and time, we cannot even think (§3404), because our body and therefore the thoughts rising out of our physical senses exist within time. However, angels do not exist within time and space, so they think in terms of state. That is why increments of space and time in the Word symbolize states; see §§1274, 1382, 2625, 2788, 2837, 3254, 3356, 3827.

[2] There are two types of states: one that corresponds to space, and one that corresponds to time. The one that corresponds to space is a state

of existence, and the one that corresponds to time is a state of emergence (§2625).

There are two things in our makeup: existence and emergence. Our
existence is nothing but a container for the eternal quality that radiates
from the Lord, because people, spirits, and angels are simply vessels or
forms for receiving life from the Lord. It is the reception of life that is
ascribed to emergence.

We believe that we exist, and exist on our own, when in reality we do
not exist but emerge on our own, as mentioned before.

Existence, [or beingness,] exists only in the Lord and is called Jehovah.
From beingness, or Jehovah, comes everything that *seems* to exist. The
Lord's beingness, or Jehovah, cannot be shared with anyone in any
way, only with the Lord's humanity, which became divine beingness, or
Jehovah. (On the point that the Lord is Jehovah in regard to both his
natures, see §§1736, 2004, 2005, 2018, 2025, 2156, 2329, 2921, 3023, 3035.)

[3] Emergence is also ascribed to the Lord, but only for the period
when he was in the world, where he clothed himself in divine beingness.
Now that he has become divine beingness, emergence can no longer be
ascribed to him except as a kind of influence radiating from him. What
radiates from him is what looks like emergence in him, but rather than
existing in him, it comes from him and causes people, spirits, and angels
to emerge—in other words, to live.

Emergence in a person, spirit, or angel is life, and life is eternal happiness. The happiness of eternal life is what eternity on the highest level
corresponds to, eternity being a product of the Lord's divine beingness.

Clearly the inner-level symbolism of good fortune is the happiness of
eternal life, and its outer-level symbolism is pleasurable feelings, so these
need no explanation.

[4] It is the pleasure of a desire for truth and goodness (corresponding
to the happiness of eternal life) that is symbolized.

All desires have their pleasure, but the nature of the desire determines
the nature of the pleasure. The desire for evil and falsity has its pleasure,
and until we regenerate and accept from the Lord a desire for truth and
goodness, this seems like the only kind of pleasure. The illusion is so strong
that we do not believe any other kind of delight exists. If it were taken
from us, we think that we would be utterly destroyed.

People who receive from the Lord the delights of a desire for what is
true and good gradually see and sense that the delights of their previous life,

which they considered irreplaceable, are comparatively worthless and even vile. The further we enter into the pleasures of a desire for truth and goodness, the more we start to feel disgust and eventually loathing for the pleasures of a desire for evil and falsity.

[5] In the other world I have sometimes talked to individuals who enjoyed evil and falsity. "You won't come alive," I have been given the opportunity to tell them, "until you have been stripped of your pleasures."

"If we are stripped of them, we won't have any life left," they say, as people like them in the world do.

"That is the point at which life starts," I have been allowed to answer, "and with it, a happy life like the life in heaven, which is more or less indescribable." They cannot understand, though, because people dismiss anything with which they are unfamiliar.

The same thing holds true for all in the world who love themselves and their worldly advantages and therefore lack neighborly love. They know how gratifying the former love is, but not the latter, or neighborly love. So they have no idea at all what charity is. Still less do they realize that we can find pleasure in charity, when in reality that pleasure fills every corner of heaven, rendering it blissful and happy. Believe it or not, it even produces understanding and wisdom and the pleasures associated with these qualities. You see, the Lord flows into the joy of charity with the shining light of truth and the burning flame of goodness and so with understanding and wisdom. Falsity and evil reject, choke, and twist that inflow, bringing about stupidity and madness.

This clarifies the identity and nature of the pleasurable desires that correspond to the happiness of eternal life.

[6] The people of our era believe that if we only have confidence in our beliefs at the moment of death, we can go to heaven, no matter what our attitude throughout the course of our life. I have in fact spoken from time to time with individuals who adopted and lived by this creed. When they come into the other life, at first they have no idea they cannot enter heaven. They gloss over the way they have lived up to that point. They gloss over the fact that this life has endowed them with the pleasures of a desire for evil and falsity—evil and falsity produced by the self-love and materialism that constituted their goals. I have been allowed to tell them that anyone can be let into heaven, because the Lord denies heaven to no one, but that if they were admitted they would be able to tell whether they could live there. Sure enough, some who had never wavered in this belief

were let in, but when they arrived, they started to suffer, because the life there is one of love for the Lord and love for one's neighbor, which make up the whole, happy atmosphere of heavenly life. In such an environment they could not breathe. Then they started to smell the stench of their own desires and consequently to experience the tortures of hell. So they rushed off, saying they wanted be far away, and wondering how something could be heaven that was hell to them. This account makes it clear what each of the two kinds of pleasure is like. It shows that people who delight in a desire for evil and falsity cannot possibly live among those who delight in a desire for goodness and truth. They are opposites, just as heaven and hell are. See §§537, 538, 539, 541, 547, 1397, 1398, 2130, 2401.

[7] To examine the happiness of eternal life further, when people with a desire for goodness and truth are living in the world, they cannot perceive that happiness, but in its place a kind of pleasure. The reason is that in our bodies we focus on worldly cares and are therefore beset by anxieties that prevent the happiness of eternal life inside us from manifesting itself in any other way. When eternal happiness flows from deep within into the worries and troubles that are external to us, it lands among those worries and cares, where it turns into a hint of pleasure. Still, the pleasure contains a sense of good fortune, which contains happiness. That is what being content in God is like. When we rid ourselves of our body and of these worldly concerns, the happiness that lay hidden in the shadows of our inner self emerges and reveals itself.

[8] Since desire has come up so many times, I need to say what is meant by it. A desire is nothing but love, specifically an extension of love. We respond with love either to evil and falsity or to goodness and truth. Because love stands behind and within every single part of us, it is not perceived as love but constantly varies with the matter at hand, conditions, and any change in conditions, in everything we will, think, and do. This extension of love is what is called desire, and it is what governs our life. It generates any pleasure we have, and as a result it generates our life itself, because our life is nothing but the pleasure belonging to our desires, so it is nothing but the desires connected with what we love. Love constitutes our willing, so it constitutes our thinking, and accordingly it constitutes our doing.

3939   *And she called his name Asher* symbolizes its nature. This can be seen from the symbolism of *calling a name* as the quality, as above. The quality itself is what Asher represents.

In the original language, *Asher* means good fortune, but it involves everything symbolized by the speech of his mother, Leah, "In my good fortune! Because daughters will call me fortunate." That is, it involves pleasant feelings corresponding to the happiness of eternal life. This is the fourth general means uniting the outer self with the inner. When we sense such a corresponding pleasure in ourselves, our outer self starts to bond with our inner self. The pleasures of a desire for truth and goodness are what unite the two selves. Without the pleasures of desire, no bond forms, because those desires bring us life. For desires as the means to all union, see §§3024, 3066, 3336, 3849, 3909.

The *daughters* who were to *call* Leah *fortunate* symbolize religions. To see that on the Word's inner level daughters mean religions, see §2362.

The phrase is uttered here by Leah because the children the slaves bore symbolize general truths, which are middle grounds serving to create a union that enables religion to emerge in a person. When we feel that pleasure or those desires, we start to become a church, and that is why the text says this about the fourth and final son born to the slaves.

[2] The Word mentions Asher in various places, but in those passages he symbolizes the nature of the subject under discussion, as the other sons do. That is, each symbolizes the nature of people in the state the passage is describing. Their nature is also reflected in the order in which the sons are named. Because the nature and quality of the first person listed extends and passes into those that follow, a list that starts with Reuben, or faith, implies one thing; one that starts with Judah, or heavenly love, implies another; and one that starts with Joseph, or spiritual love, implies another. Their symbolism varies, then, in the passages where they are named.

Here, where their birth is the topic, they symbolize general attributes of the church and consequently all facets of faith and love that make up the church. They have this symbolism because the preceding material deals with human rebirth, or the states we go through before we become a church. In the highest sense it deals with the Lord and the way he made his humanity divine. So it deals with the ascent of the ladder that Jacob saw in Bethel, leading all the way to Jehovah.

Genesis 30:14, 15, 16. *And Reuben went in the days of the wheat harvest and found dudaim in a field and brought them to Leah his mother; and Rachel said to Leah, "Please give me some of your son's dudaim." And [Leah] said to her, "Is it a little thing that you have taken my husband, and will you* **3940**

*also take my son's dudaim?" And Rachel said, "Then he will lie with you
tonight, for your son's dudaim." And Jacob came from the field in the evening,
and Leah went out to meet him and said, "You shall come to me, because I
have indisputably hired you with my son's dudaim." And he lay with her on
that night.*

Reuben went in the days of the wheat harvest symbolizes faith and the
state of the love and charity connected with faith. *And found dudaim
in a field* symbolizes reflections of marriage love in the truth and goodness belonging to charity and love. *And brought them to Leah his mother*
means applying them to the desire for outer truth. *And Rachel said to
Leah* symbolizes a perception of desire and a longing felt by inner truth.
Please give me some of your son's dudaim means for that which marriage
love has to offer, with which it would mutually and reciprocally unite.
And she said to her, "Is it a little thing that you have taken my husband?"
means that there is a longing for marriage. *And will you also take my son's
dudaim?* means that under the circumstances it would abolish the marital relationship between earthly goodness and outer truth. *And Rachel
said* symbolizes consent. *Then he will lie with you tonight, for your son's
dudaim* means that it would be united. *And Jacob came from the field in
the evening* symbolizes goodness-from-truth in a state that is positive but
dim—a state typical of earthly goodness. *And Leah went out to meet him*
symbolizes a longing on the part of a desire for outward truth. *And said,
"You shall come to me,"* means that the one would unite with the other.
Because I have indisputably hired you with my son's dudaim means so it was
settled, from foresight. *And he lay with her* symbolizes union.

3941   *Reuben went in the days of the [wheat] harvest* symbolizes faith and
the state of the love and charity connected with faith. This can be seen
from the representation of *Reuben* as the faith with which regeneration
starts (dealt with in §§3861, 3866); from the symbolism of *days* as states
(discussed in §§23, 487, 488, 493, 893, 2788, 3462, 3785); and from the
symbolism of *wheat* as love and charity (discussed below). A *wheat harvest*, then, means an advancing state of love and charity.

The account of Jacob's four sons by the slaves had to do with the
means by which the outer self unites with the inner. The current account
concerning the remaining sons has to do with the union of goodness and
truth, so it starts with the dudaim, which symbolize this union or marriagelike tie.

A wheat harvest means an advancing state of love and charity because
a field symbolizes the church and therefore attributes of the church, and

seed sown in a field symbolizes aspects of goodness and truth. The produce of that seed—wheat, barley, and so on—symbolizes aspects of love and charity and also of faith. So sowing and reaping are used as a simile and metaphor for the state of the church in regard to those qualities, as in Genesis 8:22 (§932).

[2] The meaning of *wheat* as facets of love and charity can also be seen from the following passages. In Moses:

> Jehovah makes them ride on the heights of the earth and feeds them with the produce of the fields. He makes them suck honey from a crag, and oil from a boulder of rock; the butter of the herd and the milk of the flock, together with the fat of lambs and of rams—the sons of Bashan—and of goats, *together with the fat of the kidneys of wheat;* and the blood of the grape you drink as unmixed wine. (Deuteronomy 32:13, 14)

In an inner sense these verses speak of the ancient church and its condition at its founding, depicting in a symbolic way every form of love and charity that it possessed, and every teaching of faith. The fat of the kidneys of wheat means heavenly love and charity. Fat or grease symbolizes something heavenly (§353) and wheat symbolizes love, so they are paired in various places in the Word, as in David:

> If only my people were obeying me! Israel would walk in my ways; [Jehovah] *would feed them with the fat of the wheat,* and with honey from the rock I will satisfy them. (Psalms 81:13, 16)

And again in the same author:

> Jehovah, who makes your border peaceful, *satisfies you with the fat of the wheat.* (Psalms 147:14)

[3] The meaning of wheat as love and charity is visible in Jeremiah:

> Many shepherds destroyed my vineyard, trampled my field allotment, reduced my field allotment to a desert wilderness. Over all the hills in the wilderness have come the destroyers, because Jehovah's sword is devouring from the end of the earth to the end of the earth; there is no peace for any flesh. They *sowed wheat,* and thorns they have harvested. (Jeremiah 12:10, 12, 13)

The vineyard and field stand for the church; the desert wilderness, for its spiritual devastation; the devouring sword, for the stripping away of truth; "no peace," for a lack of any goodness that touches the heart; the sowing of wheat, for the good effects of love and charity; and harvesting thorns, for harvesting the evil and falsity that result from self-love and materialism. A vineyard means a spiritual religion (§1069). A field means the goodness in a religion (2971). A wilderness means spiritual devastation (1927, 2708). A devouring sword means the stripping away of truth (2799). Peace means a touching goodness (3780). [4] In Joel:

> The field was devastated, the ground mourned, because the grain was devastated, the new wine dried up, the oil droops. The farmers were put to shame, the vinedressers wailed, *over the wheat* and *over the barley,* because the *harvest of the field* was destroyed. Gird yourselves and lament, priests; wail, you ministers of the altar! (Joel 1:[10,] 11, 13)

Anyone can see that this passage depicts the condition of a devastated religion. The field and the ground, then, mean the church; the grain means its goodness, and the new wine, its truth (§3580); the wheat, heavenly love; and the barley, spiritual love. Since the subject is the condition of the church, the text says, "Gird yourselves and lament, priests, and wail, you ministers of the altar!" [5] In Ezekiel:

> The spirit of Jehovah said to the prophet: "*Take yourself wheat* and barleycorns and bean and lentils and millet and spelt, and you are to put them into a single vessel; and make them into bread for yourself. With human dung you shall make a cake before their eyes. In this way shall the children of Israel eat their bread unclean." (Ezekiel 4:9, 12, [13])

This is about the profanation of what is good and true. The wheat, barleycorns, bean, lentils, millet, and spelt stand for varieties of goodness and therefore of truth. The bread made from them, or the cake containing human dung, stands for the profanation of all of them. [6] In John:

> I looked, when there! A black horse! And one sitting on it, having a balance in his hand. I heard a voice from the midst of the four living creatures, who were saying, "*A choinix of wheat for a denarius,* and three choinixes of barley for a denarius. But do not hurt the oil and the wine." (Revelation 6:[5,] 6)

This passage also deals with the devastation of what is good and true. A choinix of wheat for a denarius stands for the rareness of love. Three choinixes of barley for a denarius stands for the rareness of charity. [7] In Ezekiel:

> Judah and the land of Israel were your merchants, *in minnith wheat and pannag;* and for honey and oil and balsam they gave you trade. (Ezekiel 27:17)

These words describe Tyre, which symbolizes knowledge of goodness and truth. Different kinds of loving or charitable goodness, and the happiness they produce, are the *minnith wheat* and pannag, and honey, oil, and balsam. Judah is a heavenly religion, and the land of Israel is a spiritual religion, which are the source of that goodness and happiness. Trade is the acquisition of them. [8] In Moses:

> *A land of wheat and barley,* and grapevine and fig, and pomegranate; a land of olive, oil, and honey. (Deuteronomy 8:8)

This describes the land of Canaan, which in an inner sense means the Lord's kingdom (§§1413, 1437, 1585, 1607, 3038, 3705). Goodness that comes from love and charity in that kingdom is the wheat and barley; goodness that comes from faith is the grapevine and fig tree. [9] In Matthew:

> . . . whose winnowing fan is in his hand; and he will thoroughly clear out his threshing floor and *gather his wheat into the granary,* but the chaff he will burn with unquenchable fire. (Matthew 3:12)

These are John the Baptist's words describing the Lord. The wheat stands for goodness that comes from love and charity. The chaff stands for people devoid of goodness. In the same author:

> Let both grow together till the harvest, and in the time of the harvest I will say to the harvesters, "First collect the tares and bind them into bundles to burn them, *but gather the wheat into my granary."* (Matthew 13:30)

The tares stand for evil and falsity; the wheat, for what is good. They are metaphors, but all metaphors in the Word come about through spiritual symbolism.

And found dudaim in a field symbolizes reflections of marriage love **3942** in the truth and goodness belonging to charity and love. This can be seen from the symbolism of *dudaim* as attributes of marriage love (treated of below) and from that of a *field* as the church and consequently as religious truth and neighborly kindness, since these constitute the church (as discussed in §§368, 2971, 3196, 3310, 3500, 3508, 3766).

Translators [of the Bible] do not know what dudaim are. Supposedly they were a kind of fruit or flower, and the translators each have an opinion on its identity, but what the exact type was does not matter. What is important is that all fruits and flowers had symbolic value for the ancients in the church. They knew that the whole material world was a theater representing the Lord's kingdom (§3483) and that each and every object in its three kingdoms, including individual fruits and flowers, represented something specific in the spiritual world.

The symbolism of the *dudaim* as a marriagelike bond between goodness and truth can be seen from the series of ideas in the inner meaning here and from the derivation of the word in the original language. *Dudaim* comes from *dudim,* which means "loves" and union through those loves. This derivation of *dudaim* and the fact that it symbolizes something connected with marriage is evident in the following:

> We will rise early to the vineyards; we will see if the grapevine has flowered, has put out a grape, [if] the pomegranates have blossomed. There I will give my loves *[dudim]* to you. *The dudaim have given off a fragrance.* (Song of Songs 7:12, 13)

This shows what dudaim are.

[2] The book from which this quotation comes, the Song of Songs, is not among those referred to as Moses and the Prophets, because it does not have an inner meaning. Nevertheless it was written in the ancient mode, full of symbols garnered from books of the ancient church— most of the symbols being used by that church to stand for heavenly and spiritual love, particularly marriage love. Further evidence that this is the nature of the book is visible in its literal meaning, which unlike that of the books referred to as Moses and the Prophets is erotic in many places. However, since it is packed with images symbolizing the love found in heaven and in marriage, it also apparently contains a mystical undercurrent.

[3] From the symbolism of dudaim you can now see that *Reuben found dudaim in a field* symbolizes something marriagelike in the truth and goodness that belong to love and charity—in other words, something that can be united. In a spiritual sense, anything having to do with marriage simply means the kind of truth that can unite with goodness and the kind of goodness that can unite with truth. This is also the source of

all marriage love (§§2728, 2729, 3132). Real marriage love, then, is possible only for people devoted to goodness and truth and therefore to the heavenly marriage.

And brought them to Leah his mother means applying them to the **3943** desire for outer truth. This can be seen from the meaning of *bringing* here as applying and from the representation of *Leah* as a desire for outer truth (discussed in §§3793, 3819).

And Rachel said to Leah symbolizes a perception of desire and a long- **3944** ing felt by inner truth. This is established by the symbolism of *saying* as perceiving (discussed in §§1898, 1919, 2080, 2619, 2862, 3395, 3509) and by the representation of *Rachel* as a desire for inner truth (discussed in §§3758, 3782, 3793, 3819). What follows next also shows that it means a desire and longing felt by that truth, because Rachel says, "Please give me some of your son's dudaim."

Please give me some of your son's dudaim means (a desire and longing) **3945** for that which marriage love has to offer, with which it would mutually and reciprocally unite. This is established by the symbolism of *dudaim* as attributes of marriage love (discussed above in §3942). The presence of desire and longing is evident from §3944. For marriage love as a mutual, reciprocal union, see §2731.

And she said to her, "Is it a little thing that you have taken my husband?" **3946** means that there is a longing for marriage. This can be seen from the symbolism of *taking a husband* who also belongs to another woman, as Jacob belonged also to Leah. The symbolism involves the love shared between them. That is why the clause *is it a little thing that you have taken my husband?* symbolizes a longing for marriage.

And will you also take my son's dudaim? means that under the circum- **3947** stances it would abolish the marital relationship between earthly goodness and outer truth. This is established by the symbolism of *taking* as abolishing; by that of *dudaim* as something marital (dealt with in §3942); and by that of a *son* as truth (dealt with in §§489, 491, 533, 1147)—in this case outer truth, since the words are Leah's. Leah's symbolism as outer truth was demonstrated earlier.

And Rachel said, "Then he will lie with you tonight, for your son's dudaim," **3948** symbolizes consent to the union. This can be seen without explanation.

And Jacob came from the field in the evening symbolizes goodness-from- **3949** truth in a state that is positive but dim—a state typical of earthly goodness. This is established by the representation of *Jacob* as the goodness that comes of earthly truth (discussed in §§3669, 3677, 3775, 3829); by the symbolism of a *field* as the church in respect to goodness (dealt with in §2971) and therefore as goodness; and by that of the *evening* as something dim (dealt with in §§3056, 3833).

3950   *And Leah went out to meet him and said, "You shall come to me,"* symbolizes a longing on the part of a desire for outward truth that the one unite with the other. This can be seen from the representation of Leah as a desire for outer truth, dealt with above. The longing for union is clear without explanation.

3951   *Because I have indisputably hired you with my son's dudaim* means so it was settled, from foresight. This can be seen from the symbolism of *indisputably hiring* as a settled bargain, as the material leading up to this shows. The settlement was marked by foresight because all union of truth with goodness and of goodness with truth in a person results from foresight—in other words, from the Lord's providence. The text here is talking about the union of goodness with truth and of truth with goodness, and accordingly about the goodness that we adopt as our own. Goodness is not good in us until it unites with truth. Since everything good—that is, every appropriation of goodness through its union with truth—comes from the Lord, it is described as being from foresight. The Lord's providence revolves chiefly around this union, which makes us human and distinguishes us from brute animals. The more we gain from the union, or the more we allow the Lord to carry out the process, the more human we become. So this is the goodness in us. There is no other goodness that is spiritual and lasts forever.

[2] The blessings of our outer self, which form the central pleasures of our life when we are living in the world, are good to the extent that they have this kind of goodness inside them. Take the blessing of riches. The more our wealth has spiritual goodness inside it—that is, the more we aim to benefit our neighbor, our country (the public good), and the church—the more beneficial it is.

On the other hand, people make a serious mistake when they decide that the spiritual goodness described above is impossible in the presence of worldly wealth and therefore convince themselves they have to renounce wealth in order to make room for heaven in their lives. If they renounce their money or deprive themselves of it, they cannot benefit anyone, and they themselves necessarily live a miserable life in the world. They can no longer make the good of their neighbor, their country, or even the church their goal but only themselves and their salvation, with a view to becoming greater than others in heaven. As an added consideration, when they give up worldly advantages, they also expose themselves to a contempt that makes them despicable in the sight of others. So they render themselves useless for serving others or performing their duties. When service is our goal, we also seek as our purpose (or as a means) a state in which we can achieve that goal.

[3] The situation is exactly the same as with nourishment. The point of feeding ourselves is to have a sound mind in a sound body. If we starve our body of sustenance, we also rob ourselves of the state we are aiming for. When people are spiritual, then, they do not look down on food or on the pleasure it provides. Neither do they make it their goal but rather a means that serves the goal.

Conclusions can be drawn from this example about other kinds of goodness.

And he lay with her on that night symbolizes union, as can also be seen without explanation.

3952

For the last few verses, the explanation has been limited mostly to the inner-level symbolism of the words because by its very nature it cannot be understood unless it is presented as a single series. The text describes the union of truth with goodness and of goodness with truth, and this union is a marital one, taking the word in its spiritual sense. In other words, this union creates the heavenly marriage in an individual and in the church.

The passage depicts and reveals hidden details concerning the heavenly marriage, which are as follows: The heavenly marriage (to repeat) is a union of goodness with truth and of truth with goodness. However, it is not a union between goodness and truth on one and the same level but between goodness and truth on a lower and higher level. That is, it is not a union between goodness in the outer self and the truth there but between goodness in the outer self and truth in the inner self. To put it yet another way, it is not a union between goodness in the earthly self and the truth there but between goodness in the earthly self and truth in the spiritual self. This union is what creates the marriage.

[2] The case is the same in the inner or spiritual self. No heavenly marriage takes place between the goodness and truth in that self but between goodness in the spiritual self and truth in the heavenly self, which is on a relatively higher plane. Nor is there a heavenly marriage between goodness and truth in the heavenly self but between goodness in the heavenly self and divine truth radiating from the Lord.

It is also clear, then, that the divine marriage itself in the Lord is not between divine goodness and divine truth in his divine humanity but between goodness in his divine humanity on one hand and his divinity itself on the other, or between the Son and the Father. The goodness of the Lord's divine humanity is what the Word calls the Son of God, and divinity itself is what it calls the Father.

[3] These are the secrets contained in the inner meaning of the account concerning the dudaim.

Anyone can see that the story contains some kind of secret, because if there were not something divine hidden there, it would be too trivial to form part of any scriptural narrative. It would be too trivial to mention that Reuben found dudaim in a field; that Rachel wanted them; that in exchange for them she promised Leah that their husband would lie with Leah; that Leah went to meet Jacob when he came from the field in the evening; that she said she had hired him in exchange for the dudaim. But just what the divine secret hidden there is, no one can see without knowing what Jacob's sons and the tribes named for them symbolize. It is also necessary to know the sequence of meaning in the inner sense. And since it is the theme, it is necessary to know what the heavenly marriage is: the union of goodness in the outer self with a desire for truth in the inner self. [4] But to reveal this secret more clearly, let me offer additional light on it.

The truth in our outer self consists of secular and doctrinal knowledge that we pick up first through our parents, then through our teachers, then through books, and finally by our own studies. The goodness in our outer self consists of the pleasure and delight we sense in that knowledge. The knowledge (truth) and the pleasure (goodness) unite with each other, but they do not create a heavenly marriage in us. Knowledge—including doctrinal knowledge—combines with pleasure even in people who love themselves and their worldly advantages and who consequently immerse themselves in evil and falsity. The pleasure is that of self-love and materialism, which is also capable of having truth unite with it, but people like this stand outside the heavenly marriage.

The union of the pleasure in our outer, earthly self with the secular and doctrinal knowledge of our outer, earthly self creates the heavenly marriage in us under the following circumstances: The delight or pleasure that is the goodness in our outer, earthly self has to spring from spiritual love—love for our neighbor, our country (the public), the church, and the Lord's kingdom—and more particularly from heavenly love, or love for the Lord. These two kinds of love have to flow from our inner, spiritual self into the pleasure of our outer, earthly self, creating that pleasure. This process cannot happen in evil people, only in good people—that is, people who have such a process as their goal. To learn about the inflow of the inner, spiritual self into the outer, earthly self, see earlier discussions at §§3286, 3288, 3314, 3321.

[5] Once these facts are known, it is possible to see the meaning of the individual phrases for which only a word-by-word explanation of the inner meaning is given above. For instance, there is the statement that Reuben (faith's truth, with which regeneration starts) found dudaim; that he brought them to his mother, Leah (a desire for outer truth); that Rachel (a desire for inner truth) longed for them, and they were given to her; and that Leah therefore lay with her husband, Jacob (goodness that comes of truth in the earthly self). Later on there is the fact that two sons, Issachar and Zebulun, were born to Jacob by Leah. They symbolize and represent facets of marriage love and so of the heavenly marriage. And then there is the birth of Joseph, who symbolizes and represents the Lord's spiritual kingdom, which *is* that marriage, and this becomes the theme.

Genesis 30:17, 18. *And God listened to Leah, and she conceived and bore Jacob a fifth son. And Leah said, "God has given me my reward because I gave my slave to my husband." And she called his name Issachar.*   **3953**

God listened to Leah symbolizes divine love. *And she conceived and bore Jacob a fifth son* symbolizes acceptance and acknowledgment. *And Leah said, "God has given me my reward because I gave my slave to my husband,"* on the highest level symbolizes goodness-from-truth, and divine truth-from-goodness; on an inner level, heavenly marriage love; on an outer level, mutual love. *And she called his name Issachar* symbolizes its nature.

God listened to Leah symbolizes divine love. This can be seen from the symbolism of *listening to* someone, when *God* (the Lord) is said to do it, as divine love. To listen to another is to do what that other prays and wishes for, which comes from divine goodness, and divine goodness comes from divine love. So divine love is what listening to someone symbolizes on the highest level.   **3954**

When the Word's literal meaning climbs to heaven, it enters an environment in which everyone thinks from the Lord and about the Lord and his qualities. In the end, angels perceive it in its inner meaning, which *is* the Word for them. The literal meaning serves the inner meaning as a grounds or springboard for thought. The literal meaning cannot reach the angels, because in many places it deals with worldly, earthly, and bodily concerns, which angels cannot think about, since they are involved in spiritual and heavenly concerns and are therefore far above such things. So we have been given a Word that can serve both humans and angels. In this respect the Word differs from all other writing.

3955 *And she conceived and bore Jacob a fifth son* symbolizes acceptance and acknowledgment. This is clear from the symbolism of *conceiving* as acceptance and of *bearing* as acknowledgment, discussed above in §§3860, 3868, 3905, 3911, 3919.

3956 *And Leah said, "God has given me my reward because I gave my slave to my husband,"* on the highest level symbolizes divine goodness-from-truth, and divine truth-from-goodness; on an inner level, heavenly marriage love; on an outer level, mutual love. This can be seen from the symbolism of a *reward*. The Scriptures speak of reward in various places, but few know what it means there.

The churches know that we cannot earn credit by the good we do because the good we do is not ours but the Lord's. They know that the issue of credit directs attention to the person and accordingly joins forces with self-love and with thoughts of superiority, and therefore with contempt for others. Deeds that are done for the sake of reward, then, are not intrinsically good because they do not well up from the genuine spring of charity for one's neighbor. Charity for our fellow humans involves wishing as well to them as to ourselves, and among angels it involves wishing better to others than to oneself. This is also what the *feeling* of charity is like. So the feeling of charity opposes all credit and therefore any good deed that seeks a reward. The reward for people who have neighborly love is the ability and opportunity to do good and the reception of the good they do. This is the pleasure and in fact the bliss of people moved by charity. These considerations show what a reward mentioned in the Word means; it means the joy and blessing that a feeling of charity yields. In other words, it is the joy and blessing of mutual love (§3816), because a feeling of charity is the same thing as mutual love. See previous remarks on this subject in §§1110, 1111, 1774, 1835, 1877, 2027, 2273, 2371, 2380, 2400. This shows that on an outer level the reward symbolizes mutual love.

[2] On the next level above that, the inner level, the symbolism of a reward as heavenly marriage love becomes clear from previous discussions of the heavenly marriage at §§2618, 2739, 2741, 2803, 3024 at the end, 3132, 3952. These discussions show that the heavenly marriage is the union

of goodness and truth and that mutual love results from that union or marriage (§§2737, 2738). In an inner sense, then, a reward means heavenly marriage love.

[3] In the highest sense a reward clearly means divine goodness-from-truth, and truth-from-goodness, because this is the source of the heavenly marriage. A union of the two exists in the Lord and issues from him, and when this union flows into heaven, it creates a marriagelike bond between goodness and truth, through which in turn it creates mutual love.

These remarks and earlier ones demonstrate the inner-level symbolism of Leah's words here, "God has given me my reward because I gave my slave to my husband." The slave symbolizes an affirmative middle ground serving the union of the outer and inner selves (§§3913, 3917, 3931). So until the [truth] symbolized by the slaves' sons has been affirmed and acknowledged, no union of goodness and truth can occur, and neither can mutual love. The affirmations have to come first.

That is what these words mean.

And she called his name Issachar symbolizes its nature. This can be seen **3957** from the symbolism of *calling a name* as the quality, as above in §§3923, 3935. Issachar's name comes from the word for reward, so it involves everything said above about reward and everything symbolized by the rest of Leah's message.

Given that "Issachar" means a reward, that on an outer level a reward symbolizes mutual love, and that on an inner level it symbolizes the union of what is good and true, it is worth noting that very few Christians today know these are what reward means. They do not know because they do not know what mutual love is, let alone that goodness has to unite with truth if one is to experience the heavenly marriage. I have been allowed to discuss the subject with large numbers of people in the next life who came from the Christian world, including the better educated. Astonishing to tell, hardly any of the people I had the opportunity to talk to knew anything about it. If they had only been willing to use their rational mind, they could have learned a great deal about it on their own; but they did not worry about life after death, only about life in the world, so the subject did not interest them.

[2] The following is what they could have learned on their own if (again) they had been willing to use their rational mind.

First: When we slough off our body, we gain the use of much greater intellectual light than we enjoy while living in our body, because when we are in our body, bodily and worldly concerns monopolize our thoughts, generating darkness. When we shed our body, these concerns no longer stand in the way. We become like those who engage in deep thought by withdrawing their mind from their outward senses. From this fact the people I talked to could have seen that conditions are much clearer and brighter for us after death than before. They could have seen that when we die, we pass from comparative shadow into light because we pass from the realm of the world to that of heaven, from the realm of the body to that of the spirit. Surprisingly, although such people can understand these concepts, they think the opposite. They imagine that conditions during life in the body are relatively clear, while conditions during life after shedding the body are dim.

[3] *Second:* If only they use their reason, they can tell that the life we acquired for ourselves in the world follows us; we live the same life after death. After all, they can see that without dying altogether, no one can get rid of a life built up from infancy. Such a life plainly cannot transform at once into another life, let alone into its opposite. For example, if we built ourselves a life of deceit and found the core pleasure of our life in fraud, we cannot divest ourselves of such a life. No, we live that life after death as well. For another example, we might wallow in self-love and therefore in hatred and vengeance against people who do not serve us, or in similar passions. After bodily life we keep those passions because they are what we love. They constitute the central pleasure of our life and consequently our very life itself, so they cannot be taken from us without the obliteration of all the life in us. And so on.

[4] *Third:* We can see for ourselves that we leave much behind when we cross into the other world: concerns over food, clothing, and housing, and over making money and amassing wealth. None of this exists in the other world, and neither do concerns over the positions we seek to be promoted to and spend so much time thinking about during physical life. Other concerns unconnected with any earthly kingdom take their place.

[5] *Fourth:* As a result we can see that if these are the only things we thought about in the world—if we were obsessed with them, if they were all we enjoyed in life—we are not fit to live among those who enjoy thinking about heavenly matters.

[6] *Fifth:* As a further result, if bodily and worldly superficialities are taken from us, we are then such as we were inside; we are then such as we think and will. If our deepest thoughts formerly consisted of plots to deceive people, of aspiration to rank and wealth and to the prestige these

bring, of hatred and vengeance, and so on, we continue to focus on the same things and thus on the affairs of hell. It does not matter whether we hid our thoughts from others for just those purposes, appearing upright on the outside and leading others to believe we did not fixate on such things. Those outward appearances, those pretenses of honor, are in fact stripped from us in the other world, as can also be known, because when we shed our body we shed superficialities, which are no longer of any use. What kind of person will then be visible to the angels is something anyone can figure out independently.

[7] *Sixth:* It can also be known that heaven (or the Lord through heaven) is constantly at work, flowing in with goodness and truth. If we then have no plane to act as soil or grounds for receiving goodness and truth in our inner self (the part of us that lives on after physical death), the inflowing goodness and truth cannot be received. So while we are alive in the world, we ought to make sure we provide ourselves with such an inner plane. The only way we can acquire it is by thinking, wishing, and therefore doing well to our neighbor, and by obtaining the highest pleasure of our lives from such activity. We acquire this plane through charity for our neighbor, or mutual love, and the term for it is conscience. Goodness and truth from the Lord can flow into this plane and be received there, but not where charity and therefore conscience are lacking. Where they are lacking, inflowing goodness and truth pass right through and turn into evil and falsity.

[8] *Seventh:* On our own we can see that love for God and love for our neighbor are what make us human, as distinguished from animals. We can see that they constitute heavenly life, or heaven, and that their opposites constitute hellish life, or hell.

People do not know these things because they do not want to know (since the life they live is just the opposite) and because they do not believe in life after death. Another reason is their adherence to principles of faith but not of neighborly love. They believe, as many people teach, that if life does continue after death, they can be saved by faith no matter how they have lived, as long as they embrace faith in the final hour before they die.

Genesis 30:19, 20. *And Leah conceived again and bore a sixth son to Jacob. And Leah said, "God has gifted me, me, with a good gift; this time my husband will live with me, because I have borne him six sons." And she called his name Zebulun.*

3958

Leah conceived again and bore a sixth son to Jacob symbolizes acceptance and acknowledgment. *And Leah said, "God has gifted me, me, with a good gift; this time my husband will live with me, because I have borne him six sons,"* on the highest level symbolizes the Lord's divinity itself and his divine humanity; on an inner level, the heavenly marriage; on an outer level, marriage love. *And she called his name Zebulun* symbolizes its nature.

3959   *Leah conceived again and bore a sixth son to Jacob* symbolizes acceptance and acknowledgment of truth. This can be seen from the symbolism of *conceiving* as accepting, and of *bearing* as acknowledging (mentioned above in §3955), and from that of a *son* as truth (dealt with in §§489, 491, 533, 1147, 2623, 3373).

3960   *And Leah said, "God has gifted me, me, with a good gift; this time my husband will live with me, because I have borne him six sons,"* on the highest level symbolizes the Lord's divinity itself and his divine humanity; on an inner level, the heavenly marriage; on an outer level, marriage love. This can be seen from the symbolism of *living with* and from the rest of Leah's speech here.

On the highest level *living with* or living together means the Lord's divinity itself and his divine humanity because his divinity itself (the Father) is in his divine humanity (the Son of God) mutually and reciprocally. To quote the Lord's own words in John:

> Jesus said, "Philip, whoever has seen me has seen the Father; believe me, that I am in the Father and the Father is in me." (John 14:9, 10, 11; 10:38)

This oneness is the divine marriage itself (see §§3211, 3952). It is not a living together but is expressed that way on the literal plane. Things that are one are presented in the literal text as two (Father and Son, for instance) or even as three (Father, Son, and Holy Spirit) for many reasons, which will be examined elsewhere, the Lord in his divine mercy willing.

[2] On an inner level *living with* or together means the heavenly marriage because the heavenly marriage comes from the divine marriage, which is the oneness of the Father and the Son, or of the Lord's divinity itself with his divine humanity. The heavenly marriage is a name for the Lord's kingdom and for heaven because heaven comes from the divine marriage, which is the Lord. This is the inner-level symbolism of living

together, and because of it, heaven is also called God's dwelling place, as in Isaiah:

> Look out from the heavens and observe from *your holy* and *beautiful dwelling place*. Where are your zeal and your strength? The stirring of your inward parts and your compassions toward me have kept on. (Isaiah 63:15)

A holy dwelling place stands for the heavenly kingdom, and a beautiful dwelling place for the spiritual kingdom. *Dwelling place* here comes from the same word as *living with* and *Zebulun.*

[3] On an outer level living with or together means marriage love because real marriage love never comes from any other source than the heavenly marriage of goodness and truth, which comes from the divine marriage, or the Lord in respect to his divinity itself and his divine humanity. See previous discussions on this topic: The heavenly marriage stems from the divine goodness in the Lord and the divine truth radiating from him (2508, 2618, 2803, 3132); it is the source of marriage love (2728, 2729); partners who have true marriage love live together at the deepest levels of life (2732), so they live a life of love for what is good and true, since goodness and truth are the inmost depths of life; marriage love is fundamental to all love (2737, 2738, 2739); a marriage of goodness and truth exists in heaven, in the church, in every individual there, and in every part of nature (718, 747, 917, 1432, 2173, 2516, 2712, 2758); it exists in every part of the Word (683, 793, 801, 2516, 2712), so in the highest sense it is the Lord himself; the name Jesus Christ symbolizes the divine marriage (3004).

[4] That is the meaning not only of living together, or of the clause "This time my husband will live with me," but also of the previous clause, "God has gifted me, me, with a good gift." The former symbolizes the truth that comes of goodness, and the latter, the goodness that comes of truth. Each makes a heavenly marriage.

Since this is an ending, the text says, "Because I have borne him six sons." In this case six symbolizes the same idea as twelve: all facets of faith and love. Half and double a number have the same symbolism in the Word when the topic of discussion is the same.

And she called his name Zebulun symbolizes its nature. This can be seen **3961** from the symbolism of *calling a name* as the quality, as above. *Zebulun* was named for living together, so the name involves everything said just above at §3960 about living together and everything symbolized by the rest of Leah's message.

3962   Genesis 30:21. *And afterward she bore a daughter and called her name Dinah.*

Afterward she bore a daughter symbolizes a desire for all of these things, and a religion centered on faith that contains goodness. *And called her name Dinah* symbolizes its nature.

3963   *Afterward she bore a daughter* symbolizes a desire for all of these things, and a religion centered on faith that contains goodness. This can be seen from the symbolism of a *daughter* as a desire and as a religion (discussed in §2362). The object of the desire, and the nature of the religion, becomes clear from any modifiers. For instance, the addition of "Zion" shows that it is a heavenly religion, which is called the daughter of Zion. The addition of "Jerusalem" shows that it is a spiritual religion, which is called the daughter of Jerusalem. And so on. In the current verse, where no modifier is added, the daughter symbolizes a religion centered on faith that contains goodness.

The theme up to this point has been general truths belonging to a faith that contains goodness, and the acceptance and acknowledgment of these truths, which, as has been shown, are symbolized by the ten sons of Jacob discussed above. Since the text mentions the birth of a daughter right after talking about the sons, the sequence shows that she stands for a religion embracing them all.

[2] It is all the same whether you speak of a religion centered on faith that contains goodness or of a spiritual religion, or again of a desire for all the general truths. After all, religion grows out of a desire for truth that contains goodness and goodness that produces truth. It does not grow out of a desire for truth lacking in goodness or out of a desire for goodness that does not produce truth. People who say they have religion and who desire truth but ignore the goodness intrinsic to truth (that is, do not live by the truth) are badly mistaken. They stand outside religion, even if they are members, because they want what is wrong, and truth cannot unite with evil. Their response to truth does not come from the Lord but from themselves, because they concentrate on themselves, seeking to gain a reputation and consequent rank and wealth from their knowledge of the truth. They do not focus on the church or the Lord's kingdom, let alone the Lord.

People who desire a goodness that does not produce truth are also not part of the church, even if they are members, because they are devoted to earthly rather than spiritual goodness. They let themselves be led into all kinds of evil and falsity, provided only that the evil is made to look good, and the falsity, to look true. For more on this, see §§3470, 3471, 3518.

And called her name Dinah symbolizes its nature. This can be seen [3964] from the symbolism of a name and *calling a name* as the quality, as above. The nature of everything in a religion centered on faith that contains goodness is what *Dinah* represents and symbolizes, as discussed just above. The same meaning is also evident from the derivation of her name. In the original language "Dinah" means judgment. The Word speaks of judgment in connection with faith's truth (see §2235), and in an inner sense, judging means sacred faith, while in an outer sense it means a good life (§3921). These are aspects of religion.

Genesis 30:22, 23, 24. *And God remembered Rachel, and God listened* [3965] *to her and opened her womb. And she conceived and bore a son and said, "God is gathering up my disgrace." And she called his name Joseph, saying, "Jehovah add to me another son!"*

God remembered Rachel, and God listened to her symbolizes foresight and providence. *And opened her womb* symbolizes a capacity to accept and acknowledge. *And she conceived and bore a son* symbolizes acceptance and acknowledgment. *And said, "God is gathering up my disgrace"; and she called his name Joseph, saying, "Jehovah add to me another son!"* on the highest level symbolizes the Lord's spiritual divinity; on an inner level, the spiritual kingdom, or the goodness that goes with faith; on an outer level, being saved, as well as being fruitful and multiplying.

God remembered Rachel, and God listened to her symbolizes foresight [3966] and providence, as the following shows. *Remembering,* when God is said to do it (as in this case), symbolizes foresight, because remembering someone means turning one's [mental] gaze on the person, and in the highest sense, sight means foresight (see §3863). And *listening to* someone, when God is said to do it, symbolizes providence, as noted in §3869.

And opened her womb symbolizes a capacity to accept and acknowl-[3967] edge. This can be seen from the meaning of *opening the womb* as granting the capacity to conceive and give birth and so in an inner sense as the capacity to accept and acknowledge—accept and acknowledge the goodness inherent in truth and the truth inherent in goodness. The symbolism of conceiving and bearing as acceptance and acknowledgment has been demonstrated in several places above.

And she conceived and bore a son symbolizes acceptance and acknowl-[3968] edgment, as above in §§3919, 3925, 3955, 3959.

3969   *And said, "God is gathering up my disgrace," and called his name Joseph,*
saying, "Jehovah add to me another son!" on the highest level symbolizes
the Lord's spiritual divinity; on an inner level, the spiritual kingdom, or
the goodness that goes with faith; on an outer level, being saved, as well
as being fruitful and multiplying. This can be seen from the representation of *Joseph* in the Word, discussed below, and from the symbolism of
God is gathering up my disgrace and *Jehovah add to me another son,* since
Joseph was named for *gathering* and *adding.*

God is gathering up my disgrace means that Rachel was no longer infertile and so would not be dead, as she told Jacob she would be in verse 1 of
this chapter (§3908). Rachel represents a desire for inner truth, or truth in
the inner self (3758, 3782, 3793, 3819). Truth and goodness in the inner
self are essentially dead if there is no corresponding goodness and truth
in the outer, earthly self (see §§3493, 3620, 3623). [2] The inner and outer
self have to form such a close bond on both sides that they are not two but
one self together. The bond cannot form until the earthly, outer self has
been prepared—until it accepts and acknowledges the general truths symbolized by the ten sons Jacob had with Leah and the slaves, and until
goodness in the earthly self has united with the truth there. This union
is symbolized by the last son Jacob had with Leah, Zebulun, whose name
came from a word for living together (3960, 3961). Once this union comes
about, the inner and outer self enter into the heavenly marriage described in
§3952, which they cannot do any sooner for a deeply hidden reason: Goodness in the inner self is what then unites with goodness in the outer self and
through this with the truth there. It also unites with goodness and with
truth in the outer self through the inner self's desire for truth. So it forms
both direct and indirect ties. (On its direct and indirect connections, see
§§3314, 3573, 3616.) Then for the first time the inner self unites with the
outer self. Until they unite, the inner self is more or less a nothing and
therefore dead, as noted above. That is why the text says, "God is gathering
up my disgrace." This, then, is the symbolism of the disgrace God is said to
have gathered up—that is, removed, or delivered Rachel from.

[3] The next phrase for which Joseph was named, *Jehovah add to me*
another son, symbolizes a second secret, which is this: Joseph represents
the Lord's spiritual kingdom, so he represents a spiritual person (since
every spiritual individual has the spiritual kingdom inside). There are two
elements composing a spiritual person, namely, charity and faith, or goodness and truth. Charity as the source of faith, or goodness as the source

of truth, is what Joseph represents. Faith that contains charity, or truth that contains goodness, is what the second son symbolizes, and it is represented by Benjamin, who is told about in Genesis 35:16, 17, 18. So Joseph means a spiritual heavenly person, and Benjamin means a heavenly spiritual person. The nature of the difference can be seen from frequent earlier discussions of the goodness that produces truth and the truth that contains goodness. This now is what Rachel's second sentence, "Jehovah add to me another son," symbolizes.

Only people whose faith has led to charity can see these secret meanings, though, because their inner depths are bathed in heaven's light, and heaven's light brings understanding. People who enjoy only the world's light cannot see them, because the world's light does not bring understanding, except to the extent that it contains heavenly light. For the angels living in heaven's light, such ideas are some of the most familiar.

[4] The above evidence now shows that on the highest level the words "God is gathering up my disgrace" and "Jehovah add to me another son" symbolize the Lord's spiritual divinity. On an inner level they symbolize his spiritual kingdom, which is to say the goodness that goes with faith, since this is the spiritual side of his kingdom. On an outer level they symbolize being saved, as well as being fruitful and multiplying, because this is the result (§3971).

A definition of the Lord's spiritual kingdom can be found in what has been said and shown many times before about that kingdom: It consists of people imbued with charity and therefore with faith. It is different from the Lord's heavenly kingdom, which consists of those imbued with love for the Lord and therefore with charity. The latter make up the third and inmost heaven, while the spiritual make up the second, intermediate heaven.

[5] The verse mentions God first ("*God* is gathering up my disgrace") and then Jehovah ("*Jehovah* add to me another son") because it focuses first on the climb from truth to goodness and then on the return from goodness down to truth. Spiritual people are devoted to the goodness associated with faith, or goodness that produces truth, but before they become spiritual they are devoted to the truth associated with faith, or truth that contains goodness. "God" is mentioned when the theme is truth, but "Jehovah," when the theme is goodness (§§2586, 2807, 2822, 3921).

[6] Joseph's representation as the Lord's spiritual kingdom, or a spiritual person, and so as goodness inspired by faith, can also be seen from

other passages in the Word that mention him, as for instance the prophecy of Jacob, who by then was Israel:

> The child of a fertile woman is *Joseph,* the child of a fertile woman beside the spring; daughters [each] stepped over the wall. And the archers will vex him and shoot arrows and hate him. And he will sit in the firmness of his bow. And his arms and hands will be strengthened by the hands of mighty Jacob, from whom comes the Shepherd, the Stone of Israel; by the God of your father, who will assist you; and with Shaddai, who will bless you with the blessings of the sky from above, with the blessings of the underlying abyss, with the blessings of breasts and womb. The blessings of your father will prevail over the blessings of my forebears, even to the desire of the age-old hills; they will be on the head of *Joseph* and on the crown of the head of the Nazirite among his brothers. (Genesis 49:22–26)

On the highest level these prophetic words contain a description of the Lord's spiritual divinity, and on an inner level, of his spiritual kingdom. The explanation of that chapter, with the Lord's divine mercy, will say what the individual words involve [§§6416–6438]. [7] Likewise in a prophecy by Moses:

> To *Joseph* he said, "A blessing from Jehovah on his land in the precious worth of the sky, in the dew, and in the underlying abyss; and in the precious worth of the sun's produce; and in the precious worth of [many] months' yield; and in the first fruits of the eastern mountains, and in the precious worth of the age-old hills; and in the precious worth of the land and its abundance; and the good pleasure of the one dwelling in the bramble. They shall come on the head of *Joseph* and on the crown of the head of the Nazirite among his brothers." (Deuteronomy 33:13–17)

[8] Since Israel represents the Lord's spiritual church (§§3305, 3654), Jacob, who by then was Israel, said to Joseph before dying:

> Your two sons, who were born to you in the land of Egypt, before I came to you, into Egypt, will be mine; *Ephraim* and *Manasseh* will be like Reuben and Simeon. May the angel who redeemed me from every evil bless the boys, so that my name can be given to them, and the name of my fathers, Abraham and Isaac; and may they grow into a throng in the middle of the land. (Genesis 48:5, 16)

There are two elements to a spiritual religion: intellect and will. Ephraim represents the intellect, and Manasseh, the will. This explains why Jacob, or Israel by then, adopted Joseph's two sons and acknowledged them as his own. Ephraim's name comes up frequently in the Word, especially the prophetic parts, and in those places he symbolizes an understanding of what is good and true, which is the mark of a spiritual religion. [9] In Ezekiel:

> Jehovah said, "Son of humankind: Take yourself one stick and *write on it, 'For Judah* and for the children of Israel, his companions.' And take one stick and *write on it, 'For Joseph:* the stick of Ephraim and of the whole house of Israel, his companions.' And join them, one to the other for yourself, into one stick, so that they will both be one in my hand." This is what the Lord Jehovih has said: "I, yes I, am taking *Joseph's stick,* which is in the hand of Ephraim and of the tribes of Israel, his companions, and I will add them onto *Judah's stick* and make them into one stick, and they will be one in my hand. And I will make them into one nation in the land, on the mountains of Israel. And one monarch will serve them all as monarch, and they will no longer be two nations, and they will no longer be split into two kingdoms again." (Ezekiel 37:16, 17, 19, 22)

The theme here is the Lord's heavenly and spiritual kingdom—his heavenly kingdom being Judah (§§3654, 3881, 3921 at the end), his spiritual kingdom, Joseph—and the promise that the kingdoms will not be two but one. So this is what actually happened when the Lord came into the world. [10] On the point that the Lord's Coming saved the spiritual, see §§2661, 2716, 2833, 2834. They are the ones the Lord speaks of in John:

> And other sheep I have that are not from this fold. Those too I need to bring, and they will hear my voice, and there will come to be one flock and one shepherd. (John 10:16)

That is what is symbolized by the two sticks, Judah's and Joseph's, which will be joined into one and will be one in the Lord's hand. Heavenly individuals, you see, make up the third and inmost heaven, while the spiritual make up the second, intermediate heaven. They are united there, because the one (the heavenly) flows into the other (the spiritual). The spiritual kingdom forms a kind of platform for the heavenly kingdom, stabilizing both of them. The heavenly divine quality in the third or inmost heaven is love for the Lord, and the spiritual heavenly quality there is charity. The latter, charity, is the main element in the second, intermediate heaven, where those who are spiritual are to be found. This clarifies the nature of the inflow and the way it creates stability. Wood symbolizes goodness—both the goodness of love for the Lord and the goodness of charity for one's neighbor (§§2784, 2812, 3720)—which explains the command to write "Judah" and "Joseph" on the sticks that were to become one. [11] In Zechariah:

> I will empower the *house of Judah,* and *the house of Joseph* I will save, and I will settle them, because I pitied them, and they will be as though I had not abandoned them, because I am Jehovah their God and I will answer them. (Zechariah 10:6)

This is also about the two kingdoms, heavenly and spiritual (the heavenly kingdom being Judah, and the spiritual, Joseph), and the salvation of the spiritual. [12] In Amos:

> This is what Jehovah has said to the house of Israel: "Seek me and you will live; seek Jehovah and you will live, to keep him from invading the *house of Joseph* like fire and consuming, and no one to quench it. Hate evil and love goodness, and establish judgment in the gate; perhaps Jehovah, God Sabaoth, will have mercy on the *remnant of Joseph.*" (Amos 5:4, 6, 15)

Here too Joseph symbolizes the spiritual. The house of Israel means a spiritual religion (§§3305, 3654). Joseph means the goodness in that religion, which is why the passage says, "Jehovah has said to the house of Israel, 'Seek me and you will live, to keep [Jehovah] from invading the house of Joseph like fire.'" [13] In David:

> Shepherd of Israel, turn an ear, *as you lead Joseph like a flock;* as you sit upon the guardian beings, shine out before *Ephraim* and *Benjamin* and *Manasseh.* Arouse your might and go save us! (Psalms 80:1, 2)

The meaning is the same. Here too Joseph means a spiritual person. Ephraim, Benjamin, and Manasseh are three aspects of that religion. [14] In the same author:

> Lift a song and give [voice to] the tambourine, the pleasant harp with the lute; blow a horn for the month, for the festival on the day of our feast, because it is a statute for Israel, a judgment by the God of Jacob.

He made it a *testimony for Jehoseph* in his going out against the land of
Egypt. I heard a language I did not know. (Psalms 81:2, 3, 4, 5)

Jehoseph means a spiritual religion or a spiritual person, as the individual
words and expressions show. Constantly, throughout the Word, there
are words that express spiritual qualities and words that express heavenly
ones. This passage contains words expressing spiritual qualities—words
such as *song, tambourine, harp with lute, blowing a horn for the month, for
the festival on the feast day.* Once again, then, it is evident that the theme
is a spiritual religion, which is Joseph. [15] In Ezekiel:

> This is what the Lord Jehovih has said, "This is the border to which
> you will inherit the land in accord with the twelve tribes of Israel: *To
> Joseph, ropes.*" (Ezekiel 47:13)

The Lord's spiritual kingdom is the subject here, so the text says, "To
Joseph, ropes."

The Lord's spiritual divinity is what is also called his kingliness, since
his kingliness is divine truth, while his priestliness is divine goodness
(§§2015, 3009, 3670). The Lord's actual monarchy is what Joseph represents in his becoming king over the land of Egypt, a representation to
be discussed where that event is described, with the Lord's divine mercy.

[16] The Lord's spiritual divinity, or his divine truth, represented on
the highest level by Joseph, does not exist in the Lord but comes from him.
The Lord is pure divine goodness, but divine truth issues from divine goodness. The situation resembles that of the sun and its light, since the light is
not in the sun but radiates from it. In other words, it resembles fire, since
there is no glow in fire, only a glow radiating from it. What is more, the
Word uses the sun and fire as a simile and metaphor for divine goodness
itself. The Lord's heavenly kingdom lives off the goodness that comes
from the Lord, but his spiritual kingdom lives off the truth that comes from
him. So in the other world the Lord appears as a sun to the heavenly but
as a moon to the spiritual (see §§1053, 1521, 1529, 1530, 1531, 3636, 3643).
Warmth and light emanate from the sun, the warmth resembling a loving goodness, which is also called heavenly and spiritual warmth, and the
light resembling the resulting truth, which is also called spiritual light
(see §§3636, 3643). The heavenly warmth and spiritual light that radiate
from the Lord as the sun in the other world contain love's goodness and
faith's truth, so they contain wisdom and understanding (§§1521, 1522,

1523, 1542, 1619–1632, 2776, 3138, 3190, 3195, 3222, 3223, 3339, 3485, 3636, 3643, 3862). Anything that comes from the Lord, after all, is alive.

[17] From this discussion it can be seen what spiritual divinity is and what the spiritual and heavenly kingdoms spring from. It can also be seen that the spiritual kingdom is faith-related goodness, or charity, which flows in directly from the Lord and indirectly through the heavenly kingdom.

The spiritual divinity that comes from the Lord is called the Spirit of Truth, in the Word, and consists of sacred truth [John 14:17; 15:26; 16:13]. It does not belong to any spirit but to the Lord and is sent by the Lord through a spirit, as the Lord's own words in John indicate:

> When he—the Spirit of Truth—comes, he will lead you into all truth, since he will not speak from himself but will speak whatever he hears; he will also proclaim the future to you. He will give me glory, because he will take from what is mine and proclaim it to you. (John 16:13, 14)

❋   ❋   ❋   ❋

3970   Genesis 30:25, 26. *And it happened when Rachel had borne Joseph that Jacob said to Laban, "Send me and let me go to my place and to my land. Give me my women and my children, because I served you for them, and let me go, because you know my service with which I have served you."*

It happened when Rachel had borne Joseph symbolizes an acknowledgment of the spiritual dimension represented by Joseph. *That Jacob said to Laban* symbolizes goodness based on earthly truth addressing a side branch of goodness that stemmed from a divine origin, which was the means of union for the inner levels. *Send me and let me go to my place and to my land* symbolizes the longing then felt by the earthly plane (represented by Jacob) for a state of union with divine rationality. *Give me my women* means that a desire for truth belonged to that plane. *And my children* means that the resulting truth did too. *Because I served you for them* means by his own power. *And let me go* symbolizes union with divine rationality. *Because you know my service with which I have served you* symbolizes work and study done under his own power.

3971   *It happened when Rachel had borne Joseph* symbolizes an acknowledgment of the spiritual dimension represented by Joseph, as the following shows: *Bearing* symbolizes acknowledging, as discussed in §§3905, 3911, 3915, 3919. *Rachel* represents a desire for inner truth, as discussed in §§3758, 3782, 3793, 3819. And *Joseph* represents the spiritual kingdom and therefore a spiritual person, as discussed in §3969, so he represents the spiritual dimension. Since the spiritual dimension comes from the Lord, it is what creates a spiritual person and the spiritual kingdom.

The preceding verses, under the figures of Jacob's sons by the slaves and Leah, spoke of the acceptance and acknowledgment of general truths and finally about their being united with, or internalized by, the inner self. So the chapter has been dealing with a person's rebirth to the point of becoming spiritual. Joseph means this spiritual person. The next verses talk about the fruitfulness and multiplying of truth and goodness, symbolized by the flock Jacob acquired for himself through Laban's flock. After the inner self unites with the outer, or the spiritual self with the earthly, goodness becomes fruitful and truth multiplies, because that union is the heavenly marriage in a person, and from it are born goodness and truth. This is another reason why Joseph on an outer level symbolizes fruitfulness and multiplying (§§3965, 3969). Goodness is said to be fruitful, and truth, to multiply (§§43, 55, 913, 983, 2846, 2847).

That Jacob said to Laban symbolizes goodness based on earthly truth **3972** addressing a side branch of goodness that stemmed from a divine origin, which was the means of union for the inner levels. This can be seen from the representation of *Jacob* as goodness based on earthly truth (discussed in §§3659, 3669, 3677, 3775, 3829) and from that of *Laban* as a side branch of goodness from a divine origin (discussed in §§3612, 3665, 3778). Union at deeper levels is accomplished through that goodness, as explained already several times; see §§3665, 3690, and other sections.

This goodness is also what is symbolized by Laban's flock, through which Jacob built up his own flock—a subject to be discussed below.

Send me and let me go to my place and to my land symbolizes the longing **3973** then felt by the earthly plane (represented by Jacob) for a state of union with divine rationality, as the following indicates: Jacob, the speaker here, represents goodness based on earthly truth, as noted just above in §3972. A *place* symbolizes a state, as discussed in §§2625, 2837, 3356, 3387. And *land* in this case symbolizes divinity on the rational plane, because *my land* means his father Isaac and his mother Rebekah, since it was to them that he wanted to be sent and to go. Isaac means goodness in the divine rationality (see §§2083, 2630, 3012, 3194, 3210), and Rebekah means divine truth united with divine goodness on the rational plane (§§3012, 3013, 3077).

The longing for union is clear from the emotion in the words.

Give me my women means that a desire for truth belonged to that plane; **3974** *and my children* means that the resulting truth did too. This can be seen from the following: *Women* symbolize a desire for truth—Jacob's woman Leah symbolizing a desire for outer truth, and Rachel, a desire for inner truth—as noted many times before. And *children* symbolize the truth that results from it. Offspring symbolize truth (§§489, 491, 533, 1147, 2623, 3373), and those explicitly described as born to women symbolize truth resulting from a desire for it.

The ancients decreed that the women given to male slaves, and the children born to them, would be the property of the master they served. This can be seen in Moses:

> If you buy a Hebrew slave, for six years he shall serve and in the seventh go out free, for nothing. If his master has given him a woman, and she has borne him sons or daughters, the woman and her children shall be his master's, and he shall go out with [just] his own body. (Exodus 21:2, 4)

Since this rule existed in the ancient church, it was known to Laban, so he claimed Jacob's women and children for himself, as is clear in the next chapter:

> Laban said to Jacob, "The daughters are my daughters and the sons are my sons and the flock is my flock, and everything that you are seeing—it is mine." (Genesis 31:43)

Because Jacob knows this, he says to Laban, "Give me my women and my children."

The rule Moses wrote about in the quoted passage represented the right of the inner, rational self to the goodness and truth the outer, earthly self had acquired for itself. A slave represented earthly truth such as it is at first, before genuine truth is injected into it. This first truth is not true, though it seems so, but it still serves as a means of introducing real truth and goodness, as already shown [§§3665, 3690]. So when goodness and truth have been instilled through that truth as a slave, it is sent away, and the genuine qualities gained in the process are kept. To represent this, the law above concerning slaves was laid down.

[2] Jacob, however, was not a purchased slave but belonged to a more illustrious family than Laban. In fact, by the service he performed Jacob bought Laban's daughters and consequently the children born to them, since he took them in lieu of pay. Laban's opinion on the subject, then, did not match the facts. Moreover, a male Hebrew slave symbolized truth that serves to introduce actual goodness and truth, and his woman symbolized

a desire for earthly goodness. This was not the case with Jacob. He represents goodness based on earthly truth, and his women represent a desire for truth. Neither does Laban represent the rationality that the master in the cited law concerning a Hebrew slave represents. On the contrary, he represents a side branch of goodness (§§3612, 3665, 3778), which by its very nature lacks genuine goodness but instead *appears* to be good and serves to introduce truth (§§3665, 3690). This truth therefore belonged to Jacob.

[3] Hardly anyone will be able to understand the points just brought forward, admittedly, since most people do not know what truth and goodness on the earthly plane are, or that they differ from truth and goodness on the rational plane. Still less do they know that goodness and truth that are not genuine but appear genuine serve to introduce genuine truth and goodness, especially at the beginning of rebirth. Yet that is what is contained in the inner meaning of the current words and those that follow, telling about Laban's flock and Jacob's acquisition of his own flock from it, so they must not pass unmentioned. Maybe some people will understand it. Anyone who longs to know such things—who has a desire for spiritual goodness and truth—receives enlightenment in them.

Because I served you for them means by his own power. This can be seen from the symbolism of *serving* as work and study (discussed in §§3824, 3846). When these are attributed to the Lord, they mean his power, because the Lord used his own power to acquire divine goodness and divine truth for himself and to make his humanity divine. See §§1616, 1749, 1755, 1921, 2025, 2026, 2083, 2500, 2523, 2632, 2816, [3381,] 3382. **3975**

And let me go symbolizes union with divine rationality. This can be seen from the symbolism of *going*—going to his place and to his land, as above in §3973, which symbolizes a longing for union with divine rationality. **3976**

Because you know my service with which I have served you symbolizes work and study done under his own power. This symbolism can be seen without further explanation from the remarks and citations just above in §3975. **3977**

Any further meaning here can be found in the discussion above at §3974 and in what follows.

Genesis 30:27, 28, 29, 30. *And Laban said to him, "Please, if I have found favor in your eyes, . . . I have learned by experience that Jehovah has blessed me because of you." And he said, "Name the wage you claim of me and I will give it." And [Jacob] said to him, "You know how well I have served you and how your property has fared with me. Because what you had previous to me was* **3978** *little, and it has burst into abundance, and Jehovah has blessed you at [every step of] my foot; and now, when shall I also do for my household?"*

Laban said to him symbolizes a perception yielded by the goodness Laban symbolizes. *Please, if I have found favor in your eyes* symbolizes a positive leaning. *I have learned by experience that Jehovah has blessed me because of you* means from the Divine, on account of the earthly goodness it was to minister to. *And he said, "Name the wage you claim of me and I will give it,"* means it would willingly give what was wanted. *And he said to him, "You know how well I have served you,"* means that [the side branch of goodness] knew the disposition and power of [earthly goodness]. *And what your property has been like with me* means that this was also from the Divine. *Because what you had previous to me was little* means that its goodness is barren before it is internalized, or united. *And it has burst into abundance* symbolizes its fertility afterward. *And Jehovah has blessed you at [every step of] my foot* means that it comes from what is divine on the earthly plane. *And now, when shall I also do for my household?* means that as a consequence its goodness will now become fruitful.

3979　　*Laban said to him* symbolizes a perception yielded by the goodness Laban symbolizes. This is established by the symbolism of *saying* as perception (dealt with in §§1898, 1919, 2080, 2619, 2862, 3395, 3509) and from the representation of *Laban* as a side branch of goodness originating in the Divine (dealt with in §§3612, 3665, 3778).

The reason "Laban said to him" symbolizes a perception yielded by that kind of goodness is that people in the Word have a purely symbolic meaning. On the highest level they symbolize divine traits in the Lord; on an inner level, the human traits under discussion. So two individuals symbolize two characteristics in a person.

3980　　*Please, if I have found favor in your eyes* symbolizes a positive leaning. This can be seen from the symbolism of *finding favor in someone's eyes* as a positive leaning. When the goodness that Laban symbolizes wants to be present, it is said to have a positive leaning. Those who reflect or are capable of reflecting on the feelings they have for what is good and for what is true, and on the pleasure and satisfaction they receive from each, will notice they lean more strongly toward one than the other. But unless we reflect on it, this inclination and others like it are invisible.

3981　　*I have learned by experience that Jehovah has blessed me because of you* means that it was from the Divine, on account of the earthly goodness it was to minister to. This can be seen from the symbolism of *learning by experience that Jehovah has blessed* someone as knowing for sure that it was from the Divine. *Because of you* means that it was on account of the earthly goodness it was to minister to. Jacob means the goodness that comes of earthly truth (§§3659, 3669, 3677, 3775, 3829), and Laban means a side branch of goodness that serves (as shown above in several places, and see below at §§3982, 3986).

And he said, "Name the wage you claim of me and I will give it," means it would willingly give what was wanted, as can be seen without explanation.   **3982**

What has been said so far cannot be explained in a clear and intelligible way, for two reasons. First, the mind cannot turn instantly from the story of Laban and Jacob to the spiritual themes dealt with in the inner meaning. The narrative always clings and fills the reader's thoughts, but it needs to disappear if nonnarrative elements are to be understood in sequence. Second, it is necessary to have a clear notion of the goodness represented by both Laban and Jacob and to see that the goodness that Laban represents is a mere tool for introducing genuine truth and goodness. Once it has performed its function, it is left behind.

The nature of that goodness has been described before. It resembles an immature structure in newly formed fruits that introduces the juice and then shrivels when it has done its job. Meanwhile the fruit is brought to ripeness by other fibers and finally by fibers containing the real juice. [2] People recognize that during our childhood and youth the sole purpose of many things we learn is to serve as a means to more useful knowledge, which in turn is simply a means to still more useful knowledge and finally to knowledge about eternal life. When we acquire this knowledge, the earlier kinds are almost completely erased.

Likewise, when we are being born anew from the Lord we are led by many kinds of desires for goodness and truth that are not desires for real goodness and truth. They are simply useful in our gaining a handle on the real ones and then steeping ourselves in them. Once we have absorbed them, we forget the earlier forms and leave them behind, because they had merely served as a means.

The situation is the same with goodness that branches off to the side, symbolized by Laban, as compared to the goodness that comes of truth, symbolized by Jacob and by the flock of each man, as discussed below.

[3] These are the secrets contained in the current verses and those that follow. They are presented in narrative form to allow even the young and the uneducated to enjoy reading the Word, so that while they are feeling reverent pleasure in the story, the angels with them are experiencing the

holiness of the inner meaning. The inner meaning is suited to angelic intelligence; the outer meaning, to human intelligence. The result is a fellowship between people and angels, though we are completely unaware it exists and experience it only as a certain sense of delight tinged with awe.

3983   *And he said to him, "You know how well I have served you,"* means that [the side branch of goodness] knew the disposition and power of [earthly goodness]. This can be seen from the sequence of ideas in the inner meaning. Knowing what someone is like obviously means knowing the person's disposition. Knowing what that person is like as a servant, or *knowing how well I have served,* means knowing the person's power. This can be seen from the current symbolism of *serving* as autonomous power (discussed in §§3975, 3977). After all, Jacob represents goodness-from-truth on the Lord's divine earthly plane, which has power.

From this it follows that *what your property has been like with me* means that this was also from the Divine.

3984   *Because what you had previous to me was little* means that its goodness is barren unless it is internalized, or united, as also becomes clear from the sequence in the inner meaning. The subject is the nature of the goodness represented by Laban before it unites with the goodness-from-truth that is Jacob. It is not very useful, which is to say that it is barren.

What comes next will expand on this topic.

3985   *And it has burst into abundance* symbolizes its fertility afterward. This can be seen from the symbolism of *bursting into abundance* as fertility—fertility that follows union.

3986   *And Jehovah has blessed you at [every step of] my foot* means that it comes from what is divine on the earthly plane, as the following shows: *Jehovah's blessing* someone means receiving the gift of goodness (as noted in §3406) and being united (§§3504, 3514, 3530, 3565, 3584). So Jehovah's blessing someone means receiving divine goodness as a gift, through union—in this case, union with the earthly goodness represented by Jacob. The *foot* symbolizes what is earthly. (For this meaning of the foot, see §§2162, 3147, 3761. The same thing will become clear from the way the universal human corresponds to everything in the human body, as discussed at the chapter ends.) Plainly, then, *Jehovah has blessed you at [every step of] my foot* means coming from what is divine on the earthly level.

[2] Few if any know the secret hidden here and in the preceding verses, so it needs to be revealed.

Goodness differs radically among people both within the church and outside the church. It differs so profoundly that no one person's goodness is exactly like another's. The variations are due to the truth with which goodness forms a bond, since all goodness takes its quality from truth (while truth takes its vital essence from goodness). The variations are also due to the desires that make up each individual type of love—desires that are rooted in and adopted by us through the life we live. Even inside the church, people know very little real truth, and people outside the church know even less, so it is rare to have a feeling of desire for that truth. [3] Nonetheless, people who live good lives, or lives of love for God and charity for their neighbor, are saved. They can be saved because the Lord's divinity resides within good done out of love for God and charity for one's neighbor. Where divinity is present, everything is arranged in a pattern that enables it to unite with the real goodness and real truth that exist in the heavens.

The truth of this statement can be seen from the countless communities that make up heaven. Each and every one has a different kind of goodness and truth, but taken together they form a single heaven. They resemble the limbs and organs of the human body, which all differ from each other but still constitute a single person. A single whole consisting [of] many parts is never composed of identical units but of varied units joining in harmony. All oneness is the result of varied elements joining in harmony. It is the same with different versions of goodness and truth in the spiritual world; although they differ so markedly that they are never the same in one individual as in another, the Divine still makes them into one through love and charity. Love and charity are spiritual union; their variety is heavenly concord, which creates such harmony that in the Divine, or the Lord, they are one.

[4] In addition, no matter how widely truth or the desire for truth differs, good done out of love for God and good done out of love for one's neighbor are still open to genuine truth and goodness. They are not hard or resistant, so to speak, but soft and yielding. They allow themselves to be led by the Lord, so they permit themselves to be bent to what is good and, through that goodness, to be turned toward him. Not so for people immersed in self-love and materialism. They do not let themselves be led and turned by the Lord or to the Lord but staunchly resist. They want to lead themselves—especially the ones who have hardened themselves in false principles. As long as they stay like this, they refuse to let the Divine in.

[5] Such considerations now show the inner-level symbolism of these words spoken by Jacob to Laban. Laban symbolizes goodness that is not

genuine because it does not have genuine truth planted in it but is still capable of having genuine truth unite with it and of containing the Divine. This is the kind of goodness that typically exists in young children before they acquire real truth. It is also the kind of goodness that exists among the uneducated in the church, who know little religious truth but live lives of neighborly love. Again, it is the kind of goodness that exists among upright people outside the church who worship their own gods with reverence. Such goodness can introduce real truth and goodness, as evidenced by remarks at §3690 on the young and the untaught within the church, and at §§2598, 2599, 2600, 2601, 2602, 2603 on upright nations outside the church.

3987   *And now, when shall I also do for my household?* means that as a consequence its goodness will now become fruitful. This can be seen from the symbolism of a *household* as something good (discussed in §§2233, 3128, 3652). *My household* here symbolizes the goodness that Jacob also symbolizes. *Doing for* this household symbolizes the consequent fruitfulness of what is good, as is clear from the fact that the theme is now how goodness becomes fruitful and truth multiplies. That fruitfulness is symbolized by Joseph, the most recent child (§§3965, 3969, 3971), and is depicted in the flock Jacob amassed for himself through Laban's flock, as described below.

Goodness does not become fruitful and truth does not multiply until the outer self unites with the inner. After all, the role of the inner self is to wish what is good for another and so to think about what is good, while the role of the outer self is to do what is good and therefore to teach it. If we do not unite doing what is good with wishing what is good, and teaching what is good with thinking about it, there is no goodness in us. Evil people can wish evil and do good, and they can think about what is evil and teach what is good, as anyone can see. Hypocrites and profaners excel others in that study and art, to the point where they can impersonate angels of light, despite being devils inside. Plainly goodness cannot become fruitful in anyone, then, unless doing what is good unites with wishing what is good, and teaching what is good with thinking about it. That is, it cannot become fruitful until the outer self unites with the inner self.

3988   Genesis 30:31, 32, 33. *And he said, "What shall I give you?" and Jacob said, "You won't [have to] give me anything if you do this word for me: let me return [and] pasture [and] guard your flock. I will pass through your whole flock today removing from it every speckled and spotted animal, and every black animal among the lambs, and the spotted and speckled one among the she-goats, and it will be my wage. And my righteousness will answer for me on a future day, when you come concerning my wage [that is] before you; all* *that which is not speckled and spotted among the she-goats and black among the lambs—it is stolen with me.*"

He said, "What shall I give you?" symbolizes knowledge. *And Jacob said* means the answer. *You won't [have to] give me anything if you do this word for me* symbolizes what goodness-from-truth for its part will bring about. *Let me return [and] pasture [and] guard your flock* means that the goodness that Laban symbolizes is to be put to use. *I will pass through your whole flock today* means that [the Lord] perceives what all goodness is like. *Removing from it every speckled and spotted animal* means that any goodness and related truth that is tinged with evil (the speckled) or falsity (the spotted) will be separated out. *And every black animal among the lambs* symbolizes an innocent sense of autonomy—a mark of the goodness symbolized by Laban. *And the spotted and speckled one among the she-goats* means that any truth-based goodness tinged with falsity or evil will then be his own. *And it will be my wage* means that it will come from himself. *And my righteousness will answer for me* symbolizes the divine holiness that is the Lord's. *On a future day* means forever. *When you come concerning my wage [that is] before you* symbolizes what is his own. *All that which is not speckled and spotted among the she-goats* symbolizes any of the goodness meant by Laban that is present in truth-based goodness and is not tinged with evil and falsity. *And black among the lambs* symbolizes the first stage of innocence. *It is stolen by me* means that it would not be his.

He said, "What shall I give you?" symbolizes knowledge. This symbolism is evident because it is a question seeking information on the type and amount of wage Jacob wanted.   **3989**

And Jacob said means the answer, which needs no explanation.

You won't [have to] give me anything if you do this word for me symbolizes what goodness-from-truth for its part will bring about. This can be seen from the symbolism of *not giving anything* as not being brought about by the goodness that Laban represents but by the goodness that Jacob represents, which is goodness that grows out of truth (§§3669, 3677, 3829). What was to be brought about will be described below.   **3990**

Let me return [and] pasture [and] guard your flock means that the goodness that Laban represents is to be put to use—in introducing real goodness and truth, as shown above [§§3974, 3982, 3986]. The symbolism can be seen from that of the *flock*—Laban's flock—as the goodness that Laban represents. *Returning, pasturing, and guarding his flock* means putting it to use, and what follows will make this clear, because Jacob used Laban's flock to build up his own. It served him as a means, so it served a use.   **3991**

3992   *I will pass through your whole flock today* means that [the Lord] perceives what all goodness is like. This becomes clear from the symbolism
of a *flock* as something good (discussed in §§343, 3518) and from that of
passing through the whole of it as perceiving and knowing what it is like.

3993   *Removing from it every speckled and spotted animal* means that any
goodness and related truth that is tinged with evil (the speckled) or falsity
(the spotted) will be separated out. This can be seen from the symbolism
of *removing* as separating out, and from that of an *animal,* or the smaller
livestock—the she-goats and lambs, in this case—as goodness and truth
(discussed in §§1824, 3519).

Obviously these details and others to follow in the current chapter
hold secrets, because few of them would be worthy of mention in the
Word of God if they did not contain something more arcane than appears
in the letter. It would not be worth mentioning that Jacob requested as
his wage the speckled and spotted animals among the she-goats and the
black among the lambs; that he then took rods of hazel and sycamore
peeled down to the white and put them in the channels in front of Laban's
flocks when they went into heat; that what he did with the lambs was to
turn the faces of the flock toward the mottled and the black in Laban's
flock; and therefore that he enriched himself with deplorable rather than
laudable skill. Nothing divine is evident in these scenes, and yet the Word
is divine in each and every respect down to the smallest jot. Knowing
this story makes not the smallest scrap of difference to our salvation, and
yet the Word, being divine, contains nothing that does not contribute
to salvation and eternal life. [2] These particulars and others like them
elsewhere can lead anyone to conclude that the text contains a hidden
meaning, and that although the details of the literal meaning seem trivial,
they carry something more divine inside.

What they carry inside is absolutely impossible to see without the
inner meaning—that is, without knowing how they are viewed by angels,
who focus on the spiritual meaning when we read the earthly narrative.
How far apart the two meanings appear to stand (although they are tightly
bound together) becomes strikingly clear from these and the other story
elements.

Of course the actual secret contained here and in the remaining part of
the chapter can be seen to some extent from previous remarks about Laban
and Jacob—that Laban means the kind of goodness that can introduce
real goodness and truth, and that Jacob means goodness based on truth.
But few know what earthly goodness corresponding to spiritual goodness

is, and fewer know what spiritual goodness is, or that there ought to be a correspondence. Still fewer know that a certain kind of apparent goodness is a means of introducing real goodness and truth. As a result, it is not easy to explain the secrets involved in these subjects intelligibly, because the intellect is in the dark concerning them. It is like a person talking in a foreign language; no matter how clearly the speaker explains the matter, the listener fails to understand. Even so, the explanation still needs to be made, because it is important to reveal what the Word hides in its inner meaning.

[3] In its highest sense, the text is dealing with the way the Lord made his earthly level divine. In a representative sense it is telling how the Lord regenerates the earthly dimension in us and reduces it to correspondence with our inner self—that is, with the part of us that will live on after physical death. This part is then called our spirit, and on release from the body it takes with it everything belonging to the outer self except the flesh and bones. If correspondence between our inner and outer selves does not develop in the temporal world, or during the life of our body, it does not occur later. The union of the two through rebirth from the Lord is the subject of the inner meaning here.

[4] First the discussion dealt with the general truths we have to accept and acknowledge before we can be reborn, Jacob's ten sons by Leah and the slaves symbolizing these truths. Then it dealt with the union of our outer with our inner self, or of our earthly with our spiritual self, after we have accepted and acknowledged these truths, Joseph symbolizing that union. Now, continuing in order, it concerns the increased fruitfulness of goodness and the multiplying of truth, which first takes place when the union has been achieved. The fuller the union, the more they become fruitful and multiply. These are the ideas symbolized by Jacob's acquisition of a flock through Laban's. The flock symbolizes what is good and true, as it does in many other scriptural passages. Laban's flock symbolizes the goodness that Laban represents, whose nature has been described above. Jacob's flock symbolizes the genuine goodness and truth acquired through that goodness. What is being depicted here is the *way* we acquire genuine goodness and truth.

[5] No one can understand this, however, without knowing the inner-level symbolism of the speckled, the spotted, the black, and the white, so I need to start by discussing them. What is speckled and spotted consists of black and white. Broadly speaking, black symbolizes evil; more narrowly it symbolizes human selfhood, since human selfhood is unmitigated evil; darkness symbolizes falsity, and specifically false premises. White, on

an inner level, symbolizes truth. Strictly speaking, it symbolizes the Lord's righteousness and merit and accordingly his righteousness and merit in us. This white is described as dazzling, because it gleams with light from the Lord. In an opposite sense white symbolizes our own self-righteousness, and our own personal merit. Truth devoid of goodness carries a sense of personal merit with it, because when the good we do is not inspired by truth-based goodness, we always want a reward for it; we are doing it for our own sake. When goodness inspires us to act on truth, though, it is lit with light from the Lord. These considerations clarify the meaning of the *spotted* as truth mixed with falsity, and of the *speckled* as goodness mixed with evil.

[6] Real colors are seen in the other world, and they are so beautiful and radiant that they cannot be described (§§1053, 1624). They result from changing amounts of light and shadow falling on white and black. Although the eye sees the light in that world as light, it is not like the light in this world. The light in heaven contains understanding and wisdom, because divine understanding and wisdom from the Lord presents itself as light there and illuminates all of heaven (§§2776, 3138, 3167, 3190, 3195, 3222, 3223, 3225, 3339, 3340, 3341, 3485, 3636, 3643, 3862). Shadow in that world, too, looks like shadow but is unlike shadow in this world. The shadow there is an absence of light, so it is a lack of understanding and wisdom. This, then, is the origin of white and black. Since they result from the light there, which holds understanding and wisdom, and from shadow that is a lack of understanding and wisdom, white and black plainly have the symbolism given above. This, then, is the origin of color, which is a modification of light and shadow playing on whites and blacks as their palette. The resulting variations are what are called colors (§§1042, 1043, 1053).

[7] From this evidence it can now be seen that something *speckled,* or marked and dotted with black and white speckles, means goodness mixed with evil, and that something *spotted* means truth mixed with falsity.

These are the elements taken from Laban's stock of goodness to serve for introducing real goodness and truth. Just how they can serve is a secret. The secret can be revealed clearly to those who see by heaven's light, because again, this light contains understanding. It *cannot* be revealed clearly to those who see by the world's light, unless their worldly light glows with heaven's light, as it does in people who have been reborn. Everyone reborn sees goodness and truth by heaven's light within her or his earthly glimmer, because heaven's light creates such a person's intellectual sight, while the world's weaker glow creates physical sight.

[8] A few words need to be added to explain the situation. Pure goodness—goodness unmixed with evil—does not exist in a human being, nor does pure truth, or truth unmixed with falsity. The human will is nothing but evil, and falsity constantly flows from it into a person's intellect. As is recognized, we carry with us by inheritance the evil gradually accumulated by our ancestors. From this store we ourselves bring evil out into act and make it our own, and then we pile our own evil on top of it. The evil we possess comes in various kinds, though. There is evil that cannot mix with goodness, and evil that can. The same with falsity. If it were not so, no one could ever regenerate. Evil and falsity incapable of mixing with goodness and truth are what oppose love for God and love for one's neighbor. It includes hatred, vengefulness, cruelty, resultant contempt, and the distorted convictions growing out of these. The evil and falsity capable of mixing with goodness and truth is that which does not oppose love for God and love for one's neighbor.

[9] For example, we might love ourselves more than others and be inspired by this love to work at outshining others in moral life and civic life, in secular and doctrinal knowledge, in acquiring high position and more wealth than they have. If we nevertheless acknowledge and revere God, serve our neighbor from the heart, and conscientiously do what is just and fair, the evil of this self-love is the kind that can mix with goodness and truth. It is the kind of evil that is natural to the human being, the kind we are born into. To snatch it from us would be to damp the first fires of our life. On the other hand we might love ourselves more than others and be inspired by this love to despise others in comparison with ourselves, hate those who fail to honor and essentially worship us, and therefore satisfy our hatred in cruel and vengeful ways. The evil of this love is the kind that cannot mix with goodness and truth, because they are opposites.

[10] For another example, we might believe ourselves to be free of sin and therefore clean (like a person rinsed of dirt) once we repent and fulfill the penance imposed on us, or hear a confessor say so after we confess or attend Holy Supper. If we live a new life full of desire for what is good and true, that falsity is the kind that can mix with goodness. On the other hand, if we live a life devoted to the flesh and the world as before, it is a kind of falsity that cannot mix with goodness.

[11] For another, if we believe we are saved by believing in what is good and not by willing it and yet we do will it and therefore do it, that is a falsity to which goodness and truth can attach; but not if we do not will and therefore do what is good.

For another, we might not know that we rise again after death, so we might not believe in resurrection; or we might have heard but doubt and almost deny it. If we live a life of truth and goodness nonetheless, that is another falsity that can mingle with goodness and truth. If we live a life of falsity and evil, though, goodness and truth cannot mingle with that falsity, because they are opposites. Falsity destroys truth, and evil destroys goodness.

[12] For another, pretense and cunning that seeks the good of a neighbor, the country, or the church is a form of prudence, and the evil that tinges it can mix with goodness for the sake of the overall goal. In contrast, pretense and cunning that seeks evil is not prudence but guile and deceit, which cannot possibly unite with goodness. Deceit, which is the mark of a wicked goal, coats everything inside us with hellishness. It puts evil at the center and casts goodness off to the periphery, which is the characteristic arrangement in hell.

And so on, without limit.

[13] The existence of evil and falsity capable of linking with goodness and truth can be seen simply from the fact that there are so many different dogmas and doctrines, most of which are thoroughly heretical, and yet each has adherents who are saved. It can also be seen from the presence of the Lord's church even among nations outside the church. Their inhabitants have misconceptions, but those who live a life of neighborly kindness are saved (§§2589–2604), which could never happen if there were no evil that could mix with goodness, no falsity that could mix with truth.

The Lord takes the mixed evil and goodness and the mixed falsity and truth and arranges them in a marvelous pattern. They do not unite, much less merge into one, but form links and attachments that set goodness with truth in the middle, or at the center. The kinds of evil and falsity described come at various stages out toward the edges or circumference. That is why the latter are lit up by the former and are turned into various colors by light from the middle or center, as white and black are. This is the heavenly pattern.

That is what the speckled and spotted symbolize on an inner level.

3994   *And every black animal among the lambs* symbolizes an innocent sense of autonomy—a mark of the goodness symbolized by Laban. This can be seen from the symbolism of *black* as selfhood [or autonomy] (discussed just above in §3993) and from that of a *lamb* as innocence (discussed below).

To comment on the innocent sense of self symbolized by the black among the lambs: Goodness has to contain innocence in order to be good. Charity is not charity without innocence, still less is love for the Lord really love for the Lord, so innocence is the actual essence of love and charity and consequently of goodness.

Innocent selfhood is the awareness, acknowledgment, and belief—not on the lips but in the heart—that all we produce is evil and that everything good comes from the Lord. So an innocent sense of self is the awareness, acknowledgment, and belief that our insistence on self-direction is totally black, whether it is self-direction of our will (evil) or of our intellect (falsity). When we confess and believe this from the heart, the Lord flows in with goodness and truth and instills in us a heavenly autonomy, which is a bright, shining white. We cannot possess true humility until we acknowledge and believe this at heart, because that is when we become self-effacing, self-averse, and in the process, self-forgetful. So that is when we have a welcoming attitude toward the Lord in his divinity. Accordingly, the Lord brings goodness to a heart that is humble and contrite.

[2] Such is the innocent selfhood symbolized by the black among the lambs, which Jacob chose for himself. The white among the lambs symbolizes the merit equated with good deeds. The meaning of white as merit was given above at §3993. Jacob declined it because it goes against innocence. People who take credit for their virtues acknowledge and believe that everything good comes from themselves, because they focus on themselves rather than the Lord in the good they do, so they self-righteously demand a reward. As a result they also despise and even condemn others in comparison with themselves, and to the extent they do so, they stray from the heavenly pattern—in other words, from what is good and true.

These considerations show that charity for one's neighbor and love for the Lord can exist only if they have innocence in them and therefore that no one can go to heaven without possessing some share of innocence. In the Lord's words:

> Truly, I say to you: anyone who does not accept the kingdom of God like a little child will not enter it. (Mark 10:15; Luke 18:17)

A little child here and elsewhere in the Word symbolizes innocence. See previous remarks on the subject: Childhood is not innocence; rather, innocence resides in wisdom (2305, 3494); the nature of childhood's innocence and the nature of wisdom's innocence (2306, 3183); the nature of human selfhood when it is enlivened by the Lord with innocence and charity (154); innocence makes goodness good (2526, 2780).

[3] The symbolism of lambs as innocence becomes clear from many passages in the Word. Let me quote the following examples as proof. In Isaiah:

> The wolf will stay with the lamb, and the leopard will lie down with the kid, and the calf and the young lion and the ox [will live] together, and a little child will lead them. (Isaiah 11:6)

This is about the Lord's kingdom and the state of peace and innocence there. The wolf stands for people who oppose innocence and the lamb for those who possess innocence. Likewise elsewhere in the same prophet:

> The wolf and the lamb will pasture together, and the lion like the ox will eat hay, and the snake will have dust as its bread. They will not do evil or cause destruction anywhere on my holy mountain. (Isaiah 65:25)

As above, the wolf stands for people who oppose innocence and the lamb for those who possess innocence. Since a wolf and a lamb are opposites, when the Lord was sending out the seventy [disciples] he said to them (in Luke):

> Here, I am sending you as lambs in the midst of wolves. (Luke 10:3)

In Moses:

> He makes them suck honey from a crag, and oil from a boulder of rock, the butter of the herd and the milk of the flock, together with the fat of lambs and of rams—the sons of Bashan. (Deuteronomy 32:13, 14)

In an inner sense this is about the heavenly qualities of the ancient church. The fat of lambs stands for innocent charity.

[4] The original language has a variety of words for lambs, symbolizing different levels of innocence. To repeat, goodness has to contain innocence in order to be good, so truth also has to contain innocence. The word for lambs here is the same one used for sheep in such places as Leviticus 1:10; 3:7; 5:6; 17:3; 22:19; Numbers 18:17; and it symbolizes the innocence in faith, which is the innocence in charity. Other words are used elsewhere, as in Isaiah:

> Send the lamb of the land's ruler from the rock by the wilderness to the mountain of Zion's daughter. (Isaiah 16:1)

Yet another word is used in the same author:

> The Lord Jehovih comes in strength, and his arm will rule for him. He will pasture his flock like a shepherd; *he will gather the lambs* into *his arm* and carry them in his embrace; he will lead the unweaned. (Isaiah 40:9, 10, [11])

The lambs being gathered into his arm and carried in his embrace stand for people who have charity imbued with innocence. [5] In John:

> After revealing himself, Jesus said to Peter, "Simon of Jonah, do you love me more than you love these?" [Peter] says to him, "Yes, Lord; you know that I love you." [Jesus] says to him, *"Pasture my lambs."* He says to him again, "Simon of Jonah, do you love me?" [Peter] says to him, "Yes, Lord; you know that I love you." [Jesus] says to him, *"Pasture my sheep."* (John 21:15, 16)

Here as elsewhere, Peter symbolizes faith; see the prefaces to Genesis 18 and 22, and §3750. Faith is not faith unless it comes from charity for one's neighbor and therefore from love for the Lord, and charity and love are not charity and love unless they stem from innocence. That is why the Lord first asks whether Peter loves him (whether faith contains love) and says, "Pasture my lambs" (people who have innocence). Then after the same question he says, "Pasture my sheep" (people who have charity).

[6] The Lord is innocence itself—the innocence in his kingdom—because every trace of innocence comes from him, which is why he is called the Lamb, as in John:

> The next day John the Baptist saw Jesus coming to him and said, "Look! *The Lamb of God,* who takes away the sin of the world." (John 1:29, 36)

And in Revelation:

> They will fight *with the Lamb,* but *the Lamb will defeat them,* because he is Lord of Lords and King of Kings; and those with him are the called and chosen. (Revelation 17:14)

There are other passages in Revelation as well, such as 5:6; 6:1, 16; 7:9, 14, 17; 12:11; 13:8; 14:1, 4; 19:7, 9; 21:22, 23, 27; 22:1, 3.

In the highest sense, the Passover lamb is the Lord (as is known), because the Passover symbolized the Lord's glorification, or the robing of his human part in divinity. In a representative sense it symbolizes human rebirth, and the Passover lamb symbolizes the vital element in rebirth, which is innocence. No one can be regenerated except by charity that contains innocence.

[7] Innocence is the primary feature of the Lord's kingdom and is what makes it heavenly. Since sacrifices and burnt offerings represented spiritual and heavenly qualities of the Lord's kingdom, innocence, the most essential feature of that kingdom, was represented by lambs. Accordingly lambs were used for the perpetual or daily burnt offering—one in the morning and the other between the evenings (Exodus 29:37, 38, 39; Numbers 28:3, 4). Two were offered on Sabbath days (Numbers 28:9, 10), and even more on appointed feasts (Leviticus 23:12; Numbers 28:11, 17, 19, 27; 29:1–end).

A woman who had just given birth and completed the days of cleansing was to offer a lamb and a pigeon chick or turtledove as a burnt offering (Leviticus 12:6) for two reasons. One was to symbolize the results of marriage love—and marriage love is innocence (see §2736). The other was that babies symbolize innocence.

3995   *And the spotted and speckled one among the she-goats* means that any truth-based goodness tinged with falsity or evil will then be his own. This can be seen from the symbolism of the *spotted* as falsity and that of the *speckled* as evil (which are discussed just above at §3993), and from that of *she-goats* as the goodness that comes of truth, or the charity that comes of faith (see §3519). The fact that it will all be his is symbolized by the next clause, "And it will be my wage."

[2] Truth-based goodness, or the charity that comes of faith, must be defined briefly. When we are in the process of rebirth, faith's truth seems to come first, and charity's goodness, to come after it. When the process is complete, though, charity's goodness plainly comes first and faith's truth plainly comes after it. On the point that what happens first is an appearance but that the latter is how things really are, see §§3539, 3548, 3556, 3563, 3570, 3576, 3616, 3603, 3701. When we are being reborn, we do good because of the truth we have learned, since truth teaches us what is good; but a goodness within is what brings this about. Goodness flows in from the Lord along an inner path, or the path of the soul, you see, while truth flows in along an outer path, or the path of the physical senses. Truth entering along this route is adopted by the goodness inside and unites with it—increasingly so, until we are reborn. Then a reversal takes place and we act on truth because of goodness. These remarks identify the goodness that comes of truth and the truth that comes of goodness.

That is why so many people these days describe charitable goodness as the fruit of faith; that is how it appears at the beginning of regeneration. The appearance leads them to this conclusion. They have no idea it is not so, because few regenerate, and no one can know it is otherwise except a person who has been reborn—a person with a desire for goodness, or charity. A desire for goodness, or charity, enables people to see and even perceive it clearly. People who have not been reborn do not even know what this desire or charity is but reason about it as something foreign to or outside themselves. In consequence they call charity the fruit of faith, when faith actually results from charity.

Still, it is not very important for the uneducated to know what comes first and second but only to live charitable lives, because charity is the life of faith.

[3] The "animal" mentioned in this verse means lambs, ewes, kids, she-goats, rams, and he-goats, but only lambs and she-goats are named, because lambs symbolize innocence, and she-goats, the charity that comes of faith—these being the focus of the inner meaning.

It is for this reason that "the spotted" is expressed in the original language by a word that also means lambs, as in Isaiah 40:11, and "the speckled" by a word that also means a sheep breeder, as in 2 Kings 3:4, Amos 1:1.

And it will be my wage means that it will come from himself. This **3996** can be seen from the meaning of the *wage* as being Jacob's in return for his service, which means by his own power, or from himself; see above at §§3975, 3977, 3982.

And my righteousness will answer for me symbolizes the divine holi- **3997** ness that is the Lord's. This can be seen from the symbolism of *righteousness* [or justice] as referring to what is good (discussed in §§612, 2235). When attributed to the Lord, as it is here, it symbolizes divine holiness, since all spiritual and heavenly goodness issues from the Lord's holy divinity.

On a future day means forever, as stands to reason from the meaning **3998** of *a future day*.

When the Word speaks of yesterday, today, or tomorrow, in the highest sense it means eternity. "Yesterday" means from eternity, "today" means eternity, and "tomorrow" means to eternity. (For the meaning of "today" as eternity, see §2838.) In the Word, periods of time—centuries, years, months, weeks, days, hours—symbolize states, as shown many times before [§§482, 893, 2788]. The Lord does not have states, though; everything in him is eternal and infinite. Clearly, then, *a future day* means forever.

3999   *When you come concerning my wage [that is] before you* symbolizes what is his own. This is established by the symbolism of a *wage,* when it is said to be the Lord's, as what is his own—that is, what he acquired by his own power, as discussed above in §§3975, 3977, 3982, 3996.

4000   *All that which is not speckled and spotted among the she-goats* symbolizes any of the goodness meant by Laban that is present in truth-based goodness and is not tinged with evil and falsity. This can be seen from the discussions above at §§3993, 3995, where similar words occur.

4001   *And black among the lambs* symbolizes the first stage of innocence. This can be seen from the symbolism of *black* as human selfhood and from that of a *lamb* as innocence (dealt with just above at §3994).

The *black among the lambs* means the first stage of innocence because human selfhood reigns supreme at first in those who are being reborn, since they imagine they are doing good under their own power. They *have* to do it seemingly on their own, so that they can receive the gift of a heavenly sense of self (see §§1712, 1937, 1947, 2882, 2883, 2891). As a result, the black among the lambs symbolizes the first stage of innocence.

4002   *It is stolen by me* means that it would not be his, as is self-evident.

The literal meaning here does sound rather harsh, but when the sentence passes into heaven, the harshness is erased, turning soft and gentle. The same happens where the Lord is described in Matthew:

> Be watchful! Because you do not know at what hour your Lord is to come. Recognize this: if the householder knew at *what hour the thief was to come,* he would certainly be watchful and not let his house be broken into. (Matthew 24:42, 43)

In John:

> If you are not watchful, *I will come upon you like a thief,* and you will not know at what hour I am to come upon you. (Revelation 3:3)

In the same author:

> Here, now, *I come like a thief;* fortunate are those who are watchful and keep their clothes! (Revelation 16:15)

"Like a thief" simply means by surprise and unexpectedly.

In an inner sense, *stealing* means claiming for oneself what is actually the Lord's—namely, goodness and truth. Everyone does this at the beginning of regeneration, and it is the first stage of innocence (see just above in §4001), so the word is milder than it sounds in the letter. *Stolen by me,* then, means that it would not be his.

Genesis 30:34, 35, 36. And Laban said, "Here, by all means let it be ◼ **4003**
according to your word!" And on that day he removed the mottled and spot-
ted he-goats, and all the speckled and spotted she-goats, every one in which
there was white; and every black one among the lambs; and gave them into
the hand of his sons. And he put a journey of three days between himself and
Jacob; and Jacob was pasturing Laban's remaining flocks.

Laban said, "Here, by all means let it be according to your word!" symbolizes consent. *And on that day he removed the mottled and spotted he-*
goats means that truth-from-goodness sprinkled and tinged with evil
and falsity—truth proper to the goodness symbolized by Laban—would
be separated out. *And all the speckled and spotted she-goats* symbolizes the
goodness that comes of that truth, which has evil and falsity mixed in.
Every one in which there was white symbolizes truth. *And every black one*
among the lambs symbolizes an innocent sense of autonomy. *And gave*
them into the hand of his sons means that these qualities would be handed
over to truth. *And he put a journey of three days between himself and Jacob*
symbolizes the state of these qualities, entirely separate. *And Jacob was*
pasturing Laban's remaining flocks means that from what was left [the Lord]
would take the goodness and truth that would bond together.

Laban said, "Here, by all means let it be according to your word!" sym- ◼ **4004**
bolizes consent, as is self-evident.

And on that day he removed the mottled and spotted he-goats means ◼ **4005**
that truth-from-goodness sprinkled and tinged with evil and falsity—truth
proper to the goodness symbolized by Laban—would be separated out, as
the following shows: *Removing* means separating out. *He-goats* symbolize
truth-from-goodness, as discussed below. The *mottled* symbolize what is
sprinkled and tinged with evil, as also discussed below. And the *spotted* symbolize what is sprinkled and tinged with falsity, as discussed above [§3993].

He-goats are mentioned first here, and she-goats second, because he-
goats symbolize truth based on goodness, while she-goats symbolize goodness based on truth. For the difference between them, see above at §3995.

[2] The Word maintains a careful distinction between males and
females. This is clear from the sacrifices and burnt offerings, for which
there are commandments specifying whether the offering was to be a male
or female lamb, a she-goat or he-goat, a ewe or ram, and so on. These
commandments show that a male symbolized one thing, and a female,
another. Males in general symbolized truth, and females, goodness. So
the he-goats mentioned here symbolize truth that comes of goodness,
and the she-goats mentioned next symbolize the goodness attached to that
truth. Because they differ this way, the text says that [Laban] removed the

mottled he-goats, not the speckled ones, as it says of the she-goats. What is mottled symbolizes truth sprinkled and mixed with evil, but what is speckled symbolizes goodness sprinkled and mixed with evil (as noted above at §3993). Strictly speaking, truth mingled with evil belongs to the intellect, and goodness mingled with evil belongs to the will; that is the difference.

This mixed truth obviously comes from the goodness symbolized by Laban, since the goats came from Laban's flock. In the Word, a flock symbolizes goodness and truth, or to put the same thing another way, people with goodness and truth, and therefore people in the Lord's church.

[3] This secret cannot be explained any further because the only mind that can see into it is one instructed in truth and goodness and also enlightened. It is necessary to know what the truth that develops out of goodness is and what the resulting goodness is, and to know that the single kind of goodness represented here by Laban can be separated into so many varieties. If you do not know these things, you also do not know that every type of goodness contains countless others—so many different types that even the most knowledgeable person would have a hard time separating them into their general categories. There are different kinds of goodness acquired through truth, truths born from those kinds of goodness, and a further range of goodness acquired through these truths. There is truth born from goodness, and so on in its own series. There is goodness mixed with evil, and truth mixed with falsity, as discussed above in §3993, and there are blends and compounds of these in such variety and abundance that the number exceeds hundreds of millions. Goodness also differs throughout the stages of life, which vary generally with a person's age and specifically with a person's every mood.

From these considerations it can be gleaned to some extent that Laban's goodness was able to be divided into all these different varieties, some of which link with the truth symbolized by Jacob's sons, and some of which are left behind. From them stem yet other varieties.

As just mentioned, though, these are ideas that can be grasped only by an intellect both instructed and enlightened.

4006   *And all the speckled and spotted she-goats* symbolizes the goodness that comes of that truth, which has evil and falsity mixed in, as the following shows: *She-goats* symbolize goodness-from-truth, as mentioned in §3995, and in this verse they symbolize goodness linked to the truth described just above in §4005. The *speckled* symbolize goodness with evil mixed in, and the *spotted* symbolize truth with falsity mixed in, as discussed in §§3993, 3995.

Every one in which there was white means in which there was truth. **4007**
This can be seen from the symbolism of *white* as truth, though more
properly as the Lord's righteousness and merit, and therefore as his righteousness and merit in us (discussed in §§3301, 3993).

White has this symbolism because heaven's light, which shines from
the Lord and gives off a brilliant white radiance, symbolizes truth. Whatever is lit by that light and its brilliant white radiance, then, is what is
called the Lord's righteousness and merit in us. People who acknowledge the Lord's righteousness, accept it in a sincere way, and reject self-
righteousness are the ones specifically symbolized by "the righteous" whom
the Lord mentions in Matthew:

> The righteous will glow like the sun in the Father's kingdom. (Matthew
> 13:43)

[2] This symbolism of shining white is also clear from other Scripture
passages, as in Moses:

> He had eyes redder than wine and teeth *whiter* than milk. (Genesis 49:12)

This is about Judah, who represents the Lord and his divine love, or on
a lower level his heavenly kingdom, and therefore a heavenly person; see
§3881. "Eyes redder than wine" symbolize divine wisdom; "teeth whiter
than milk" symbolize divine righteousness. In David:

> You will purify me with hyssop, and I will be clean; you will wash me,
> and *I will become whiter than snow.* (Psalms 51:7)

Washing and becoming whiter than snow stands for being purified of sin
by accepting and taking on the Lord's righteousness. In John:

> In the middle of the seven lampstands, one like the Son of Humankind—
> his head and *hair white,* like *white wool, like snow,* and his eyes like a
> fiery flame. (Revelation 1:13, 14)

[3] In the same author:

> You have a few names in Sardis who have not defiled their clothes and
> will *walk with me in white* because they are worthy. Those who con-
> quer will be *dressed in white clothes.* (Revelation 3:4, 5)

In the same author:

> I advise you to buy from me gold purified by fire, so that you will grow
> rich, and *white clothes, so that you will be dressed.* (Revelation 3:18)

In the same author:

> To each soul under the altar were given *white robes*. (Revelation 6:9, 11)

In the same author:

> I saw people standing before the throne and before the Lamb *dressed in white robes*. One of elders said to me, "These, *dressed in white robes*—who are they, and where did they come from?" To whom I said, "Lord, you know." He said to me, "These are the ones coming out of great affliction, and they washed their robes and *whitened their robes in the Lamb's blood.*" (Revelation 7:9, 13, 14)

In the same author:

> . . . angels *dressed in white and shining linen* and circled around their chests with golden sashes. (Revelation 15:6)

In the same author:

> I looked, and there! A *white horse!* And one sitting on it, having a bow, who was given a crown. (Revelation 6:2)

And in another passage:

> Afterward I saw heaven opened, when look! A *white horse!* His armies in heaven followed him on *white horses, dressed in fine linen, white* and clean. (Revelation 19:11, 14)

[4] In all these places, white symbolizes religious truth; white clothes and white robes have no other meaning. However, people who believe that they acquire faith for themselves and therefore that they gain wisdom on their own do not possess religious truth, only those who believe they do so under the Lord's power. The latter receive faith and wisdom, because they do not attribute any truth or goodness to themselves, let alone believe any truth or goodness in them makes them deserving or—still worse—righteous. No, they attribute it all to the Lord alone and therefore to his grace and mercy. That is what it means to wear white clothes and to have [their robes] whitened in the Lamb's blood.

All who go to heaven discard two things: self-sufficiency with its over-confidence, and a sense of merit, or self-righteousness. These they replace with a heavenly sense of self, given by the Lord, and with the Lord's merit or righteousness. The more they take these on, the deeper into heaven they go.

This is the specific symbolism of red and white. Red is the loving goodness they then have, and white is the religious truth.

And every black one among the lambs symbolizes an innocent sense of autonomy, as is evident from the discussion above at §3994, where the same words occur.

4008

And gave them into the hand of his sons means that these qualities would be handed over to truth. This can be seen from the symbolism of *sons* as truth (discussed in §§489, 491, 533, 2623, 3373). *Giving them into the hand* of the sons means handing them over to truth's control and authority, because a *hand* symbolizes power (§§878, 3387).

4009

The truths that the sons symbolize are what are called sense impressions, because they are the product of the senses and are on the most superficial plane of the earthly mind. Our earthly dimension communicates on one side with the senses, which belong to the body, and on the other side with reasoned thinking, which belongs to the rational mind. Through this middle ground we make a kind of ascent from the body's senses, which open toward the world, to the rational mind's thinking, which opens toward heaven. We also make a descent from the latter—that is, from heaven to the world. This happens only in people.

This ascent and descent is the theme of the inner meaning in the current chapters. Every aspect of it needs to be expressed as a representation, so the rational level is represented by Isaac and Rebekah, the earthly level, by Jacob and his two women, and the sensory level, by the sons born to Jacob and his women. However, the prior levels are all present in the sensory level as the last of their series, so each son represents a general attribute containing those levels, as shown above.

And he put a journey of three days between himself and Jacob symbolizes the state of these qualities, entirely separate, as the following indicates: *Putting a journey* means being separated. *Three* symbolizes the last part, completion, or end, as noted in §§1825, 2788, so it means *entirely* separate. And *days* symbolize states, as discussed in §§23, 487, 488, 493, 893, 2788, 3462.

4010

And Jacob was pasturing Laban's remaining flocks means that from what was left [the Lord] would take the goodness and truth that would bond together. This can be seen from the symbolism of *flocks* as goodness and truth (discussed in §§343, 2566, 3767, 3768, 3772, 3783). What follows will show that *pasturing the remaining flocks* means taking them—the goodness and truth that would bond together—from what was left, since that becomes the subject.

4011

4012   Genesis 30:37, 38, 39, 40. *And Jacob took himself a fresh rod of poplar, and hazel and sycamore, and peeled white peelings on them, a baring of the white that was on the rods. And he stood the rods that he had peeled in the channels, in the water troughs, where the flocks came to drink, opposite the flocks, and they went into heat as they came to drink. And the flocks went into heat at the rods, and the flocks bore mottled, speckled, and spotted [offspring]. And Jacob separated the lambs and turned the faces of the flock toward the mottled and [toward] every black one in Laban's flock and gave himself droves for himself alone and did not put them into Laban's flock.*

Jacob took himself a fresh rod of poplar symbolizes the inherent power of earthly goodness. *And hazel and sycamore* symbolizes the resulting power of earthly truth. *And peeled white peelings on them, a baring of the white that was on the rods,* symbolizes a rearrangement by the power of inner truth. *And he stood the rods that he had peeled in the channels* symbolizes further preparation. *In the water troughs, where the flocks came to drink,* symbolizes a desire for truth. *Opposite the flocks, and they went into heat as they came to drink* means to a pitch of burning desire for their union. *And the flocks went into heat at the rods* symbolizes the effect achieved by inherent power. *And the flocks bore mottled, speckled, and spotted [offspring]* means that from the intermediate goodness symbolized by Laban, real earthly goodness therefore acquired such things. *And Jacob separated the lambs* means in respect to innocence. *And turned the faces of the flock toward the mottled* means toward truth sprinkled with evil and falsity. *And every black one* means toward that kind of state. *In Laban's flock* means within the goodness symbolized by Laban. *And gave himself droves for himself alone* symbolizes the isolation of goodness and truth by [the Lord's] own power. *And did not put them into Laban's flock* symbolizes utter isolation from the goodness symbolized by Laban.

4013   *Jacob took himself a fresh rod of poplar* symbolizes the inherent power of earthly goodness. This can be seen from the symbolism of a *rod* as power and from that of *poplar* as goodness on the earthly level (discussed below).

A *rod* [or staff] is often mentioned in the Word, where it always symbolizes power. The symbolism arose both because shepherds used a rod [or crook] for exercising power over their flocks and because it served to support the body. It also substituted for a right hand—a hand symbolizing power (§§878, 3387). Ancient monarchs used a staff on account of this symbolism, which is why a short staff and scepter are royal insignia.

Moreover, it was not only royalty who used a staff but priests and prophets such as Aaron and Moses as well, in order that their use of a staff could also symbolize the power they had. Accordingly Moses was often commanded to stretch out his staff, or at other times his hand, when miracles took place, because a staff and a hand symbolized God's power. The symbolism of a rod as power was also the reason Egyptian magicians used rods when performing magic, which is why modern magicians are represented with wands in their hands.

These facts show that rods symbolize power.

[2] The original language has different words for the staffs of shepherds, monarchs, and priests and prophets. The word in the current verse is that for a walking stick and also for a shepherd's crook, as is clear from other passages using the term, such as Genesis 32:10; Exodus 12:11; 1 Samuel 17:40, 43; Zechariah 11:7, 10. Of course the rod in this verse is not mentioned as a prop for the hand but as a switch cut from a tree—poplar, hazel, and sycamore—to put in the troughs before the faces of the flock; but it still has the same symbolism. In an inner sense it depicts the power of earthly goodness and so of earthly truth.

[3] As for the *poplar* of which the rod was made, it needs to be known that trees in general symbolize perceptions and religious knowledge—perceptions when they relate to a heavenly person, and knowledge when they relate to a spiritual one (see §§103, 2163, 2682, 2722, 2972). So specific trees symbolize different kinds of goodness and truth, since these are the objects of perception and religious knowledge. Some varieties, such as olive trees and grapevines, symbolize profound forms of goodness and truth belonging to the spiritual person. Some, such as poplar, hazel, and sycamore, symbolize shallower forms of goodness and truth belonging to the earthly person. Since each tree symbolized some type of goodness and truth to the ancients, they based their worship in groves on the species of trees there (§2722).

The poplar mentioned in the current verse is white poplar, named for its whiteness, from which the word derives [in the original language]. That was why it symbolized the good that comes of truth, or (what is the same) goodness-from-truth, as also in Hosea 4:13—though in that verse it symbolizes a falsified form.

And hazel and sycamore symbolizes the resulting power of earthly **4014** truth. This can be seen from the symbolism of *hazel* and *sycamore* as earthly truth.

This symbolism of the trees does not become as clear from other passages in the Word because they are not mentioned elsewhere, except for an instance of the sycamore in Ezekiel:

> The cedars did not hide it in the garden of God; the firs were not equal to its branches, and the *sycamores* did not rival its branches. No tree was equal to it in its beauty. (Ezekiel 31:8)

This speaks about factual knowledge and rational ideas in an adherent of a spiritual religion. The garden of God means a spiritual religion; the cedars mean rational ideas; and the firs and sycamores mean earthly concepts—firs, earthly concepts of goodness, and sycamores, earthly concepts of truth.

4015   *And peeled white peelings on them, a baring of the white that was on the rods,* symbolizes a rearrangement by the power of inner truth, as the following shows: *To peel* and *peelings* symbolize a rolling back of the surface to reveal what is inside, so they symbolize a baring. *White* symbolizes truth, as discussed above in §§3993, 4007. And a *rod* symbolizes power, as discussed just above in §4013—here, inner power, because the white was under the bark on the rods.

A rearrangement by the power of inner truth is by the power our inner self exercises over our outer self, or the power our spiritual self exercises over our earthly self. All rearranging of goodness and truth in our earthly self comes from our spiritual self, or rather from the Lord through our spiritual self, and in fact through the truth there. The Lord acts on the goodness in our spiritual or inner self and through the truth there on our earthly self. He does not act directly through goodness until we have been reborn. So all reorganization of our earthly self comes from inside. [2] That is the only possible way our earthly level or earthly self can be reorganized—in other words, be reborn. Clearly it has to come from inside, because an acknowledgment of truth is not an acknowledgment unless it comes from inside. The same thing is clear from conscience— which is an inward acknowledgment of truth—and from perception.

Since rearrangement from within happens through truth, power is predicated of truth. It is attributed as well to a rod, which symbolizes power, and to a hand, which also symbolizes power (§3091), as can be confirmed by many passages in the Word—not that power is inherent in truth. Power is inherent in goodness, so truth obtains its power from goodness, or rather from the Lord through what is good. This discussion clarifies to some degree what it is to be rearranged by the power of inner truth.

In the highest sense, which deals with the Lord, a rod symbolizes inherent power. Divinity has its own power, since it receives power from no other.

And he stood the rods that he had peeled in the channels symbolizes further preparation. This can be seen from following sections, which discuss the effect that the power of inner truth has on the earthly self. *Rods* symbolize power (§§4013, 4015). *Peeling* means rearranging from inside (§4015). And *channels* symbolize goodness-from-truth on the earthly level (§3095).

4016

In the water troughs, where the flocks came to drink, symbolizes a desire for truth, as can be seen from the following: *Water* symbolizes religious and secular knowledge, which is the earthly form of truth, as discussed in §§28, 2702, 3058. *Troughs* or watering places contain water, so on an inner level they symbolize the goodness that comes of truth, since goodness is a container for truth (as noted in §3095). And *coming to drink* symbolizes a desire for truth. The reason *coming to drink* symbolizes a desire for truth is that it involves thirst, and in the Word, thirst symbolizes an appetite, longing, and therefore desire for knowing and imbibing truth, since water symbolizes truth in general. Hunger symbolizes an appetite, longing, and desire for assimilating what is good, because bread (which is assumed to mean food in general, §2165) symbolizes goodness. It is apparent, then, that these words symbolize a desire for truth.

4017

Opposite the flocks, and they went into heat as they came to drink means to a pitch of burning desire for their union. This can be seen from the symbolism of *going into heat as they came to drink* as a burning desire. *Going into heat* means burning, of course, and *coming to drink* means a desire for truth (see just above at §4017). *Opposite the flocks* symbolizes an intent that truth and goodness on the earthly plane unite, because it implies a viewpoint and the desire aroused by the view from that point, since this is how spiritual qualities are united. What is more, truth and goodness are always implanted and united by desire. When we learn about truth and goodness but are not touched by them, they do enter our memory but stick as lightly there as a feather on a wall, which slips away with the slightest breath of air.

4018

[2] When ideas enter our memory, they land in its shadows if they enter without our desire, but in the light there if they enter with our desire. The ideas standing in light spring into clear and vivid sight and vision whenever something similar stirs them, but those lying at the shadowy edges do not. That is what love and its desire carry with them.

These considerations show that desire is always what implants truth and unites it with goodness. The greater the desire, the stronger the union. The burning desire mentioned here is a very deep desire. [3] However, the only desire that can implant truth and unite it with goodness is a desire for what is good and true. The springs from which this desire wells up are those of charity toward our neighbor and love for the Lord. Evil and falsity are implanted and united by a desire for evil and falsity, which wells up from the springs of self-love and materialism.

This being the case, and the theme of the inner meaning here being the union of goodness and truth in the earthly self, the current verse and those that follow talk about the flock's going into heat when it came to drink, since that is the symbolism.

4019   *And the flocks went into heat at the rods* symbolizes the effect achieved by inherent power. This can be seen from the symbolism of *going into heat* as an effect—the effect of desire (§4018)—and from that of *rods* as inherent power (discussed above in §§4013, 4015).

4020   *And the flocks bore mottled, speckled, and spotted [offspring]* means that from the intermediate goodness symbolized by Laban, earthly goodness therefore acquired such things, as can be seen from the following: *Bearing* symbolizes acknowledgment and union (as noted in §§3911, 3915). The *mottled* symbolizes truth tinged with evil (§4005). The *speckled* symbolizes goodness tinged with evil, and the *spotted* symbolizes truth tinged with falsity (both of them discussed in §§3993, 3995, 4005). That is what the animals symbolize and what passed from the goodness symbolized by Laban to the goodness represented by Jacob—the goodness that comes of earthly truth.

4021   *And Jacob separated the lambs* means in respect to innocence. This can be seen from the symbolism of *lambs* as innocence (discussed above in §3994).

The phrase "*in respect to* innocence" is used because the next few sections have to do with the way earthly goodness and truth are disposed to receive and incorporate innocence.

4022   *And turned the faces of the flock toward the mottled* means toward truth sprinkled with evil and falsity. This is established by the symbolism of the *mottled* as truth sprinkled and tinged with evil (dealt with at §§4005, 4020).

4023   *And every black one* means toward that kind of state—the state symbolized by the *black* among the lambs; on that state, see §§3994, 4001.

4024   *In Laban's flock* means within the goodness symbolized by Laban. This is established by the symbolism of a *flock* and the representation of *Laban* as goodness, specifically the intermediate goodness through which the earthly

dimension acquired different kinds of goodness and truth (discussed above
[§4020]).

And gave himself droves for himself alone symbolizes the isolation of
goodness and truth by [the Lord's] own power. This can be seen from
the symbolism of the *droves* of the flock as goodness and truth, and
from the meaning of *giving himself for himself alone* as isolating what he
had obtained by his own power.

In its highest meaning this passage has to do with the Lord and the
way he made his earthly dimension divine, using his own power but also
using the proper means in the proper order. The goodness and truth he
made divine within himself are the droves that were for himself by himself.

And did not put them into Laban's flock symbolizes utter isolation from
the goodness symbolized by Laban, as can be seen from the preceding
discussion without further explanation.

Divine goodness and truth are absolutely separate from goodness and
truth that draw at all on what is human, because they transcend what is
human and become infinite.

What has been unfolded so far in regard to the inner meaning of the
words is too deep and therefore too arcane to be explained clearly and
intelligibly. In its highest sense it concerns the Lord and the way he made
his earthly level divine, and in a representative sense it concerns the way
the Lord renews our earthly level when he regenerates us. All of this is
presented fully in the inner meaning of the current passage.

[2] By their very nature, the contents of the passage's highest meaning—
concerning the way the Lord made the earthly dimension in himself divine
by his own power—surpass even an angel's ability to understand. A frac-
tion of them can be seen reflected in human regeneration, because our
rebirth is an image of the Lord's glorification (§§3138, 3212, 3296, 3490).
Of human rebirth we can form some concept, but only if we have been
reborn. Even at that, the concept will be vague as long as we are living in
our body, because the bodily and worldly concerns with which we also
live are constantly pouring forth fog and dragging our mind down.

If we have not been reborn, we cannot understand anything at all
about it. We are barred from knowledge because we are barred from perception. We have absolutely no idea what rebirth is and consider it impossible. Even the feeling of neighborly love (through which we are reborn)
is completely unknown to us, as is conscience, not to mention the inner
self, and the correspondence of the inner with the outer self. We can be
familiar with the terms—and many are—but we are ignorant of the reality behind them. Since any notion of these items is lacking, then, it does

not matter how clearly the hidden contents of the inner meaning here are explained; it would still be like making a visual presentation in the dark, or talking to the deaf. Besides, the desires belonging to self-love and materialism that reign supreme in us prevent us from learning or even listening to any of it, since they immediately spurn and reject it.

It is different when we feel love for our neighbor, though. Then we take pleasure in ideas like these, since when we immerse ourselves in them, the angels with us are very happy, because they are pursuing thoughts that involve the Lord (in whom they live), neighborly love, and human regeneration. When people who feel love for their neighbor read the text, pleasure and bliss flows into them from the angels, or rather from the Lord through angels. It flows in even more strongly when they believe the material has something holy in it, and most of all when they grasp some part of the inner meaning.

[3] The current passage touches on the following themes: the Lord's inflow into goodness in the inner self and his inflow through that goodness into truth there; his inflow from the inner self into the outer, earthly self; the desire for goodness and truth that he stimulates; the acceptance of truth and its union with goodness on the earthly level; and the goodness that serves as an intermediary, symbolized in the current passage by Laban and his flock.

To angels, who focus on the Word's inner meaning, or for whom the inner meaning *is* the Word, these subjects yield boundless insights and perceptions, hardly any of which are accessible to the human intellect. Concerning those that *are* accessible, we are in the dark. That is why the material has not been explained in more detail.

4028   Genesis 30:41, 42. *And it happened at every onset of heat in the flock (those mating first) that Jacob put rods before the eyes of the flock in the channels, for it to go into heat at the rods. And at the later mating of the flock he did not put [the rods there], and [the offspring] of those mating later were Laban's, and [the offspring] of those mating first were Jacob's.*

It happened at every onset of heat in the flock (those mating first) symbolizes those that were willingly adopted. *That Jacob put rods before the eyes of the flock in the channels, for it to go into heat at the rods* means summoned and united by [the Lord's] own power. *And at the later mating of the flock he did not put [the rods there]* means adopted under force. *And [the offspring] of those mating later were Laban's* means that they would be left behind. *And [the offspring] of those mating first were Jacob's* means that what was willingly or freely adopted would be united.

It happened at every onset of heat in the flock (those mating first) sym-   **4029**
bolizes those that were willingly adopted, as the following shows: *Going
into heat* symbolizes burning desire and its effect (discussed above at
§§4018, 4019). A *flock* symbolizes what is true and good (also mentioned
above [§§3992, 4025]). And *those mating first* symbolize what is willingly
adopted.

The symbolism of *those mating first* as what is willingly adopted
becomes clear from the interconnection of ideas in the inner meaning. It
also becomes clear from the fact that anything done with desire is done
willingly. What is done with the burning desire symbolized by a heat is
done with the greatest possible will, and that is why the verse speaks of
the heat twice. The same thing can be seen from the root of the word in
the original language, which means union through the deepest love. The
current theme is the union of truth and goodness on the earthly plane,
which is accomplished only through what is voluntary—that is, only in
freedom. It stands to reason, then, that *at every onset of heat in the flock
(those mating first)*—every instance when the first-mating members of the
flock went into heat—symbolizes truth and goodness that were adopted
willingly, freely, or with the strongest desire. Anything that springs from
love or desire is free (see §2870); truth and goodness always unite in a
state of freedom, never under force (2875, 3145, 3146, 3158); so reformation and rebirth is accomplished only through freedom (1937, 1947, 2876,
2877, 2878, 2879, 2880, 2881); if it could be accomplished through force,
everyone would be saved (2881).

That Jacob put rods before the eyes of the flock in the channels, for it to   **4030**
go into heat at the rods means summoned and united by [the Lord's] own
power, as the following indicates: *Rods* symbolize power, and in connection with the Lord, his own power (as discussed in §§4013, 4015). And
putting them before the [flock's] eyes in the channels, to go into heat means
summoning them to unite, as is clear from the remarks above at §4018
and elsewhere concerning the symbolism of these words.

And at the later mating of the flock he did not put [the rods there] means   **4031**
adopted under force, as can be seen from the symbolism of the *later mating.* Mating first symbolizes something willing or free, as shown above
in §4029. This symbolism and the interconnection of ideas in the inner
meaning make it clear that *mating later* means what is forced or nonfree.

The same thing can be seen from the absence here of the word *heat,*
which was used of those mating first. Being in heat symbolizes desire,
and in this case a burning desire. Anything done without desire is done

without willingness or freedom, since all willingness or freedom comes from desire or love (§2870).

It can also be seen from the root of the word in the original language, which means a failing, because when burning desire fails, freedom ends, and what comes next is called nonfree and (in the end) forced.

[2] The sections cited above in §4029 show that all union of truth and goodness, and therefore all reformation and rebirth, happens in a state of freedom, or voluntarily. Clearly, then, no union and so no rebirth can be brought about in a state of nonfreedom, or through force. (For what freedom is and where it comes from, see §§2870–2893, which discuss human freedom.)

When people do not know that human freedom is prerequisite to the union (or adoption) of truth and goodness, and accordingly to rebirth, they plunge into deepest shadow and therefore into serious error in reasoning about the Lord's providence, human salvation, and the damnation of many. They imagine the Lord can save everyone, if he wants, and that he has endless means to do so: miracles; the resurrection of the dead; direct revelation; angels who would keep us out of trouble and openly, forcefully compel us to be good; various conditions that reduce us to repentance; and so on.

[3] They do not know, however, that these means are all coercive and cannot reform us. Nothing that compels us sparks any desire in us; or if it does, it binds with an evil desire. It looks as though it inspires awe, and actually does so, but when our mood shifts, we go back to our old desires—that is, to evil and falsity. The sense of awe then unites with the evil and falsity and turns into something profane, which by its very nature brings us into the gravest hell of all. First, you see, we acknowledge and believe in what is holy and feel drawn to it, and then we deny and even oppose it. People who both acknowledge something at heart and afterward deny it are profaners, but people who do not acknowledge it at heart are not; see §§301, 302, 303, 571, 582, 593, 1001, 1008, 1010, 1059, 1327, 1328, 2051, 2426, 3398, 3399, 3402, 3898. So obvious miracles do not happen today, only subtle, inconspicuous ones, which are such that they do not flood us with reverence or rob us of our freedom. As a consequence, the dead do not rise, and direct revelation and angels do not withhold us from evil or come right out and force us into goodness. [4] It is our freedom that the Lord works with and that he uses to bend us.

All freedom has to do with our love, or desire, so it has to do with our will (§3158). If we do not freely accept what is good and true, we cannot adopt it, or make it our own. Nothing we are forced into is ours; it belongs to the person who forces us, because we do not do it on our own, even if it happens at our hand. At times, as for instance during spiritual trials and battles, it looks as though we are compelled to be good, but our freedom is stronger during those periods than outside them (see §§1937, 1947, 2881). It seems as though we are being forced into goodness when we force ourselves into it, but it is one thing to compel ourselves and another to be compelled. When we compel ourselves, it comes from something free inside us, but when we are compelled, it comes from something nonfree.

This being so, you can see what shadows people can plunge into and therefore how far they can stray when they reason about the Lord's providence, human salvation, and the damnation of many without knowing that the Lord works through freedom and never through force. If sacred matters are not freely accepted, coercion in them is dangerous.

And [the offspring] of those mating later were Laban's means that those adopted under force would be left behind; *and [the offspring] of those mating first were Jacob's* means that what was willingly or freely adopted would be united. This can be seen from the remarks just above in §§4029, 4031.

4033

"What was adopted under force" means what did not and could not unite; "what was willingly adopted" means what united and also what was capable of uniting. It includes elements that *could* unite because willingness depends on desire, and on the nature of one's desire.

After the goodness symbolized by Laban and his flock serves the purposes described earlier, it is separated. The next chapter talks about this separation.

Genesis 30:43. *And the man spread out greatly, greatly, and he had many flocks and female slaves and male slaves and camels and donkeys.*

4034

The man spread out greatly, greatly symbolizes multiplication. *And he had many flocks* symbolizes the resulting inner kinds of goodness and truth. *And female slaves and male slaves* symbolizes intermediate kinds of goodness and truth. *And camels and donkeys* symbolizes truth-from-goodness that is close to or right on the surface.

And the man spread out greatly, greatly symbolizes multiplication—the multiplication of goodness and truth. This can be seen from the symbolism of *spreading out* as multiplying. *Greatly, greatly* means beyond measure.

4035

4036   *And he had many flocks* symbolizes the resulting inner kinds of goodness and truth. This can be seen from the symbolism of *flocks* as goodness and truth (discussed in §343) and as inner kinds (§§2566, 3783).

4037   *And female slaves and male slaves* symbolizes intermediate kinds of goodness and truth, or the earthly dimension proper. This can be seen from the symbolism of *female slaves* as different kinds of desire on the earthly plane and so as goodness there (discussed in §§1895, 2567, 3835, 3849) and from that of *male slaves* as facts, which are the truths of the earthly self (discussed in §§2567, 3019, 3020, 3409).

4038   *And camels and donkeys* symbolizes truth-from-goodness that is close to or right on the surface, as can be seen from the following: *Camels* symbolize the general facts in the earthly self (as discussed in §§3048, 3071, 3143, 3145)—general facts being truth-from-goodness on a relatively low or superficial level. And *donkeys* symbolize truth based on earthly goodness on a still lower level, or right on the surface (as discussed in §2781). An idea of inner, intermediate, and relatively or completely superficial goodness and truth may be had from the comments at §4009.

[2] People have three overall dimensions: the bodily, the earthly, and the rational. The bodily dimension is on the outside, the earthly is in the middle, and the rational is inside. To the extent that one dimension dominates over another in us, we are described as being body-centered, earthly, or rational.

These three parts of a human communicate in a marvelous way— the bodily part with the earthly, and the earthly with the rational. As newborns we are conscious only on the bodily level, but we possess the ability to be perfected, so later we wake to the earthly level, and at last we become rational. It can be seen, then, that each part communicates with the next. The bodily dimension communicates with the earthly dimension through the senses—in one way through the senses that belong to the intellect, and in another way through those that belong to the will. Both kinds have to be perfected in us if we are to become and remain human. The senses of sight and hearing play a particular role in perfecting the faculty of the intellect, and the other three senses relate particularly to the faculty of the will.

Through these senses our bodily level communicates with our earthly level, which is the middle level, as noted. Whatever enters through our senses stores itself in our earthly part in a kind of container, which is our memory. The delights, pleasures, and appetites there belong to our will and are called earthly goodness, but the facts there belong to our intellect and are called earthly truth.

[3] Through the items just listed, our earthly part communicates with our rational part, which is the inner dimension, as noted. Whatever rises up from there to the rational level stores itself in our rational part, again in a kind of container, which is our inner memory (treated of in §§2469, 2470, 2471, 2472, 2473–2480). The bliss and happiness there belong to our will and embody rational goodness, while deep insights and perceptions belong to the intellect, and the concepts seen and perceived are called rational truth.

These are our three constituent parts, and communication exists among them. Our outer senses link our bodily plane with our earthly plane, and our inner senses link our earthly plane with our rational plane. So what exists in our earthly part and draws on our outer senses (the senses belonging to our body) is what is called truth-from-goodness on or near the surface. What draws on our inner senses (the senses belonging to our spirit) and communicates with our rational part is what is called inner goodness and truth. What lies between the two and partakes of both is what is called intermediate kinds of goodness and truth.

These are the three dimensions symbolized on an inner level by the flocks, the female and male slaves, and the camels and donkeys, going in order from the inmost.

The Universal Human and Correspondence (Continued): Correspondence with the Cerebrum and Cerebellum

THE end of the previous chapter [§§3883–3896] dealt with the correspondence of the heart and lungs with the universal human, or heaven. Now the topic is to be the correspondence of the cerebrum, the cerebellum, and the medullas attached to them. A discussion of the correspondence, though, must be prefaced by some remarks on the overall form of the brain, the reasons for that form, and its representation.

4039

4040   When the skull and the membranes covering the entire surface of the brain are removed, one can see in the brain wonderful twistings and windings that hold what are called the cortical substances. The fibers making up the brain's core run from the cortex through the nerves into the body, where they function at the beck and call of the brain.

All of this matches the form of heaven perfectly, because the Lord imprints that form on the heavens and therefore on the parts of a human being, especially on the human cerebrum and cerebellum.

4041   The form of heaven is astounding and completely mind-boggling, because it far surpasses any concept of forms we can possibly develop by looking at worldly objects, even when we analyze them. All heavenly communities are organized into that form, and amazing to say, they exhibit a circular motion that accords with it, though angels and spirits do not feel the motion. The situation resembles the earth's daily rotation on its axis and its annual revolution around the sun, which the inhabitants do not sense.

I was shown what the form of heaven is like in its lowest realm; it resembled the pattern of folds seen in human brains. A perceptible view of its flow or circular motion was granted to me, the demonstration lasting several days.

From this experience I could tell that the form of the brain matches the pattern of movement in heaven. The deeper parts of the brain, invisible to the eye, match the deeper structures of heaven, which are totally incomprehensible. The angels said this shows that we were created to reflect the structure of the three heavens. So the image of heaven is imprinted on us in such a perfect way that we are a miniature heaven at its smallest scale, which is why we have a correspondence with the heavens.

4042   A consequence is that only through humankind is there a descent from the heavens into the world, and an ascent from the world to the heavens. The brain and its inner depths provide the means of descent and ascent because they contain the actual rudiments or starting and ending points from which absolutely everything in the body stems and flows. The brain's inner depths are also the source of the thoughts in our intellect and the emotions in our will.

4043   The forms that are still deeper—and more universal—are incomprehensible, as noted, because the word *forms* carries with it the notion of space and of time. At the depths where heaven exists, nothing is perceived in terms of space and time (because they are proper to the material world) but in terms of state, and of variations and changes in state. However, we also cannot conceive of variation or change apart from the attributes of form and, to repeat, we cannot conceive of form apart from the attributes of space and time—although heaven lacks both. So you can see how incomprehensible such things are, and how indescribable. In fact, all the human words in which these ideas must be described and understood involve earthly qualities and are therefore unsuited to expressing those ideas. In the heavens they are presented as variations of the heavenly light and heavenly fire coming from the Lord, in such great and marvelous fullness that thousands upon thousands of the ideas perceived [by angels] could hardly be reduced to a single idea perceptible by us.

Despite this fact, what is presented in the heavens is presented over again in the world of spirits in forms bearing some resemblance to those that appear in our world.

Representations are nothing but images of spiritual realities in physical objects, and when the former are truly represented in the latter, they correspond. **4044**

People who do not know what the spiritual but only what the earthly plane is might think that such representations and correspondences are impossible. They might say to themselves, "How can something spiritual act on a piece of matter?" However, if they are willing to reflect on what is happening inside them every moment, they can form some idea of it for themselves. They can consider how their will is able to act on the muscles in their body and trigger actual movement. Their thoughts can act on their speech organs, activating their lungs, windpipe, throat, tongue, and lips to produce speech. Their emotions can act on their face, creating such an accurate self-portrait there that another person can often tell what they are thinking and wishing. These examples can provide some picture of representations and correspondences.

Now because these parallels show up in us, and because nothing exists that can survive on its own but only by depending on something else, which in turn depends on something else and finally on what is first, through a chain of correspondences—because of all this, people who enjoy any breadth of judgment can come to the conclusion that there is correspondence between humankind and heaven, and between heaven and the Lord, who is the First.

Since this kind of correspondence exists, and heaven is divided into many smaller heavens, and these into even smaller ones, and the whole into individual communities, there are heavens that relate to the entire cerebrum and cerebellum, and they contain heavens relating to various parts or components of both. There are those relating to the dura mater, **4045** the pia or soft mater, the sinuses, and various brain structures and cavities, such as the corpus callosum, corpora striata, smaller glands, ventricles, infundibulum, and so on.

The nature of the heavens connected with this or that part was therefore revealed to me, as the following will show.

4046   A large number of spirits appeared above my head a short distance away. Their united action resembled a heartbeat, though there was a kind of ebbing-and-flowing, up-and-down motion, accompanied by a cool puff of air on my forehead. This led me to believe that they were of an intermediate sort, belonging to the region of both heart and lungs, and that they did not have much depth. The same spirits later generated a fiery light at first, garish but illuminating nonetheless, which appeared under the left side of my chin; then a light under my left eye; then a light over my left eye that was dim but ruddy rather than white, which told me what their nature was, because different kinds of light indicate different feelings and different levels of intelligence.

[2] Afterward, when I put my hand to the left side of my skull, or head, I felt a pulse under my palm, again rising and falling—a sign by which I knew they were connected with the brain.

When I asked who they were, they did not want to say. Others told me that these spirits do not speak voluntarily. In the end, forced to talk, they said that if they did speak, they would be exposing their character. I sensed that among them were some who make up the area of the dura mater, a membrane covering a large part of the cerebrum and cerebellum. I could tell what they were like, because I was allowed to learn their nature from talking with them. They did not think or talk about spiritual and heavenly affairs, any more than they had as people on earth, because—although they did not admit this—they naturally disbelieved in anything other than the earthly realm, since they could not penetrate any further. Nevertheless, like others they worshiped the Divine, took time to pray, and were good citizens.

[3] Later there was a different group of spirits acting on my pulse, not with an undulating, up-and-down motion but crosswise. Then there was yet another group, which did not use an alternating motion at all but a more continuous one; and another, which forced my pulse to jump from one place to another. They said that they related to the outer layer of the dura mater and that they were the types who had thought about spiritual and heavenly subjects, although they based these thoughts on objects of the outward senses. That was the only way they could grasp deeper

entities. To me they sounded female. People who start with their outward senses and therefore with worldly and earthly evidence in reasoning about things of heaven, or about the spiritual properties of faith and
love, confuse the two and make them into one. The more they do so, the
farther they move toward the surface, all the way to the scalp, which is
what they represent. If they have lived a good life, they are still within the
universal human, but on its very outermost surface. After all, everyone
who lives a good life out of the desire to love her or his neighbor is saved.

Other spirits also appeared above my head, and when they flowed in,
their movement over my head generally streamed across from front to back.
And there appeared still others whose inflowing motion traveled from each
temple in toward the midbrain. I sensed that they belonged to the region
of the pia mater, which is a second covering, more directly enveloping the
cerebrum and cerebellum and communicating with them through strands
extending from itself.

Their nature I was able to learn about from their speech, since they
talked with me. As in the world, they did not trust their own thinking
much. So they did not narrow down to any definite opinion on sacred
subjects but depended on others' beliefs, without challenging the validity
of those beliefs.

[2] This character of theirs was also demonstrated to me when their
perceptions flowed into the Lord's Prayer as I was reading it. I could
always tell what the various spirits and angels were like from the Lord's
Prayer by noticing the influence their thoughts and feelings exerted on the
content of the prayer. So I perceived that these spirits were the kind I
have described. I also perceived that they could serve the angels as intermediaries (since there are mediating spirits between the heavens through
whom the heavens communicate), because their thinking was not closed
but open minded. They allowed themselves to be controlled, readily receiving and accepting the influences on them. They were also modest and
peaceful, and they said they were in heaven.

Once there was a spirit near my head talking to me, and from his
tone I perceived that he was in a calm state, like that of a peaceful sleep.
He asked one question after another, but with such good sense that he
could not have done better wide awake. I could tell that angels at a deeper
level spoke through him and that his state allowed him to understand
and convey what they said. I asked about his state, describing it to him.

"I do not say anything that is not good and true," he answered. "I can
tell when it is not, and if something that is not comes to mind, I do not

let it in or verbalize it." He said of his state that it was peaceful, and I had the opportunity to feel it when he communicated it to me.

I was told that spirits like this relate to the [dural venous] sinuses or major blood vessels in the brain, and that others like him relate to the longitudinal fissure between the brain's two hemispheres, where conditions are quiet, no matter how turbulent the brain is on either side.

4049   There were some spirits above my head and slightly in front who talked to me, speaking pleasantly and exerting a fairly gentle influence on me. They were distinguished from others by their constant longing and desire to go to heaven. I was told that their kind relates to the brain's ventricles, or its larger cavities, and belongs to the region of these ventricles. The reason for the relationship was added: the better type of lymph in the ventricles is that way; it returns to the brain, in the course of things, and therefore has a drive to return there. The brain equates with heaven, and the drive, with the spirits' longing and desire. Such is the nature of correspondences.

4050   One time, I at first saw a face over a blue window, but the face soon withdrew and a star appeared in the general area of my left eye, then more stars, twinkling, and gleaming with a white light. Afterward I saw some walls but no ceiling—the walls standing only on the left side. Finally there was a kind of starry sky. Because these objects showed up in a place where there were evil spirits, I considered it a dreadful thing to be shown such a sight. Soon the wall and sky disappeared, though, and there appeared a well from which a kind of white cloud or mist issued. It also looked as though something was being pumped out of the well.

[2] I asked what it all symbolized and represented and was told that it represented the infundibulum in the brain, with the brain (symbolized by the sky) on top. What I saw afterward was the duct itself symbolized by the well and named for a funnel. The cloud or mist pouring from it was the lymph that flows through and is siphoned off. The lymph is of two types: the type that mixes with the soul-fluids in the usable portion of the lymph, and the type that mixes with the watery fluids in the portion of the lymph to be excreted.

[3] Then I was shown the nature of the spirits who belong to this region, but only the more inferior ones. I also saw the spirits themselves, who run here and there, attach themselves to anyone they see, listen to everything, pass on what they hear, and are suspicious, impatient, and restless, like lymph in the infundibulum that shunts back and forth. Their

rationalizations equate with the fluids there that represent them. But these are an intermediate sort of spirit.

[4] The spirits who relate to the waste lymph there are the ones who demote spiritual truth to earthly truth and drag it through the dirt. For instance, there are those who hear something about marriage love and apply it to promiscuity and adultery, reducing the former to the latter; and so on. They appear some distance out in front on the right.

The good sort, though, are similar to the ones described just above in §4049.

Some communities relate to the area in the brain called the isthmus, and also to the clusters of nerve fibers in the brain that look like glands, from which fibers extend for various purposes. The fibers act in unison at their glandlike starting points, but each has its own function at its far end.

4051

One community of the spirits to whom these structures correspond presented itself to me, and here is the story: The spirits came forward and addressed me, saying they were people.

"You are not the kind of people who have a body, but spirits," I was permitted to answer. "So you are also people, since everything in a spirit aims after what is human—including a form like that of an embodied person—because the spirit is the inner person. And since understanding and wisdom are what make people human, not shape, good spirits and especially angels are more human than people who still have their bodies, because they have more of wisdom's light."

[2] They then said that they have a populous community in which no individual is like another. Since it seemed impossible to me that a community of unlike spirits could exist in the other world, I talked with them about it and eventually learned that although they are dissimilar, they have a common purpose, which brings them together. They went on to say that by nature they each act differently and speak differently than the others, but wish and think the same. This they also illustrated by an example: One individual in the community will say that a certain angel is the least important in heaven; another, that the angel is the most important; and a third, that the angel is neither the least nor the most important; so there is a lot of variety. Their thoughts are in unison, though: Angels who want to be the least are the greatest, so by comparison they *are* the greatest. At the same time they are neither least nor greatest because they do not think about rank. And so on. They come together in their fundamental principles, then, but take independent action on the outermost level.

They placed themselves at my ear, saying that they were good spirits and that this was their manner of speaking.

I heard that no one knows where they come from and that they drift among various communities.

4052   Moreover, the correspondence of the brain with the universal human is like this: People who start with goodness relate to the parts of the brain that are its beginnings, which are called the cortical glands or substances. Those who start with truth relate to the parts of the cerebrum and cerebellum that extend from those beginnings, which are called fibers. There is a difference, however. Those who correspond to the right side of the brain are the ones intent on what is good and therefore on what is true, but those who correspond to the left side of the brain are those who understand what is good and true and therefore appreciate it. This difference exists because people to the Lord's right in heaven are those whose will inspires them to goodness, while the ones to his left are those whose intellect does. The former are called heavenly; the latter, spiritual.

4053   No one has yet known that these correspondences exist, so I realize that when people hear it they will wonder, because they do not know what the inner self or the outer self is; that the inner self is in the spiritual world, and the outer self, in the physical world; or that the inner is what lives in the outer, flows into it, and controls it. Yet from these facts and from the evidence offered in §4044 it can be seen that spiritual inflow and correspondence do exist. The idea is quite familiar in the other world, as is the concept that a physical object is simply a representation of the spiritual forces creating and sustaining it, and that what it corresponds to is what it represents.

4054   The brain, like heaven, exists in an environment of purpose, useful purpose. Anything that flows in from the Lord embraces as its aim the salvation of the human race. This is the goal that reigns supreme in heaven and therefore in the brain as well. After all, the brain, where the human mind resides, has a goal for the body—that the body serve the soul, enabling the soul to be happy forever.

On the other hand, there are communities whose members have no useful purpose—only that of joining their male and female friends in having fun. So they do nothing but indulge and pamper themselves. If they happen to have any concern for private or public interests, it is with the same end in view. More groups of these spirits exist today than could possibly be believed. As soon as they approach, the atmosphere they carry with them goes into action, snuffing out any desire others may have for truth or goodness; and when this is extinguished they enjoy their friendships to the utmost.

[2] Such spirits clog the brain and make it stupid.

Many groups of these spirits have been with me, and a dullness, sluggishness, and absence of emotion has let me know they were present. Several times I also talked with them.

They are plagues and banes, although while they were in the world they seemed in public to be good, charming, polite, and clever people, because they know appearances and how to use them to worm their way in—especially in winning friends. What it is to befriend goodness, or what friendship on a good basis is, they do not know and do not want to know.

A grim lot awaits them. They end up living in squalor in such gross stupidity that hardly a trace of human intelligence remains. The purpose makes the person, and the nature of the purpose determines the nature of the person and therefore the nature of the person's humanity after death.

More about the universal human and its correspondence appears at the end of the next chapter [§§4218–4228].

4055

[CONTINUED IN VOLUME 6]

Biographical Note

EMANUEL SWEDENBORG (1688–1772) was born Emanuel Swedberg (or Svedberg) in Stockholm, Sweden, on January 29, 1688 (Julian calendar). He was the third of the nine children of Jesper Swedberg (1653–1735) and Sara Behm (1666–1696). At the age of eight he lost his mother. After the death of his only older brother ten days later, he became the oldest living son. In 1697 his father married Sara Bergia (1666–1720), who developed great affection for Emanuel and left him a significant inheritance. His father, a Lutheran clergyman, later became a celebrated and controversial bishop, whose diocese included the Swedish churches in Pennsylvania and in London, England.

After studying at the University of Uppsala (1699–1709), Emanuel journeyed to England, the Netherlands, France, and Germany (1710–1715) to study and work with leading scientists in western Europe. Upon his return he apprenticed as an engineer under the brilliant Swedish inventor Christopher Polhem (1661–1751). He gained favor with Sweden's King Charles XII (1682–1718), who gave him a salaried position as an overseer of Sweden's mining industry (1716–1747). Although Emanuel was engaged, he never married.

After the death of Charles XII, Emanuel was ennobled by Queen Ulrika Eleonora (1688–1741), and his last name was changed to Swedenborg (or Svedenborg). This change in status gave him a seat in the Swedish House of Nobles, where he remained an active participant in the Swedish government throughout his life.

A member of the Royal Swedish Academy of Sciences, he devoted himself to studies that culminated in a number of publications, most notably a comprehensive three-volume work on natural philosophy and metallurgy (1734) that brought him recognition across Europe as a scientist. After 1734 he redirected his research and publishing to a study of anatomy in search of the interface between the soul and body, making several significant discoveries in physiology.

From 1743 to 1745 he entered a transitional phase that resulted in a shift of his main focus from science to theology. Throughout the rest of his life he maintained that this shift was brought about by Jesus Christ, who appeared to him, called him to a new mission, and opened his perception to a permanent dual consciousness of this life and the life after death.

He devoted the last decades of his life to studying Scripture and publishing eighteen theological titles that draw on the Bible, reasoning, and his own spiritual experiences. These works present a Christian theology with unique perspectives on the nature of God, the spiritual world, the Bible, the human mind, and the path to salvation.

Swedenborg died in London on March 29, 1772 (Gregorian calendar), at the age of eighty-four.